U0120595

赵元任 著

石 锋 潘韦功 译

连续性：
方法论的研究

上海教育出版社
SHANGHAI EDUCATIONAL
PUBLISHING HOUSE

赵元任哈佛时期照片

The undersigned, a committee of the Division of

Philosophy

have examined a thesis entitled

Continuity

A Study in Methodology.

presented by

Yuen Ren Chao.

candidate for the degree of Doctor of Philosophy,

and hereby certify that it is worthy of acceptance.

Edward V. Huntington

L. J. Henderson

H. M. Sheffer

原件之一

CONTINUITY

A Study in Methodology

Yuen Ren Chao

Cambridge, Mass.,

April 13, 1918

原件之二

of one's life by a very steep curve. The phenomenon of
biological mutation was spoken of as part of the continuity of evolution (foot-note, p.18, Ch.Ⅵ). But talking
in another order of magnitude, mutation is steep enough
to be called a jump.

3. Stable Equilibrium

Why, it may be asked, are things separated by
intervals or by steep variation? Perhaps some light
may be had by a study of a generalized conception of
equilibrium, in so far as it bears on the problem of difference. To put it schematically, we may let x represent
a generalized variable (which need not be spatial), and y
a generalized "potential", which tends (physically, socially, etc.) to be a minimum. The rate of variation,
or the slope of the y-x curve, will then represent the
generalized "force", which measures the tendency to go
down hill. In Fig.1, of balls
on hills, A is in "stable equilibrium", in that if it is slightly displaced, it will return
to the valley. B is also in
stable equilibrium, tho the
"base" within which it may be
displaced and return is small.
C is in "neutral equilibrium", in that it will be not
be urged forward or brought back, by any force, but remains neutral. D is in "unstable equilibrium", in that
if it is dispalced, however slightly, the displacement
will be favored by a force, so that it will tumble down
hill. E is not in equilibrium, as there is a force urging it to move down. So much, then, for what is familiar
ground.

If now a shower of falls on these hills, is it not
evident that the drops will be automatically classified

原件之三

equal. A walker looking for a trolley car will not tarry
slowly between two stops because the chance of missing a
car at one is the same as at the other. Buridan's ass between the hay and the water may be equally hungry and thirsty,
if such a case were possible, but a gentle slight breeze from the
side of the hay will attract him slightly to one side and
then the unstable equilibrium ceases to be an equilibrium.
An infinite number of factors can exactly balance only in
a scholastic universe of discourse.

In the spirit of continuity, one might say that every
little counts, but more carefully, one should say that every
little may count, but need not count, unless it is enough to
cross a ridge, or threshold of difference. In physiology,
there is the principle of "all or nothing"*, according to

*See W. M. Bayliss, *Principles of General Physiology*,
1914, p.383.

which if the nerve of a muscle is stimulated, the muscle
will not respond at all until the intensity attains a minimum threshold beyond which ~~the~~ it will respond with full
force. Similarly, to light a candle for a plant kept indoors
is of absolutely no help to its metabolism. For, below
1/100 part of the noraml light that a plant receives, any
light is as good as no light. Again, slowing oozing water
will not fall until the weight of the water exceeds the hold
of ~~the~~ its surface tension, when the whole drop comes off.
Electric charge gather relatively continuously from the
combs of a static machine, but will discharge by units across
the knobs. According to the quantum theory of radiation,
energy is continuously absorbed, but when gathered to a degree which its carrier cannot hold, it will be radiated as
a unit.

A point of unstable equilibrium may be crossed
by the multiplication of a secondary factor connected
with the primary factor by a sort of trigger or lever ~~action~~

原件之四

译 者 序 言

石 锋

从《赵元任全集》各卷的陆续出版，到《好玩儿的大师——赵元任影记之学术篇》，现在又有 46 卷的《赵元任日记》，使世人能够饱览一代文艺复兴式巨匠的风采。赵元任先生一生的学术成就不仅在中国历史和学术史上，而且在世界历史和学术史上都是巨大的贡献，其重要历史意义将会随时间的推移而愈加显现出来。随着赵元任档案的整理出版，大家来读赵元任和重新认识赵元任的不断进展，赵先生的各种超前的学术理念和研究方法将会极大地促进我们现在的学术创新。

1. 学术生涯的奠基之作

赵元任先生早年从美国康奈尔大学转入哈佛大学哲学系(1915年)，至 1918 年获得博士学位。他的博士论文《连续性：方法论的研究》按照惯例一直保存在哈佛大学。商务印书馆出版《赵元任全集》，把这篇极为重要的博士论文收录在第 14 卷，使我们得以看到赵先生对连续性方法论所做的全面系统的开创性阐述。这在当时是非常超前的现代科学思维方式，是各种科学研究的普适性方法论，至今仍居世界学术前沿。连续性思维是从哲学意义上重新认识世界，是学术观念和研究范式的全面革新。这不仅是现代科学的方法论，还是为人处世的大智慧。

赵先生的博士论文《连续性：方法论的研究》是他总括早期学术研究的结晶和升华，既是他全部学术生涯的奠基之作，又是他超前于学界的杰出代表作。他早期的知识素养、发表的各种文章以及个人的生活历练，都在他的博士论文中得到体现，其中有多处显示出他对人类语言的基本观念和后期研究的创意萌芽。他在博士论文中详细论证的研究理念和研究方法，奠定了他一生的学术方向和研究风格，贯穿他一生的学术研究实践。这在他后来的所有论著中都是随处可见，贯穿始终的，如《语言问题》《中国话的文法》等。

赵先生在博士论文中写道："希望每一位智力的禀赋和受过的训练跟笔者相似的读者，都会发现这种处理方式有着高度挑战性且极具启发性……"的确如此！连续性的思维方式有着高度挑战性且极具启发性。我们翻译赵先生的博士论文，也是进一步向赵先生学习的实践过程。翻译赵先生的博士论文，使我们深受感染，极为震撼。他对世界对人生看得那么通透豁达，高出我们所知道的任何人，确实如沈家煊老师所说："深感如果早读赵元任，就可以少走很多弯路。"

2. 超前的现代科学思维方式

赵先生在博士论文中写道："从历史上看，基于连续性的思考在不同地方都出现过。例如：莱布尼茨和伽利略。但是莱布尼茨把它看成为一个哲学原则，而伽利略则只是在偶尔遇到其他问题时使用它。因此，连续性还没有被作为一种方法进行系统研究过。"

大约是赵先生博士论文发表 20 年以后，维特根斯坦（Ludwig Josef Johann Wittgenstein）后期的"家族相似性"才跟连续性思维发生联系。可以看出，赵先生的连续性思维超越时代，领先学界，比维特根斯坦还要超前。维特根斯坦后期的特点类似于赵先生的论述风格，都是把哲学从哲学家的书斋中解放出来，并把哲学跟大众的日常生活相结合，从普通的常识中阐发深刻的哲学道理。

赵先生的连续性思维（1918）和后起的原型范畴理论（prototype theory）密切关联。传统的经典范畴理论认为：范畴是离散的，有着明确的边界；一个成分只有符合这个范畴的特征才能属于这个范畴；所有范畴成员的地位相同。而后起的原型范畴理论（Rosch 1978）却反其道而行之。原型范畴理论认为：范畴具有内部和外部的连续性,范畴边界模糊;所有范畴成员具有家族相似性;范畴成员有中心和外围之分,中心成员具有更多的共同特征;最常见的状态或最中心的成员被定义为范畴的原型。原型范畴理论跟60年前赵先生阐述的连续性观念是一致的。

赵先生的连续性观念(1918)还是近年来的量子逻辑含中律的先驱。基于经典物理学的经典逻辑跟经典范畴理论相联系,有三原则:(1)识别原则,如:A就是A;(2)对立原则,如:A不是非A;(3)排中原则,如:不存在既是A又是非A的第三方。经典物理学认为,粒子不是波,波也不是粒子。然而在量子层面上,粒子同时可以是波。于是,经典逻辑的排中原则被打破,让位给量子逻辑的含中原则:存在一个同时既是A也是非A的T值,可以具有A、非A、T三个真值(Nicolescu 2002)。这种主体、客体、主客体交互作用的三分法,明显区别于主体、客体的形而上学的二分法(Nicolescu 2008)。赵先生的连续性观念就是强调中间态的重要性。量子逻辑的含中律出现在赵先生对连续性进行系统论述之后约90年。

3. 语言中的连续性

在自然界和人类社会中,到处都存在着连续性。连续性主要表现为分布模式的连续,包括时间上的连续或空间中的连续。人类语言中同样普遍存在连续性,语音、语义、语法、词汇、语用,都是如此。例如,词和非词之间,动词和名词之间,元音和辅音之间,轻声和非轻声之间以及语法化的过程和词汇化的过程,都是连续的,没有截然分开的界限。拉波夫(W. Labov)说:"在本书第二卷,我们将看到许多在相当长的一段时间内变异都保持连续性的例子。"(《语言变化原理:内部因素》中文版,商务印书馆,2019)他的《语言变化原理》三卷巨著中,用调查和实验展示出大量的语言连续性变化的实例。

赵元任先生讲的多能性,即非唯一性。对于连续性的语言事实如何划分,可以从不同的角度有不同的解决方案:可以是分离式的范畴;可以是交叠式的范畴;可以是蕴含式的范畴。这都只是好坏的问题,而不是对错的问题。比如,汉语普通话的上声是低平调还是低降调? 都可以。应该是字本位还是词本位,还是短语本位和句本位? 都可以。我们讲过,所谓的本位都是个人的本位。连续性的方法是发现语言事实的方法。至于对发现的语言事实怎样去看,赵先生对别人的观点是很宽容很开放的,并不要求别人都要同意自己的看法,他常说"这未始是不可的事情"。

我们从赵先生的连续性观念可以得出语言连续性法则:语言中普遍存在着连续性。研究语言的任务,就是要从这种连续性当中发现同一性和差异性,找出其中的奇点和阈限,从而掌握语言的真髓,破解语言的奥秘。首先是弄清这个问题的各个要素在时间上或在空间中的分布,把它们排列为一个连续统。这样就从整体上对这个问题有了全局的把握,同时也就为解决这个问题打下了坚实的基础,创造了良好的条件。这个问题就会迎刃而解。

4. 连续性和离散性

沈家煊说:"赵元任的学识、贡献和境界远远超越结构主义语言学,还超越语言学,有许多创见超越时代,先知先觉,经历时间的考验和科学的证明。"(沈家煊《大家来读赵元任》,《实验语言学》第 12 卷第 1 号,2023 年)赵先生在博士论文中全面系统论证连续性方法论,就是最具重要性和最有代表性的实例。我们没有见到哪位结构主义语言学家论述连续性问题,因为结构主义以及后结构主义的各家理论都是强调离散性而忽视连续性。

连续性和离散性是同一事物的两个方面,总体上,连续性更多的是客观自然状态,离散性更多的是主观认知加工。直到现在,还有不少学者坚持离散性而排斥连续性。其实连续性和离散性相互联系,彼此对应,就像一枚硬币的两面。儿童开始初级认知的事物都是离散的范畴,随着逐渐成长,进入高级认知,才看到事物内部和外部的连续性。如果只看到事物的离散性而看不到连续性,就意味着还停留在初级认知阶段。维特根斯坦的家族相似性,以及前面讲的原型范畴理论和量子逻辑的含中律,都是从离散性向连续性认识的发展。

连续性思维强调两个方面:第一是强调对中间状态的研究,中间状态的表现丰富多彩,引人入胜,最有价值;第二是不仅注意类别的差异,更加关注程度的差异,程度的差异需要更仔细的观察和更深入的探索才能获得。认识了连续性,才能更清楚离散性的来由;知道了程度的差异,才能懂得类别的差异的原因。

赵先生还很看重黄金均值的意义,注意奇点和阈限,特别多次提到词语和语句所处的语境和论域对于语义的决定性作用。为节省篇幅,这里就不逐一赘述了,请读者找到书中的有关章节和段落细细研读。

5. 翻译工作的说明

以我们有限的学识和能力翻译赵元任先生的博士论文,是远远不足的,真是知其不可而为之。因此我们在翻译过程中唯恐有误,如临深渊,如履薄冰,多方查考,不断修改,至今还不敢完全放心。请读者多加关注,若发现哪里有误,就及时告诉我们。

赵先生博士论文的总体布局跳出一般学位论文的窠臼,一开头就列举出十二种连续性的实例,清新别致,独具一格。文章的写作风格轻松幽默,全篇极少超过一行的长句,没有冗长的理论说教;除必需的极少术语,都是日常英语口语的词句;采用很多实例说明深刻的道理。翻译赵先生论文就是向赵先生学习请教,好像是在听赵先生如数家珍、侃侃道来地讲课。我们反复阅读原文,努力逐词逐句弄清原意,在尽量保持原句的结构和语气的情况下译成可读的中文,力求做到既保持作者原文的意思,又方便读者看懂。从初稿到定稿,虽然经过多次修改,有的句段还是不能令人满意。后面附上赵先生博士论文的英文原文,就是为了使能够阅读英文的读者便于进行英汉对照,准确理解。

赵先生学识渊博,在论述中引证大量科学史上的实例,还有他亲身经历的体验和发表在《科学》等刊物上的科普文章。其中不时会有一些赵先生喜欢的风趣诙谐的文字游戏，含义深刻、耐人寻味。我们随文添加了很多译者脚注，希望能够帮助读者看懂赵先生论述的深刻道理。

6. 关于数学的证明

赵先生博士论文中有一些涉及数理逻辑方面的数学推理和证明，对于文科的老师和同学来说，这可能是最感到困难的。这些数学方程式的推理和证明，是为了说明连续性方法论的各个环节的严密性和科学性。尤其是赵先生为论证连续性思维方法论的科学可靠性，专门创立"连续数学归纳法"，并给出了严谨的证明。赵先生以此为基础，全面系统论述连续性方法论，做出了开创性的研究工作。此后近百年中，先后有十余位数学家又陆续发表过"连续数学归纳法"的证明，但是除少数论文外，多数都没有标明赵先生的首创之功。这在科学史上是有过先例的。当年奥地利的孟德尔（Gregor Johann Mendel）做了 8 年豌豆杂交实验，1866 发表《植物杂交试验》，直到他逝世 16 年后，世人在 1900 年才重新发现孟德尔遗传学定律。这个遗传学的开创性定律被尘封 34 年，原因就是：太超前了。

连续性源于数学，从数学领域实数的连续性，扩展到自然现象的连续性，因为数就是具体事物的抽象；再扩展到科学研究中数据的连续性，因为研究对象都是客观的。这都是连续性观念应用的领域很自然的扩展。在赵先生列出的数学算式中，数学变量的定义极为宽泛：一个事物、一个人物、一件事情、一个场景，都可以成为数学变量。出乎很多人的意料，数学的应用竟会是如此普遍。赵先生非常清楚：一个法则的定义和应用是不一样的。在赵先生那里，抽象性和具体性，科学性和人文性，纯粹性和世俗性，这些不同视角的对立面，是二者兼顾而不是分割开来。这种高超的智慧，在文中随处都可以显现出来。目前在中外语言学界，理解并应用连续性方法论的学者并不多,这也表明赵先生连续性观念和方法的超前性,至今仍居前沿位置。

语言学正面临着人工智能飞跃发展的巨大冲击。为此,我们请三位美国的朋友分工合作,利用 ChatGPT 把赵先生博士论文的英文原稿全部译为中文,作为附录放在书后。有兴趣的读者可以跟我们翻译的内容相互对照,看看二者之间的异同之处,会有很多感触和启示。据我们初步感觉,有个别词句,ChatGPT 译得更好些,如:我们译"天真的实用主义"不如它译为"朴素的实用主义";但是有很多地方不能令人满意,如:identity 在这里应译为"同一性",而它却多译为"身份"。类似情况还有不少。看来人工智能还有很长的路要走哦。

马克思认为:"一种科学只有在成功地运用数学时,才算真正达到完善的地步。"(转引自拉法格《忆马克思》)其实,现代语言学就是数据之学,这跟基于大数据的人工智能在大方向上是一致的。人类学习语言都是基于概率匹配的动物本能,这跟新一代人工智能的基本算法依据概率匹配的原理总体上也是一致的。王力先生受教于赵先生,晚年曾经感慨:"我一辈子吃亏就吃亏在我不懂数理化。"非常深刻! 有些语言学先驱已经走在前面了。人工智能已经在做语言学家应该做的事情了。其实,人工智能的挑战正是给语言学学者提供了最佳机会——从象牙之塔走出来,跟上时代的步伐,把人工智能作为研究的利器。

使语言学走上科学的道路,达到完善的地步。这就是我们翻译赵先生博士论文的初衷和愿望。让我们大家一起努力!

石锋

写于 2023 年 6 月 1 日

目　　录

连续性：
方法论的研究

Yuen Ren Chao

赵元任

马萨诸塞州剑桥市

1918 年 4 月 13 日

概　　要

问题与方法

第一章和第二章。——这项研究，正如以论文的形式所呈现的，是在某些论述形式、发现方法、做事方法和某些实际困境方面几个不断发展中的思路的一个阶段。在现在的阶段，最好是用"连续性"这个术语来描述它，它的意义是从最模糊的含义到它在应用中所能接受的最高数学严密性。

正是本文研究的方法本身被用来作为研究它们的方法，试图表明循环并不总是恶性的。一般来说，方法被认为是用一部分现实去对抗另一部分现实，以确保方法论的杠杆作用，无论是机械上的、智力上的还是道德上的。

连续性研究和使用的典型方法包括以下几个阶段：(1) 具体案例，(2) 分级，(3) 系列排序，(4) 极限点，(5) 明确定位，(6) 中间环节，(7) "夹挤"，(8) 变换。

抽象地说，这整个研究可以作为一个连续变量函数的方法论的理论。它不是一项数学研究，因为它关注的是前提跟它们的解释、应用或示例之间的联系，而忽视去使这些联系的严密性比最弱的联系有任何增强。

专题章节的成果

第三章，概念分级。——当我们发现一些概念被完全采用时，最好是问一下它们对程度、阶段、色度或等级的允准程度。一些特定的应用包括：

举例、图示、类比、比喻等是构成概念的具体定义的不同等级的元素。

　　数学中的一个参量，允许不同等级或顺序的可变性，其中变量和常数作为它的极端情况。这种顺序通常是为了实验的方便。

　　用一条曲线表示的数学函数只不过是把值的高度限制在一个区域、一条带或者一根管内而已。当其他因素的变化对问题中的重要现象没有影响时，剩下的那个因素就是这个现象的"唯一"起因。

　　第四章，系列排序。——任何两件事物都可以按照任意定义的序列顺序进行比较。具体事物的序列可比性不是一个是与否的问题，而是或多与或少的问题。

　　只要使用中的波动和科学上的"偶然"失误低于一个相关的阈值，我们就能够不使用重言式去陈述序列顺序，这样，我们称呼一件事物的时候，就可以不止于用它的定义来称呼它。

　　第五章，极限点。——"通过连续性进行论证"，人们总是能够得出结论，一个极限案例至少也是一个案例。但一个极限案例至少在作为*极限*案例这一点上是奇特的。因此，每个具体问题的答案都要取决于进一步的考虑。

　　数学的精神在于把下限也称为一个案例。哲学的精神在于把通常的事物延续到它们的上限。科学和生活占据着中间位置。但通过转换的方法，可以看出这两个极端在哪些方面是相通的。与形式上的虚无相比，无限的事物，如实际的、绝对的、事实的等等，具有无限性。正是实际的天赋、善意、资本、能量等等，使得循环成为并非恶性的循环。

　　在特定问题中，上限阈值和下限阈值（"M"和"ε"）会取代极限的位置。因此，有人提议重新解释那些真正跟实际问题相关的阈值所构成的极限。这跟现在严谨的数学中使用的极限的对应定义是一致的。在这个意义上，我们说，意义或定义是标准的极限，真理是真实的极限，道德准则是现实道德的极限，等等。

　　这一程序与"奥卡姆剃刀"不同的一个重要方面是，它声称没有终结性或排他性。为了某些目的或为了某些人，客观对象可能会被"简化"为一类有限的感知数据。但从循环的角度来看，我们对物理学家或生理学家有同样的尊重和同情,他们认为把感知数据"简化"为其他人曾试图简化的术语是有启发性的。

第六章和第七章,连续性中的同一性和差异性。——同一性和差异性问题是把跟每个问题相关的各个方面都区分开来的一个问题。

连续性的概念有助于看到同一性,前提是明智地选择变量 x,其中,事物在某个非平凡的方面被看作是合并在一起的。

一个倾向于隐藏同一性的背景中的差异可能是某种奇点,例如,零点,它可能是一个很大的程度差异,也可能是一个小的程度差异,把某人目前立足点的重要性夸大为超过其他的点。

一种特殊数学兴趣的偶然结果是"连续数学归纳法"定理,这是源自楔形细端的一个熟知论点的数学公式。它的形式证明是基于(1)阿基米德公理和(2)一般数学归纳法。但是这一论点的实际强度跟所有论点都一样,取决于它的前提的强度。

差异不只是单纯的差异,而是意味着分类、事件的交替问题、概念或感觉的差异、行动方式的决策等等。

一个差异可能是来自变量 x 的大幅度变化,或陡峭的曲线,或用单个点标记,特别是用稳定和不稳定的平衡点标记。

一个点可能会只因为它本身值得关注而跟其他点不同,例如主要因素被平衡抵消而次要因素有了重要性的情况。案例连续性的概念(连续函数的一般定义)在这方面是很有用的。如果 $f(a) < 0$ 且 $f(b) > 0$,那么 a 和 b 之间存在 ε,这种中间环节的性质使得 $f(\varepsilon) = 0$ 也会有应用之地,尤其是在物理和心理测量中。

第八章,结论和进一步的问题。——大自然是连续的吗? 这要看情况。非连续性和连续性具有不同程度的数学准确性和方法有效性,都是在科学与生活中有用也可用的概念。自然作为一个时间函数的连续性,可能在于我们相对成功地塑造了对时间的科学认知,从而使时间函数得以连续。这又是一个并非恶性循环的案例,有待修订。

　　进一步的问题是通过对变量和函数具体理解的考察,在方法论中制定出函数的一般理论。从另一个角度来看,这将构成一种"具体数学"。这里仅仅触及一些特殊的应用,但它们本身值得进一步研究,如平衡问题、最佳点或广义黄金平均值、相关性阈值、术语原则、道德和法律问题的界限、效率、运动技能的素质、音乐技巧以及现实中的其他一切,只要摆弄这些概念,就会导向我们力量的增强,而不是减弱。

赵元任

马萨诸塞州剑桥市

1918 年 5 月

正文目录

第一章 引　言

1. 问题：中间态

池塘边的一块石头上，一只青蛙正在歇息。突然间，这青蛙顺势向前一跳[①]：在水面的波纹漫向四周之前，它已经潜入池底。然而，这只青蛙在某个时间、在某个位置曾经处于刚刚穿过水面的状态，这一点难道不是不言而喻的吗？

人们告诉我，我每年都会长高两英寸。如果在除夕夜里通宵不睡就能发现我这两英寸是在哪个时刻长出来的，并且能体会这种变化是怎样的感觉，那是不是很开心呢？但是人们说，成长就是一种成长的过程。比如说，如果你想做个好人，那你就必须从现在开始养成好的习惯。如果你说："我可以现在先放任轻松，等长大了我自然就会认真负责的。"那么，你长大成人也还将当不上好人。但是劝告有什么用处呢？那些听从劝告的人不需要去劝告，而那些不听劝告的人劝了也没用。然而，我或许正好是在中间，似乎坏到需要很多的劝告，又好到可以听从一些劝告。

然而，我们真的总是能够找到事物之间的中点吗？我这排座位花 1.5 美元似乎有些不值，可我后面一排座位只要 1 美元，肯定物超所值。真遗憾没有 1.25 美元的票价。有个人住在长江与黄河的分水岭上，却总是抱怨没有鲜鱼可吃也没有水路可通。每当下雨的时候，水不是流进黄河，就是流入长江。多奇怪，在两条相邻的峡谷之

---

① 译者注："顺势向前一跳"，其实原文是 nature makes a leap，这是源自拉丁语的格言 natura non facit saltus（nature does not make leaps 大自然不会跳跃）。莱布尼茨、林奈、达尔文都把它作为自然哲学的一个重要原则。作者在这里反其意而用之，是一种幽默的文字游戏。

间没有再加一条峡谷！也许有些时候这样的情形也是好事。如果一个演奏长号的人在每两个音符之间都进行连奏①，会是怎样的情况？如果用水银代替硬币作为货币，又会是怎样的情况？

有时候，让我感到讨厌和尴尬的，是在来不及考虑的情况下就必须做出决定。"香烟，口香糖，冰激凌，晚报！"火车站台上小贩在叫卖着。我想在其中挑一个最好的。但如此多样的几种物品之间，该怎样比较哪个更"好"呢？这时候火车"突特，突特"地开动了，带着我和我的思考一起离开了。或许我没选择冰激凌是件好事，因为我曾得到过这样的建议："不要在两顿饭之间吃东西，除非你饿了。如果你不确定饿还是不饿，那就不要吃。"而刚刚正是我不确定的情况。然而当一件事情是否不确定的本身也是不确定的时候，又该如何呢？然后就以此类推循环下去。

当然，不管怎么说，没有选择香烟总是好的。如果我已经最后一次冒犯了别人，没理由不再最后冒犯一次——毕竟每一次冒犯都是最后一次。记住，吸一口烟和吸一整包烟没什么不同。那么吸入别人吐出的烟和自己吸烟，有什么种类的差别和程度的差别呢？种类的差别和程度的差别之间的差别，到底是种类的差别还是程度的差别，抑或两者都是呢？这些完全不同的事情又是如何写满这一页纸的呢？最后一次冒犯别人，又与一只跳入水中的两栖动物有什么关联呢？

上面的这些，就是对本研究所关注的问题所做的一个并不学术而又十分冗长的"定义"。我愿意选用这种表述方式，而不用另外的方式。即，当一个人有许多特别的事情要说时，一般都会先从总体上讲这是一种哲学上的缺陷，然后继续给出这种情况的一般原因。而这里的介绍主题的杂乱方式正是"实例法"的反思性应用。某些思路似乎汇聚到某个模糊感觉到的问题上，或者更准确地说，似乎

---

①　译者注：连奏(legatissimo)，音乐术语，也叫"最连音"，指以最连贯、圆滑的方式演奏，程度高于连音(legato)。

是在一组可能存在的问题的网格中连接起来的。不管原则或原则的统一性如何，人们都会去寻找更多似乎与此有关的"实例"，尽管这里的"实例"是非常模糊的事物。

尽管这种方法不是一种理性主义的方法，它让一切都取决于，也就是说，悬挂在一个或几个钉子上；它也不同于那种依靠几条腿的经验主义，比如感觉的材料和有关系的想法。这种方法联系到从事物的中间开始，比如颜色混合、元素周期律、火车上的饥饿，以及人群的分布。

只靠随意罗列不同的事物是无法描述一个问题的。如果不对所讨论的客观事物、提出的问题、使用的方法和得出的结论做一个限制，那么这一讨论就会涵盖整个哲学领域甚至更多内容，并且没有"理论上"的理由不让人们漫无边际地去追随自己的目标。然而，一种天真的实用主义认为，现实中的一些部分应该被标记出来，以便可以在单一体量的范围内加以处理：在讲台上用三个小时讲完，在一本书的两个封皮之间呈现，或者特别是写成学术论文，并进一步划分为几个子问题，再分别在不同章节中进行讨论。或许上述所有问题的产生和定义都是从行为角度而言的，但本文的明确意图并不是为哲学的实用主义辩护。

为了应用分级和序列的方法（第三章第 31 页，第四章第 45 页[①]），我们可能需要把问题按照概括程度进行排列——从口腔护理和烹饪白菜到布尔代数和一般性分析。从这个角度看来，在本文开头那一段内容说明的实例占据了一个中间的位置。更加准确地说，这个问题似乎比物理学或是心理学这类自然科学更为概括，而又没有数学分析那么概括——至少我希望它们是这样。

然而，如果我们想把问题这样定位，那么首先需要解决两个反对意见。第一个反对意见是，"我们是否总是能够找到事物之间的

[①] 译者注：为了方便读者，中文译稿中的有关参阅页码，已经按照本书排版页码做了适当修改。

中间点?"尽管可能没有任何问题会自然地汇聚起来,稳定地统一在这样一个中间的主体附近(参见第七章第 99 页),但考虑到哈佛大学诸位先生宽宏大量的程度,尤其是这样一个各种事物的混合体,也许永远也不会允许作为一项研究课题而通过:对于哲学来说太肤浅,对于科学来说太不准确。答案是,仅仅是这种中间类型研究的缺乏本身,就可能证明需要接受这种研究,也可能证明这种研究自然是不可行的。因此,这种研究的实际执行将会或多或少证明自身肩负的合理性。此外,它在一般性的观点上与归纳逻辑和方法论的历史领域非常接近,这也正是本文题目的由来。

第二个反对意见是,概括性并非分类问题的唯一原则,除非我愿意承认它与形式逻辑的一致性,否则连哲学本身的位置也值得怀疑。依照本研究的精神,我在此声明,选择概括性作为变量 x,仅仅是为了对问题进行定位而做出的一项个人决定。但是,如果因为考虑它们的困难程度、人性的诉求、可推广性、使开心性或是其他什么方面出现问题时,我们没有理由不可以采用变量的"转换方式"。

实际上,需要更多的考虑而不是一般的概括,以便把本研究限制为"连续性"研究,这跟其他方法论问题相对不同。既然在开头部分已经提供了活生生的实例,于是尝试着正式陈述问题就不会有多大的风险了。使用"下限法",我将从零开始。但是,"无中生有",所以我不得不从一个模糊的事物开始。问题是:怎么办? 换句话说,我如何理解它,欣赏它,或是正确对待它? 为超越这种模糊,可能会注意到事物的某些特征或方面,很感兴趣或似乎很重要;当我们观察整个世界时,会发现跟最初的事物在那些方面不同的或者是相似的其他事物。在认识论语言中,我们已经获得了"那个",并通过跟"其他"对比而把它定义为"什么"。在数学语言中,我们有一个特定的项,接着去寻找自变量,而随着变量的变化,我们可以找到一个对应的函数,那个特定的项就是这个函数值之一。从这个角度对问题进行系统的研究,可以称为方法论中的函数理论,它将涉及与主题相关的所有艺术和科学,并将借鉴所有对问题有足够影响的数学函数理论。

　　然而,目前的研究范围相对来说要窄得多。首先,它主要只涉及一个变量 x 的单值函数,它在相关问题中可以处理为足够接近一个连续体。其次,主要重点只放在划分层级的连续性(第三章)、序列顺序的比较(第四章)、极限情况的考察(第五章)、连续性和非连续性相通的同一性等问题上(第六、七章)。多变量函数的问题,以及最大值和最小值、统计变量等的问题都不单独考虑。但由于连续性作为一种具有弹性的可扩展的方法,其中有些问题确实进入了我们有限的视野,因此这项研究并不像表面上看起来那么狭窄。

2. 方法: 内在的

　　由于问题是从事情的当中开始的,所以我们采用的方法就像前一节所讲的,主要是内部的,或者是反思性的。在对连续性和非连续性进行区分时,我会问一问,它们是否不可相容,它们是否相互限制。在看到这项研究和所有其他研究之间的连续性时,我会问,或者至少其他人会问我,我该在哪里画这条界线?借用电学中的说法,问题、方法和结论在这里并不是“串联”,而是“并联”的。如果我们不喜欢它们相互预设的悖论,我们也许可以武断地选为它们彼此共设(consupposition)①的悖论。在问题开始时存在着方法,在开始正确的方法时存在着问题,而在“好的开始是成功的一半”中存在结论。这样说来就像是在原地兜圈子,或者像是要用自己的鞋带把自己拉起来。但是,正如第二章中关于方法的部分所述(第13—14页),有些圈子绕起来并不是无意义的,而有些用鞋带提拉自己的努力也不是徒劳的。

　　普通数学中所用到的方法和结论将会自由地应用于本研究,但它们的使用受到“某些性”(someness)精神的影响。说某件事物是

---

　　①　译者注:“consupposition”查无此词,疑似作者将词缀“con-”(共同的)和“supposition”(推断)拼合创造。

"某些性"的，这意味着两件事：第一，确实有这样的事物，这是经验的动机，——这需要注意具体的案例；第二，也可能有不是这样的事物，这是分析动机，——它需要关注抽象的概率。在数学里可以说，*如果a 那么b*，并且把它确定为普遍命题是完全安全的。但是，由于在本研究中，还要关注具体情况是否符合这个假设或那个假设的问题，因此这种安全性并不具备。因此，数学定理的使用范围比数学概念要小得多，而且从来没有被"证明"过，只有"连续数学归纳法"（第六章第 91—92 页）一例除外，就作者对数学文献的狭隘了解而言，这是原创的。数学证明把一个假设跟另一个假设相联系，如果后者不太容易得到经验的直接支持，那么数学证明可能是方法论上的失败。

　　一种方法或一组方法声称应用范围没有限制，我似乎需要为其有效性进行辩护。(1) 首先，我要承认任何方面的连续性概念都只能在它适用的范围内应用。这个范围有多大，只有本文中这些无效的以及有效的(如果有的话)尝试才能显示出来。一些理想主义者和实用主义者认为现实是不确定的或是灵活的，而更好的说法是把它说成可塑的。像丝线或水一类的事物是柔性的，不会抵抗，会屈服于任何力量；像钢或蒸汽这样的事物在抵抗和屈服方面都是有弹性的，在一定程度上取决于所施加的力。思想的任意性有一定的自由度。但当我们采用一种方法去解决一个问题时，我们都要为自己的做法负责。当适用范围缩小到难以察觉的地步时，比如试图用对着铁棒叹息的办法来把它折弯，就说明我们在使用错误的方法。因此，认识到一种方法的局限性就等于提供了一个安全阀。这样，每当那么多可塑性的现实超出我这个方法论的小锅炉的容量，就可以泄流出来，而不会造成教条主义的伤害。

　　(2) 其次，这种把事物看作是具有连续性和非连续性的一个变量的函数的观点只是看待事物的可能的视角之一。手里有一把智能之锯，人们自然应该要想着"在钢琴上"、在门上、在所有其他家具上试着用它来锯一锯，甚至梦想着去锯锯子。但这并不意味着所有的事物都必须以它的可锯性(sawable)为唯一的定义。抛开这个比喻的局限性，我可能会认为，转换的方法将会把解决一切问题所需要的新想法都包括进去。但这只不过是一个试图以虚空为代价，从无限概括中获得安全的例子而已(见第五章)。一种更为安全的态度是，希望每一位智力的禀赋和受过的训练跟笔者相似的读者，都会发现这种处理方式有高度挑战性且极具启发性，并同时认识到，研究中发现的只是一系列形式主义和牵强附会的思维方式的合法性存在。

3. 术语：混合的

在阅读后面的章节时，除去有几个经常出现的惯用语，人们可能会有词语的使用缺乏一致性的感觉。其实，本文原则上是在刻意避免这种一致性。另一方面，语言修辞的使用非常随意，并且有时是混合的。有人确实认为，整个研究是把数学的类比应用于非数学或半数学的对象。这种说法是正确的。如果本研究不是一种特殊的类比方法，那么所有的方法都可以不看作是类比了。正如第三章(第31页)所示，实际案例、"真实"类比与隐喻之间，仅仅是程度上的区别。因此，使用多种不同的术语、各种各样的数字和示例，可以呈现出这个概念的本质定义。实际上，考虑到语言的本质是诸多事实中的一个事实，一种与其他活动有关联的人类活动，除了使用形式上的重言式[①]之外，有没有一种字面意思和指代内容完全符合的语言，这是值得怀疑的。因此，当语义的轻重与我们需要考虑的问题无关的情况下，我就不用再费心去列出一连串的同义词。"绝对的、无条件的、无限的、具体的、范畴的"不需要在同一个语境中加以区分，尽管它们在其他一些方面可能有重要的区别。

本文尽量避免或非常谨慎地使用以下这些词语。"理论上"和

---

① 译者注：重言式(Tautology)又称为永真式，是逻辑学的名词。如果给定一个命题公式，无论对分量作怎样的指派，对应的真值都为真(True)，就称为重言式。一般语言上可以理解为同义重复。

"实际上"很少出现在讨论中，因为每当有机会可以使用它们时，会发现其他一些词更令人满意。"主观"和"客观"这两个词在本次提及之后几乎不会再出现，并不是认为它们是无效的概念，而是因为它们碰巧没有涉及这些问题。"真"和"假"在本文中发挥的作用并没有它们的普遍适用性那样重要。每当有机会用到它们时，通常会给出适当的（或不适当的）解释。多数时候，"有用""有结果""有效""有意义"和"人为性""无用""无结果""无意义"足以描述所讨论的情况。本文尝试用惯用语甚至口语词的表达方式使词语的意思更加明确，并利用词语在上下文中丰富联想的重心来消除可能存在的歧义。若是这些方法还不足以解决，本文将给出解释或定义。

下文是解释一些常见的术语：

*事物*几乎总是跟"某物"这个词一样具有广泛的含义。它似乎和实体、事项、客观起同样的作用，并且在许多（不一定是哲学的）讨论中，它确实有着更普遍的意义。

点，在正式讨论的语境中使用时，并不一定是指几何意义上的一个点，而是指一个系列中的任何元素，也就是任何事物。因此，在第五章中，开头的那句格言就是一个限制性的"点"，或者在第六章（第83页）中，一场完整的体育比赛也是一个"点"。

想法、观念、概念、构想，除在特定的语境中或习惯用法中必须分开之外，没有区别。

*阈值*和*阈限*可交替使用。ϵ 用于表示下限阈值，而 M 用于表示上限阈值。

*奇点*从广义上讲，是指任何一个特别感兴趣的点。用 ξ 表示。

论域[1]意味着有某种明确特征的事物，而*语境*意味着有某种模糊联系的事物。但是，如果二者的映射相互重叠，并且区分不重要，

---

① 译者注：论域（universe of discourse），一般是指在一定文句或对话中涉及的客观事物，即论题所包括的同类事物的总和。同时，在科学研究中，任何科学理论都有它的研究对象，这些对象构成一个非空集合，称为论域。

则可以互换使用。

无限大,正如在第五章所讨论的,仅用于代表变量的意义,跟数学分析中的用法一致。在本研究中还没有用到完全的、静态的无限大或超限数的概念。

一个函数的值,在数学的语境中,代表且仅代表当变量 x 取一个常数值时,对应函数的一个常数解。因此,当 $x=3$ 时,函数 $f(x)=x^2+17$ 的值为 26。要避免使用这个严格建立的数学用法是很困难的,但本研究属于边界研究,特别需要明确指出的是,在常数 26 中不需要存在任何价值,且函数 $f(x)=x^2+17$ 中也不需要存在任何目的性。当然,在不同的语境下,我们可以谈论呼吸功能的重要价值,或者国家功能和社会功能的政治价值。

最后也是最重要的一点,"连续性"这一术语需要解释。在本研究中,级数[①]的连续性和函数的连续性这两种数学意义都将被使用。因为适用性属于一个程度问题,这些术语将用于仅仅是近似连续的事物。细心的数学家会坚持认为连续性的这两个含义之间彼此无关,可能存在一个变量的连续函数,它只是稠密的,而不是连续的[②]。但是,我们通过以简驭繁可能把两者混在一起。那么连续统就被作为连续函数 $x'=x$ 的特例。

连续统具有两种特性:第一个是所谓的戴德金[③]式的封闭性,它相当于填充了每一个极限点的空间;第二个是密集性,也就是连续统的区间可以无限细分。现在让我们把前者跟连续函数会通过

---

① 译者注:此处用词为与此前"序列"相同的 series。此处只具数学意义,故译为"级数"。

② 见 F. W. Hobson, *Theory of Functions of a Real Variable*,第 222—223 页。

③ 译者注:戴德金原理(Dedekind principle)亦称戴德金分割,是保证直线连续性的基础,其内容为:如果把直线的所有点分成两类,使得:1. 每个点恰属于一个类,每个类都不空。2. 第一类的每个点都在第二类的每个点的前面,或者在第一类里存在着这样的点,使第一类中所有其余的点都在它的前面;或者在第二类里存在着这样的点,它在第二类的所有其余的点的前面。这个点决定直线的戴德金切割,此点称为戴德金点(或界点)。戴德金原理是德国数学家戴德金(R. Dedekind)于 1872 年提出的。

所有中间值的性质①相混合；把后者跟连续函数的另一个性质相混合，即在变量的差值接近零时，函数的差值也接近零。这样，我们就可以讨论一般的连续性了。

这种悄然移动过的类比当然经不起严密的数学证明的考验。例如，连续函数的两个特性是相互独立的，而连续统的两个特性则不是独立的。但是，类比是在部分差异的事物中寻求部分同一性的过程，而对这些数学上的差异无差别地使用"连续性"和"连续的"这两个词时，在多大程度上或潜意识中导致这种方法论出现无效或混乱的结果，只有通过实际案例才能确定。

4. 资源：多方面的

如果研究是包括对一个主题已发表的所有内容进行系统和详尽的调查，再加上一点新东西，那么本研究大概就配不上那样的研究。因为本研究的*典型*素材来自观察青蛙、戒掉香烟、陷入实际的困境、收集文字游戏和变通数学。这在某种意义上是一种探索，但很难称得上是研究。

另一种研究材料来源是我接受的科学训练，主要是物理和数学。这就解释了本文中物质科学的例子远多于其他自然科学②，而科学中的实例又远多于其他领域的原因。同样的*原则*可以适用于所有其他学科领域，这样说很容易。但从实例是构成原则的重要部分这样的信念来看，如果是其他学科，比如更多地利用生物学题材，那么总体计划很可能会做出很大的改变（参见第 120 页结论概要）。

从历史上看，基于连续性的思考在不同地方都出现过。例如：

---

①　这通常是通过夹挤法来证明的，很令人怀疑。见第二章，第 21 页上端。

②　译者注：物质科学（physics）据作者本人译名。西方把自然科学分为生命科学和物质科学两大分支，并且还有更细的划分。中国早期引入时曾以"格致"指代 physics。作者当时应该是受到这种影响。

莱布尼茨①和伽利略②。但是莱布尼茨把它看成为一个哲学原则,而伽利略则只是在偶尔遇到其他问题时使用它。因此,连续性还没有被作为一种方法进行系统研究过。可以肯定的是,本文中直接呈现的许多观点,甚至可能是大多数想法,要么是对他人曾经更好、更充分地表达过的观点的不完全复述,要么只是对过去阅读中被无意识灌输的观点的回忆。因此,没有充分的致谢,标志的不是傲慢,而是无知。

　　然而,在许多情况下,本文是在有意避免直接引用。文中尽可能用好的标准英语列出一些概括性的陈述,然后在适当的地方绘制一些有意义的图示来说明,从而展现出某种思路。但如果有人非要说:"嘿,这不过是笛卡尔③解析几何的伪装。"或者,"这只不过是把黑格尔④的正反合理论又重复一遍。"那么,一个历史知识丰富的人就会立即把对作者全部图示的联想,转向他熟悉已久的子领域。现在,如果图示构成了观念,那么旧观念的新图示将不太可能与旧观念的本意完全一致;而新的图示就像两个山谷之间分水岭上的水一样,并没有处于稳定的平衡态,它们必将流入已有的河道,除非它们能获得一个机会,聚集在山边的蓄水池中,从而开辟出新的溪流(参见第七章第 101 页及后文,论平衡态)。因此,无论无知是真实的还是假装的,在无知造成的损失中,都有可能存在着新鲜感带来的

---

　　①　译者注:莱布尼茨(G. W. Leibniz, 1646—1716)是德国哲学家、数学家,被誉为 17 世纪的亚里士多德。他和牛顿先后独立发现了微积分,还发现并完善了二进制。

　　②　译者注:伽利略(Galileo di V. B. de Galilei, 1564—1642)是意大利天文学家、物理学家和工程师,欧洲近代自然科学的创始人,研究了速度和加速度、重力和自由落体、惯性、弹丸运动原理,描述了摆的性质和静水平衡等,因提倡日心说遭罗马教廷异端裁判所判罪管制。

　　③　译者注:笛卡尔(René Descartes, 1596—1650)是法国哲学家、数学家、物理学家。他是影响 17 世纪的欧洲哲学界和科学界的巨匠之一。他把几何和代数相结合,创立了解析几何学。在哲学上,他那句"我思故我在"最为著名。

　　④　译者注:黑格尔(G. W. F. Hegel, 1770—1831)是德国古典哲学的代表人物之一。他提出的辩证法可以说就是由正题、反题与合题组成的。他的名言是:存在即合理。

收获。

　　本文最后给出了一份参考文献列表(第 127—129 页)。但是，列出那些完全用到或是所用并不足道的作品似乎也有助于学术诚实，如果更仔细地察看这些作品，可能会改进或极大地修改本研究的结果。

　　最后，谈话、通信和讨论对本研究的助益甚至大于阅读文献。特别感谢亨德森(I. J. Henderson)教授，他通过"实例法"保持了我的科学兴趣，特别是指导我注意伽利略使用过的科学方法；亨廷顿(E. V. Huntington)教授让我见识了许多数学上的概率，并帮我做了很多细节的修正；还有谢费尔(H. M. Sheffer)博士[①]帮助我完成了本文的总体规划，并建立了清晰和准确的高标准。因为如果清晰只是程度的问题，那么根据每个问题的要求，它至少必须高到足以跨越所需程度的阈值。除此之外的致谢难以全部列出。但是，正如上文提到的，正是哈佛大学哲学和心理学系的科学自由主义，继承了罗伊斯(Royce)教授[②]的传统，使得在不同学科的边界地带进行这种研究成为可能。

　　[①]　译者注：谢费尔(H. M. Sheffer)博士是指导本博士论文的导师。他曾在康奈尔大学任访问讲师。作者认为"谢费尔的讲课是我听过的最好的讲演"，"完全是个享受。"

　　[②]　译者注：罗伊斯(J. Royce)为哈佛大学著名教授，于 1916 年去世。作者深受其影响，极为怀念。

第二章 方 法

1. 方法：杠杆

方法，从广义上讲，可以说就是用一部分现实去对付另一部分现实。用来描述方法的词可以有很多：中介的、间接的、话语的、形式的、人为的、机械的。这些描述跟立即的、直接的、直觉的、实质的、自然的、自发的形成对比。一只乌鸦没有办法立刻喝到一个高水罐里的水。它捡起小石头扔进水罐里，于是水位上升到了它能够喝到的程度。这就是方法。在自然的各种基本力量面前，人本来是一种无助的生物。可是，通过科学技术，人延伸并加强了自己的手臂，使这些力量成为自己的仆从。这就是方法。

于是，方法也可以说是杠杆。给定一个我可以自由使用的有限的力 ε，需要克服一个更大的力 M。采用的方法就在于找到一个杠杆 n，使得 $n \times \varepsilon$ 大于 M。同样，方法也可以比作触发扳机的动作。我不能把球扔到 200 英尺以外；但我可以制造枪和火药，然后扣动扳机，把球送到几英里之外。

在方法论中，有一点儿类似于用自己的鞋带把自己拉起来①。把鞋带绕过一个滑轮，然后往下拉。这样用一半的力就可以拉起全部的重量②。这就是科学一直以来在做的事情。对小行星谷神星③的几次观测确定了它具有某种运行轨道。因此，先前记录的某颗"星球"一定是谷神星。而如果它是谷神星，那么它一定有更精确的

---

① 译者注：用自己的鞋带把自己拉起来 Pulling oneself up by one's bootstraps，俗语，原指自食其力。这里是取字面意思。

② 见 *Scientific American*，1917 年 10 月 20 日。

③ 译者注：谷神星(Ceres)是太阳系中最小的、也是唯一位于小行星带的矮行星。由意大利天文学家皮亚齐(Giuseppe Piazzi, 1746—1826)发现。

某种运行轨道，而不是最初记录的那样。因此，我们在走过合理的循环中，获得了一种对现实的*把握*。

但方法不仅仅是方法，方法也是问题。一个体重 300 磅的人不太可能有 150 磅的力气。因此，他必须解决方法的*应用*问题。也许他可以再加装一个滑轮，这样就只需要 75 磅的力就足够了。或者他可以把鞋带缠绕在电机上，再扳动开关，这就只需要几盎司①的力量。

培根②似乎认为，科学方法论一旦完善，任何人都可以应用。但是，只有在方法的使用者有着足够的智慧，能够明智选择并有效使用的情况下，方法才是方法。按照重要程度的顺序安排几个业务项目是一件很简单的事情。因此，我们把它称为用于业务调度的系列排序法。但是，当涉及对于某些人员的任职资格进行评级时，我们就进一步采用加权因子的方法来解决排序*问题*。每一种方法都可能存在问题。每种方法都允许并且可能需要有一个*用于它的*方法。

然而，仅仅是对方法进行改进并不会导致方法的应用。杠杆可以加长，触发扳机可以更加精巧，但它们还需要一些有限的力量来启动。培根对于方法的概念和笛卡尔关于触发自由意志的论点都是基于这样一个假设：我们用 n 乘以 0，可以得到某个有限的结果 m。一个用鞋带自缢的人是无法把自己提起来的，因为他已经没有力气了。没有现实可言，循环就是恶性的。

因此，方法的作用并不是*取代*直觉、直接经验、判断或者任何这一类的东西，而是把它们跟问题的解决联系起来。一个人在某个领域拥有的想象力、天赋、技能和经验越多，他就越能准确和有效地使用正规的方法。如果说方法是用现实的一部分跟另一部分相对立，

①　译者注：1 公斤约等于 2.2 磅，1 盎司约为 28 克。

②　译者注：培根(Francis Bacon, 1561—1626)，英国文艺复兴时期散文家、唯物主义哲学家，现代实验科学的创始人。他把经验和实践引入认识论，努力实践"复兴科学"的志向。

那它绝不是一无所有与空无一切相对立，而是使用者拥有的现实越多越好。

2. 方法

对方法的一般性讨论就到此为止。现在我们要讲到具体的方法。本文开始研究的方法只涉及方法论领域中的一个小的角落。但对于这些方法适用于哪些问题则没有限制。当我们遇到那些以任何意义上的连续性思想都无法有效解决的问题时，这种适用性才会消失。

（1）实例法

要清晰地定义一个问题，我们必须收集足够且适当的样本。除非问题有了清晰的定义，否则我们无法判断什么样的样本是适当的，有多少样本才算充足。但是在科学研究和日常生活中，问题的现实存在能够帮助我们脱离这样的循环。即使我们还不确定问题的定义，我们也可以从问题的历史发展中，模糊地感觉到我们所要做的事情。因此，我们可以通过观察世界来收集"案例"，尽管我们还不知道什么样的案例是足够和适当的。

因此，当我们遇到精神上和物质上、思想上和身体上等等的问题时，实例法将会寻找诸如愤怒、恐慌、财富、体质、音乐喜剧、陨石、噪音等例子。如果我对某些事情感到悲观，我可能是在寻找诸如科学成就、战争、剥掉的橘皮、小孩的噪音、哲学、酣睡、难吃的晚餐、唱歌合拍和走调等等情况。

这种方法当然只是一个最初的步骤，一般来说它并不会定义一个问题，也不用说是解决问题。它告诉我们要深入事情的本质，寻找那些自然存在的实例。避免过早陷入问题和系统的定式中。随着人们工作的进展，可能会找到一些理由去把此前的问题加以细分，或者把它跟其他问题结合起来，甚至可以认为它已经不成问题。

（2）分级法

寻找具体案例是任何称为经验主义的方法都会有的一个过程。

当我们在一个概念的不同阶段、不同程度或不同层次上寻找具体案例时，连续性的思想就进入了。这就是莱布尼茨①所说的形式的连续性，即：任何两个不同类的事物之间都存在中间状态的事物。作为一种哲学，它认为中间形式总是在某种意义上存在的。但作为一种方法，我们只是满足于去想象并尝试采用层级理念是否有好处，就可以了。由于这一方法将在第三章中进一步展开，我在这里不再赘述。

（3）系列排序法

当我们定义一个等级 x 时，就可以在某种意义上把案例按照优先等级进行比较，分级法就转变成为排序法。当 x 接近一个数学上的连续统时，这个方法有一些最为重要的应用——尽管这一方法也适用于其他系列，例如整数列。对于那些认为不应轻易地把事物进行量化的反对意见，我通常都是这样回答：在很多情况下，这种适用性会减弱，任何两种或更多事物的排序比较可能会在意想不到的情况下成为一个实际问题，并作为一种有效的方法。第四章将对这一主题进行更全面的论述。

（4）极限法

当我们把一个问题构想为根据条件 x 得到结果 y 的形式时，把变量 x 设为不受限制的极端值往往是一种富有成效的方法。对于极端情况下的考虑，往往会引出一些在其他情况下表现为不确定或不明显的事实。因此，在系列的比较中，人们很难判断出哪个更优秀或哪个更健康，但在极端情况下，一个智障者不如天才，或者一个运动员比一个癫痫患者更健康，则是显而易见的。

然而，在说事情"显然"会是某种结果的时候，我们必须保持经验上的谨慎态度。例如，人们可能会认为，在从银行只取两美元的极端情况下，如果柜员还是把两张钞票翻过来，沾湿手指，按常规方式点钞，那将是"荒谬的"。但事实是，出于职业习惯，他还是会这么

①　见 Bertrand Rursell, *The Philosophy of Leibniz*, 1900，第 64—65 页。

做。因此,*反证法不需要去证明任何事情是错误的*。

普遍性的命题通常是基于少数的案例得出的,科学规律也往往是通过小范围的事实推断出来的。因此,有必要采用极限法对结果进行检验。伽利略发现的重力加速度是一个常量;但牛顿发现,在地月距离这种极端状态下,重力加速度会随着距离的平方增大而减小。托勒密①和阿尔哈曾②都进行过光线折射的实验,并发现了入射角与折射角的大致关系;尽管他们没能发现正弦定律,但他们发现了∠β 总是大于∠α(见图 1)。尽管他们可能想象过使用极限法,也就是把高密度介质中的∠α 增大到极端数值来看看可能会发生什么,但直到开普勒③才发现∠α 超过临界值会导致∠β=90°,也就是全反射现象。

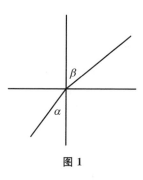

图 1

氧气在一般环境下被认为是一种"非磁性"的物质,但在极低温度下,当氧气为液态时,它就会有很强的磁性。超低温的实现为新的物理现象打开了一片广阔的视野。在莱顿大学进行的那项最为出色的研究④就是极限法在这一领域里的一次伟大的应用。

函数的定义都是一个试探性的而且只能或多或少说得上准确的事情,它的有效性取决于问题的进展和结果(参见第三章第 39 页以及其后各页,关于函数)。极限法不仅可能导致函数公式的修改,

---

① 译者注:托勒密(Claudius Ptolemaeus,约 90—168)是古罗马数学家、天文学家、地理学家和占星家。地心说的集大成者。他对光学也作过研究,认为光线在折射时入射角与折射角成正比关系。

② 译者注:阿尔哈曾(Alhazen,965—1039)是中世纪阿拉伯最重要的一位物理学家。他最感兴趣的领域是光学,完成了影响世界的重要实验:小孔成像、眼睛成像原理。

③ 译者注:开普勒(Johannes Kepler, 1571—1630)是德国天文学家、物理学家与数学家。他提出了行星运动三大定律。同时他对光学、数学也作出了重要的贡献,是现代实验光学的奠基人。

④ 译者注:指莱顿低温实验室发现超导性。

还可能导致函数转换为完全不同的变量。也就是说，在极端情况下，原本的函数可能会失效，而另外的次要因素可能会突显出来。例如，对于一根小电线中的电学问题，可以用一个相对简单的公式来充分描述发生的现象①。但在跨越大西洋的长电缆这样的极端情况下，由于电容和电感等因素变得重要起来，那个公式就失效了。

极限法可以作为稍后将要描述的夹挤法的一个预备性步骤，正如，"你不能过于这样，也不能过于那样"通常是个错误的建议。但若是前往极端状态，人们往往会走过平均值的另一侧。然后，当钟摆向回摆动时，人们就做好了它会回到平均值的准备。

因此，一个大学新生使用化学天平称重量，一开始用的砝码太轻，再加 1 克砝码，发现还是不行，再加 500 毫克，再加 1 厘克，如此等等，却始终测不出准确的重量。正确的方法当然是先添加较大的砝码，直到它明显过多，然后再改用更小的砝码。

许多人都有在钢琴上弹奏伪琶音②的毛病，就是左手按键比右手稍早一点。一种有效的纠正方法是有意识地去犯相反方向的错误，从而体会到右手按键过早是怎样的感觉。这样，学会双手同时按键就会更容易些。这可以追溯到亚里士多德（Aristotle），他把这种想法比作扳直一根弯曲的手杖要做的事情。③

极端的方法当然不需要都在物理科学中实现。这可以通过假设和想象的方式来完成，以便了解接下来会发生什么情况，也可以通过实际进行实验来获得经验的结果。一位医学研究者并不需要

---

①　译者注：如欧姆定律的公式，导体中的电流跟导体两端电压成正比，跟导体的电阻成反比。见 41 页注①。

②　译者注：琶音（arpeggio），指从低到高或从高到低依次连续奏出的一串和弦音。这里的"伪琶音"（pesudo-arpeggio）指本文提及的按键错误听起来像是琶音而不是真正弹奏出的琶音。

③　见 *Nichomachean Ethics*，Book II，Chapter IX，在 J. E. C. Welldon 译本第 56 页。

摄入过量的氯仿①来确认它的效果，一位经济专业的学生也不需要在一片土地上投资一百万来验证收益递减规律。

　　极限法的极端形式就是极值法，通过这种方法，我们可以了解当测量条件接近下限或无限增加时，会有什么结果。例如，一个空类在广义上也称为一个类。公式：

$$\int_a^b y\,dx + \int_a^b z\,dx = \int_a^b (y+z)\,dx$$

在 b 为无限大时也可能成立。通过使用极限法，我们可以获得心理概念上或语言表述中的普遍性、对称性和简单性，或者发现事物在什么条件下会变得不同。我们将在第五章进一步详述这一想法。

　　（5）明确定位法

　　为了充分理解一个事物，我们必须重视它与其他事物之间的位置。在本研究中，我们将使用标尺去衡量一个事物的位置，正如前面的分级法和排序法所定义的那样。

　　例如，一个国家可能对国民的健康程度没有明确的概念。通过调查，可能会发现，这个国家的国民平均健康水平在各国中属于非常低的。总的来说，统计学工具对于弄清楚曾被忽视或错误认识的位置，是非常有效的。

　　明确的位置是找出黄金均值（golden mean）的起始点。我在八个月里看了两部戏。这个数量接近平均值吗？如果不是，那它是在平均值的哪一边呢？这个方法能够揭示出许多隐藏着零值的情况。一个人可能做的运动量是零，携带私人信件的数量是零，在实验室工作的时间是零，一起游戏的孩子数量是零，一年内跟人争吵的次数是零，为各种事业捐款的数目是零，用外语说话的次数是零，喝酒

　　①　译者注：氯仿，学名三氯甲烷，音译为"哥罗仿"，是一种有机化合物，无色透明、有甜味、易挥发的液体。在医疗上曾跟乙醚一样用作麻醉剂，并被广泛使用。

的酒量是零。从这些例子的混合性质来看,很明显,零不一定就是不足或过量。关键在于,明确定位法会激起人们的疑问,是这样吗?可以肯定的是,有很多问题都是微不足道的,可以忽略不计,或者最好是根本不提。这时必须依靠常识,或是亚里士多德所说的"实践的智慧"①。正如前文所说,一个方法不会自己说明什么时候最适合应用它②。

(6) 中间态法

极限法试图把我们的函数使用范围扩展到初始范围之外;中间态法是在已知案例之间寻找值得注意的案例。这两种方法分别对应于外推法和内插法,但是它们的适用范围更广,因为它们不一定像外推和内插那样要求"外部或内部都是一样的情况",而只是简单地问:在未经标尺检验的部分中,什么是真实的。

更确切地说,中间态法是建立在连续函数的性质上的,这简单地表示为它会经过所有的中间值的性质。这一方法也可以说是分级法的发展。因此,一发炮弹在某个时刻从大炮射出,而在另一时刻又在几英里之外,那么必定在某个瞬间,它位于炮口前仅一英尺的位置。我们很难想象这一瞬间的情况,但一张快速曝光的照片会捕捉到这个中间态。

我们常常认为中间态的存在是理所当然的,尽管我们对它们的理解可能是错误的。在早期的电影史上,迈布里奇③通过连接在悬线上的相机,拍摄了马奔跑时的一系列照片,揭示了有趣而令人惊讶的事实,展现出动物在运动过程中间位置的实际形式。随着现代

---

① 译者注:亚里士多德(Aristotle,公元前 384—前 322)是古希腊哲学家,被誉为西方哲学的奠基人之一。他认为,人的本性是求知的,人的目的是追求真理和智慧;人类的智慧是通过经验和理性的相互作用获得的。

② 参见 Samuel C. Crothers, *The Pardoner's Wallet*(第一篇散文)。

③ 译者注:迈布里奇(Eadweard Muybridge, 1830—1904),英国摄影家。后到美国,以最早拍摄动物及人类动作的分解照片而著称。1878 年,他使用 24 台照相机拍摄马奔跑时的连续照片《奔跑中的赛马》,证明马奔跑时四蹄腾空。

摄影技术的完善,把中间态法应用于鸟的飞行也成为可能的事情。

在对中间态的探索中,谨慎选点往往可以避免无结果的尝试。如果巧妙地用数学函数定义为研究的问题,那么在数学方面某些具有特异性的点,在具体问题中也可能具有重要意义。这类点的例子包括 $-\infty$、0、$1/2$、$+\infty$、已知点之间的中点、两点之间的算数平均值和其他平均值、习惯点、自然倾向点、在定义问题时所给出的点,等等。可以看到,列出的这些点也包括了极限法所用到的例子。

(7) 夹挤法

当我们的兴趣不仅仅是一般的中间态,而是转向具体到一些特殊的情况时,我们就使用所谓的夹挤法,因为没有更优雅的名字。

已知在一种情况下有一个结果,在另一种情况下会有另一个结果;我们让二者相互接近,并探寻二者差异接近于零的临界情况下会发生什么。可以看出,这可以归结为极限法的一种特例,但因它的特殊重要性而需要专门考虑。

这种方法的数学形式可以通过以下定理表现:在区间 (a, b) 中,
若:(1) $a \leqslant a_1 \leqslant b_1 \leqslant b$,
$a_1 \leqslant a_2 \leqslant b_2 \leqslant b_1$,
$a_2 \leqslant a_3 \leqslant b_3 \leqslant b_2$,
……

图 2

且:(2) $\lim_{n \to \infty} (b_n - a_n) = 0$,
则存在点 ξ,使得:

$$\lim_{n \to \infty} a_n = \lim_{n \to \infty} b_n = \xi$$

事实上,这是证明连续函数的介值性的一种方法(或者说我们通过这种方法证明了一个引理[①],进而又通过这一引理证明了这一

————————

① 译者注:引理是为证明某个定理或解决某个问题所要用到的命题。引理和定理没有严格的区分。

性质）。

　　寻找黄金均值的过程可以采用夹挤法的方式进行。在调整显微镜聚焦时,我们先采用极限法把目镜从一个过高的位置开始。接着把镜筒逐渐降低,到物镜几乎要压碎标本或者玻片,以确定我们已经越过了平均点。然后我们拉回镜筒,尝试越来越精细的位置调整,直到获得最佳的聚焦效果。

　　通过夹挤法来估测数量,得到的结果通常比直接用直觉更加准确。一位机械师曾根据亲身经验说,比如当他想设计一根用于某种目的的杆子,而又猜不出正确的尺寸时,他就会先(在纸上)画一根细得可笑的线条,再画一个短粗可笑的圆柱体。接下来,他会在旁边画一根仍然很细,但稍粗一点儿的杆,再画一个仍然很粗,但不那么笨重的杆。就这样,他不断地缩小 a_n 与 b_n 之间的差别,直到看不出它们分量的差别。然后他取二者各项尺寸的算术平均数,称之为他的平均值 ξ。这个方法经过实际使用证明十分有效。

　　因此,通过夹挤法得出黄金分割点的过程,可以跟钟摆的减幅振动进行比较。人类总是在平均值的一侧或另一侧犯下极端的错误,历史也总像是钟摆一样在摇摆中前行,如果我们知道有些钟摆的运动是减幅的,我们就不必为这样的事实而失去信心。

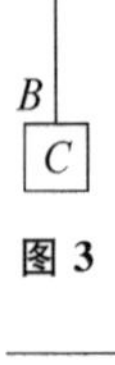

　　伽利略在一些论证中使用了夹挤法：已知长绳比短绳要脆弱,假设有一根绳子会在重物 C 的作用下于 D 点断裂(见图 3),那么在这根绳子以比 D 点高一点点的 F 点作为悬挂点时,绳子依然会在 D 点断裂。同样地,假如重物被挂在比如说 E 点,一个只比 D 点低一点的位置,那么绳子也没理由不在 D 点断掉。因此,一根绳子的脆弱程度只相当于它的最弱点,不论这根绳子长如 AB 还是短如 FE。[①]

　　尽管这种方法在证明跟连续函数有关的数学定理方面起着重要作用,但它并不是对于任何问题的连续性都会有用处。

图 3

──────────
① 指伽利略的重力实验与斜面实验。

如果存在非连续性的情况,这个方法也将跟找出其他感兴趣的点一样确定它的位置。对奇点的更全面的处理参见第 6 章和第 7 章关于同一性和差异性的描述。

(8) 转换法

到目前为止,我已经说明了一些方法的发展,这些方法并不超出一个特定变量或者一个特定函数的范围。但是,由于没有绝对理由要我们必须留在最初提出问题时的观点之中,如果改变视点似乎可取,那我们就可以求助于转换的方法。例如,在把视野清晰度作为显微镜目镜位置的函数问题中,当我们达到接近焦点的临界状态时,发现不存在一个"焦点",而只是对应于标本不同层次的不同聚焦程度。这样,在问题中就引入了一个新的 x。

考虑到陈述和概念的简明性,我们可以把分级法看作是转换法的下限。在第一个例子中定义函数 $y = f(x)$ 也是如此。这在数学中是很地道的表达方式;举例来说,如下的"线性变换":

$$w = Az + B.$$

实际上,这只是在表达 w 是 z 的一个线性函数。因此,如果我们要在转换中达到完整性的上限,就应该把本论文的整个范围,甚至更多内容都考虑进去。因此,有必要在本节中对转换进行一个粗略的描述。

首先是转换的目的。从形式上来说,进行转换的目的包括:确保

1) 函数的连续性

2) 函数的非连续性

3) 曲线的平坦度

4) 曲线的陡度

5) 函数的线性

6) 数量的有限性

但对于一个不懂数学的人来说,很容易看出这些不是自己最关

心的,而只有工具价值。进行转换的*科学性*目的更能够被认为是"目的"。下面列举一些最重要的目的,转换可能是为了:

1)更为充分地定义最初引发问题的模糊意图

2)容易理解

3)便于进行数学的或逻辑的"操作"

4)便于进行文字方面的表述

5)提高结果的准确性(有效性最佳化)

6)发现新因素和新结果的一般目的

关于转换本身,我们可以把它们划分为变量 x 的变化和函数 y 的变化。在很多情况下,这二者会有重合之处。例如, x 乘以 n ,这等同于 y 除以 n 。因此,差异是重点之一。

变量 x 的变化——以下是最重要的几种 x 的变化形式:

描述	一般形式	特殊形式
1)乘	ax	$nx, x/n, -x$
2)加	$x+a$	$x+a, x-a$
3)幂次	x^a	$x^n \cdot \sqrt{x}, 1/x$
4)指数	a^x	e^x
5)三角函数		
6)其他		$x' = x_1/(x_1+x_2),$ $x' = x/\sqrt{x^2+1}$
7)新因素		

为了说明其中的一些形式,我们发现了一个使用乘法的例子,当伽利略使用一个斜面替代自由下落的球体,从而把

$$v = gt$$

转变为

$$v' = g(\sin \alpha)t'$$

(α 为斜面的倾角)。也就是说,他延长了时间,以使时间曲线变平,

从而便于(文字叙述的)操作,并借助于减缓球的移动速度,提高了观测球在即时位置的准确性。

3)取倒数是幂 x^a 的一种特殊情况,此时 $a = -1$。例如,与其说电流与电阻成反比,这会产生一组难以控制的双曲线,不如说电流与电导率成正比,这就会得到一条直线。

7)引入新的因素尤其重要,因为极限法和夹挤法往往会导致这一步。前文已经讲到跨越大西洋电缆中的电容和电感的例子,以及显微镜的不同聚焦程度的例子。此外,某个函数在某一点上的非连续性,可能会在另一个函数中转换为连续性,这将在后面的章节中详细说明(参见第七章第 110 页及后文)。

函数 y 的变化——y 的变化可以分为两种:对 y 本身的常量操作和不同函数的复合,其中后者对应于引入新因素的方法。

常量操作——

描述	一般形式	特殊形式
1) 乘	$af(x)$	$nf(x)$, $f(x)/n$, $-f(x)$
2) 加	$f(x)+a$	$f(x)+a$, $f(x)-a$
3) 幂次	$f(x)^a$	$f(x)^n \cdot \sqrt{x}$, $1/f(x)$
4) 指数	$a^f(x)$	$e^f(x)$
5) 对数	$\log f(x)$	
6) 三角函数		
7) 符号函数	$\operatorname{sgn} f(x)$	
8) 导数	$f^{(n)}(x)$	$f'(x)$, $f''(x)$
9) 阶梯函数		$E[f(x)]$

5)例如,在统计学中绘制相关曲线时,会取对数以使曲线变得平直。

7)$\operatorname{sgn} f(x)$ 仅表示是 $f(x)$ 的符号。这一函数可以用于标记差异,这将在第七章第 107 页得到更充分的讨论。

8)我们可以考虑把衡量一只钟表的准确程度作为取导数的一

个例子。一个儿童或一个无知的人可能会有的最为天真的看法,是:

a) 如果一个钟表走得不准,那它就是坏的。也就是说,如果我们把基于时间 t 的函数 $f(t)$ 作为时钟表示的时间,那么只要 $f(t)$ 偏离 t,就可以判定为时钟坏了。

b) 但一个更聪明的人会说,时钟走得不准可以调整,又或者误差可能在容许范围内。重要的是它走的速度要正确,不能太快也不能太慢。换句话说,他考虑的是 $f'(t)$,并且能够使他满意的情况只是:

$$f'(t) = 0$$

c) 但一个曾经用过准确时钟的人会说,如果走的速度错了,也可以调整,重要的是错的速度要一致。换句话说,速度变化的速度要为零,或者说

$$f''(t) = 0$$

因此,大多数钟表的真正缺陷是它们运动的二阶导数不为零。

9)可以认为采取非连续步骤就是利用 sgn y 把一个函数转换为两个值的一种广义形式。例如,在绘制统计曲线时,我们不绘制数据太少的连续曲线,而是把数据分组,例如,5 英尺 5 $\frac{3}{4}$ 英寸和 5 英尺 6 $\frac{1}{4}$ 英寸都归入五英尺半这个类,从而把平滑曲线转化为直方图,也就是具有方形顶部的曲线,如图 4 所示。

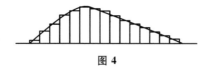

图 4

函数复合——

描述	一般形式	特殊形式
1) 乘	$f_1(x) \cdot f_2(x)$	

乘 x　　　　　　　　　　　　　　　　$xf(x)$

乘以降低非连续程度　　　　　　　　　$(x-a)f(x)$

除以 x　　　　　　　　　　　　　　　$f(x)/x$

2）加　　　　　　　$f_1(x)+f_2(x)$

加特性　　　　　　　　　　　　　　　$f_1(x)+f_2(x)$

减去 x　　　　　　　　　　　　　　$f(x)-x$

1）函数 y 经常与 x 相乘以确保其线性。因此,假设我们有

$$xy = a + bx$$

则,设

$$y' = xy$$

有

$$y' = a + bx$$

这是一个很有用的变换,例如,用在相关曲线中。

　　2）为了说明除以 x,让我们回想一下拉斯金(Ruskin)的说法:如果一本书值得阅读,它就值得购买[1];或者是老生常谈的建议,如果一件事值得做,它就值得做好。现在的问题不是更多的收益是否来自投入更多的时间、精力、金钱等,而是收益是否成正比。换言之,比起第一个例子中出现的函数 $f(x)$,更重要的是变换函数 $f(x)/x$。因此,总的来说,如果从鸟瞰图中得出:给予十分之一的额外时间,可以获得十分之一以上的额外收益,那么这条值得研究的曲线就值得进行最后的检验。图 5 以一般方式表示了这种联系,此时:

$$\frac{f(x_2)}{x_2} > \frac{f(x_1)}{x_1}. \text{(由于 } \tan\theta_2 > \tan\theta_1\text{)}$$

---

[1]　Sesame and Lilies, section 32(Harvard Classics, vol. 28,121 页)。

但是，一份报纸只值得在开始读几分钟，而当我们看到"心灵鸡汤"和廉价促销的栏目时，回报递减法则的影响就开始显现出来。在这种情况下，如图 6 所示，对于 $x_1 < x_2$，我们有：

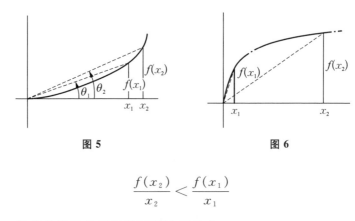

图 5　　　　　　　　　　　　　　图 6

$$\frac{f(x_2)}{x_2} < \frac{f(x_1)}{x_1}$$

很多值得做的事情并不都值得做完。

2)通过加法进行复合时，被加上去的函数常常以忽略结果的形式出现。从自然的角度来看，这种过程被称为减法。因此，在扩大一家工厂时，不仅要考虑总收入的增加，还要从中减去运营费用的增加。有远见的改革者倾向于关注如果现在就完成改革将会带来的好处。但保守派呼吁他们注意必须从受益中减去浪费、风险和危险的代价，因为克服传统、习惯，以及有关的其他不合理的机构会危害真实价值。

在整个方法论的研究中，人们可能会提出反对意见，即为了提高准确性、确定性等，为了发现最佳行动方案，搭建智力支架的总体费用可能会带来这样那样的浪费、风险和无关的多余过程，这种打了折扣的结果带来的将是优势的缩小而不是放大。

对这种异议的回应是承认它。通过下限法，我们可以把没有方法也视为一种方法，这可以称为观察直觉法或直接判断法（见第四章第 51 页）。一个合理的方法论不会建议用蒸汽驱动的起重机来捡起一块鹅卵石,也不建议在睡梦中阅读亚里士多德的《伦理学》[1],然后再决定什么时候是停止睡觉和醒来的最佳时间。

3. 方法的阶段性

以上是这些方法的概述,下面章节中将逐步阐述。总起来看,我们可以把这些方法看作是连续性这一种方法的不同的自然阶段,随着涉及问题的深入,这种连续性方法也随之逐渐深入。我们从具体的案例开始,从中发现分级,并按顺序加以排列,向外探索极端案例,向内探索中间案例,把我们的注意力集中在特别感兴趣的点上。当这些步骤似乎还不足以解决问题时,我们通过转换法重新表述关注的问题,转换法是包含着无数个可能的子方法的一个类别名称。

然而,这些只是形式上的表述。在实际应用中,我们可能会对其中某个阶段最感兴趣,认为某个阶段最为重要;那么我们就可以说是正在使用这个或那个子方法。

同样,有的问题可能是需要以不同的顺序应用这些方法,或者多次重复应用相同的方法。这并不奇怪,因为我们可以在任何适宜的时候改变我们的观点,并重新考虑这个问题,或者,因为我们甚至都不能把"问题"说清楚,我们也许就会转而全力去处理新的问题。

尽管这些不同的阶段有着自然的顺序,但并不要求它们严格按照逻辑前后相承。很可能其中一个阶段虽然在某些方面非常松散和牵强,可是对现实有很好的作用。因此,按事物的重要性排列顺序的方法是一个相当有效和明确的过程,尽管衡量重要性的变量 x 是一个极其模糊的东西。或者,又比如夹挤法可能非常有启发性,

---

① 译者注:亚里士多德(Aristotle,公元前 384—前 322)是柏拉图的学生,亚历山大的老师。亚里士多德的著作构建了西方哲学的第一个广泛的系统,包含道德、美学、逻辑和科学、政治和玄学。

即使数学证明它仅适用于数学连续统 x，我们却不得不用它来处理从更精细的角度来看甚至不"密集"的系列。

简而言之，如果我们认为方法是面对一个问题时解决问题的有效工具，那么它是否能有效地解决另一个问题也就无关紧要。当然，在越来越精确的领域中，还需要有更为严格、详尽、准确和全面的方法。这些领域，无论是二重唱和赋格曲①，还是天体力学，都始终是从明确的角度加以规定的。但是，如果想要提出唯一真正或有效的普遍方法的问题，我们就将会超出本论文计划的范围之外了。

---

① 译者注：赋格(fugue)又称"遁走曲"，是结构严谨、音乐内容丰富的一种音乐体裁，属于复调音乐。赋格的结构与写法比较规范。

第三章　概　念　分　级

1. 概念分级与系列排序

所谓概念分级,我指的是一些具有层级、等级、层次或阶段的事物。概念分级的研究与系列排序的研究不同,后者来自两个或多个对象和一个尺度;而前者来自某个既有的概念,我们要探究是否可以找出可能的或实际的分级和排序。例如,用同一种材料绘制两幅图形,问:"A 比 B 高吗?"是一个排序问题;而"A 是高个子吗? 他长得如此之高。"则是概念分级的应用。对系列排序的问题来说,在数学上准确地定义用于衡量的标尺,通常是十分重要的,这将在下一章中讨论。但是,当我们对分级的概念本身感兴趣时,它们之间具体的形式关系并不总是那么重要。因此,人们不必对发明创造的贡献程度进行数字评分也能认同蒸汽机发展的阶段性。于是,我们下面将要研究的等级可能是一个密集系列的连续统,或者可能仅仅是一连串的离散项,甚至可能是一系列各自没有明确定义的项。

2. 分级的问题和方法

如果我们要给一个概念分级,最明显的方法就是打开我们的思想和身体的眼睛,去寻找分级的具体案例("实例法")。我们可以在给定的概念中选择某个方面 x 作为向导,这样随着 x 的变化,就会产生不同的层级。一般来说,要找到一个概念的某种层级是一件简单的事情,但带来的结果是否微不足道,则是个更进一步的问题。

然而,对于一个已经在脑海中占据已久的非黑即白的概念,人们通常很少寻求去分级。给一个概念分级,与其说是一个问题,不如说是我们用来尝试解决问题的一种方法。我们可以称之为挑战性问题。这样的一种判断可能带来什么样的结果呢？

　　1）首先，找到的具体案例可能会帮助我们发现未知的事物，或是注意到此前我们忽略的事物。当人们谈论精神和物质时，很可能会提到"愤怒、恐慌、美丽、财富、罢工、战争"[①]这些干扰二元和谐的事情。

　　2）分级可能是"明确定位"（第二章第19页）的预备步骤，也就是说，我们在一个分级的系列中，往往会对已有概念的位置有更好的理解。一个人从法语课程毕业，并认为自己"已经学会法语"，但如果他考虑到"学习看菜单、阅读科学文献、看小说、说法语、听讲座、写作、与儿童聊天，吵架，用法语梦想或做乘法，看懂一部法语的说唱歌舞剧（vaudeville）"这些等级，他可能就会惊讶地发现，自己所处的位置并不是"学会法语"这个短语所应表达的地方。

　　3）我们最初对于概念的层级作出的定义，可能需要更加精确地描述，或把定义加以修订，甚至可能需要放弃原来的定义。"智力行为"有时被定义为有能力应对新情况的行为。把红色和食物联系到一起只是单纯的联想，而能认出"从左数第二扇门"的能力才称为智力。但是，如果我们把排列颜色、形状、大小、位置、顺序、门的状态等元素的复杂程度和普遍程度都考虑到，进行可能的分级，那么，显而易见，事物"新"或"非新"的定义就需要进一步细化了。在这里，分级法只是提出了一个新问题，而没有保证只靠自己就能解决它。

　　4）一个常识性的概念，尤其是用一个词包裹起来的时候，可能会被穿透而引出它的优势意义。因为在一个词的周围往往会聚集一些联想，有的不适于它所使用的上下文语境，就会导致理解错误。如果我们把一个人属于某个教会这件事表达为"他是个基督徒"，那么所有基督徒应有的品质就都倾向于归到他身上。但是，如果我们考虑到教会内和教会外的人在一周七天中表现出的基督教精神的

---

　　① 参见 H. L. Hollingworth, The Psychophysical Continuum, *Journal of Philos*, *Psy and Sci*, XIII7, 182 及后文。

等级,我们或许就会对这个人有另外的看法。

类似地,我们可以把诸如重要的／不重要的、非常有趣／不太有趣、近期的／非近期的、必要的／多余的、保守的／自由的等等,这类二分性概念都进行分级。如果这些词在上下文语境中的意义是明确无误的,那么就是使用适当;如果它们导致人们的错误理解,那么这些词就属于误用。

5) 立法决定的陈述同样也受到定义不确定性的影响,因为陈述就涉及定义。因此,通过分级法,我们应该看出诸如"一切有智力的人都有权获得人道待遇","除非必要,否则不要说话","只读重要的书",这种简单陈述规则的不足之处。

6) 从以上内容可以看出,对概念进行分级可能是夹挤法①的准备步骤,也就是说,从两个不同条件下的两个不同结果开始,逐渐让两个条件接近,然后检查结果的改变是在何处产生以及如何进行的。

7) 对骆驼鼻子的争论(第六章第 92 页)也可以作为概念分级的准备。因此,如果有人说我们看不到分子的运动,我们可以说,如果我们可以透过眼球的晶状体"看到"一把椅子,我们没有理由不能用望远镜"看到"远处的一棵树。所以我们可以用一副观剧望远镜"看到"舞台上的"歌手",通过光学显微镜"看到"一个细胞,通过几秒钟内的静止照片"看到"一朵花,通过福柯钟摆②"看到"地球的转动,通过天文望远镜"看到"几年前那个方向上的一颗 12 等星,通过布朗运动③"看到"分子的运动。当然,仅仅具有概念分级的可能性,并不是充分的论据。在所有这些争论中,如果没有骆驼身体的实质力量支撑,骆驼鼻子的形式就毫无意义。

---

① 参见第二章第 21—22 页的示例说明。

② 译者注:让·福柯(Jean Foucault)是法国物理学家。他于 1851 年用钟摆展示出地球的自转。这项成功的实验,使得福柯钟摆成为很多国家科学博物馆的标志性特征。

③ 译者注:布朗运动因由英国植物学家布朗(Robert Brown)在 1827 年发现而得名。它是指悬浮在液体或气体中的微粒所做的永不停息的无规则运动。

8) 事物同一性的某些方面往往可以通过划分等级来表现出来。因此,在后面的一节中(第 35 页),我将试图表明,图示、类比、隐喻等实际上都是某些广义概念的组成部分,从这个角度来看,所有这些都属于实例。同样,如果我们能够划分出对自然进行不同程度干涉的例子,从制造化合物,通过嫁接鲜花,到观看流星,我们就会发现,除了在人为干预①程度上有所不同之外,实验和观察都具有相同的性质。而通过连续性对同一性进行充分的讨论是第六章的主题。

9) 对一个概念进行分级可以取一个案例的概括形式,把其中某个常量特征(如 0 或 1)视为一个变量,或者从另一个角度,在这个案例的某个变量取某个特定值时,把它作为一个系列中的一项。因此,区域限制(第 39 页)的操作相当于把相关系数为 1 的严格函数的情况推广到相关系数不为 1 的情况。或者,在上一个例子中,如果鲍桑葵②屈尊使用我的术语,他可能会用人为控制程度为零的广义实验来作为观察的定义。

10) 到目前为止,我一直在讨论分级的连续性方面。但既然概念都已经是分级的,它们的结果怎么能不分级呢? 有的方面是相同的,并不排除其他方面有差异。把观察视为实验而把某个变量减少到为零的程度,并不妨碍我们把控制程度小于特定值 ε 的某类实验归到"观察"的名称下,并在逻辑、方法、学术或财务上给它们以特殊待遇。

所有的罪犯都一样是罪犯,但社会却发现最好是根据罪行的等级来分级惩罚。所有考试及格的学生都一样通过,但教育实践表明,他们应该以 A、B、C 等成绩通过考试,这有时会带来不同的结果。作为一个微不足道的实例,我可以进一步讲,在练习早起的过

---

①　参见 Bosanquet, *Logic*, 2nd ed. II, 141 页。

②　译者注:鲍桑葵 (Bernard Bosanquet, 1848—1923)是英国哲学家、美学家。他认为,个人组成集体,但集体大于个人之和。他主张国家对个人应该使用一个合适的干涉限度。

程中,记录不同等级的先到和后到,要比每次早上起床迟到时只打个叉更有效。对懒惰程度进行分级,可以防止有人因为没能做到最好就去做最烂。

对于分级处理的方法,我们需要一个精确的分级尺度的操作定义,换句话说,就是系列排序。因此,我们要超出本章所考虑的分级法的范围之外。就像任何其他方法一样,分级法从一个问题的某个地方开始,如果它对问题产生了影响,就会使问题向前迈进一步,却永远无法解决生命和宇宙的最终问题,而且往往无法把有限的问题解决到预期的程度。关于概念分级的总体讨论就到此为止。在以下章节中,我们将讨论几个特别感兴趣的案例,即:逻辑概括度;变量、参数和常量;数学函数与区域限制;以及智力进程。

3. 分级逻辑的概括度

我们对于"生物、动物、人、希腊人、苏格拉底"这种系列分级逻辑的概括度都很熟悉。然而,人们经常忘记,在这类系列中,一个概括的概念和例子只是两个相对的术语。如果有 n 项事物按概括度顺序排列为 a_1、a_2、……a_n,则我们可以取任意两个 a_i 与 a_j,并说"a_i,例如 a_j",其中 a_i(在序列中)先于 a_j。因此,在一个这样系列中:一个事件、一个过去的事件、一项科学发现、一个物理定律的发现、牛顿对冷却定律的发现,我们可以说"一个过去的事件,例如,一个物理定律的发现"。

有些人似乎喜欢用模糊的例子来说明自己的想法。他们会说"一个事件,比如说,一个历史事件","一个科学发现,例如化学中的一个发现","一个定理,例如数学中的某个定理"。其模糊之处就在于用来说明的事物和被说明的事物之间的概念等级没有太大差别。因此,人们不应被"例如说"这一类表达误导而感到满意,因为这是一种承认等级的概念,很可能因等级差别太低,而没有达到考虑问题所要求的水平。

还有一个跟刚才提到的系列类似的分级系列是:实例、案例、例子、示例、类比、比喻、文字游戏。地球和太阳之间的关系是万有引力的一个例子。在现代课堂上重复卡文迪许①的实验被称为万有引力的示例，这例子本身并不是很重要的，而是有助于使这个概念具体化。把万有引力跟声、光和热进行对比就是类比。恩培多克勒②关于爱情的理解可作为一个比喻。而我可能使出浑身解数，也想不出一个聪明的文字游戏来完成这个序列。在这里，我建议把分级视为逻辑概括度的上升序列。这样，引力、光、声、热等等，都归入了强度成平方反比这一概念之下。

　　一个比喻，如果它是一个好的比喻，除了明显的构成依据之外，还应该有其他的相似点。如果这样说来，把引力和爱情归为同一类的相似点还真不少。对于一个好的文字游戏，通常既有逻辑上的共同点，也有文字上的共同点。结论是，我们不应该毫无理由地画下一条界线，并把"示例"之前的内容看得至关重要，而轻视之后的序列元素，认为是偶然的。它们在某种*程度*上全都至关重要。它们全都是概念的*组成*部分。

　　从概括度的角度来看，我们可以看到形式含义和实际含义之间的关系。由于二者含有显性或隐性的可变项，形式含义所连接的两个陈述并不是命题，而是命题函项。根据二者的具体程度不同，可以说这个形式含义有不同程度的"形式度"③。但是，当系列中所有的项都具体化，使我们都拥有两个命题，即显著陈述时，就会达到实

---

　　① 译者注：卡文迪许（Henry Cavendish, 1731—1810）是英国化学家、物理学家。在牛顿发现万有引力定律之后，他测出引力常量，并推算出地球平均密度，计算出地球的质量，被誉为第一个称量地球的人。

　　② 译者注：恩培多克勒（Empedocles，约前 495—约前 435）是古希腊哲学家，他认为有一种循环存在着：当各种元素被爱彻底地混合之后，斗争便逐渐又把它们分开；当斗争把它们分开之后，爱又逐渐地把它们结合在一片。

　　③ 考虑到"形式度"（formality）没有在分级意义上使用过，因此在术语上用它指形式含义取值的可变性并无不妥。这一可变程度如何测量，是否可以测量，以及这一可变程度是否能够用显性以及隐性变量的数量和取值范围表示，可能是一个重要的问题，但对这里讨论的问题而言并无必要。

际含义的极限。示例如下：

1）"x 是 a"，意味着"x 不是非 a"。（非常形式化）

2）"x 在一个地方"意味着"x 不在另一个地方"。

3）"一个人在一个地方"意味着"一个人不在另一个地方"。

4）"一个人在英国"意味着"一个人不在美国"。

5）"伯特兰·罗素[①]在英国"意味着"伯特兰·罗素不在美国"。（含有隐性可变项时间）

6）"伯特兰·罗素 1918 年 4 月 1 日在英国"意味着"伯特兰·罗素 1918 年 4 月 1 日不在美国"。（实际含义）

这只是含义问题的一个方面。它并没有说明可变程度为零的事实会有什么不同，或者说，实际含义为什么是一个有用的概念（参见第五章第 61 页）。

4. 变量、参量、常量

初学数学的学生通常很难接收常量和变量的概念。直到熟悉感扼杀了好奇心之后，他才会明白为什么 C 是一个比 x 更确定的数，正如丙是比天更为确定的数一样。参量的概念则是更像一个悖论：它既是一个常量，也是一个变量。即使是数学老师，有时候也会把参量说成是一种奇怪的东西。然而，在下文中，我将试图证明参量是数学领域中的常规，而不是例外。

在介绍字母的使用时，老师告诉我们，在同一个"讨论"（或同一个论域）中，每个字母代表的数字都不变。但是，一次讨论是由什么构成的呢？显然，从一个表达式的一部分到整个数学，有着各种不同程度的包括范围。现在考虑一下表达式 $x + x = 2x$，为什么我们不写 $x + x = 2y$？因为 x 在对"$x + x = 2x$"简短的讨论中，需要做

---

① 译者注：罗素（Bertrand Arthur William Russell，1872—1970）是英国哲学家、数学家、逻辑学家、历史学家、文学家，分析哲学的主要创始人，世界和平运动的倡导者和组织者。他曾于 1920—1921 年来中国讲学，赵元任那时给他做中文翻译。

常量,应该保持不变。但在更广泛的讨论"' $x + x = 2x$ '对每个 x 均为真"中,每次我们在讨论" $x + x = 2x$ "时, x 都可能会取不同的值。这样,它就成为一个变量。因此,即使是对于变量 a ,也有一些参量性的成分。可能正是变量那不变的一面,解释了不同变量 x 、 y 、 z 等令人困惑的自我认同。它们之所以被称为变量,是因为它们不变的一面虽然被认可,而它们可变的一面则被强调了。

另一方面, 在圆的方程 $x^2 + y^2 = R^2$ 中,只要我们在 x 和 y 改变的同时保持 R 不变, R 就是个常量。但如果我们扩大讨论范围,考虑到不同数值半径的圆,那么 R 就成为一个参量,对应于某个半径的值,比如2,就成为一个常量。但在讨论半径的数值时,比如说2时,我们不会在一个方向上测量2英寸,在另一个方向测量2厘米,而是设定单位是常数,这只有在更广泛的讨论中才把它当成变量。因此,甚至"2"也可以被视为一个参量,作为"2 个单位"的一种缩写方式。

因此,我们可以说,在整个数学领域中,所有术语项的处理都涉及一个潜在的参量。因此在讨论中提到所谓的参量时,我们指的是一个在其他项变化时保持不变,但又可能在整个讨论中产生变化的项。一个自身不变时,其他项也不变的项是一个变量,而一个相对于讨论中的任何项都不变化的项则是个常量。在这两者之间,可以存在任意数量不同等级的参量。对于任何一个研究过数学问题的人来说,这种观点的本质当然不是什么新鲜事;但是,在头脑中明确认识可变性或参量性的程度,会有助于对基础分析的教学,也将有助于研究连续性趋向的一致性、级数的积分和微分以及其他双重极限等这类问题。这一领域过大,在这里无法全面说明。

尽管我们有一种感觉是,所有的论域都是任意的,但在我们实际的理论生活中,处理问题的过程自然培养了我们的某些习惯或偏见。因此,在我们看来, x 就像一个变量,作为参量也是个不错的字母,而 K 和 C 通常是问题中的常量。 $x^2 + y^2 = R^2$ 和 $K^2 + y^2 = p^2$ 之间没有逻辑上的差异。然而,后一个方程会立刻让我们产生一种冲动去改变半径和纵坐标,保持横坐标 K 不变,然后在更广泛的讨论中,会因为 K 取不同的值,而把它考虑为不同的垂直线。

在物理问题中,可变性的排序通常有一种"自然的自然性"。在钟摆的方程式中:

$$x = A\cos\left(2\pi\sqrt{l/gt}\right)$$

x 和 t 是变化最大的量,因为钟摆是随着时间而移动,而振幅 A 和周期不变。然后再看,A 自然是比摆绳长度 l 更可变的参量,因为我们可以很容易地把钟摆拉到不同的位置或给它不同的推力来改变振幅,并且进而在一系列不同振幅的实验中保持其他东西不受干扰。最后,重力加速度 g 自然是一个比 l 更稳定的参量,因为比起搬着器械设备到不同纬度的地方去实验不同的 g,人们当然更喜欢完成一系列摆绳长度不同的实验。但假如有一个人足够富有、悠闲和愚蠢,他也可以飞来飞去地旅行,来改变 g,而保持 A 和 l 不变,然后在巡游世界完成之后,再改变他的 A 和 l。因此,参量的可变性甚至并不是一个固定的序列顺序,而是可能随着所提出的问题而变化的。

5. 数学函数与区域限制

如果我们在宇宙中随机选取两个变量[①] x 和 y,那么其中一个是另一个的数学函数的可能性很小。例如,一堵有裂缝的墙壁的颜色不会由生长在上面的花朵的花枝分叉数量决定。但通常情况下,变量 x 可能会对变量 y 的变化产生一定的限制。因此,尽管长笛吹奏的音符音高和强度总体上是独立的,但它不可能吹奏低 C 的*最强音*(fortissimo)或是一个非常高的*最弱音*(piano)。用图示来说明(见图 1),使 x 表示音符的音高,y 表示音符的响度,那么尽管可能存在的组合不是如同线 AB 所代表的那样,严格地一一对应的函数

---

① 为简洁起见,此处只取 2 个变量。通过把整个带视为一个 n 维管并进行其他的对应调整,我们可以轻松地将这一讨论扩大到 n 个变量。

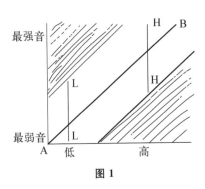

图 1

关系,但它们会被限制在一个带或一个区域内(图 1 中没有阴影的部分)。因此,对于低音,变奏被限制在 LL 范围内,永远也不会达到强音(forts),而对于高音,变奏则被限制在 HH 范围内,从来也不会达到最弱音。

同样地,虽然美德和知识之间没有严格的关联,但如果一个人知识太少,他既不能成为圣人,也不会成为大恶人。因此,这种限制如图 2 所示,接近 0 点处就是所谓的白痴状态,这种人既不可能很好,也不可能很坏。

再次,可以举出第四章系列排序中关于温度等级的讨论为例(第 53 页),我们依次缩小了温度变化跟它的各种物理解释之间的限制区域(图 3)。

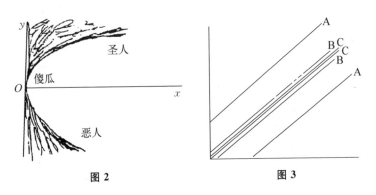

图 2　　　　　　　　　　　　　　　图 3

最后,在两个变量 x 和 y 之间的所有统计相关性之中,各个实例并不是位于一条单一曲线上,而是根据 x 和 y 的相关系数的大小,或多或少地分散开来(图 4)。对某个"单一"量级进行非常精确测量的结果只是简单的相关性,即,由于其中一个因素占据主导地位,而其他"偶然"或"无关"的因素被最小化,所以各点只是位于一个非常狭窄的区域内。[1]

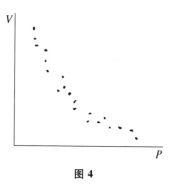

图 4

从这些例子中,我们可以说,如果我们随机选取两个变量 x 和 y,它们之间就存在一定程度的限制区域。在限制区域的下限,两者有完全的独立性(如果有的话)。在上限,两者之间有严格的函数关系(如果有的话)。在这两个极端之间,我们可以提出一个方法论问题:如同统计相关系数一样,发明一个区域限制系数的通用定义,或是广义函数系数的特殊定义。这样,我们对于每一个问题都可以决定,需要达到多大程度的限制才把它实际称为一个函数。

注记。——人们可能会对这种关于函数的宽松看法作出一个合适的评论,即这种宽松来自一个未指明的"隐性坐标"或"隐藏因素"的存在。例如,对于给定的导电体,通过它的电流 I 和它承受的电压 V 大致成正比。这种关系不是一条曲线而是一个带状,因为我们没有确定第三个因素温度,它的变化使电流在相同的恒定电压下略有变化。对此,我可以说,确定温度这一重要因素的结果,只是一种更高等级的限制或一个广义的函数。因为谁能说每四分之一个世纪不会新出一个霍尔[2]来发现一个新的因素,比如磁场对电流的影响呢?因此,欧姆定律[3],作为规定有限数量的因素的一个重要断言,它只是一定程度的区域限制;而作为仅是电阻的定义,因为比值

---

[1] 见 K. Pearson, *Grammar of Science*, 3ed.,关于原因的章节。

[2] 译者注:霍尔(Edwin. H. Hall, 1855—1938)是一位美国物理学家,于 1879 年发现著名的霍尔效应,定义了磁场和感应电压之间的关系。

[3] 译者注:欧姆定律(Ohm's law):在同一电路中,导体中的电流(I)跟导体两端的电压(V)成正比,跟导体的电阻(R)成反比。由德国物理学家欧姆(Georg Simon Ohm, 1789—1854)于 1827 年提出。

V/I 集中了所有已知和未知的可能因素，从而成为一个严格的数学函数，其代价就是成为一个重言式（参见第四章关于系列排序的结论一节）。

6. 智能的进展

提出下面这些问题是完全合理的："是谁发明了第一台蒸汽机？""笛卡尔知道第三运动定律吗？""是谁第一个使用函数这个术语？""贝多芬①是一位原创作曲家吗？"但是不要忘记，在这些问题的答案中通常隐含着限定的条件。因此，最好是提出相对的阶段性概念，而不是那种认为在某个发现之前什么都没有，从那以后就有了一切的观念。

（1）发明。——蒸汽热量转化为机械能可以追溯到亚历山大利亚的希罗②；在瓦特③之前不久，就有了伍斯特侯爵和纽科门④等人的蒸汽发动机；而在我们这个时代，帕森斯爵士发明的蒸汽涡轮机是一个不小的进步。如果希罗、伍斯特、纽科门、瓦特和帕森斯各位先生站成一排，那么应该提名瓦特先生作为蒸汽机的正式发明者。他的这个头衔是为了提醒人们他所做的这些改进的重要性，而不意味着他是从无到有创造了一切。

（2）对真理的认识。—— 对于一个人或一个时期是否"已经知道"某个定律或概念的问题，可以用不同的认识程度来说明往往会解决得更好。早在人们知道如何用船篙撑船的时候，就已经在实用

① 译者注：贝多芬（Ludwig van Beethoven, 1770—1827）是德国著名音乐家，维也纳古典乐派代表人物之一。

② 译者注：希罗（Hero of Alexandria）是古罗马数学家、发明家，居住在罗马行省的亚历山大利亚。他发明了一种叫汽转球的蒸汽机。他还发明了风轮，是最早利用风能的设备。

③ 译者注：瓦特（James Watt, 1736—1819），英国发明家、企业家，第一次工业革命的重要人物。1776 年制造出第一台有实用价值的蒸汽机，使人类进入"蒸汽时代"。

④ 译者注：纽科门（Thomas Newcomen）是英国工程师，蒸汽机发明人。他发明的常压蒸汽机（纽可门机）是瓦特蒸汽机的前身。

程度上理解了牛顿的第三运动定律①。笛卡尔的运动守恒定律只是动量守恒学说在代数上前进的一步,动量守恒是第三运动定律的本质。现在,我们对于质量和惯性的概念还在发展,我们对这个定律的认识也仍在进行相应的改进。

（3）首次提到与概念。——首次命名一个概念的行动通常是十分重要的,因为它会对这命名概念的未来发展作出反应。但是,例如,是莱布尼茨第一次把某种关系命名为"函数",在他之前有诸如多项式和三角变量等方面的研究,在他之后是傅立叶②和魏尔斯特拉斯③发明的函数的广义概念,他本人很难把这些定义视为自己合法的智力后代。实际上,仅仅提到或记下一个概念,往往意义不大。如果一个系统的构建者只是回答这个系统的反对者,说他的概念在系统中某个地方曾被提到,那是不会满足的。同样,如果一个人开始用一个私人博物馆来收藏偶然的想法,可以简单地记下它们,供偶尔引用作参考。但随着这些记录变得越来越多,难以操控,博物馆往往会变成一个墓地。因此,我们在提出一个概念时,要么是必须系统地进行许多交叉的引用,要么是立刻把它展开,阐述到高度明确而详尽的地步,否则它就会丢失。因为只是把它放在厚厚的剪贴簿里,这样带来的欣慰感,就跟把经常放错地方的手表掉到了海里一样:至少现在我知道它在哪里了。

（4）原创性。——原创性的标准可能需要根据具体问题来提出,正如在艺术品收藏中把复制品与原件进行分类。例如,一篇博

---

① 译者注:牛顿三大运动定律:第一定律说明了力的含义——力是改变物体运动状态的原因;第二定律指出了力的作用效果——力使物体获得加速度;第三定律揭示出力的本质——力是物体间的相互作用。

② 译者注:傅立叶(Baron Jean Baptiste Joseph Fourier, 1768—1830)是法国著名数学家、物理学家。他提出任一函数都可以展成三角函数的无穷级数。他提出的一种特殊的积分变换称为傅立叶变换。注意另有一位空想社会主义者傅立叶。

③ 译者注:魏尔斯特拉斯(Weierstrass, 1815—1897),德国数学家,被誉为"现代分析之父"。

士论文可能会因"非原创"而被完全合理地拒绝。但总的来说，原创性可能会有程度的不同，从绝对的原创到新的概念组合，对未完全成型的旧概念做新的处理或解释，再到评论、模仿，最后到抄袭和机械复制。以音乐为例，一个人不可能在拥有一个新的心理物理有机体的意义上具有绝对的独创性。要求创造一种新的音乐模式的独创性，这也太苛刻了：甚至德彪西①的全音音阶都是由已知成分的组合构成的。如果我们分析贝多芬所有作品的短旋律②，很可能会发现它们全都在此前某个作曲家那里出现过。因此，若是一个人想要做到高度批判性，那么音乐中没有什么是原创的，除非他真的去听"色彩交响乐"之类的东西。另外，即使对于一个弹奏五指练习曲的孩子来说，也有一定程度的独创性，以此类推。我通过这个音乐的例子是想说明，智能进程中的所有原创性都可以在两个假设的极端之间进行分级，在这方面我们主要的并不是去关注它们的存在（参见第五章）。

---

① 译者注：德彪西（Achille-Claude Debussy, 1862—1918）是法国作曲家、革新家，他的"印象主义"音乐对欧美各国的音乐产生了深远的影响。

② 译者注：motive 又称"乐汇"。它是乐段内部可划分的最小组成单位。这里跟 short 合译为短旋律。

第四章 系 列 排 序

当我们提出这个问题：我们就有了一个系列排序的问题。这样的概念可以被称为"程度的比较""优先的顺序""线性尺度上的排列"，或者任何其他涉及连接、传递和非对称关系的术语。系列排序的形式逻辑已经得到了很好的发展，如亨廷顿的《连续统》(1917)一书[①]。本章主要关注这一概念在方法上的应用。首先，我将尝试详解系列排序的含义，然后澄清一些系列排序中常见的谬误。接下来，我将考虑如何建立系列排序的方法，随后把系列排序视为可以应用于进一步解决问题的方法。在总结部分中，将从阈限概念的角度进一步发展系列排序的含义。

1. 系列排序的含义：它是什么

二分法观点——当我们问"是 A 比 B 更 x，还是 B 比 A 更 x？"时，我们经常听到这样的回答："A 和 B 真的可以在 x 这方面进行比较吗？"我们可以问："伦敦是不是比巴黎更受欢迎呢？"但是不能问："没赶上火车是不是比吸入二氧化硫[②]更愉快？"于是，根据这种观点，在一个维度 x 上，两件事要么是可比的，要么是不可比的。

连续性观点——以下分级的案例包括并超越了这个观点，提供考虑：

（1）如果我们被问到，两个人中哪一个更重，那么，这是一个意

---

① 译者注：应是指《连续统和其他序列类型（*The Continuum and Other Types of Serial Order*）》一书，作者 Edward. V. Huntington。

② 译者注：二氧化硫是最常见、最简单的硫氧化物，化学式为 SO_2，为无色透明气体，有刺激性臭味，是大气主要污染物之一。

义非常明确的问题，可以得到一个简单的答案。因为体重有一个简单明确的含义。

（2）对于 m/n 和 q/p 两个分数哪一个更大这个问题来说，答案就是不那么简单了。因为每个分数都有两个元素需要考虑。定义分数的相对大小的一种方法是，根据 mp 大于或小于 qn，来得出 m/n 大于或小于 q/p。事实上，由于各种合理的原因，这也是公认的定义。因此，分数的大小已经得到了很好的定义。

（3）现在对于两个职业中哪一个更"适合"于某人去从事的问题。我们感觉这个问题应该有一个含义和一个答案。然而，我们必须首先确定一个适合的标准。我们应该对于天赋、兴趣、可用的教育设施、已有的业绩、社区的需求等等，分别给予多大的权重呢？在这里，尽管人们还没有一个公认一致的适合度定义，但我们仍然相信适合度是存在的。因此，职业的适合程度被认为是某种事物，但仍有待定义和标准化。

（4）如果现在有人问我们，对于中国人来说，英语发音更难还是德语发音更难，那么我们可以给出一个永远正确的答案："这要看情况。"从发音的难度来看，德语要困难得多；而从拼写中识别正确读音方面的难度，英语当然超过了大多数语言。因此，不存在"发音困难"，而只有具体意义上的困难。

（5）再次，可能有人会问我们："谁先发现的海王星，是亚当斯还是勒威耶①？"考虑到可能问的是研究工作的先后，或出版发表的先后，或者是在知识界产生影响的先后，我们会说："用年、月、日等表示出三种情况的优先度，把它们相加再除以三，这样以结果为先后。"在这个过程中，我们自然会说，这个方法在"逻辑上"没有问题，但这将只是个"任意的"或"微不足道的"定义优先权

---

　　① 译者注：亚当斯（John Couch Adams, 1819—1892）是英国天文学家。1845 年与勒威耶同时独立用数学方法推算出当时尚未发现的海王星位置。勒威耶（Urbain Jean Joseph Le Verrier, 1811—1877）是法国天文学家。

的办法。

(6) 最后,当我在餐桌上走神,思考各种不同的系列排序时,可能会听到这样一个问题:"你喜欢要冰淇淋还是李子布丁?"如果对这个问题没有充分的理论思考,我可能只是简单地附和一句"李子布丁",而实际上并没有感觉到更倾向于它。我选择它并不是因为我在任何意义上都更喜欢它,而是我说更喜欢它只因为我碰巧要接受它[①]。这里的偏好顺序只是*临时*定义的,是一种同义重复的重言式。

总之,我们可以按照一种尺度标准对事物进行比较,尺度标准有:(1) 广为人知的,(2) 定义明确的,(3) 理论上可以定义,但还没有明确定义的,(4) 只有在特定情况下才确定的,(5) 任意定义的,(6) 重言定义的。因此,序列的可比性不是一个是与否的问题,而是一个或多或少的问题。

然而,以上六种重要程度的分类其实并不重要。实际上,即使是情况(1)中的体重标准也可能会有争议。虽然在大多数情况下,并不在意体重的意义和测量的微小变化,但在某些情况下,次要因素会变得突出。于是,A 在中午可能比 B 更重,但由于 B 更能吃,他在下午两点可能就比 A 更重了。如果出于任何原因需要更精细地比较,我们必须细化和重新定义体重,比如说,在规定的时间内六周的平均重量。因此,我们现在面临着踏入这种人为性的等级的风险。另一方面,如果我们只取极端的情况,那么微小的差别就不会产生主要的影响了。因此,不论是从哪一个互不兼容的排序定义来看,我们都可以说,中国人比欧洲人更早发现了磁偏角[②]。下面的两项提供了一个新的转折意义的哲理,即:

---

① 愉快和不愉快行为学意义。

② 译者注:沈括的《梦溪笔谈》最早记载了人工磁化的简便方法,即"以磁石磨针锋",造出指南针。他第一个指出地磁场存在磁偏角,即磁针所指"常微偏东,不全南也"。西方学者比沈括的发现晚 400 年。

事物之间的差异越 $\begin{cases}小\\大\end{cases}$，把它们区分开来就越 $\begin{cases}困难\\容易\end{cases}$。

2. 系列排序中的谬误：它不是什么

在这里，跟其他地方一样，是否存在谬误是一个程度问题。在一个极端上，我们可能不加选择地对事物随意进行比较，从而陷入混乱；在另一个极端上，我们可能会否认所有事物之间的比较，并在那令人困惑的多维现实的具体性面前举手投降。然而，我们的天性自然倾向于进行各种比较，如果保持谨慎行事，这就是一种很有用的方法。

（1）*单一维度的谬误*。——然而，当有人问到"谁是你最好的朋友？"的时候，我可能会感到不知所措，在自己日常生活中的伙伴、道德上的恩人和终生的导师诸位之中，不知道该怎样作出选择。但只要一个人不需要作出选择，那么却只用单一的标尺去对多方面的友谊进行排序，有什么意义呢？同样，我们也会发现类似的问题：一个健康的小女孩和一个生病的运动员，哪个更强壮？谁的音乐水平更高，是一个把"四级"曲目演奏得很差的人，还是一个把"二级"曲目演奏得很完美的人？90°的经度差距是大于还是小于 30°的纬度差距？乌鸦更像写字台还是更像茶盘①？

在这些问题中的每一个问题中，

1）我们有两个*表面上*在几个方面都不同的事物。例如，纬度和经度是不同的地理维度。

2）对尺度 x 的理解有待于明确的定义。

3）似乎没有任何意图或目的可以用来定义一个比较的标准。因此，这个问题可以认定为"一维的谬误"而放弃。（这里也隐含着②

---

① 参见 Lewis Carroll, *The Adventures of Alice in Wonderland*, "A Mad Tea-party(疯茶会)"。译者补注：见《赵元任全集》第 12 卷，第 55 页。商务印书馆，2023 年。

② 译者注：此处原文为 Seclusically，疑为古词，暂译为"隐含着"。

所用术语未能满足连通性假说①的意思。)

（2）*标准混淆*。——然而，对于这种认定，人们可能会申辩说，离开具体背景提出的任何问题都可能显得愚蠢或毫无意义。如果我们在讨论天气时提出上述地理问题，那么 30°纬度差距可能比 90°的经度差距更大。换句话说，是*语境*提供了条件才使比较具有意义。（在上文提到的极端情况的"明确定义"问题，如对分数的关注中，其语境是整个数学领域或其他更大的领域，视情况而定。）但是，由于语境通常是隐含的，而且往往非常模糊，当我们把比较得出的结果放在不同的语境中时，就可能发生混淆比较标准的风险。

因此，假如我在为一台望远镜研磨透镜，球面像差和色差就远比场曲率更为重要。所以，我主要通过避免前两种像差的影响程度来衡量镜片的"好坏"。由于我在研磨店的职业或业余爱好对我来说已经提供了足够的语境，所以我不需要特别用形容词"望远的"或"色彩的"来形容镜头的"好坏"。但是，由于"好坏"这个词在其他语境中有着很多联想，当我在邻居制作*摄影*镜头的商店里，而那里镜头的好坏在很大程度上取决于图像的平坦度时，我可能就会忘记这个前提，仍然习惯于对于镜头好坏的"有色"判断。除非我们明确表达出各自的评判标准，否则我们之间的争论永远不会结束。于是，我们在这里就有把一个标准跟另一个标准相混淆的例子。

我们应该从这里吸取的教训，不是总要对每一件事物都明确地定性，这既没有必要，也不是总能做到的，甚至往往也不可取；而是应该意识到，每当问题出现困难时，都有可能存在着这样的混淆。

（3）*无关的辐射②*。——同样，在某些情况下，基于多个因素进行的比较可能会无意识地只用在其中的一个因素上，甚至用在完全

---

①　译者注：连通性是点集拓扑学中的基本概念，把"连通性"定义如下：对于拓扑空间 X,(1) 若 X 中除了空集和 X 本身外，没有别的既开又闭的子集，则称此"拓扑空间 X 是连通的"。(2) 若 E 作为 X 的子空间，E 在诱导拓扑下是可连通的，则称拓扑空间 X 的子集 E 是连通的。

②　参见"Fallacies of Composition and Division"（合与分的谬误）。

无关的事物上。因此，如果从伟人的成就来看，A 国总体上比 B 国更伟大，这并不一定就是 A 国最伟大者比 B 国最伟大者更伟大。换句话说，最伟大的国中的最伟大者并不一定是最伟大的。同理，如果富兰克林①总体上比你我更加杰出，那么至少我们希望，这并不意味着你我在各方面的排序都不如他。如果一个人在工厂管理方面很出色，并不意味着他在国际事务上的判断总是可靠的。

关于重要性的争论往往落入这一谬误。由于总的来说，爱国主义高于艺术，如果必须作出排他性的选择，人们会认为，任何与爱国主义有着松散相关的事情，例如某个曲子的陈词滥调，都应该优先于一个伟大的艺术组织的存在。类似地，一个逃课的学生可能会找出借口去城里买铅笔而不参加钢琴课，是因为他认为写作比音乐更重要。

正如我们不能从整体论证到部分一样，我们也不能总是反向论证。因此，如果我基于一系列考虑决定了我一生的工作，就不应该因为偶尔发现其他工作比我从事工作更有吸引力而动摇。

在这些导致标准混淆的辐射谬误的情况下，总是要求对"整体"的含义进行准确的限定，同样既是没有必要的，也是不可能的和不可取的，因为这会导致徒劳无益。回顾本章第一节关于极端案例的最后一句话，我们可以说，如果一个人，比如在物理学方面取得了卓越的成就，那么他在数学能力方面也会很高，还有理由认为他语言运用得也会相当好，他不太可能道德败坏，尽管偶尔我们会发现像吉尔拉莫·卡尔达诺②那样的人。事实上，我们这里有一个统计相

---

①　见 *Autobiography*, virtue no. 3(Harvard Classics, vol. 1, p. 83)。译者加注：富兰克林·罗斯福(Franklin Delano Roosevelt, 1882—1945)是任期最长的美国总统，带领美国赢得第二次世界大战胜利。

②　译者注：吉罗拉莫·卡尔达诺(Gerolamo Cardano, 1501—1576)是意大利文艺复兴时期百科全书式的学者，古典概率论创始人。他死后发表的《论赌博游戏》一书被认为是第一部概率论著作。不过他性情喜怒无常，精神错乱，时常挥霍。他的姓氏英文旧译Cardan(卡当)。

关系数的降序列表。对待这些谬误采取的中庸态度是,认识到概念的"干扰带"可能会受到不安全或不相关的辐射,同时我们可能会自由而富有成效地、并带有一定风险地对标准作出解释。

（4）*否认比较*。——跟单一维度的谬误相反的一种错误,就是否认任何事物在任何标准上存在可比性（普遍的）,或者否认在应该比较的时候去进行比较（特定的）。由于学生的天分能力、应用实践和成绩专长各不相同,所以老师拒绝只按分数标准进行排序。事实上,所有犹豫不决的情况都在于无法在不同"质量"的事物之间作出偏好选择。这种谬误的哲学在于断言,由于所有具体的事物在许多方面都有所不同,并且所有的序列比较标准都包含一定程度的任意性和人为性,因此所有这些比较都是人为的,并且永远不应该进行。我们不妨说,任何小于无穷大的东西都必须是零!

3. 系列排序中的方法：它从哪里来

在关于方法的那一章中,我曾试图表明,（对于）每一个方法来说,都有一个用于它的方法。因此,在处理系列排序法的应用之前,我将会探寻系列排序是如何建立的。

观察。——有些时候,"A 是不是比 B 更 x?"这个问题是如此清晰,答案是如此明显,以至于我们可以不用任何"方法",答案就一目了然。天蓝色比一套新的哗叽西服颜色更亮,野心比绝望更好,飞机比空气更重。我们可以称为观察法或直觉法,它是方法中的零,或者说是方法中的下限。这种方法的意义在于,无论复杂的方法论机制有多少步骤参与了问题的解答,总要在某个地方有这方面的观察、直觉或直接借助经验,都必须应用这种方法。（参见第二章第15—16页）

定义 x 。——如果标度 x 不能轻易判定,那么我们就必须找到比较 x 用的标准。换句话说,使 x 的含义更加明确。问黄金是否比白银更重,是指二者在相同体积下的重量比较,或是同样地看它们在水中减掉了多少重量。所以我们把它们放入水中称量来得出答

案。因此，方法的介入推迟了观察天平读数的行为，却增加了准确性的作用。

x 的选择。——但很多情况下，我们无法确认在出现问题的语境中，哪种意义才是值得考虑的，从而导致这个问题得不到解答。即，我们称它为"单一维度谬误"。另一方面，x 概念的使用和作用可能告诉我们，我们能够从这个更 x 的问题中获得一些内容。现在的问题是，能获得什么，怎样才能获得呢？

极限。——尝试使用极值法是一种方式（第二章第 16 页）。无论是通过实际的还是假设的（如果出于安全需要），我们都会通过观察来作出判断，并明确需要考虑哪些不那么突出的因素。

加权因素。——接下来，我们必须把这些因素结合起来，并问：我们所说的结果 x 到底是什么意思。例如，通过考虑一些标准测试来评定智力，并通过某种方式整合这些结果来获得最后分数。在这里，我们对智力的等级① x 有一个概念，但只有当我们建立了一个标尺时，我们才能对 x 有一个可行的明确含义。因为"智力"的含义过于宽泛，不能满足在心理科学中的应用。

用法。——比较的标准导向是什么？这个问题的答案，就像一般的定义一样，是用法和效用。"用法"在理论家那里是个很不受欢迎的词。"一个名称里有什么内容？"但除非这个问题无足轻重到无须考虑，否则这个定义不清的问题一定会带来一些粗略的概念。"A 和 B 哪个是更好的镜头？"这个问题在一定范围内是模棱两可的。但这个范围并不是无限的。这里用的"好"被限制在一个弹性有限（也许定义不清）的范围内。我们要把镜片的好坏定义为表面有大量划痕，还要把划痕定义为超过"完美弹性极限"。这就是用法，首先告诉我们是在哪里做什么，并使我们开始出发。

稳定性。——如果用法过于不确定，不能满足我们的目的，那

---

① 译者注：degrees of intelligence，一般译作"智商"。此处出于前后呼应的考虑译作"智力的等级"。

么就要考虑到效应。对于我们的问题而言,最重要或最少主观武断的定义 x 的方式是什么? 如果认为效用是一个令人不快的术语,我们可以称之为逻辑稳定性。通常在解决实验中的实际问题,或建构真正的定律的过程中,用什么样的标准化方法才可能产生序列顺序 x 呢?

通常情况下,一个科学上非常稳定或有用的 x 的定义,在实际使用中会跟 x 的平均含义相差甚远。如果相差太大,那么出于用法的考虑,我们可以使用技术来衡量,或者选用其他术语,或者简单地只是把出现这个术语的科学论著封皮和封底之间的全文作为适合的语境。于是,冷和热在使用中有一个大概的标准;后来,它以液体的膨胀程度来定义,再后来又以气体的膨胀程度来定义,最后是用热力学的关系,这是物理学中对于温度最"稳定"的定义。如果我们发现一个 60℃ 的勺子比一个 61℃ 的杯子更热,那么我们可以给它定性,说这只是心理上的冷暖,而不是物理上的温度。

一般来说,我们可以说使用可能会引发问题,但效用会把我们引向要去的地方。如果我们找到理由走得更远,那就让我们把它说出来,使它一目了然。否则,我们就可能会混淆标准,把坏的说成好的,而把好的说成坏的。

4. 系列排序法:它是为了什么

系列排序是一种方法,因此它本身要得到应用执行,从而实现进一步的目的。

(1)*优先顺序。*——在选择行动方案、事物或人选时,我们必须把各个选项按照偏好的程度进行比较。很多时候,仅仅是排序的过程就是很重要的一种方法。当一个仓促的决定总比没有决定更好的时候,就是这种情况。如果一个人对需要做的一系列各种事情感到困惑,不知道要先做哪个,那么,一个比较现实的解决方法就是简单地按照任意的优先顺序把它们排列出来,然后一件一件完成。在这种"排队"的实践过程中,顺序就不是那么随意了。因为在这里,

"提供服务"的顺序被定义为"即将发生"的顺序。

（2）位置。——系列排序也可以帮助人们把某件事物按照一种尺度来定位。对一个班级的很多学生进行评分，一种方法是先按照成绩的顺序排列，然后，比如说，给全班前 3％的学生评 A，接下来21％的评 B，再后面 45％的评 C，等等。尽管在第一次根据观察进行排序有"主观"的成分，对于一个大班级来说，这样一种程序的结果，比仅仅直接把某张试卷称为是 B 级或者 D 级要"客观"得多。另一个例子是按字母顺序排列事物的做法，如词典中的单词，或按数字顺序排列事物，如书中的页面。这都显而易见，不需要讨论。

定义。——在系列排序过程中，可以定义某些模糊的概念。例如，节俭不一定意味着保留这点或放弃那点，而可以被定义为我们应该依据常识，或用进一步的方法，依据"合理的"顺序或重要性的顺序，安排可能的费用支出，把总的费用规模缩小到自己能够承受的范围。

"可能性"，在实用意义上，也可以考虑一个尺度。"我不可能在明天之前完成那件事"，这意味着如果我把事情按照紧急程度的先后排序，那么我完成排在"那件事"之前的事情所需用的总时间将会超过明天。

事实。——但正如前面三节内容所讲的，系列排序最重要的应用却是系列排序本身的含义。只要明确定义了一个系列的顺序，就会引发相关的事实：我们可以背诵关于 x 的定理；我们现在可以按照这个尺度演奏曲调了。如果 A 比 B 更重，那他摔倒时就会受到更大的冲击，他的行动需要消耗更多的能量，他的裁缝能赚到的利润更少，他在薄冰上滑冰时会更不安全。还有很多关于体重的其他事实。根据常识，比起心理测量这种科学手段或是概率和熵的抽象理论，"排队"似乎更有意义。因而，这些概念在科学中是有用的，因为它们不仅仅是除了自己的定义之外，就没有任何真实的释义。它们绝非人为虚构的，而是进入了相关的规律和真实的命题，这些规律和命题所包含的具体意义，跟胖人对肥胖意义的理解是同样实在的。

5. 结论：阈限[①]

生活和科学都只是近似的事情，这已是老生常谈。具体来说，"$a=b$"意味着，如果有任何更精细的比较会导致 a 和 b 之间的差异，那它也不足以引起我们注意。如果 ε 是一个问题中最小相关性的阈值，那么"$a=b$"就意味着 $|a-b|<ε$。从这个角度来看，"标准的混淆"往往是一种优点，也可能会是一种错误。由水银、气体和能量定义的三种温度可以*不用*进行修正就被视为"温度"。当微小的差异没有影响时，所有的目标都是可以允许的。从这种做法中获得的好处就在于，我们可以自由地说（在一定的幅度内）气体的膨胀与温度成正比，等等。

用法的不一致也往往是潜意识的，如果是这样，我们可以让它们在同一术语下和平共存。"人品优秀"在使用中当然会有不一致的含义，但在众多的联系中，我们不希望有一个枯燥冗长的严格定义，这将限制它的适用范围。

这些并不是为粗心大意作辩解，而是为了保留成果。我不会因为顾虑到温度的高低并不等同于感觉的冷热，而会忘记高温很热这个事实。在一定的 ε 之内，它们属于同一类的成员。只有在没有警告的情况下次要的差异变得重要时，即观点的改变或立场的转变超过阈值时，才会发生争议和出现悖论。因此，我提倡的或似乎提倡的粗心并不是天真的，而是精巧的，就像艺术中那种雕饰的天然。

现在，一个转向数学思维的人可能会提出，解决悖论的方法就在于精确的定义。因为如果数据是近似的，那么自然会引出一个问题：近似于*什么*？为什么不找出那个*什么*来作为标准呢？那么很好，我们讨厌对于温度的那些不一致的不科学的概念，让我们采用理论物理学用的温度的热力学定义。于是，简单气体定律 $PV=RT$

---

① 参见第五章（特别是第 3、4 节）第 66 页及后面的部分。

只对"理想气体"①成立。可是实际上没有气体是理想的。因此，我们得到一个可悲的结果：没有任何气体符合这个气体定律，也没有任何气体可以适合用来测量温度。但有人会来催促，如果你完善你的理论和实验，你就会发现一个用于实际温度的真实气体定律，比如用范德华方程②所表示的那样：

$$(P + \frac{a}{V}a)(V - b) = RT$$

这个方程考虑到了分子并不是完全弹性的，也不是几何上的点。而这不就是通过对 ε 的缩减达到一种更高程度的改进吗？研究发现，范德华也无法把严格的理论施加在实际的气体之上。如果我们坚持对温度本身的严格定义，那么我们就只能说，除了它的定义之外，没有什么是正确的：能量关系的测量容易出现意外误差；范德华方程是不精确的；简单的气体定律是错误的，热和冷的感觉是虚幻的。由此会得出，在开尔文爵士③的热力学温度标准出现之前，所有关于温度计和诸如此类的研究都是不科学的，或者与温度本身无关的，甚至在热力学温度标准提出之后也是如此。同样，由于目前对质量概念的讨论尚未达成最终定义，我们所有的质量概念也都与质量无关。当亨廷顿教授④用力和其他具体关系来解释质量时，他受到了

---

①　译者注：理想气体(Ideal gas)的定义：忽略气体分子的自身体积，将分子看成是有质量的几何点；假设分子间没有相互吸引和排斥，即不计分子势能，分子与器壁之间发生的碰撞是完全弹性的，不造成动能损失。这种气体称为理想气体。从宏观上看，理想气体是一种无限稀薄的气体，它遵从理想气体状态方程和焦耳内能定律。

②　译者注：范德华方程是荷兰物理学家范德瓦耳斯(van der Waals, 1837—1923)于 1873 年提出的一种实际气体状态方程。范德华方程是对理想气体状态方程的一种改进。

③　译者注：开尔文(Lord Kelvin, 1824—1907)是英国物理学家、发明家。他对物理学的主要贡献在电磁学和热力学方面，是热力学的主要奠基者之一。他于 1848 年创立了热力学温度标准。

④　见 *America Math*, *Monthly*, 1918 年 1 月。

一些人的指责,说:"质量就只是*质量*。"因此,根据逻辑,T 是 T,且 T 不是非 T。证明完毕[①]。

但是,只要允许有近似裕度[②]的存在,也许是在黑格尔哲学的意义上,那么我们就可以说 T 不是 T,也就是说,我们可以谈论某些事物的某些性质了。在大多数常识性的语境里,这个阈限比在科学上更为宽松。但在科学中,它也从来不是零。科学是在一个系列中对事物进行比较而达到逐步完善。这并不包括通过宣布 $\varepsilon = 0$ 得到一种无益的精确性,同时却使真理的数量缩减为零;而是通过尝试缩小 ε 的同时,保留 ε 中很多真实的原理,这样来确保有益的准确性。

如果把这个观念放在几张图表中,也许会比放在几页论述中更清楚。用 T 表示抽象温度,则有重言式 $T = T$,它可以用直线 $y = x$ 来表示(图1)。然后再用 T' 表示基于物理定律的测量结果。由于定律和测量都只是近似的,相同的温度可能会有不同的读数,而相同的读数又可能温度不同,因此 T 和 T' 实际上是彼此的多值函数,而 $T < T'$ 的图也不会

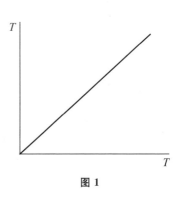

图 1

是一条曲线,而是一条带(图2)(参见第40页图1)。接下来,用 T'' 代表对我们皮肤的粗略猜测,它比温度计受到更多干扰的影响。于是,对温度的判断将更加粗略,表现为一条更宽的带(图3。当然,这条带不一定要有明确且笔直的边界)。

---

① 译者注:原文为 Q. E. D. 即拉丁语 quod erat demonstrandum,指证明完毕。

② 译者注:裕度(margin),统计学术语,指留有一定余地的程度,允许有一定的误差。

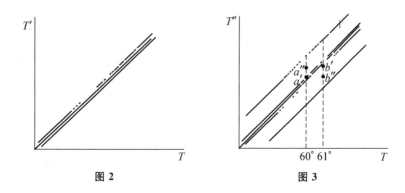

图 2　　　　　　　　　　　　图 3

以 60℃的勺子和 61℃的杯子为例。我们的第一个温度计会给出读数 a' 和 b'，由于其差值只有 1 度的很小一部分之内，结果将显示杯子更热。但是，我们的嘴唇受到热传导的影响，则可能会把勺子估计为 a'' 而把杯子估计为 b''，从而使得它的结果与温度计的结果不一致[①]。

现在的重点是，在极端情况下，即使是皮肤的感觉也总是能得出正确的结论。另一方面，在差异很小的临界情况下，即使是一个好的温度计也会显示不出差异。因此，皮肤和温度计之间的差异可以被视为程度的差异。每条带在某种程度上实际上都是一条曲线。

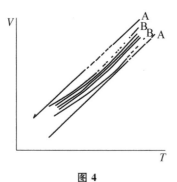

图 4

在它的宽度范围内，所有的差异都是无关紧要的。

因此，与幅度相关的事实在于，同一条所谓的"话语带"里面包括有若干条小的带。在图 4 中，假设简单气体定律在较宽的带 AA 内成立，那么这意味着代表实际观测真实气体的较细的带（标记为实心黑色）都位于宽带之内。现在，作为对近似程度的进一步提升,我们把这条原理的适用范围细化,比如说,限定在一条符合范德华方程的更窄的带 BB 内,它仍然包括了所有的细带。这就意味着进步。但是,如果我们只是通过画一条线而不是一条带来给温度设定一个限制标准,那么显然,它将不包括任何一条实际测量出来的带。科学的目的在于找到一条既窄而又包含许多其他带的带;是一条具有包容性的窄带,而不是一条线性的排他性曲线。

以上这些就是对"有益的准确性"与"无益的精确性"的图形译解。如果我们采用 n/ε 这样的概念,来测量系列排序的效用或逻辑稳定性,用 n 表示包含的带的数量,除以表示带宽度的 ε。那么有益的准确性将意味着一个很大的 n 除以一个很小的 ε;而无益的精确性却通过让 $\varepsilon=0$,使得 n 也成为 0,从而导致无意义的 $0/0$,这已经是跟逻辑稳定性相去甚远了。

第五章　极　限　点

1. 极限点的一般性质

"如果你不能拥有你喜欢的,那就喜欢你所拥有的。"但如果我真的喜欢我所拥有的,那我不就是*拥有了我所喜欢的*吗?换句话说,通过把我对生活的要求降低到一个下限点,我的满意度就自动提高到百分之百的上限点。这种推理并不是为了把斯多葛主义[①]归结为荒谬之论或者是合乎理性,而是为了说明研究中设想的极限点的两面性。

极限点的性质在形式上可以用 C, 1, ∞ 等术语来表示,或者可以方便地用任何其他表示尺度极限的术语。下限的概念可以用 0 来表示,称为"零拥有",也可以表示为 1,即"思想就是自己跟自己对话"。上限的概念可以用 1 或者 100% 表示,为"全部论域",也可以表示为 ∞,如"相关因素的总和"。

从斯多葛的例子更进一步,我们可以应用简单的数学技巧,把一个标度上的任何区间 (a, b) 转换为任何其他区间 (ε', b'),特别是转换为 $(0, \infty)$;通过设置任何一种一一对应的关系,使 a 对应 0,而 b 对应 ∞,或者反向对应。例如,从一位教授的角度来看,一位大一新生可能有一定程度的智力 a,四年后的智力略高出的程度为 b;但在大四老生经过反向转换的眼睛里,大一新生代表着无知和愚蠢的上限,而在四年内,无知和愚蠢应该消失殆尽,也就是,a 变为 ∞,而 b 变为 0。

---

① 译者注:斯多葛主义(stoicism),源自希腊,即对痛苦默默承受或泰然处之的坚忍行为。斯多葛哲学源自 Stoa Poikile,指雅典中心广场的绘画长廊,因创始人古希腊哲人芝诺常在这里讲课而得名。

　　这种可转换性使得对极限点的研究比那些特殊符号的意义更为普遍。例如,所有两个事物相等的情况都可以被认为是二者之间差异的下限。实际上,特别是在处理复杂变量的情况下,数学中的一种常用技术,是处理为 $a-b=0$,而不是 $a=b$。

　　然而,在许多情况下,对观点的选择有一种自然的偏好,除非以方法论的影响力为不必要的代价,这种偏好的弹性范围是难以克服的。因此,在一个充满奋斗和成就的世界里,我们自然会把斯多葛主义作为一个理想程度为 0 的立场,而对于它的完全实现也不会觉得有什么重要的意义。所以我们称之为一个下限的例子。对于下限的一个典型表达是"至少可以说"。每个人都可以有一些可以实现的理想,至少可以说是零。

　　现在,以一个具有常识的人来说,他没有意识到自己做事需要日程表和规划,也就是说,他处于方法的下限;但他只是知道自己能把事情办成,也就是,他处于直觉的上限,直觉显然是从无到有,一下就跳到了现实的"1"。对于上限的一个典型表达是"最终"。因此,最终,无论有没有方法,一个人都必须有一些实际的意志力来付诸行动,并有一定的直觉来了解现实。

　　无论是上限还是下限,极限点的中心问题都是同一性和差异性问题。极限在哪些方面跟系列的其他部分是相同的? 在哪些方面又是不同的? 我将在以下的章节中按顺序说明这些问题。

2. 极限点的同一性

　　仅仅把事物称为极限点,然后就到此为止,似乎确实是定义功能的下限。因此,要求给这些空洞的概念填充更多的意义是合乎情理的。

　　(1) *形式的概括性*。——最初的回答是,"没有"。我扩展了一个尺度,把两个不合时宜的事物包括在内,并把它们分别放在我这尺度里的零和无穷大的位置,就像一个关于概括性的实验一样,用增加陈述的简洁性或对称性,从逻辑上保住我的脸面。实际上,这就是形式逻辑和数学的精髓。由于我们并不总是能够确定 S 是 P，为了保险起见，我们至少可以说 A 是 A。空类就只是一个成员数量为 0 的类。如果 A 是 B 或 C 的有限析取是不确定的，那我们至少可以建立一个无限析取：使 A 是 B 或 C，或*两者皆非*。

　　如果我们把讨论的范围扩展得足够宽泛，我们可以说美德不是正方形的，或者至少可以说，在任何情况下都有 A 不是非 A。*在同样的总体条件下*，同样的起因会产生同样的效果。所有于 1917 年 6 月 5 日，在美国登记了(身份)的外来移民，精神病人等等，都属于兵役登记的五类人员之一①。在每一个"具体"的问题中，你都必须考虑到所有"具体的""实质的"因素。永远记住要"看情况"。一切真实的事物都是独一无二的。至少可以说，一枚刚从铸币厂造出来的新硬币不是另一枚硬币。换句话说，这个原则的目的在于，通过把尽可能多的事物包括进来，从而获得一个逻辑上的鸟瞰图，而不介意我目前能说的有多么少。

　　有一类有趣的案例，使我们更喜欢跳过一道鸿沟来完成一个宇宙。我们不说支出减去收入等于赤字，而是说收入加赤字等于支出。类似地，设 F_e 和 F_w 分别为向东和向西的作用力的总和，a 为向东的加速度，m 为受加速度作用的质量；然后，达朗贝尔②不说 $F_e - F_w = ma$，即，两个力相差的量为 ma，而是这样写：根据他的原理，$F_e - F_w - ma = 0$。也就是说，所有力的总和达成相互平衡，这在某种意义上(不很严重)是把结论假设为前提。同样，我可以通过把我的未分类的物品归入未划分的类别来完成宇宙，而不把那些不属于任何类别的物品留在空气中。因此，设立"杂项"这个标题总是

----

① 译者注：指 1917 年美国《义务征兵法》对登记过的全体国民的分类，从优先服兵役的 I 类，到彻底免服兵役的 V 类。作者曾到美国兵役局登记，因属于非美国公民的 V 类，而未被征入伍。

② 译者注：达朗贝尔(Jean Le Rond d'Alembert, 1717—1783)是法国著名的物理学家、数学家和天文学家，提出达朗贝尔原理，可以把动力学问题转化为静力学问题处理，使一些力学问题的分析简单化，而且为分析力学的创立打下基础。

可以补充有限性，填补其余部分的无限性，或者换个说法，我可以说，如果我们在原则上寻求补偿，那么我们总会在原则中找到补偿。

如果一种形式的概括是有价值的，那么它就不是过错。但是，如果一个人试图既吃掉自己的蛋糕又同时把它留起来，那就是犯下谬误。提醒一个人应该努力工作，但是不要过分努力；只要他足够认真地对待工作，就能实现任何合理的理想。黄金法则和康德的普遍道德法则都是适用于在相同情况下的人，或者由于从来都没有绝对相同的情况，因此就是适用于在相对的相同情况下，换句话说也就是，在它们适用的情况下适用。因此，当一个陈述被安全地限定时，它的重要性也就失效了。

（2）显著概括。——但也许我能说的内容的重要性不完全是零。起初是从名义上的一种概括，而实际效果往往超出其名义。我们发现有些事情在有些情况下是真实的，而它们在极限情况下，也可能是真实的。如果是这样的话，那么这就不是一种名义上的概括了。

因此，如果空间的两个三角形构成某种立体图形，并具有某些性质，则当立体图形"降级"，即被展平为平面时，它们可能在极限情况下仍然保留这些性质。事实上，著名的德萨格定理①最初就是用这个方式证明的。

如果我们忽视数学的实际历史，我们可以从逻辑上说，我们的整个数字系统是下限的重复应用。一个复数 $a+bi$ 在 $b=P$ 时"降级"为一个实数，以此类推，直到最后，我们得到一个分母为 1 的有理正分数，即"降级"为一个正整数，这也是现代分析算术化过程的下限系列中的下限。在这里，我们知道，很多事物在高维情况下是真实的，在低维情况下也可以同样是真实的。

---

① 译者注：德萨格定理（Desargues theorem）是射影几何的重要定理之一。以法国几何学家德萨格（Gérard Desargues，1591—1661）的名字命名。定理指出：若两三角形的对应顶点连线共点（此点称为透视中心），则其对应边之交点必共线（此线称为透视轴）。

数学中有很多定理适用于特定的有限项，在改为用于无限项时也是成立的。因此，有些对于有限极限积分的定理，当一个或两个极限变为无穷大时，或者当被积函数的某些点变为无穷大时，仍适用于所谓的不适当积分。正如我们已经看到的，换一个角度来看，上限就是下限。$\int_a^{1/a} f(x)dx$ 也可以表示为 $\int_{1/a}^a g(y)dy$，其中，$y = 1/x$。

在学习通过复变量的球极立体映射时，我们经常感到烦恼的是，有些对于包括北极在内的所有点都为真的定理，不能一口气陈述和证明出来。因为北极作为一个无穷大，是一个分析上的非法之点。但通过一次简单的转换，北极就成为跟南极一样好的点。

力的平行四边形定律说，如果用两个力表示平行四边形的边长，那么它们的合力就由这个平行四边形的对角线表示。但当我们取一个面积为零的平行四边形时，即，当两个力之间的夹角为 0°或者 180°时，这个定律仍然适用。因此，考虑到极限中连续的同一性这些特征，数学家们声称平行四边形"降级"为一条直线的说法就似乎有失公平了。因为极限并不总是如此彻底地降级，以至于失去所有继承而来的特征。

（3）*心理延伸*。——事实上，任何名义上的延伸是否能够一直保持名义上的状态都是值得怀疑的。通过假装位于零点，我们经常会用一种心理技巧聊以自慰。如果我能成功地采取一种总是给予而永不索取的态度，那么我可能就会对份外得到的一点点祝福而感到惊喜。当小孩子拒绝按时上床睡觉，这位母亲就说："那就不睡吧，反正必须得听我的。"这样一来，她就可以通过使用一条零命令在逻辑上保留脸面，下次她就有更好的机会让孩子"不睡，但请安静一点"。

在试图过上完全理性的生活时，一个人经常会遇到机会和情有可原的诱惑（如果真的有这样的事情），这会打破一个人的规则和计划，而且可能根本不值得付出纪律上的代价。在这种情况下，人们可能会使用一个小技巧：在形式上承认这次对系统的破坏，并称之为系统的一部分,无论它似乎是多么离谱。因此,在繁忙的工作之中,与其懒散地发呆 15 分钟,对着日程表上写的"现在是你的工作时间"眨眼,还不如就白纸黑字地安排一个异想天开的提议,走 15 英里的徒步旅行,聊 3 个小时的八卦,然后再去上班或睡觉。

(4)*作为理想的极限*。——在处理上限的情况时,我们通常可以把它设定为一种理想,尽管我们没有达到它,但我们可能会在那个方向上获取一些事物。因此,我们可以把"为什么"定义为不同程度的"怎么样"的上限。在提问时,我们可以问"这是怎么回事",也可以问"为什么"。但是,如果我们牢记一种理想的"为什么"的感受,它可能就会激发人们对进一步的"*怎么样*"的探索,例如对引力定律的进一步解释。

同样,在实际工作中,我们只能考虑有限个数的最佳点。但是,把全部最佳点通过正确的代数符号综合为一个最佳点,是一个有用的主意,因为这样可以拓宽我们的价值领域。(参见第八章第 123 页,关于最佳点。)

总的来说,形而上学的精神似乎是,无论是哲学家还是科学家,都是通过把唯一的冠词 *the* 加在真、善、美的概念之前,以上限的形式来接受理想,而这些概念只在有限和相对中才能得到展现。

然而,这并不意味着不存在能够实现的理想。站在一个极限看向另一个极限,人们通常可以找到数量足够多的步骤来跨越过去。柏拉图①的分析方法,既适用于几何构造,也适用于定理的证明,就是

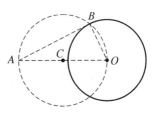

---

① 译者注:柏拉图(Plato,前 427—前 347)是古希腊伟大的哲学家,也是整个西方文化中最伟大的哲学家、思想家之一。他的著作大多是用对话体裁写成的,有《对话录》和《理想国》等。他认为:数学的对象就是数、量、函数等数学概念,而数学概念作为抽象概括或"共相"是客观存在着的。柏拉图和他的老师苏格拉底、他的学生亚里士多德并称为"希腊三贤"。

一个例子：已知点 A 和圆心为 O 的圆，要从 A 点画一条圆的切线。柏拉图首先会说："假设切线 AB 已经画好了。"这样做就只是在要求解决方案，即分析的零点。但我们并不会停留在这个光亮为零的洞穴中。我们可以稍微更进一步说，OB 垂直于 AB，因此 $\triangle AOB$ 内接于一个以 AO 为直径的圆中。所以，如果我们首先平分 AO，那么接下来的一切就都可以完成。我们就这样，无中生有，通过一些中间的事物得到了一些事物。

　　一般来说，为了确保具有最大概括性的数学精神，而冒着失去最小显著性的风险，这有时会引起人们注意到那些概括性稍低而显著性稍高的情况。性情固执的人注意不到这些情况，因为他们会习惯性地坚守最小显著性，而害怕进一步去冒险。因此，尽管人们批评数理逻辑为空洞无物，但它的详细计算过程与显著性的零点相去甚远。

3. 极限点的差异性

　　（1）*下限*。——到目前为止，我已经详细讨论了极限与其他案例的同一性。但是，至少可以说，极限是唯一的极限。并且我们已经看到，我们能够说的内容往往远不止是这个至少所能包括的。总体上来说，一个极限点所具有的特性和同一性不仅仅只是名义上的。

　　在普通的数学分析中，0 是一个具有其他数字的许多特性的数字。但它的独特之处在于：它是唯一的一个绝对值小于消失变量 ε 的任何值的常数，它没有倒数，它的 n 次方根只有一个值，以及还有许多其他方面。

　　在数学中，适用于一个变量的性质往往可能会不适用于极限的情况。因此，$\tan x$ 在 x 在 $\pi / 2$ 到 π 之间时是一个连续函数[①]，但当

---

　　① 译者注：$\tan x$ 为正切值，是指直角三角形中，某一锐角的对边与另一相邻直角边的比值。这样建立的函数称为正切函数。

$x = \pi / 2$ 时,不论对 $\tan x$ 赋予什么值,它都是非连续的。然而,这样的案例并不是什么新鲜事。只需要一个简单的转换,就可以看出它们只是零的又一个独特性。

命题,如果你喜欢的话,也可以被概括为命题函数,它是一种意义模糊的下限。但它有着或真或伪的特性,当它跟另一个命题的含义产生联系时,就会使这种含义难以理解。(参见第三章概念分级,第 31 页)

独自一人生活,作为一种下限,这只是一种单一的社会关系。这里可以肯定,值得指出的是,一个人在思考时会跟自己交谈,可以大声和自己说话,可以真的讨厌自己,爱自己,欺骗自己,为自己找借口,等等,但指出在很多方面存在着明显的差异也十分重要。

(2)*上限*。——由唯一的上限中突出的例子组成的一种极限类,是用对立面来表现的。例如,绝对与相对、无条件与有条件、无限与有限、具体与抽象、那个与什么、个体与普遍、明确的与假设的,等等。因此,无论用缝纫机为加固第一个针脚而又缝了多少针,这都是一个无限延伸的过程,直到在某处把线的末端拉过线圈来终结这个无限序列的剩余部分为止。当前提是要得出结论时,无论阿喀琉斯和乌龟[1]围绕着规则去争论多久,如果没有人实际去做,无论堆积多少一条又一条的规则,都不会得到结论。

无论一个科学家有多么复杂的方法论,要在实验室中应用它,都需要一些直觉和技巧。无论立法者在定义所有可能的案件时多么有远见,都必须有某位法官对每个特定案件来解释法律。无论一个决疑制度[2]制定得多么精细,都需要一些智慧的良知来用好它并用对它。无论一个人可以做出多长的决策链,要从最简单的一个决策开始做,都需要一定的决心。无论一个人设计的助记符系统有多

---

[1]　见 Lewis Carroll, "What the Tortoise Said to Achilles", *Mind*, 1895,第 278 页。

[2]　译者注:罗马天主教的一种决疑制度:当专家意见相左时参与者可以自行选择任何可信的意见。

完备,都需要一定的自然记忆力来记住这些符号。无论一个公设系统的无穷多个定理中有多少是一致的,要验证所有那些定理是一致的,都需要有一些具体的例证。总而言之,无论一个人的杠杆 N 有多大,都需要有大于零的一个实际的力 ϵ 来验证"阿基米德①公设",即,$N \times \epsilon$ 足以撬动地球。

我们会注意到,在上文中的形式概括性之下讨论的,如赤字与支出那样的案例、以上限为理想的案例以及唯一极限的这些案例之间,存在着一种相似性。事实上,如果说第一种例子只是在大峡谷的一边向另一边观察,那么第二种就是通过望远镜来研究对岸情况,而第三种则是实际飞过深谷并降落在坚实的地面上。

(3)下限阈值。——在研究论域中的一个部分时,人们往往会得出这样的结论,即整体与那个部分相类似。在导体和非导体的实验中,查尔斯·杜菲②发现,所有物体都在一定程度上导电,并不存在所谓的非导体,或者用我们的术语来说,导电性的下限和电阻的上限并不存在。然而,在一些特殊问题中已经出现了差别,电导率分别低于跟这些不同问题相关的不同阈值可以视为相当于零。因此,即使不存在唯一极限的情况下,也会有一个唯一的邻域或极限阈值,使得在它之下的案例需要不同的处理。

哲学洞察力常常会在无意中跨过这些阈值。所有的想法都是行动。然而,在外显性和敏捷性低于一定程度(相对于某些问题)时,"行动"最好还是看作一种想法。所有的经验都是沉思。然而,在冲突和努力高于某个程度时,就会以很不沉思的方式对这种情景进行沉思。一切事物都是独一无二的,没有两个事物是一样的。然而,在大多数问题中,一枚硬币和另一枚硬币一样好,即,面额相同。

---

① 译者注：阿基米德(Archimedes, 公元前 287—前 212),古希腊哲学家、百科式科学家、数学家、物理学家、静态力学和流体静力学的奠基人。阿基米德曾说过：给我一个支点,我就能撬起整个地球。

② 译者注：查尔斯·杜菲(Charles Francois de Cisternay du Fay, 1698—1739),法国化学家。

基督教科学家说,所有的痛苦都是想象出来的。然而,就算是那样,也会有低于某个阈值的想象的"想象出来的痛苦",以及高于那个器质性病变阈值的真实的"想象出来的痛苦"。一切真实的事物都是具体的,就像一个有机体,而不是一堆沙子。然而,若是在实践或理论上低于重要性的阈值以下,事物可能同样会弄得杂乱无章。在我们的大多数论域中,至少把一堆沙子当作一堆沙子是没有什么风险的。

常常有人提议说,无论情况糟糕到什么程度,他都可以充分加以利用;他可以从潜在的环境中选择最有效的环境,即使他的手脚都被绑住,他仍然可以随心所欲地思考。总而言之就是,没有自由度为零这回事。然而,当这个程度降低到一个可以忽视不计的 ε 时,那么尽力做好比起尽力做坏也就不会好多少了。如果我患上重病,对于充分利用这个机会研究连续性的建议,我可能就情有可原地不予理会了。

在第七章中(参见第 101 页及以后),我将试图展示,所有的物理系统,不是处于稳定平衡,就是处于不平衡状态。作为稳定平衡的下限,不稳定平衡的(广义的)稳定基础为零的情况,是不存在的。然而,如果稳定性低于某个阈值,我们就称为是一种不稳定平衡的情况,特别是当雪橇车滑行在山顶的小平台后面陡峭的急降坡的时候。于是,过分寒冷的溶液或过分饱和的空气都叫作处于不稳定平衡状态,这是因为让平衡离开稳定基础而引入的微小粒子跟由此产生的巨大变化相比,实在是微不足道的。为什么一个单独的电子不能引发整个变化呢?因为它的滑稽动作不足以把整个系统推出它那微小的稳定基础,尽管从我们通常的观点来看,这个基础也是在阈值之下的。

(4)*上限阈值*。——到目前为止,我一直在谈论阈值,好像它总是一个接近零的微小区间。但从上限的角度来看,一个在 ε 之内的邻域会包含超过某个上限阈值 M 的案例。因此,可以说,"一个电导率低于某个 ε 的物体实际上是非导体。"这等于说"一个电阻比干燥空气还大的物体实际上具有无限大的电阻。"电导率为零，百分之百绝缘，和电阻无限大，都是同义语。

在现象 y 作为无穷多个可能存在的因素的函数这样的一般问题中，我们可以说，我们只能考虑其中的一部分因素，而不存在考虑了影响现象 y 的所有因素这种事。也就是说，我们永远不可能完整地写出：

$$y = f(x_1, x_2, x_3, \cdots)$$

而对于每一个问题，只考虑有限的 M 个因素就足够了，并且说我们在问题中忽视掉的因素

$$\frac{\partial f}{\partial x_{M+1}}, \frac{\partial f}{\partial x_{M+2}}, \cdots$$

所产生的总效应可以忽略不计。也就是说，当考虑的因素数量多于 M 时，就跟考虑无限多个因素是一样的。而实际的无限多的因素也不一定是一个很大的数字。一个实用的电工只需要知道电线的长度、粗细、材质和电压就可以知道电流，所以对于他来说，无限多等于四；在一个更精细的物理问题中，人们可能还必须知道温度和磁场，加上这两个因素也才只有六个。

4. 极限点的具体含义

（1）极限作为一个类。——形式逻辑和数学处理下限，而哲学处理上限；在上文中已经提示了这种区别（第 61 页与第 65 页）。从观点的可转换性来看，我们可以说这两个极限相遇了。现在我们发现，在一些特定的问题中（有限个离散元素的情况除外），我们可以用这些问题所确定的小于下限的项和大于上限的项，来分别代替零和无穷大。那么，我们是不是要抛弃确切的极限点，并且贬低形而上学和数学呢？不是，因为那样可能会使我们在术语命名上成为失败者。

让我们应用奥卡姆剃刀①，或者更具体地说，应用罗素的抽象原理。由于我们不需要严格的零或极限，并且它们的含义是未定义的，在我们的有限问题中（当然也要适当考虑到物理以及其他单位的维度），可以直接把零定义为全部有限的 ε 组成的类，而把无穷大定义为全部有限的 M 组成的类。因此，抽象原则也可以称为具体化原则②。

把这种处理方法应用于各种极限情况，例如，我们可以说 $y=x^2$ 是所有问题中的一类，其中 x 的带宽或管径比每个案例中所取的 ε 更窄（参见第三章第 40 页）。因此，我们现在可以说："从具体的角度看，喷流的水柱是抛物线这个类的一员，即，它就是一条抛物线。"而不是说"从数学的角度来看，喷流的水柱实际上是一条抛物线"，这样，象征符号"$J \in P$"中的是动词 be 或"$\in$"的技术意义就被解释为普通意义。同样，我们可以说，温度是气体、液体、状态变化、辐射频率变化和热冷感受，以某些方式相互联系组成的类，而不是说各种现象测量出温度（参见第四章第 55 页及以后各页）。

（2）*极限数学定义的方法论解释*。——这听起来像是对零、无穷大和极限的随意闲谈，完全无视数学上的用法。现在，我必须近距离接触极限的标准定义了。教科书上说，"L 是在 x 趋向于 0 时 $f(x)$ 的极限"，意思就是，对于任何给定的 ε，都有对应的一个 δ，这样使得每当 $|x| < \delta$ 时，就有

$$|f(x) - L| < \varepsilon. ③$$

现在这定义的第一小句的语言有些半戏剧化。它把 x 和 $f(x)$ 描绘

①　译者注：奥卡姆剃刀原理（Occam's Razor）：如无必要，勿增实体。即简单有效原理。由 14 世纪英格兰的逻辑学家、圣方济各会修士奥卡姆的威廉（William of Ockham，约 1285—约 1349）提出。

②　参见 B. Rueesll, *Our Knowledge of the External World*，第 42 页。

③　以下评述同样适用于措辞有明显变化的其他的极限案例。译者注：作者在这里省略了两个默认的条件：$|x| > 0$，即 $x \neq 0$；ε > 0。

成一个赫拉克利特①过程。但在实际的数学研究中，极限的一个更可行的含义是 δ 和给定的 ε（或是 N 和给定的 M 等，视情况而定）之间的逻辑对应，从一种平均的观点来看，在任何单一对应的实例中，ε 和 δ 都不需要很小。

那么，我所做的或打算做的，只是把这种数学逻辑上的对应关系解释为方法论上的对应。数学家会说"对于任何给定的 ε"，然后就到此为止。我会问，是谁不请自来就给定了 ε？数学家并不在乎，他情愿把这个问题放过去。现在，在方法论上，也可能在历史上，实际的问题是不是预先给定某些阈值，这样，如果差异低于这些阈值，那么它们就"没有区别"了吗？

在同样的主题中，例如平衡状态下，会存在数量不确定的各种问题，分别具有不同的相关性阈值。事实上，我们并没有真的提出无限多个问题，这并不是反对这个定义，而是因为在数学上的极限定义中，我们不需要把所有的 ε 都给定并把它们在纸上写出来。

一个更为严重的反对意见是，按大小顺序排列的 ε 所组成的类可能不会收敛于零，而是收敛于某个大于零的正极限。答案是：只有在我们只取一部分 ε 而忽略其余的情况下，这才有可能出现。因为所有的有限问题中 ε 的下限，正是我们所说的方法论上的零点的意思。这种反对意见只存在于数学案例中，其中只考虑特定论域中的 ε，在一般情况下会涉及术语上的矛盾。因此，这种对极限的数学定义所做的似乎超数学的解读，毕竟还不是一个非数学的步骤，因而人们的数学良知不需要感受任何痛苦。

（3）*哲学应用*。——现在我们把这一观点应用于第 65 页第（4）节中提到的哲学理想。其中关于它的有效性的问题还悬而未决。1）哲学的目标，据说是"绝对性"（或者是它的任何变体）。2）让我

---

① 译者注：赫拉克利特（Heraclitus，约前 540—约前 480 与前 470 之间）是古希腊哲学家。爱非斯学派的创始人。他认为万物都处于不断的变化之中，持对立统一观念，是朴素辩证法思想的代表人物。

们先放弃这种绝对性,并且说,以我们有限的智力探索,其综合性和深度超出某个上限阈值 M,就应称为哲学。3) 既然不再需要绝对性,我们可以自由地把它定义为被称为哲学的那些探究和结果的类别。4) 这样,我们就把我们的哲学绝对性带回到具体性之中。

因此,如果从人文和时域的角度来看,真、善、美,可能意味着知识、道德和艺术标准演变的实际过程。这样在每个阶段,基于迄今为止已经取得的进展,再加上人们拥有的展望未来愿景的力量进行判断,人们可以实事求是地说,也就是直截了当地说出来,任何具体的事物是不是真的、善的、美的。这当然要说得很多。但我对待这种哲学观点的严肃程度,应该会低于对待极限点本身的案例,极限点理论最终还是必须要以极限点为基础,或者必须由极限点组成。我说"说得多",其实是想说"说得少";人们在看过这些"具体案例"之后,就不应该对此感到惊讶了。

第六章　连续性中的同一性

同一性和差异性。——在关于同一性与差异性、程度差异与种类差异、连续性与非连续性、量变与质变、均匀性或一致性与多样性、一与多、稳定性与可变性、持久与变化、习惯与智慧等等的哲学讨论中，我们常常会发现，没有差异性就没有同一性，没有同一性就没有差异性；没有持久就没有变化，没有变化就没有持久，等等。为了避免因为这种广泛的发现而使我们忘记这个概念的含义，最好是在我们智力的日常行为中去探寻，什么样的同一性和差异性是相容的，或者不相容的。

作为一种研究方法，为了根据可能获得的结果来证明它的合理性，我首先将会把所讨论的事物置于一个序列尺度 x 上，这一方法已经在第三章和第四章的概念分级和系列排序的说明中打好了基础。找到一种分级的尺度，无论是离散的还是实际连续的。有两件事需要比较。当我们进行分级时，要问：哪些方面保持相同？这就是本章的主题。而在哪些方面变得不同，如果不同，差异在哪里，以及是怎样的差异？这就是下一章的主题。

作为一种方法，而不是教条，这个程序既不是真的也不是假的，但可能是好的，也可能是坏的，有效的或者无足轻重的。在它无法控制好工作介质①的地方，那些东西就会从安全阀中泄漏出来。因此，拿一棵卷心菜和一位国王，考虑一下两者之间的形式等级。我们就会了解到，它们在属于同一个系列类别方面是相同的，

---

① 译者注：工作介质(working substance)是各种热机中借以完成能量转化的媒介物质。这些物质通常以可逆的相变(如气-液相变)来增大功率。如蒸汽引擎中的蒸汽、制冷机中的雪种等等。可以理解为在传动及控制中起传递能量和信号作用的媒介物质。

遗憾的是,这个类别是临时构建的。一般来说,我可以在形式上把任意两件事物 A 和 B 放进 K 类里面,往别处看一眼,然后嚯!现在 A 和 B 在属于同一个 K 类这一点上是相同的啦!另一方面,以 1918 年 4 月 13 日上午 10:16 的一座埃及金字塔和 1918 年 4 月 13 日上午 10:18 的同一座金字塔为例。随着时间的推移,这座金字塔从一座 10:17 前的金字塔变为一座 10:17 后的金字塔,这是一个决定性的差异。总的来说,我永远可以说,任何事物与任何其他事物都不同,而不论 A 和 B 多么相似。至少可以说,A 不是 B。在这些极端之间,我们发现了可以施加这种方法的感兴趣的事物。

同一性。——在本章的主题中,我们将通过在差异点 ε 或差异区间 x 的连续性来谈论 A 和 B 在 K 这方面的同一性,这是同一性的基础。这里选择采用各种介词是为了避免歧义,而不是要符合习惯用语。因此,在灰度的连续性中,我们跨过中性灰度点或中性灰度区间,得到中性色调的白与黑的同一性。

首先从事物 A 和 B 开始。"把它们放在一个尺度 x 上"意思是考虑到某一系列顺序 x,使点 x_1 与点 A 对应,点 x_2 与点 B 对应。换句话说,我们定义了一个函数 $f(x)$,使 $f(x_1)=A$,且 $f(x_2)=B$。同时,这种通过想象、观察或实际操作进行的分级法,包括了 x 的取值位于 x_1 与 x_2 之间时,所定义的 $f(x)$ 的值。

这个系列的选择既是自由的也是有限制的。在从一个 U 形管到一个碗这一渐变过程的示例中(第 82 页),很明显,使一个形状变为另一个形状的多维度变化有很大的可选范围。但是,在极限范围内,选择哪种系列的变化都一样,都可以显示流体力学关系的同一性。很多时候,几个离散项组成的系列就能够达到显示同一性的目标,因此 x 甚至不需要是一个近似的连续统。这就是自由。

另一方面,如果我们取一只蜜蜂和一只甲虫,不是用我们知道的进化中实际存在的中间体来显示生物同一性,而是画出从一只蜜

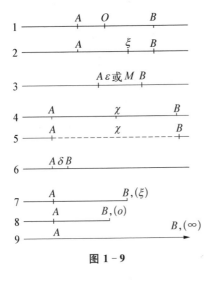

图 1-9

蜂(bee)变为一个甜菜(beet)又变成一只甲虫(beetle)的分级图示[1]，那么这个对 x 的维度的选择，至少在平淡无聊的生物学中，都是过于粗鲁唐突的。这就是限制。

本章的分节原则依据同一性隐含下的差异性背景。这种差异可能跨越一个标尺的零点，同一性从 A 处跨过零点到达 B 处(图1)。它可能会跨越某种意义的特殊点或是奇点 ξ(图2)。或者跨越差值 ε 或阈值 M(图3)，它与一个点的不同之处在于没有非常清晰的定义。(例如，听辨音高的下限阈值就是个统计学问题。)同样，背景也可能是一整段 x；不论这个 x 是实际存在的还是假设出来的(图4、5)，这段的长度足以让对面两边的事物看起来不同，尽管两者之间没有特别的兴趣点。如果在某一方面这个区间很小，那么就会出现需要特殊处理的情况(图6)。最后，在展示连续性方面，差异标记本身可能会与这一序列中的其他点相同，而这个点可能会是一般点 ξ，或 0 或 ∞(图7、8、9)[2]。

既然现在同一性在某个方面总是同一性，那么在这同一个方面之外，是不具有传递关系的。因此，如果黑色和中性灰色在色调上相同，中性灰色和某种紫色在亮度上相同，那么这并不意味着黑色和紫色在二者之中的哪个方面就会相同。因此，跟同样的事物具有同一性的不同事物之间并不总是彼此相同。

---

① 见 R. W. Wood, *Animal Analogues*，第1页。

② 关于点之间的可转换性，参见第五章第60页与第72页。

1. 跨越零点的同一性：正负号变化

　　零点两侧正负符号的差异很容易掩盖一种同一性,由于这个零点或多或少是任意的,正号与负号之间差异的显著性也会或多或少地降低。因此,所有的温度在属于同一个连续尺度这一方面上都是相同的,+1°F 和 -1°F 有些差异,但并不比 14°F 和 16°F 之间的差异更大。而 +1℃ 和 -1℃ 之间的差异更为显著,因为它对应于最重要的那种液体的状态变化,但它对许多其他物质的状态并没有影响。

　　跨越正负号变化的同一性有时在数学中被称为"连续性原理"。因此,在平常的语言里,我们说,如果两条线在一个圆内相交,它们的夹角等于被截取的两段圆弧之和的一半;而如果它们在圆外相交,它们的夹角通过所截的两段圆弧之差的一半来测量。现在,假设我们考虑从一条线到另一条线测量的弧的总和,并考虑方向。然后我们会发现,从一种情况变为另外一种情况的过程中,一条弧从正号通过零变为负号,而两条线夹角等于所截的两段弧的代数和的一半这一定律同样适用于所有情况。

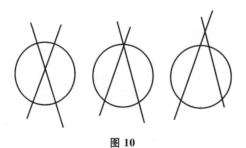

图 10

　　由于同一性总是存在的,我们不需要有任何心理顾虑,就可以在红色和绿色之间看到一个线性尺度的同一性,从饱和的红色到灰色再延伸到饱和的绿色。那么,红色就是负绿色,而绿色就是负红色。尽管这不是故事的全貌,我们至少获得了一个观点,这对处理颜色混合①、颜色适应②、视觉残像③等非常有帮助。当然，同样的同一性也适用于其他的互补色对④。

　　在做记录、计划、规则等的过程中，当正负号发生变化时，人们往往会改变一条原则。例如，我可能会开始训练自己的动作敏捷程度，并且每次落后时都准确记录下多少分钟，但是在每次准时或提前做完时却只是打个钩。可以肯定的是，提前和落后不是一回事。但是，我们也可以在标准的两侧以相同的尺度来衡量敏捷程度。问题不在于我是否应该先验地按照一致性原则而不是多样性原则行事，而在于我动作快慢的差异是偶然出现的影响，还是基于某种原因而产生的。

　　物理学中充满了通过正负号变化来实现同一性的案例，其中的差异往往会引起很大的误导。我们很自然地认为，两辆汽车之间正对面的碰撞比后面追尾的碰撞会更猛烈。但碰撞的剧烈程度完全取决于双方速度之间的代数和。如果被追尾碰撞的汽车在前面行驶，就要减去它的速度；如果是对面碰撞的车，那么就要加上它的速度。因此，每小时 30 英里的车追尾每小时 10 英里的车的冲击力，相当于每小时 12 英里的车对撞每小时 8 英里的车的冲击力（即，

---

　　① 译者注：格拉斯曼颜色混合定律（Grsassmann color law）由格拉斯曼（H. Grsassmann）于 1854 年提出：(1) 人的视觉只能分辨颜色的三种变化：亮度、色调、饱和度；(2) 两种颜色混合时的补色律和中间色定律；(3) 感觉上相似的颜色，可以互相代替——代替律；(4) 亮度相加定律：由几个颜色组成的混合色的亮度，是各颜色光亮度的总和。格拉斯曼颜色混合定律是建立现代色度学的基础。

　　② 译者注：颜色适应（color adaptation）是色觉心理现象，指人在颜色刺激下的视觉变化，即视网膜某一区域对产生某种颜色或色调的光线的强度减弱并持续一段时间的适应，这时的颜色不再保持原有的饱和度。

　　③ 译者注：视觉残像（after-images）：当外界物体的视觉刺激作用停止后，在眼睛视网膜上的影像感觉不会马上消失，这是由于神经兴奋留下的痕迹作用，也称作视觉暂留。它有正后像和负后像两种，电影就是利用的正后像原理。

　　④ 译者注：互补色（complemetary colors）分美术互补色和光学互补色两种。美术互补色：色相环中成 180°角的两种颜色；最基础的 3 对互补色有：红和绿、黄和紫、蓝和橙。光学互补色：两种色光以适当比例混合产生白光。

12－（－8）＝12＋8）。因此，对于一个开快车的司机来说，要很好地记住这个同一性法则，因为这个法则就贯穿于他与潜在受害者速度的正负号差异之中。

笛卡儿的动量守恒概念也是通过正负号的变化来观察差异的一个例子，在符号的变化中，保持着同一性。笛卡儿的弹性体碰撞理论说：让质量 m_1 与质量 m_2 分别以相对速度 v 和 $-v$ 相碰撞。如果 $m_1 < m_2$，那么碰撞后两个物体都会以速度 $-v$ 运动。如果我们采用非笛卡尔的代数动量的说法，在碰撞前的动量是 $vm_1 - vm_2$，或者说 $v(m_1 - m_2)$。在碰撞后，理论上：

$$若\ m_1 > m_2，则动量应为\ v(m_1 + m_2)$$
$$若\ m_1 = m_2，则动量应为\ v(m_1 - m_2)$$
$$若\ m_1 < m_2，则动量应为\ -v(m_1 + m_2)$$

不用莱布尼茨对案例连续性的论证（见第110页），从我们的观点看来，可以说笛卡儿把定律的差异与 $m_1 - m_2$ 的符号差异联系在一起（如果不是他有意识的话，那就是言外之意），而事实是，无论 $m_1 - m_2$ 的符号是什么，这两个物体的总动量 $v(m_1 - m_2)$ 总是同样的。

在大气和飞机之间的同一性关系上也发现了类似的情况。我相信这是一个事实，飞机可以相对于地球向前飞行，或静止不动，也可以向后飞行。但飞行员不是说，如果没有每小时大约 40 英里的最低速度，飞机就飞不起来吗？是的，但这个速度只是飞机相对于在它周围空气中的速度。当它飞在云层中，一切地上的东西对它都是无关紧要的，至少在空气动力学意义上是如此，如果不是在军事或美学意义上的话。因此，如果它以每小时 40 英里的速度在每小时 40 英里的逆风中飞行，它将静止不动；如果逆风是每小时

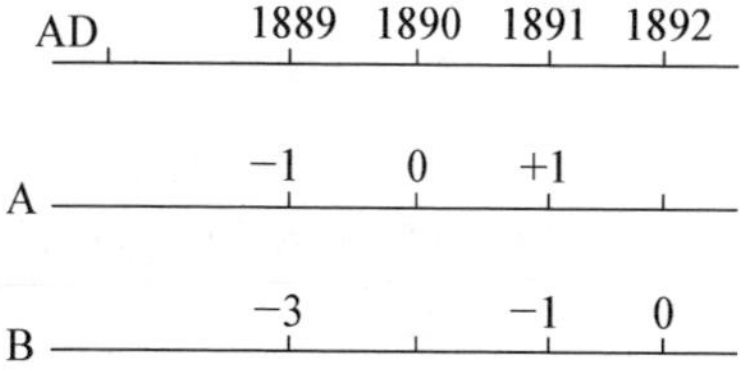

图 11

50 英里,那么在观察者看来,这台机器就是以每小时 10 英里的速度向后飞的。然而,它相对于地面速度的这种正负号差异与机翼下方空气的升力毫无关系。

最后,举一个不那么重要但是十分明确的例子,给定 A 出生于 1890 年而 B 出生于 1892 年,对于 A 来说 1889 年与 1891 年是不同的,因为他没有 1889 年的经历但是却有些 1891 年的经历;但他的意识时间零点与 B 无关。在 B 看来 1889 年和 1891 年是相同的:都是他意识时间中的负值点。

2. 跨越奇点 ξ 的同一性

在处理完零点两侧的同一性之后,我再来看某个非零的特殊点或奇点两侧的同一性。例如,水在跨越 32°F 两侧的 30.2°F 和 33.8°F 的化学成分的同一性;32°F 这一点的特殊之处在于在其两侧的水有不同的状态。等一下! 我刚刚不是用这个冰点作为零点的例子了吗? 是的,这正好引出了下一个重点,即,尽管零点看起来像是奇点的一个特例,但通过改变我们的标度,使所讨论的点成为零点,这总是可以做到的。换句话说,把参考标度适当变换,可以把所有奇点都作为零点的特例,而不是把零点视为奇点的特例。然而,对奇点进行单独处理是有原因的,即,有些点是习惯性的或方法上的方便而不作为零点,但依然具有特殊性。

因此,有这样一个几何定理:一个球缺①曲面部分的面积等于 πR^2,其中 R 表示顶点 A 到这一球缺底面周长的距离。如果这一球缺很扁,如图 12a 所示,那么它的曲面面积大约等同于一个半径为 R 的圆的面积,这看起来是合理的。但对于图 12b 中的球缺,看起来情况就不同了。连续性的方法这时主要就在于发明出分段的等级,例如通过从 A 点到球缺底面的高度 x 为标准的球缺分级(图 13),当它从 AB 变化到 AC 的过程中,我们发现在一个特殊点上,x 等于

---

① 译者注:球缺,指一个球被平面截下的部分。

球体的半径,球缺是一个半球。但在进一步的分析中,证明这种特殊性与所讨论的公式无关。所以,这一公式在经过这一奇点时保持不变。

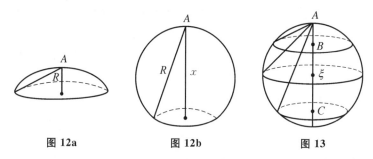

图 12a　　　　　　图 12b　　　　　　图 13

　　同样,我们都听到过一个定律:地表以上物体的重量与它和地心的距离 x 的平方成反比。但还有另一个定律:地下物体的重量,例如矿井中的物体,直接与它和地心的距离成反比[①]。这是不是说在地表这一奇点两侧有着不同的定律?从某种意义上说,当然是有的。但如果我们考虑物体和地球每一部分质量之间的关系,那么,无论是在地球内部还是外部,万有引力定律当然都是成立的。

　　拓扑关系,也就是不考虑事物形状的位置关系,通常越过另一个方面的奇点而在某个方面保持相同。因此,如图14所示的两个容器可以说是相同的,因为它们都是一对连通的容器。许多教师都做不到把托里拆利[②]的这个论点讲得

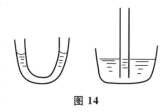

图 14

---

① 忽略地壳内不同地层中岩石密度的变化。

② 译者注: 托里拆利定律(Torricelli's Law)即在充满水的容器中,水面里小孔流出来的水,速度和小孔抵达液面的高度的平方根还有重力加速的两倍的平方根成正比。这是意大利物理学家和数学家托里拆利于 1643 年发现的。这条托里拆利定律以后被证明实际上是伯努利原理的一个特例。伯努利定律(Bernoulli's Law),是流体力学中的一个定律,由瑞士流体物理学家伯努利于 1738 年发表,描述流体沿着一条稳定、非黏性、不可压缩的流管移动时,流速越快,流体产生的压强就越小。

合情合理：当外侧容器的上端被密封和排空时,容器里的水银表面的气压会以某种神秘的方式转弯向上转动,把水银推进上端封闭的空管内。对学生来说,这个论点感觉上并不是那么可靠,而他的想象力(也是我曾经的想象力)不愿接受把容器和长管与容易理解的U 形管进行比较。

　　为了表现出同一性,有一种方法是通过想象一系列的中间状态,如图 15 - 20 中的双视图[①]。在图 15 中,我们能看到一个普通的U 形管;在图 16 中,U 形管的一端被压扁并弄弯了,但它在拓扑学和流体静力学的意义上和图 15 相同;在图 17 中,弯曲的部分进一步拢过了另一根管;在图 18 中,弯曲部分的两个端口在终点处相连从而形成一个环形,从上面看下来,图中呈现出三个圆环;在图 19 中,最内环和第二环之间的空间填满玻璃,从而形成了一个固态的环或管。这当然对液体没有影响。最后,这根管子被做得更薄,就像图20 所展现的那样,从而让我们看到了一根管和一个碗。

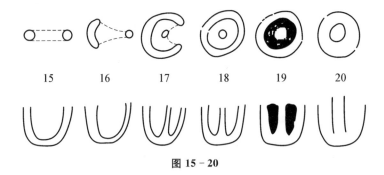

图 15 - 20

　　通过插入更多的中间形式,整个系列可以像我们喜欢的那样循序渐进。但连续性并不意味着同一性。在图 17 与图 18 之间确实发生了一个重要的拓扑变化,其中简单的有界液面变为环形液面。这

----

① 一般把主视图和俯视图称为双视图,以表示物体的结构。有时还会用到三视图、四视图。

一点非常重要,可以称之为我们问题中的真正奇点。然而,不需要太多的物理知识或想象力,就可以看出这不会影响压力关系。因此,就这一点而言,图15和图20中的情况应该看作具有同一性。

人体和环境之间的界限在许多重要方面肯定是各自独立的。但我们可以很容易地发现两者相互融合的问题。例如,当一个人在舞台上唱歌时,歌手身后的反射墙、地板和歌手的发声器官,都属于一个连续的共鸣系统,具有同一性;而如果系统的物理和生理部分都在他的控制之下,那么他选择一个糟糕的大厅去唱歌,就像选择感冒时去唱歌一样,都不是情有可原的。

当变量为时间的时候,奇点就意味着某个事物的突然变化,从而也就带来同一性的问题。物质在各种变化中的同一性就是一个重要的例子。但这种重要性往往被夸大成为同一性本身。当氢气和氧气转化为水时,它们之间的同一性仅仅存在于称为质量的力学守恒性质,以及有限的几种化学特性的变化方式。但是氢和氧依然是跟水不同的。处于动态平衡状态的系统,如尼亚加拉瀑布或任何生物,都有一些方面的同一性与物质的同一性同样重要。正是这种不合理地特别强调物质的同一性,导致了诸如织补袜子的材料跟原来买的袜子材料不一样这类同一性悖论。

能量的同一性是另一个有问题的例子。坡印廷(Poyinting)[1]和汤姆逊(Thomson)[2]在他们的《热力学教科书》(第116页脚注[3])中指出,能量的同一性是为陈述的简洁而使用的无害的形而上学概念。在严格意义上,我们应该说,例如,当一定量的动能消失时,一定量的热能就会出现。既然重要的同一性总是合格的同一性,我们为什么不把形

---

[1]　译者注:坡印廷(John Poynting, 1852—1914)是英国物理学家。1884年提出时变电磁场中的能量守恒定律被称为坡印廷定理。他1909年正式把大气的保温现象命名为温室效应(Greenhouse Effect)。

[2]　译者注:汤姆逊(Joseph John Thomson, 1856—1940)是英国物理学家,电子的发现者。以对电子和同位素的实验著称。1937年获诺贝尔奖。

[3]　译者注:这个页码是这本教科书中的页码。

而上学拉回到现实中，说不同现象的度量之间的换算比率的同一性，以及由此产生的进行共同度量的可能性，这正是我们讲到的能量同一性所要表达的意思。因此我们现在可以自由地谈论它，于是，陈述的简单性就成为一种科学的方法，而不是一个科学的借口。

有一种时间奇点很容易把连续性和同一性掩盖起来，那就是某个阶段性成就的象征性标志（参见智能的进展，第三章第 42 页及以后各页）。一张毕业证书，一场婚礼，一次民主革命，可能标志着某种事物以某种普遍的速度进展的阶段。如果这一进程类似于图 21 中的曲线（1），那么标记出 ξ 点的心理效果，是给人一种进展类似于曲线（2）的印象。根据心理反应的方式判断，未来的进展实际上可能会像走上曲线（3）一样的道路，这是现实中经常遇到的情况。把同一性误认为某一个方向上的差异，可能会导致在相反方向上的另一个差异。

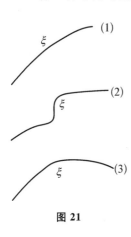

图 21

3. 跨越阈值 ε 或 M 的同一性

所谓阈值，我指的是尺度上的一个奇点，它不需要精确定位，但却标志着在某些方面的区别。例如，我可以标记出有限跟实际的无限或跟实际的零之间的区别（参见第五章第 68 页）。在对声速进行实验时，光速信号已经超过了实际无穷大的阈值。然而，在跨过这个阈值的两侧，声音和光都同样具有有限的速度，这种有限性跟恒星的像差①现象有关。

力学上说，"松弛悬挂"的柔性链是一条悬链线，其方程为

---

① 译者注：像差（Aberration），实际光学系统所成的像与理想光学系统所成的像之间的偏差。恒星像差与恒星光行差本质上是一个意思，但二者侧重强调的意思不同，前者强调恒星的虚像偏离真实位置，而光行差强调恒星的光偏离本来的方向。

$$y = a \left[\cosh\left(\frac{x}{a}\right) - 1 \right]$$

其形状如图 22。问题来了。"当链条被'拉紧'时,它是什么形状的?"我曾经真的以为"拉紧"后就一定会涉及一套完全不同的定律。但是,通过把图 23 想象为图 22 的拉长,或者类似于图 22 中标注为 tt' 的部分,很容易看出,这两种情况的不同之处仅在于支撑点处张力的垂直和水平分量之间的比率不一样,如图中的矢量所示。对于任何一个具体的问题,我们都可以设置一个比率的阈值。这样,在阈值的一侧,我们称为链条松弛;而对阈值的另一侧,我们称为链条拉紧。但这样的阈值不具有几何上的特殊性,而松和紧也只是同样的悬链线的公式中的一个参数的等级而已。

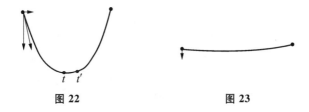

图 22　　　　　　　　　　　图 23

　　在解释一个内部为真空的玻璃球体是如何承受压力的时候,通常的方法是考虑这个球体的一小部分,如图 24 所示的 ab 部分。这个小圆盘受到周围相邻的玻璃向其中心施加的压力,但由于它是弯曲的,因此产生的未被抵消的张力成分刚好足以让这个圆盘顶住大气压力。遗憾的是,尽管这种对事实的必然性证明很有说服力,但往往无法使人在直觉上看懂它的合理性。为了把这种想象连接起来,让我们考虑一个实心玻璃球的情况。很容易想象出它是如何抵抗空气压力的。接下来,想象一下在球体中央有一个微小的真空泡(图 25)。考虑到它所受到的压力大小,还在实际零的阈值之下。然后让我们想象泡可以有各种不同的大小,直到我们得到最开始的空心球体。通过所有这些分级的变化,我们就可以生动地看到原则的同一性。

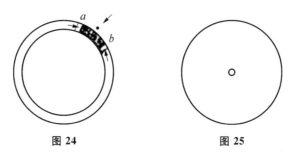

图 24　　　　　　　　　　　　　图 25

　　然而,通常情况下,我们的心理系统常常会设置一个意识范围的阈值,使我们只能在没有更为直观印象的情况下去理解同一性。因此,我们不可能听到信天翁拍动翅膀的声音和蜂鸟持续不断的嗡鸣声之间的同一性,或者从字面上*看出*颜色和从热辐射器发出的长波之间的同一性。

　　但是,这并不意味着这种同一性是"不完美的",而只是让它更有吸引力。例如,当两个音调之间每秒相差几次振动时,我们会听到节拍,如果节拍的频率高于我们的音调听觉的下限,就会引起耳蜗中的基底膜某些部分的交感振动,我们就会听到相应频率的音调。由此,人们可能在实验发现组合音调之前就预测出它的存在。然而,有些心理学家却不可思议地说,组合音调是来源于耳朵,就好像只有它是特殊地起源于耳朵,而其他音调都不是起源于耳朵。

　　.机械系统的原理通常是保持不变的,即使超出我们感觉具有决定性概念差异的点,依然如此。我们知道,一卷电影胶片(1) 在一段时间内保持绝对静止状态,(2) 然后被快门覆盖遮挡,(3) 开始移动,(4) 达到最大速度,(5) 速度减慢,(6) 停止,(7) 到达快门时被打开,(1)再次保持静止一段时间。现在,我们想象这个过程至少需要几秒钟。但真实的情况是,阶段(1)只用1/14 的2/3,或 1/21 秒,而从(2)到(7)六个阶段的整个系列大约只用了 1/14 的1/3,或1/42 秒。机械的逻辑只是简单地推演出这些连锁程序,把我们的想象力抛在了后面;并且随着现阶段的科技发展,在系统出现故障之前,也就是在突破机械性能的阈限之前,这个速率还可以进一步提高。

同样,一本关于内燃机的教科书详细解释了,如何根据电气、化学和机械原理一步接一步,构成一个完整的循环,从而让人以为内燃机就类似远洋轮船上的往复式蒸汽机那样轻松运行的印象。但是,当我们在飞机上听到这种循环合并为持续不断的嗡鸣声时,我们的想象力简直无法理解大自然是如何以如此疯狂的速度完成如此多的连锁程序的。

4. 跨越区间 x 的同一性

如果只是笼统地说,程度上的差异足够大,就会成为种类上的差异,这是不解决问题的。但这种说法让我们对这一节标题的内容有一个概念。在 a 和 b 之间有着明显的差异,尽管我们在标尺上看不出把它们分割开来的特定点。因此,这个例子中的逻辑是,看到同一性,而不是随意地选出一个区别点,或者想当然地认为存在一个明显的区别点。

因此,在统计学中,人们经常会遇到图 26 中所出现的这种曲线。统计学家把图上的那些小幅的起伏称为波动,而把较大幅度的起伏称为总体趋势。但假设我们有一条像图 27 这样的曲线,那么就会成为波动的波动和趋势的趋势。而除了对于特定问题要在波动和趋势之间画一条界线之外,它们作为数据变化这一点上都是一样的。在图 27 的后半段,甚至就连这种等级上的差异也难以辨别了。

图 26

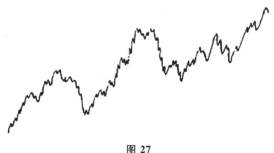

图 27

从平滑曲线和粗糙曲线的角度来看,同样的问题可能更为普遍。一个绘图员问道:"对于我的数据来说,最平滑和最接近的拟合曲线是什么?"坦率地说,这个问题在用词上是自相矛盾的。如果图 28 中的曲线 1 是最接近的拟合,那么它是最粗糙的;如果曲线 5 是最平滑的,那它也是最不接近的拟合。因此,除非我们根据横坐标的频率、纵坐标的准确性以及那些所谓相关或偶然的因素,设置一个拟合程度和平滑程度相结合的阈值,否则这个问题不会有一个全面的答案。

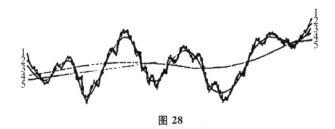

图 28

在音乐中,有时同一性会被名称或概念的差异隐藏,但可以通过具有巨大差异的不同案例之间的中间态来发现出来。因为倚音的音符①写得很小,并且要弹奏得"越快越好",所以新手经常觉得有

---

① 译者注:倚音(grace note),加在音符左上方或右上方的小音符,是竹笛、钢琴等乐器上常用的装饰音之一。一般分单倚音和复倚音两种。在乐曲中适当运用倚音,可以丰富乐曲的表现力。

点不和谐,那些大音符却是不论节奏多快,都必须明确地占据一定的时长。实际上,所有的旋律乐谱无论用什么方式写出来,都具有各种不同程度的快速性,在这一点上都是相同的。证据就是,在中间情况下,听众无法判断某个演奏片段到底是写为下面三者中的哪一个:

但他可以*倾向*于选择其中一个或另一个更为方便的乐谱。这种同一性的意义在于,它将会导致操作处理上的同一性。例如,如果普通音符的弹奏速度过快,那么倚音同样也会有过快的演奏。倚音并不是可有可无的音符。

　　和弦的同一性也常常被一些变体的巨大差异掩盖。分解和弦①或琶音②跟同步弹奏的和弦同样都是和弦。而在中间态的情况下,听众无法分辨出乐段收束的结尾处应当写作

 还是

同样的,一系列跳跃性很强的音符组合成的如下乐段:

---

　　①　译者注:分解和弦(broken chord),是一种把和弦的各和音顺次弹出的演奏方法,是和弦的装饰性或音型化处理方法之一。
　　②　译者注:琶音(arpeggio)指一串和弦音从低到高或从高到低依次连续奏出,可视为分解和弦的一种。

这是很难掌握的,但它和

 乃至于

只有程度上的差别,掌握第一种形式的教学方法就是尝试去听出它与最后一种形式之间的同一性。

　　有时候,我们没有注意到变体在 x_1 和 x_2 之间的延伸,但这并不是因为缺乏观察,而是因为中间物对理解我们的问题不存在意义,也就是说,对于这些 x 而言,$f(x)$ 没有值。这种情况下,在这段空白内的 $f(x)$ 可以通过想象、假设或实际把它创造出来进行定义。

　　因此,我们发现动物在物种上存在巨大差异。但在过去可能曾经存在的缺失环节中,我们找到了证据,并理解了整个动物王国进化的连续性①和物种起源的同一性。

　　关于动物和植物之间的区别,人们普遍认为动物会移动并对刺激作出反应,而植物则不会。现在我们知道,除了一些低等植物和敏感的植物外,所有的植物都会对刺激作出反应。向植物的一侧投射的强光会使它在短时间内转向那一侧。但这段时间是几个小时的问题,而动物的反应时间是一秒钟的问题。因为我们很少发现反应时间在一分钟左右的生物体,这之间的时间差距是惊人的。但是,如果通过单纯的想象,使反应时间的统计坐标为零,来桥接这段空白;那么,就反应的事实而言,我们就获得了两者具有同一性的概念。

　　我们发现紫外线中最短的波长约为 500×10^{-8} 厘米,而 X 光中最长的波长约为 20×10^{-8} 厘米。符合这两种辐射的电磁波理论所做的,正是跨过中等波长的空白段而看到这两种光波在重要方面的同一性。

――――――――――

　　①　取能够把突变包括在内的较宽泛的意思。

5. 跨越小增量 δ 的同一性：连续数学归纳法

数学和心理学对在一个小增量 δ 两侧的同一性特别感兴趣。假设我们有两个刺激 x_1 和 x_2，其中 $x_2 - x_1 = \delta$ 小于最小辨别阈 ε；那么 x_1 和 x_2 由于能给出相同的感觉而具有同一性。如果现在我们取 $x_3 = x_2 + \delta$，那么 x_2 和 x_3 在给出相同的感觉方面也具有同一性。但如果是 $2\delta > \varepsilon$，那么 x_1 和 x_3 就不会有同样的感觉。因此，这就是已经确认的同一性并不是传递关系的一个例子。

这只是问题的一个方面。另一方面，当类似的逻辑情形应用于没有这种有一个 ε 限制的案例时，那会自动显示出"差异"，于是惯性的力量、累积的习惯、原则的一致性等等，将会通过小得难以察觉的增量插进来，一直达到使差异成为没有差异的程度，我们才知道。（参见上一节）

这一过程的数学计算，我可以用一个定理来表述，因为没有更好的名称，我将把这个定理暂时称为"连续数学归纳法"。表述如下：

1) 设命题函数 $\varphi(x)$ 对于 $x = a$ 为真；

2) 设给定区间内有阈值 Δ，使得若 $\varphi(x')$，则 $\varphi(x + \delta)$，δ 为 0 与 Δ 之间的任意值，包括 0 与 Δ；

3) 那么，$\varphi(x')$ 对给定区间内 a 点之外的任意 x 值均为真。

证明：设 b 为任何大于 a 的 x 值。如果它与 a 的差值小于等于 Δ，则根据 2)，结论成立。

若 b 与 a 的差值大于 a，则应用*阿基米德公理*[①]，即，差值 $b - a$ 可以表示为一定数量的 Δ 加上一个分数 $\theta\Delta$（图 29）。从而存在一个整数 n 和一个真分数 θ，使得：

---

① 译者注：阿基米德公理（Archimedes' Postulate），是描述实数之间的大小关系的性质。可表述为如下的现代记法：对于任何实数 x，存在自然数 n 有 $n > x$。是一些赋范的群、域和代数结构具有的一个性质。

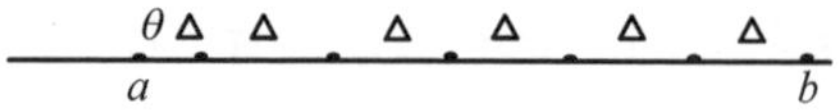

图 29

$$b - a = (n + \theta)\Delta$$

或　　　　　　　　　　$$b = (a + \theta\Delta) + n\Delta$$

接着,应用一般数学归纳法

Ⅰ. 基于假设 1)和 2),$\varphi(a + \theta\Delta)$ 为真

　　∴ 又基于 2),$\varphi(a + \theta\Delta + 1 \cdot \Delta)$ 为真。

(这里的小前提是为了 n＝1 而设的)

Ⅱ. 基于 2),如果 $\varphi(a + \theta\Delta + r \cdot \Delta)$ 在 r 为整数时为真,则对 $r + 1$ 也为真。(大前提)

Ⅲ. 因此,基于一般数学归纳法,$\varphi(a + \theta\Delta + n\Delta)$ 为真,即是说 $\varphi(b)$ 为真。证明完毕。

这一定理的严谨性和普遍性[①]可以很容易地以降低简洁程度和客观判断力为代价而得到提高。但这里可以说,它的优势和劣势都存在于第二个假设,它在超过差别阈限 ε 的负值案例中是无法实现的。现在回到应用中来:

我们让骆驼的鼻子伸进了帐篷的开口。这跟不让它进来几乎没有什么区别。然而,一旦我们允许了第一部分,就会引入第二个假设:没有理由不允许它再进来多一点,然后越来越多,越来越多,直到它整个都进入帐篷里,同一性跨过阈值。

劈开一根竹子可能很难。但是,如果楔子的细端插进去了,粗端也就会随之而进,这就是汉语中"势如破竹"这一说法。

喝半杯啤酒是无害的,也是允许的。而在喝了前半杯之后,我没有理由不再喝一小口,然后再一小口,再一小口……随着 δ 的迅

---

① 这个用命题函数的术语进行表述的定理已经比只从示例连续性视角进行处理更具有概括性。(参见第 110 页)

速增加,利用阿基米德公理获得任意数量 b 杯的啤酒也就变得越来越容易了。

在私人信件中使用一美分的公家邮票,这似乎够得上是无关紧要的小事了。但接着我也可以用两张,或者为了方便用一便士[①]的公家邮票,以此类推;于是,证明在堤坝一旦溃裂后,能保住自己不陷入腐败的重担就落到我的肩上。

我们笑对白色的谎言[②]。但是,是否存在着没有被某种程度的灰色所玷污的,真正纯白色的谎言呢?从为了取悦他人而夸大一件事,到如实说出一个事实却起到误导作用,再到一个彻头彻尾的黑色谎言,其间可能存在有限数量的有限 Δ,每一个 Δ 都不产生差别,但它们的总和确实会产生差异,在这个范围内,习惯于无差别的同一性具有很大的势头。

在开始做一件事的时候,比如改掉一个习惯,开始一项工作,或者是努力把事情做到最好,人们经常说:我将从明天开始,或者在不久的将来开始。可以肯定的是,短时间的拖延造成的影响可能是低于重要性的阈值。但我们生活在这样一个世界里,一个明天会产生另一个明天,一个未来会带来另一个未来。然而特别的情况是,今天的今天还是今天,但明天的明天却不是明天;现在的现在还是现在,但不久的将来的不久的将来却不再是不久的将来。因此,最保险的态度就是,在明天与永恒的正值一侧之间,*看到其中的连续性*,并*怀疑其中的同一性*。

在所有这些例子中,A 和 B 的结果之间有如此明显的差异,以至于智力等级的区分似乎应该能够找到一个阈值 ε,超出这个阈值的 δ 值都不应该叠加。然而,我们的心理惯性和思维习惯等,往往倾向于使连续归纳法的第二个假设成真,从而实现*实践中的同一性*。因此,把 A 和 B 同等对待会更安全、更容易。至于什么时候智

---

①　译者注:美分(cent)是美国货币单位。便士(penny)是英国货币辅币单位。

②　译者注:"白色的谎言"(white lie)是英语谚语,指善意的或无恶意的谎言。

力区分会比安全考虑更重要，或者是反过来，安全考虑会比智力区分更重要，对这个普遍性的问题，人们只能给出一个普遍性的答案："看情况"。假设都是没有经过数学验证的。

6. 奇点 ξ 的同一性

在处理了标尺不同部分之间的同一性之后，我们将考虑那些关键在于一个点本身跟其他点之间的同一性的情况，例如，抛物线与椭圆和双曲线的同一性，它们具有所有圆锥截线的那些共同特性。在这样的问题中，我们可以简单地选取一点和原标尺的一侧。然后，这个点似乎就位于新标尺的一端，它可以被转换，成为标尺的单位 1、或无穷大、或零，以适应我们的需要。因此，我们现在面对的是极限点的同一性和差异性问题，这在第五章中已经进行了讨论。在第二节(参见第 61 页及以后)中，特别是第(2)段关于显著概括，讨论了极限点与系列的其余部分可能相同的方面。为了不重复说明，我在这里只处理几个新的案例。

同样，拓扑关系在极限情况下往往还依然保持相同。因此，一个复变量的环形区域可以逐渐变化，如图 30 所示，直到最后我们得到一个连着一条细丝的简单区域。而这也展示出一些与复变量相关的定理，对 A 适用，对 B 也适用，但我们不能把这看作是理所当然的。

图 30

伽利略在他的力学中经常通过这种延伸到极限点的连续性进行推理。他发现，一个球沿着一个倾斜的平面滚下一定的高度，就会沿着另一个平面向上滚到相同的高度，因此，第二个平面坡度越平缓,球就会走得越远才停下来。于是伽利略就这样推理,在极限情况下,如果平面是水平的,那么排除摩擦导致的阻力外,球的滚动将永远继续下去。因此,他在这里含蓄地讲出了牛顿的惯性定律。

当时,由于摩擦是个令人烦恼的事情,他就在不同的介质中对下落的物体进行了实验,并发现随着介质越来越稀薄,下落速度的差异越来越小。他谨慎地得出结论,"我们有理由相信,在真空中,所有物体都很可能都以相同的速度下落。"[1]

序列中的一个点常常会看成是奇点,这是因为它恰好就是我们目前的立足点。但它可能在任何其他方面都并不特殊。因此,从这种主观的立场出发,谨慎地推断出其他奇点,并尝试通过这种方式来看待同一性,这是一个好办法。

因此,因为我身处现在,所以现在似乎具有特殊性。但超越我目前身处其中这仅有的一种特殊性之上,它还具有任何意义上特殊性吗?

如果事件按照某种进程发展,人们往往会发现这个事件与以前的所有事件都不同。是的,当然。但是在什么意义上的差异,以及差异程度有多大? 以均匀加速的自由物体为例。我们假设在物体下落一段距离后,到距离-时间曲线上的点 A(见图 31),开始对自身的事情感兴趣,并说:"现在我的状态与此前的所有状态都不同。我经过了比此前任何时候都长的距离,速度也比此前任何时候都快。"到目前为止,一切都没有问题。但它无权根据这一点就推断现在作用在它身上的力跟此前有任何不同。实际上,这个力从头到尾都是相同的,而力的变化则一直是零。因此,在图

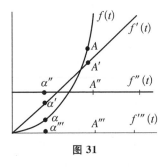

图 31

---

[1]　见 Galileo, *Dialogue Concerning Two New Sciences*,英译本,第72页。

31 中，距离 A 在大于先前所有的 a' 这一点上是特殊的，因为它的一阶导数 A'（速率）大于所有的 a''，但它在 $A''=a''$ 和 $A'''=a'''=0$ 这两点上与此前的状态是*相同的*。简而言之，这只不过是把熟悉的自由落体方程再重复一遍：

$$f(t)=\frac{1}{2}at^2$$
$$f'(t)=at$$
$$f''(t)=a$$
$$f'''(t)=0$$

在考虑历史的系列时，人们常常会忘记差异性在哪里结束，同一性从哪里开始。"我们的时代是高成本生活的时代。""我们的时代是科学的时代。"每个时代都说："我们的时代正处于启蒙的顶峰。"既然我们现在已经取得了这么多成就，怎么可能再实现任何伟大的进步呢？"问题在于"我们的启蒙比此前的任何启蒙都更启蒙，这会持续到几阶导数为止呢？

报纸专门会在奇点终止的地方旁敲侧击地指出事物的奇点。"这样那样的运动员打破了以往的纪录。此外，这次比赛打破的纪录比以往任何一次比赛都多。"但这样的报道可能每年都会重复。每走一步，我都会打破我一生的行走距离的纪录。

如果一个人交了很多朋友，可能有一天他会说："到目前为止，我爱她（或他）胜过所有其他人。"但是，仅仅有这种形式上的基础，而没有进一步的内容，在方法论上是否足够得出任何重要奇点的结论呢？

如果一个人在某些事业上有一定的进步趋势，他往往会认为，在"现在"之后，运气会发生根本性的变化。但这种变化的概率，不是等待到手的，而是努力争取的。如果我一直以四进三出的比率支付我的往来债务，那么从今天起，我就有责任用实践证明，我将会在有限的时间内还清债务。

通过连续数学归纳法进行的论证,也可以采用奇点的观念建立同一性的形式。目前这种诱惑似乎特别情有可原。"这将是我的最后一次冒犯,而最后的冒犯只能有一次。"但我必须表明,这最后一次的意义,是指它不同于未来的冒犯,它只是一系列最后的冒犯中的一个。

"这将是我最后一次生病。"长期患病的悲观主义者说。或许会如此。但它与以前的疾病在哪些方面不一样呢?

"这将是最后一场战争。"我们乐观主义者说。或许会如此。但这并不是因为这是到目前为止的最后一场战争,每一场战争进行时都必须如此。如果我们在更多的方面发现一些奇点,例如人道主义理念的发展、人民之间理解和沟通的增加、世界组织的进步、历史的自我觉醒,如果有的话,等等,从而产生的效果将使世界超过预防战争的阈限,那么一切都会好起来。如果没有(前者),就没有(后者)。

但必须增加一个条件。如果我们把一个问题设置在我们自身之外,例如,从安全距离之外看着一块石头坠落,并提问它下落的加速度是否发生了改变。我们可以通过说"如果没有,就没有"来结束。这正是特殊性结束和同一性开始的地方,我接受这一事实。但是,如果我从失事的飞机上坠落,发现我具有恒定的加速度或至少是恒定的高速(由于空气阻力),那么我就是身处问题之中。如果我想要在有奇点的地方都存在同一性,我可以从现在开始就创造一个奇点。如果我有准备,我可以打开降落伞,这样从现在开始我的速度就会大幅度改变。这个降落伞可能是为不再做最后的冒犯而额外付出的努力,也可能是为维护和平而做出的联盟,或者其他什么,以及布料制造的。在这里,就有了一个新的含义,即通过特定的连续性或是仅仅通过法则来得出差异性。逻辑法则只是重言式,但自然和人类的法则会在同一性区间的两侧产生出非重言式的差异,并为下一章的内容提供材料。

第七章　连续性中的差异性

与通过连续性得到同一性的一般陈述相对应,我们现在要在同一性 K 的范围内,以分界点 ξ 或区间 x 为参照,来讲 A 和 B 之间的差异性。因此,在色调中性的同一性范围内,通过灰色系列的连续性,我们可以参考它们跟中度灰色或位于中间的各种灰色的分界点,来区分白色和黑色。

如果我们采用跟处理同一性类似的方式来处理差异性,那么这整章的安排可能会重复跟上一章相同的标题和相同的例子。因此:

1. 零。——两辆相撞的汽车将依据其中一辆汽车的速度在零点的一侧或另一侧而处于不同的法律地位。

2. 奇点。——水和冰因为在 32°F 的两侧而有差异。

3. 阈限。——旋律不是节奏。

4. 区间。——人不是猿。

5. 连续归纳法。——约定明天做跟约定永远不做是不一样的。

6. 具有奇点。——对于所有这些来说,现在都是独一无二的。

然而,为了防止强使问题去适应形式而实现统一,在本章中,将对前面的标题进行拆分、组合、交叉,并且重新排序。

为了把通过连续性得出差异性作为一个*问题*来陈述,我们假设有两个事物 A 和 B,当某个变量,如时间、长度、速度、温度变化时,它们可能会不知不觉地相互影响。若有人问:我们有哪些感兴趣的方面,为了什么目的,应该在哪里划分界限呢?正如在下面所有的例子中将展示的,这种划清界限的行为包括把 A 和 B 作为 x 的函数,转换为一个具有两个值的新函数,其中 A 有一个,B 有另一个。而在上一章的情况是把 A 和 B 放在同一个 K 类之中。

1. 差异区间 *x*

从显而易见的案例开始,让我们来考虑由大量的程度差异所引起的差异,其中,由于缺乏远见、故意对问题进行限制,或是对事实认识有差距,没有提出在中间"划线"的问题。更为严格地,我应该说,这里也没有提出对点作出标记的问题。因为穿越一个区间的差异,不就是通过画一条线(纵向的)得出的差异吗?

有一类重要的例子是要把曲线的弱小的波动跟强大的起伏区分开来。这样,我们很容易在年度健康总体趋势的波动中,区分出哪些是季节变化导致的,哪些是持续护理的健康改善导致的,或者是持续磨损的健康受损导致的。在上一章(第 88 页,图 27)中提出的波动和趋势的同一性的普遍性问题没有在这里提出,是因为在这个健康问题中不会出现中间类别的变化。同样,地球的公转与自转是可以区分的。人们可以听辨出音乐段落中的独立重音在一般的渐强音(*crescendo*)和渐弱音(*dimiuendo*)之上;可以看到巨大的涌浪上泛起阵阵涟漪(参见第 108 页)。有人问:"既然汉语把音高的影响作为单词自身的一个语言学部分,它是怎样用音高的变化来表达呢?"答案是,一个汉语说话人可以让他的声音在波浪中上下起伏,同时那些单个的音节会产生涟漪,而无论它们的平均音高恰好是落在波浪的哪个部分。

作为统计缺环的例子,在上一章中提到了植物和动物之间反应时间的差异、光和 X 射线之间波长的差异,以及不同物种之间的差异。无论我们驯养动物干活和吃肉有什么道德的依据,这个问题理所当然地以人与动物之间的差距而大为简化。如果那些缺失的环节都活到今天,那么它们又该享有什么样的权利? 这个问题,如果不是无法回答,则必须得到回答。

由于尺度 *x* 的选择是个心智判断的问题,而 *A* 和 *B* 相对应的 *x* 的函数又是个近似的问题(见第三章的概念分级,第 39 页及以后各页),因此,尺度 *x* 上的点可能无法充分地确定这个函数。例如,对应于 200 个单词长度的文章,可能是一个名人轶事或一个短篇故事。但是,如果我们看这两种题材最大值的统计分布,就可能存在着差异,即使这两个最大值之间的分布没有断裂。然后我们可以参考其他变量来研究这个问题。于是,通过重新考虑我们选择的变量,例如,我们可能会得出结论,轶事只有一个重点,而短篇故事则需要解决几个相互冲突的元素。同样,在心理学中所谓的简单自然反应的实验中,我们发现反应时间的统计分布中有两个最大值,经过进一步的检查,证明这两个值分别对应于肌肉反应和感觉反应。

威宁格[①]在他的《性与性格》一书中说,男性和女性之间的性格区别只是存在于所谓的男性和女性中的两种性格的比例。然而,如果人们忘记了在这种比率的统计分布中,一个正常人不是以这种性格为主就是以另一种性格为主的事实,他的观点就很容易被夸大。

2. 陡峭的曲线

在上一节中,我们有一个不涉及限定问题的疑似范围。如果相对于一个问题来说,这个范围足够窄小,以至于可以忽略不计,那么我们就有了实际上的非连续性。于是,如果我们在烧瓶中混合氢气和氧气,再向里面发出一个火花,你会立即发现水,如果你能活着检查的话。烧瓶由弹性物质制成,当然先要经过一定程度的应变测试,当达到破碎点时,碎片开始逐渐分离。但是出于多种目的,这种渐进的曲线是如此陡峭,以至于我们称之为非连续跳跃,这标志出一个烧瓶和一堆碎玻璃之间的差异点。

如果我们把椅子扔向吊灯,那么在一定的速度范围内,椅子会轻轻地碰到吊灯,而不会碰碎它。这可以通过把椅子举到吊灯的高度并轻轻地敲击来验证。但是,相比于在投掷中无法控制的变量,这个安全范围太小了。实际上,我们可以说,椅子要么碰不到吊灯,要么碰到了就会把它打碎。

---

① 译者注:威宁格(O. Weininger)是奥地利学者。

在上一章中(第81页),地球表面被认为是一个奇点,这标志出内部的直接距离定律和外部的平方反比定律之间的差异。但是,如果我们真的钻了一个尺寸有限的洞,并让一个物体从洞外掉进洞里,自由下落,它受到的力的变化,即二阶导数的变化,将会是渐进的,尽管如果我们在月球距离的标尺上以英尺为单位把它绘制出来,看起来也会像是一次跳跃。

从这个角度来看,我们还发现在谈到青春期时使用"非连续性"一词是有相对理由的,青春期以一条非常陡峭的曲线作为标志,把一个人生命的不同周期划分开来。生物突变现象被认为是进化连续性的一部分(见第六章第90页,脚注)。但从另一个数量级来说,突变达到足够陡峭,就可以称为是一次跳跃。

3. 稳定平衡

人们可能会问,为什么事物之间是以分布区间或急剧变化来分隔开的?也许研究广义的平衡概念可能会对此有所启发,因为它与差异性问题有关。简单地说,我们可以让 x 代表一个广义变量(不需要是空间的),而 y 表示一个通用的"势",它倾向于(在物理上、社会上等)为最小值。变化率,即 $y - x$ 曲线的斜率,将代表广义的"力",用于测量下坡的趋势。

在图1中,在这些山丘上的小球中,A 处于"稳定平衡"状态,因为如果它稍微改变位置,还会返回谷底原位。B 也处于平衡状态,尽管可供它移位和返回的"基数"很小。C 处于"中性平衡",因为它不会被任何力向前推动或向后推动,而是保持中性。D 处于"不稳定平衡",因为如果它发生位移,无论多么微小,都会受到力的影响,使它滚下山坡。E 不处于平衡状态,因为有一股力促使它向下移动。

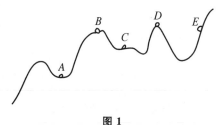

图1

那么,我们熟悉的地面,就这么多了。

如果现在有一场阵雨落在这些山丘上,那么雨水被这些山丘的起伏自动分类,并分别流入山谷,这不是显而易见的吗? 因此,稳定平衡的中心为每一个类别提供了唯一性或同一性,跟其他类别分离开来。

在化学反应中,有许多假设的中间态化合物,在放射性活动中,也有假设的元素形成。但是只有那些处于稳定平衡状态的化合物和元素才会有人去鉴定和命名。这样,我们才发现了不同种类的物质,它们不会相互融合。晶体的显著特征和生物现象,如叶序的规律性[1],在复杂性更高的层级上也有同样的概念。

在铜管或木管乐器产生旋律的过程中,或者实际上在物理现象中的任何"驻波"[2]中,都只有某些特定的频率,因非连续的音级而能够保持彼此不同。一位圆号演奏者可以试图"摆弄"他的乐器,使吹出的音稍微跑调,但他不可能像吹小号的小丑那样能做出连音(legato)的效果。但是,一个严肃的小号演奏者、小提琴手或歌手要如何准确地发出这类全音阶或半音阶的音呢? 人们有时会说,这一类的音乐家比键乐器的音乐家要困难得多,因为在无数错误的单音中,他们必须选中那个唯一正确的音。

但从稳定平衡的角度来看,他们并不像看上去的那么糟糕或是那么令人钦佩。歌手通过训练能够获得某些相对音高的平衡中心;他在实际演唱中,会稍微偏离这些中心,但如果他学会了准确的音准,那么这种偏离就不会超过平衡的基础。若超过这个基础,歌手会感到需要重新调整,或者听众会感到需要纠正。我们认为

---

[1]　见 W. M. Bayliss, *Principles of General Physiology*, 1914,第 383 页。
[2]　译者注:驻波(standing wave)是自然界一种常见的物理现象。入射波(推进波)与反射波相互干扰而形成的波形不再推进(仅波腹上、下振动,波节不移动)的波浪,称驻波。

贾维斯(Javese)①能平分五声音阶②是不可想象的,因为贾维斯训练分辨和定位这些音,而这些音对于受其他训练的那些人来说是不稳定的。

　　类似地,语音的连续分级可以通过发音器官位置的连续分级来产生。但在任何给定的语言中,都有少数的习惯性平衡中心,母语者不会偏离这些中心。如果他想学会用地道的口音说外语,他就必须习得新的稳定平衡中心,这就像欧洲人的耳朵试图学习贾维斯音阶一样。如果新的中心靠近他母语的中心,那么习得就会非常困难。把"sir"(英语:先生)发成"soeur"(法语:姐姐),或是把"parlez-vous français?"(法语:你会说法语吗?)发成"parley voo frongsay?"(英语:会谈、航班、弗龙塞),就相当于用距离最近的旧平衡中心来代替新中心的实体,从而产生了洋腔洋调的现象。一个通晓多种语言的人(polyglotte)就是习得了许多种平衡中心,他可以保持这些平衡中心的稳定又能把它们区分开来。

　　在非习惯性的事情中也可以酌情建立一种稳定的中心。在许多实例中,为合法行为和非法行为之间,或者为道德行为和不道德行为之间划定的界限可能是不一致的。但是,如果一个人一心想成为守法的人或有道德的人,他就不会偏离对于守法和道德的一种稳定的平均判断。

　　举一个一般的例子,我们可以说,思想或概念是通过它们在逻辑上或者方法上的稳定性而确定下来的。在这里,我们可以把它们定义的变体视为位移,而把其中勉强的或繁琐的部分看作是潜在的内容。例如,我们希望,"朋友"的概念应该是相当稳定的;但如果我

---

　　①　译者注:贾维斯(Javese)音乐,是专指亚洲一些民族和北美印第安人采用五音阶的原始音乐,中国古代音乐也是采用五音阶:宫、商、角、徵、羽。这是跟欧洲的七音阶音乐不同的音程划分系统。

　　②　译者注:五声音阶(pentatonic scale)是由五个音组成的一组音阶。以 C 大调为例就是 1、2、3、5、6,C、D、E、G、A。中国传统的宫商角徵羽就是五声音阶,许多国家和民族的传统音乐中都可见到这种调式。

把我的朋友定义为通常理解下的朋友加上我的狗组成的类别，那么这种偏差将会导致"我的朋友，除了我的狗"这样的表述增加使用频率，而"我的朋友"这样的表述使用频率相对减少。在这种过分滥用逻辑的情况下，有一种倾向于回到稳定平衡点的逻辑力量。也许全部定义问题的一个方面就是要找到逻辑上的稳定平衡。（参见第四章第 51 页及以后）

4. 不稳定平衡

（1）如果事物是聚集在稳定平衡的中心周围，那么处于不稳定或中性平衡状态下的事物呢？如果冰雹落在山脊的水棚或平顶上，它属于哪个山谷呢？在这里，让我们应用分级法和极限点的方法。在图 2 中，A 显然处于稳定平衡状态，B 也是一样。C 的稳定性基础很小。例如，冰雹可能被卡在岩石的一个小的浅裂缝中。在极限状态下，当基础接近零时，就是 D 这种不稳定平衡状态。现在，只有通过对任何具体问题的抽象化，我们才能把某个势能 y 称为 x 的函数。在第四章第 55 页中，我试图证明一个函数只是一个理想极限，其中一个（或极少数）因素占主导地位，而只会引起轻微变化的所有其他因素都无关紧要。同样的道理也适用于中性平衡。如果现在冰雹落在一座山脊上的平滑凸脊上，或者落在山脊上光滑的石板上，那么重力这一主要因素几乎为零，而所谓的次要因素则成为主要因素。例如，一阵微风吹来，就可能使它向一侧或另一侧移动。

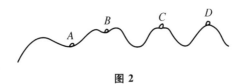

图 2

因此，处于不稳定平衡或中性平衡状态的事物实际上根本不是处于平衡状态，而是位于一条曲线的*斜率*上，也就是说，当它处于主导的稳定平衡状态时，一个作用力因为太小而无法把它推离基础，也就无法对它所在的斜率表现出任何额外的效果；但当主导因素被平衡抵消时，这就确实会产生不同的影响。

另一方面，如果空气是静止不动的，而地球的旋转也不是过于剧烈，那么平滑的石板和光滑的冰雹颗粒表面的粗糙度可能仍然足以使后者保持不动。但这只是一个稳定基础很小的稳定平衡。

因此，一般来说，我们可以说一个事物要么就是处于稳定平衡状态，要么就是根本不处于平衡状态。根据独特的阈值的区别性（第68—70页），从问题的角度出发，我们可以说，山顶上的稳定平衡若是会被偶然的或无关的因素打乱，那么它就是那个问题中的不稳定平衡。

应用这一结果形成差异的方法是这样的：我们可以通过加入新的因素来重新确定我们的问题，这种细化过程可以无限地进行下去。但是，若是当我们认为细化已经足够解决问题，却又出现了似乎是不稳定平衡的情况，那么我们可以说，靠掷硬币作出决定就可以了。因此，一个决定，无论是付诸行动还是令人沮丧，都是可能的，除非我们提出把无限数量可能存在的因素完全平衡抵消的限制性要求，而我们在任何有限的问题中都不需要这样做。

因此，在棒球场两垒之间的球员会跑向这个垒或那个垒，而不会因为似乎二者被抓住的机会相等而在那里停留不动。一个要想乘坐有轨电车的步行者，不会因为在前后两站错过电车的概率相同，而在两站中间缓慢停留。如果可能的话，在干草和水之间的布里丹之驴①可能是同样饥饿和口渴，但从干草一侧吹来的微风会把他稍微吸引过去，于是不稳定的平衡就不再平衡了。只有在学术论域内，无限数量的因素才能精确地被平衡抵消。

---

　　①　译者注：布里丹之驴（Buridan's ass）是法国著名哲学家布里丹提出的悖论：假设有一只完全理性的驴，在两堆完全一样的干草堆之间会饿死，因为它无法选择到底该吃哪一堆干草。比喻在决策的过程中，优柔寡断、犹豫不决的现象。这里的干草和水讲的应该是另一个类似的版本。

（2）本着连续性的精神，人们可以说事物的每一点都重要，但更谨慎的说法是，每一点都*可能*重要，除非它足以跨越一道鸿沟或者一个差异的门槛，否则就不需要考虑。在生理学中，有"全有或全无"的原则①。根据这一原则，如果肌肉的神经受到刺激，在强度达到最小阈值之前，肌肉完全不会做出反应，而超出阈值时，肌肉就会全力做出反应。同样，为室内的植物点起蜡烛，对它的光合作用毫无帮助。因为，低于植物正常光照的 1/100 以下，任何光照都跟没有光照一样，不会有什么区别。同样，慢慢渗出的水不会滴落，直到水的重量超过其表面张力，整个水滴就会滴落下来。电荷会相对连续地在静电起电机的电刷上聚集，但会通过旋钮在两个小球间成单位地放电。根据辐射的量子理论，能量的吸收是连续进行的，但当能量聚集到其载体无法容纳的程度时，它就会以一个单位的形式辐射出来。

（3）通过一种触发器或杠杆的作用，跟主要因素相连的次要因素可能会加倍扩增而跨越一个不稳定平衡点。因此，缓慢地描述电影的放映机制或者是内燃机的循环机制，相当于把速度从超出我们的意识范围之外降低到我们的意识范围以内。同样，我们做事的能力也可能会从某个需求的阈值之下倍增到阈值之上。我不能举起一块大石头，但我可以用杠杆使我的力量倍增；我不能准确地画出 30°的角，但通过先（徒手）画一个等边三角形，然后再把它平分，我就得到30°角，这比直接估计要准确得多。实际上，利用分析杠杆发展"手绘几何"技术是一项值得进行的研究。同样，一个人的意志力控制的成果可以通过设置触发连接点而增加。我一旦开始弹钢琴就停不下来了；当钢琴在我面前打开时，我就忍不住要开始演奏。但把钢琴锁起来，把钥匙交给一位朋友，这可能是我意志力所能够办到的。② 这样，通

---

① 见 W. M. Bayliss, *Principles of General Physiology*, 1914, 第 383 页。

② 译者注：这正是作者自己的亲身体验。在康奈尔大学读书时，因对音乐喜爱入迷，每天练习钢琴，多次在日记中提醒自己限制练琴时间。一次曾弹到很晚，引起楼下同学敲暖气管抗议。

过一种道德杠杆的作用,无法做到的事情就做到了。

　一般来说,所有方法都可以看作是杠杆,正如第二章所展示的那样。给出一个所需的标准 S(图 3)和一个有限的触发器 A,无论它是判断、技能、意志、力量、善意还是其他什么。然后,方法的问题就在于建立一种这样的连接,使 A 能够倍增到超过 S 之外的 B 点,或者,用解析的说法,把 A 转换为 B。在关于极限点的章节(第 67 页)中也讲到过这一点,当时的重点在于 A 与零点的差异,即,跟似乎是无限相比较得出的,某物与无的差异。而在这里的重点也就是从上面的阐述中给出的,A 和 B 之间相对于标准 S 的差异。

$$0 \quad A \qquad\qquad S \quad B$$

图 3

5. 关于奇点的差异

　除了形式上的意义之外,奇点一般不需要成为不稳定的平衡点。因此,取任意序列 x,再取任意点 a,我们可以通过一个纯形式的指令,称它为一个奇点,具有不稳定平衡的特性,尽管所涉及的变量可能没有任何动态特征。让我们取函数:

$$f(x) = \frac{2}{\pi}\tan^{-1}[n(x-a)]$$

其中 $\tan^{-1}$ 取第一支,n 是一个相对于问题而言的大数。然后,有点 $a-\eta$ 在 a 的左侧附近,产生结果为接近 -1 的 A;而点 $a+\eta$ 在 a 的右侧附近,产生结果为接近 $+1$ 的 B,在极限

$$f(x) = \frac{2}{\pi}\lim_{n=\infty}\tan^{-1}[n(x-a)]$$

式中,符号函数 $sgn(x-a)$ [1]如图 5 所示,其中,无论开始的触发器

---

① 见 Pierpont, *Theory of Functions of Real Variables*,第一卷,第 202 页及其后。

－η 或＋η 有多小，在 a 点左边的任何点都会向右滑入－1，在它右边的任何点也会滑入＋1。这是一种用分析方式的说法，而用直白的语言，我们可以任意选取任何点作为一个分割点，从而把在它一侧的任何事物，不管离它有多近，都放到一个类里。这就是差异显著性的下限（见上一章第 75 页关于埃及金字塔的内容）。在不稳定平衡的情况下，加入显著的动态因素作为变量。在本节中，我们将考虑其他有显著差异的案例。

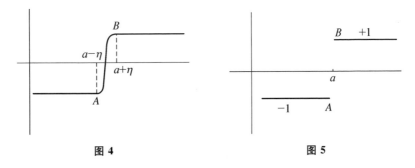

图 4　　　　　　　　　　　　　　　图 5

我们见过一些叫作波浪的事物，另一些叫作涟漪，它们之间的波长差异最大，正如本章第一节所讨论的那样。在进一步的调查中，我们发现了所有的中间状态的波长。接着，我们注意到波浪以不同的速度传播，较小的涟漪超过较大的波浪。进一步，我们发现波浪是通过表面张力、重量和惯性传播的，在最低速度的一定波长（对于水大约为 1.6 厘米）以上，波浪越长，传播的速度就越快；而在它以下，情况正好相反。因此，我们建议将这一点设为中性点，并把所有比这个点更长的扰动称为"波浪"，而那些比它更短的扰动称为"涟漪"。因此，在分割点两侧的代数符号标示的速度变化是这个逻辑上不稳定平衡的触发因素，而这种分类差异可能会导致行动和事件中出现有限的差异。

同样，在从红色到黄色再到绿色的连续光谱中，我们会在黄色中经过一个明暗"转向"的点，在颜色金字塔中用拐角表示。因此，这个奇点标记出一个系列中两个部分之间的显著差异。

在上一章中,我们说红色和绿色尽管不同,也被认为是相同的。那么在这里的重点只是说,红色和绿色尽管相同,但它们相对于零饱和度的分界点来说是不同的。如果我们把纱线分为两个篮子,其中一种或另一种颜色的轻微着色就会给纱线的命运带来有限的差异。

维护形式上的差异,就可能涵盖了很多方面的显著差异。但是,通过一种心理或法律行为,一次任意的区分就是发生的那一刻的事实的区别。在连续归纳的情况下,重点放在了 a 与 b 的同一性上。第二个假设说,"我没有理由不在另一个明天而不是下一个明天做这件事。"但我可以说:"我把第十七个明天称为奇点日,并将通过在那一天实际开始这项工作来使它成为独特之日。"当然,如果我的意志力足够强大,能够真的实现这一点,那它当然将会成为独特的日子。总的来说,由于每个点在某些方面都是独特的,所以若是通过抓住每一个机会来阻止那种令人恐惧的归纳,或者是通过警惕可能会废弃我们所需要的归纳的那种障碍,就有可能会击败第二个假设。面对"没理由为什么不做。"答案是,"没理由为什么要做。"

公约和法律之间也可以从形式上的区别造成实质上的区别。几十年前,在经度180°附近画下了一条线,因此在它东边附近的任何一点的时间读数,都比在它西边附近的任何点少 24 小时。探险家在国际日期变更线上找不到地理标记,但是当涉及日程安排、日期和电报通信等问题时,在线的两边的有限差异却实际存在着。我们从冬令时改为夏令时,在名称上也表现出事实上的区别。在某一天把时钟从早上 2 点拨到早上 3 点当然只是指针运动中的一段陡峭的曲线,但这种连续性跟这个奇点在法律上的意义无关。

6. 差异的局限性

一个显著的差异会大于它的名称所包含的内容,而小于它所不是的那些内容。因此,重新审视一下问题的另一面是很重要的。

(1) *案例的连续性*。——在对于所提出的差别进行有效性测试时，人们应该记住一种开放的可能性，即，在问题没有转换的情况下，通过检查中间状态的情况，其中有可能存在或者不存在非连续性。除非已经有了明确的非连续性标记，否则最好采用案例的连续性。因此，在上一章讨论笛卡尔碰撞理论举出的一个例子中，设定了一个位于零点处的奇点，使得质量在一个或另一个方向上的微小变化触发整个物体以 $2v$ 的有限速度差异，向一个或另一个方向运动。如果速度或动量是质量变化的连续函数，那么情况发生小的变化，就应该使它有小的改变。这实际上是莱布尼茨对笛卡尔理论的反驳[1]。在哲学上，莱布尼茨认为自然是连续的，因此笛卡尔是错误的。但在方法论上，人们会满足于说一个已有问题中的函数*可能*是连续的，(如果是这样的话)笛卡尔*可能*是错误的。以更进一步的力学事实为基础，他实际上也确实是错了。

伽利略反对[2]亚里士多德关于较重的物体下落更快的理论，他假设把两个重量不同的物体连接在一起，并推断由于物体 a 以速度 A 运动，而较重的物体 b 以更快的速度 B 运动，二者连接起来，将会以介于 A 与 B 之间的速度移动，而不是以亚里士多德理论本身为前提得出的比 B 更快的速度运动。我假装摆出亚里士多德的姿态，可能会这样回答：两个物体合二为一，实际上是一体的，因而用于两个部分之间折中效应的推理是不成立的。而一位最现代的亚里士多德派可能会引用这样一个事实，即我们不能对于通过最小的接触连接在一起的两个单独导体，进行电子作用的推理。只有当我们问到连接和不连接之间的差异时，才能感受到伽利略这个论点的分量，并展现出两个球的连接有不同的情况：从一根蜘蛛丝、一条绳子、一根链条、横穿的木杆，到焊接在一起，机械的连接不同于电学的连

---

[1]　见 Letter to Pierre Bayle, 1687, in *Philosophical Works of Leibniz*, tr. By G. M. Duncan, 1890, 第 33—34 页。

[2]　见 Galileo, *Dialogue Concerning Two New Sciences*, 英译本，第 63 页。

接,其结果实际上是一种渐进的差异。因此,这种基于案例连续性的绝对简化,已经通过事实得到了证实。这不是亚里士多德理论所暗示的存在一个奇点,而这一奇点也并不存在。

空气动力学中讲到,飞机在每小时 100 英里以下的空气阻力是跟速度的平方成正比;在 100 英里以上的空气阻力则是跟速度的立方成正比。这个公式在一定范围内的差异是合理的。但基于案例的连续性,我们发现每小时 100 英里的速度只是一个根据技术惯例的奇点,而根据精细的物理测量则不是奇点。因为速度在每小时 100 英里上下的时候,空气阻力的变化并不是一个突然甚至陡峭的变化,而下式

$$阻力 = Cv^y$$

中的指数 y 在 v 接近 100 时已经大于 2 了,而在 v 刚刚超过 100 时,指数 y 还不到 3。

(2)新变量。——在一组变量参照下明确的区分,在考虑到其他变量时可能合并为连续,或变为常量,这一事实也可能对差异构成限制。从分析角度来看,在

$$y = sgn x$$

中,A 与 B 通过分界点 O 清楚地标记出来(图 6)。但在

$$y = (sgn x) \cdot |x|$$

相当于

$$y = x$$

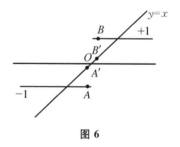

图 6

中,A' 与 B' 在 O 点附近的差异越来越小。这里只是把有限差异退回到它们的触发点去。再进行一次简单的转换,我们就又得到了同一性。

奇点的丢失也可能来自独立变量 x 的变换。例如,水的冰点标志着水和冰之间的差异。在它之下没有水,只有 100%的冰;在它之

上没有冰,只有 100% 的水(图 7)。但是,如果我们把热量而不是温度作为 x,那么,当冰中加入热量时,就会出现中间态的比例,如图 8 所示。因此通过引入另一个变量,奇点被拉伸为一条连续的曲线。同样,在从一种物质转化为另一种物质的化学变化中,如果我们在空间上从一种物质的质量穿过一个点达到另一种物质的质量,除了跨越边界的明显变化,我们是不会发现中间态的。但是如果我们考虑到从一个质量转化为另一个质量需要的*时间*,我们会发现这个变化是一个连续函数。

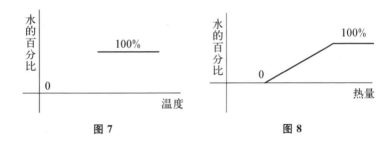

图 7　　　　　　　图 8

7. 奇点的差异性

现在我们回到奇点本身属于哪里的问题,在不稳定平衡的处理中已经给出了关于这个问题的部分答案。

(1)"*如有疑问*"。——我们经常听到这样的决定:在同一航道对向航行的船舶必须从彼此的左舷通过,但如果两者之间的距离很远则可以从右舷通过。如有疑问,请从左舷通过。

除非真的饿了,否则不要在两餐之间吃东西。如果有疑问,就不要吃。

如果近处有汽车,就不要横过马路,如果汽车在远处,就可以过马路。如有疑问,就不要过。

我要买一块秒表或一块金表,看哪一块更便宜。"在其他条件相同的情况下",我更喜欢秒表。

我们在名义上已经解决了奇点问题。但是,如果对是否有疑问的情况也有疑问怎么办? 说这事有疑问? 那么,如果对它是否有第二层疑问的情况也有疑问怎么办? 这种怀疑显然是无穷无尽的。更具体地说,假设我们在演讲赛中只根据讲稿来评判参赛者。在平等的情况下,选语言更好的。进一步平等的情况下,选演讲方式更好的。再进一步平等的情况下,选服饰更好的,以此类推。换句话说,我们知道了次要因素通过主要因素被平衡而成为主要因素的情况,正如在上文中讲到的不稳定平衡的情况。实际的结论是,我们可以通过引入更多的因素来解决问题,或者,如有疑问,继续进行,通过自行决定或随机决定,相信事情结果的统计平均值的安全性。因此,还是一个没有对糖果和冰淇淋上瘾的舌头对在两餐之间不吃东西的那个"如有疑问"的平均解释比较保险。

(2) *函数的零点。*——在上一节中,我们所考虑的点处于一种不稳定的平衡状态,无论触发器多么微小,这个点都必须倒向这一侧或那一侧。两艘相向而行的船只无论是在左舷通过还是右舷通过,都不会发生碰撞,这也是一种不稳定平衡的情况,尽管是从另一组变量的角度来看。但是,如果我们有一种形式上类似于稳定平衡的情况,若其中一个点向一侧或另一侧的轻微偏差足够小,可以认为是零,那么我们可以把这个奇点单独作为一类区分出来(参见上文关于稳定平衡作为分类中心的内容)。这尤其适用于利用连续函数经过所有中间值的性质来处理。如果函数 $f(x)$ 是连续的,且

$$f(a) < 0 \text{ 且 } f(b) > 0$$

那么在 a 与 b 之间的某个地方,存在一个点 ξ,使得

$$f(\xi) = 0$$

其中 ξ 本身可能就是一个重要奇点(见图 9)。

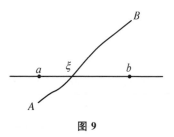

图 9

例如，一副观剧望远镜可以放大远处的事物，而缩小近处的事物。因此，肯定有一段距离，让事物透过观剧望远镜看起来和实际的大小一样。

在一座桥下，我看到潮水在一天中的某段时间冲向下游，在一天的另一段时间流向上游，那么必然会有一段时间里水是静止不动的。

在击打垒球时，如果球来的位置靠近握棒的手，球棒会产生一个朝向手的位置的震动；如果球来的位置靠近球棒末端，就会产生一个远离手的位置的震动。因此，球棒上必定存在一个完全不会震到手的 ξ 点。这个点也就是适合挥棒击球的中心点（图 10）。

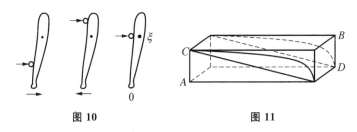

图 10　　　　　　　　　　　图 11

如果我们有一个长方体的梁 AB 在点 A 处固定支撑（图 11），那么它的强度会朝没支撑点的方向减弱。如果通过对角锯切，只剩下 CD 部分，那么朝支撑点方向的强度会增强。"既然如此，"伽利略说，"存在一条这样的切割线，在移除所有多余的材料后，会留下一个在所有点上的应力都相同的实体，这似乎不仅是合理的，而且是必然的。"[1]也就是说，这样一个实体中强度的变化量为零。他证明了这个切面是一条抛物线。

（3）*用于测量的零点*。——因为在很多情况下通过观测判断零点比判断数量更容易，我们经常会把它作为一种测量方法。例如，在海上行驶的船上，不可能直接测量地平线和太阳之间的角度。但

---

① 　同上一脚注（译者注：即 110 页②），第 141 页。

我们有一个六分仪[①],它通过反射和直接光照,把太阳和地平线拉近。在一次调节中,它们的距离是一个标志;在另一次调节中是另一个标志。因此,存在着一个使二者达到刚好接触状态的调整幅度,而这个幅度的大小可以通过观察得到相当准确的结果。

如果某些数量尚未定义,则可以通过用一个已知数量把它抵消来进行定义。例如,pb 与 $p'b'$ 的长度相比,pb 看起来更长。长多少呢?但是首先要问,长多少这个问题意味着什么?定义错觉测度的一种方法是:取一个离 p 足够近的点 a,使得 pa 明显短于 $p'b'$。因此,必然存在一个点 ξ,使得 $p\xi$ 看起来等于 $p'b'$。那么,$b\xi$ 就将是这一错觉的长度。事实上,这属于心理学中一个熟悉的领域。(a,ξ,b 三个点不应该像图 12 中那样出现在同一条直线上,这里只是出于直观示意考虑。)

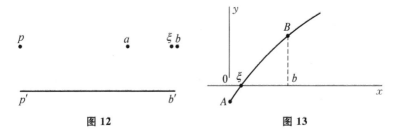

图 12 　　　　　　　　 图 13

同样的,把黄色视为负蓝色,就可以测量颜色对比度。在均匀的蓝色背景中取一条细带。设 x 为细带在正常情况下的蓝色程度,y 为在这背景下的蓝色程度。如果我们取一条灰色条带(蓝色程度 $x=0$),那么相比之下,它看起来会是黄色的(y=负蓝色)。我们由此得到了点 A(图 13)[②]。如果我们取一个确定的蓝色条带,它也会

　　① 译者注:六分仪是一种光学仪器,是重要的定位和导航工具。用六分仪测量太阳与地平面或海平面之间的夹角,再查出当天太阳直射点的纬度,就能确定观测者所在的纬度。实际上,六分仪可以测量任意两个物体之间的夹角。六分仪的原理:光线的反射角等于入射角。

　　② 参见第一章关于跳水的青蛙的讨论。

显示为蓝色，我们由此得到了 y 值大于零的点 B。现在如果 y 是 x 的连续函数，那么应该有一条中间色调的蓝色带，它在强蓝色背景中看起来会是灰色的，也就是说，会有一个 ξ 点，使得

$$y = f(\xi) = 0$$

实际上，这也是普雷托里（H. Pretori）和萨克斯（M. Sachs）研究颜色对比①以及海思（C. Hess）和普雷托里（H. Pretorie）研究亮度对比②方面所使用过的方法。

在这整个研究中，对这种奇点需要注意的是，在任何情况下，我们都不能过于严格地对待 $y = f(x)$。正如前文讲到的，当主要因素的影响变得微不足道时，次要因素的影响将不可忽视。因此，如果一条带不够窄，那么在靠近临界点的位置，我们可能会得到一条有黄色边界的蓝色带。有了一副廉价的观剧望远镜，就会有某个临界距离，使得视野中的某些部分会被放大，而其他部分会被缩小。即使在相对意义上，也不存在完全的清零，除非我们确定基于实际的考虑，对其他因素可以用诸如偶然、无关或可以忽视这种形容词来表述。

（4）*极限点*。——上一章建议要谨慎地从极限点推出奇点。因此，本章将会提出极限点不同于其他点的可能性。同样，由于这个问题已经在第五章得到了解决，因此除了使用后来的一些研究材料外，没有必要进一步详细解释。

在上一章通过连续归纳法进行的论证中，认为"一点儿"和"很多"一样成问题，其动机就在于"全无"跟"一点儿"之间截然不同。"现在"是独特的。"现在就做"与"等一会儿"截然不同。彻底的禁欲和偶尔的纵欲是截然不同的，不论纵欲时如何节制。可以肯定的是，人们不可能不通过水果摄入任何酒精粒子，也不可能在某些俱

---

① *Pfluger's Archiv（Physiol.）*，vol. 60，1895，第 71 页及之后。
② *Archiv f. Ophthalmologie*，vol. 50，No. 4，1894，第 50 页及之后。

乐部的聚会上不吸入任何香烟粒子。但是按照惯例,不跟酒杯或烟斗接触,在原则上就算是完全的零了。

从平衡的角度来看,我们可以了解到极限奇点是如何存在的。在打碎酒杯之后,一个人就已经在零点处于稳定的平衡状态了。但如果从酒杯里喝一小口,就会有一股力量把他推下山去。我们经常听说,我们永远无法确定水是不是绝对纯净的,水中可能有任何微量的物质。然而,例如,如果水里有任何游离的钠粒子,它就是完全不平衡状态,会立即变成氢氧化物①。因此,我们可以确定,水中游离(不带电)钠的量为零是一个奇点,它单独就成为一种稳定平衡。

某些生物学或社会学的力量总是会涌向作为唯一稳定平衡点的一个极限点。最高水位线不仅仅是水位上限的奇点,而且还可以通过植物的生长来进行测量:如果植物生长在这个水位以上,它们就会向下蔓延;如果是生长在这个水位以下,它们在长大之前就会被淹死,因此,它们会尽力向上生长。

在制定规则或法律时,最好要注意到事物会涌向的那个极限点。如果一种短缺商品开始公开销售,时间点并不完全一样,但人群一定会涌向这个时间的极限奇点,也就是刚开始的那个时刻。

在铁路货运中,维护成本费用如此之高,以至于其他运营费用可以忽略不计。因此,如果两条平行的线路无限制地竞争下去,就会出现恶性的竞争,走向不收取任何运费这个稳定极限。从另一个角度来看,比如说从这些线路的长远存在来看,这个极限点当然不可能是个稳定平衡的问题,正如铁路历史所表明的那样。

8. 自然的连续性

讨论过所有这些具体的同一性与差异性的实例之后,通过利用

---

① 译者注:钠和水反应生成氢氧化钠和氢气。反应时产生燃爆、发光和升温。反应现象是钠浮在水面上,四处游动,熔成闪亮的小球,并发出嘶嘶的响声,属于强烈的化学反应。

连续与非连续相互之间的转换，人们可能还想问，在最后的诉求中，大自然究竟是不是连续的。一个答案是，方法论不会诉诸最后一种方法。只有当我们选择了变量和函数时，连续性才是重要的，不论它是准确的连续还是近似的连续。水的形态和温度的关系是非连续的；水-冰比例与热量的关系是连续的。从总体上简单说，水和冰的关系是连续的还是非连续的，都没有意义，有待于进一步的定义。因此，总的来说，自然界既不是连续的，也不是非连续的。因为只有函数才可以是连续的[1]，而作为自然界的自然并不是一个函数。我们可以通过适当的转换，自由地、冒着风险使自然的一个方面连续或非连续；如果我们成功地抓住了方法论杠杆的长端，那么结果就是有启发性和有用的；而如果我们碰巧抓住的是杠杆那错误的一端，那么这个结果就是人为的而徒费力气。

然而，如果我们仔细研究这一问题的动机，并试图通过适当的陈述使它具有重要意义，那么我们就还不能放弃自然的连续性问题。实际上，最重要的动机在于把时间的连续性作为自变量。问"自然是连续的吗？"通常是意味着，"通过充分的提炼，是否总是有可能把对任何现象的测量结果表示为一个时间的连续函数，而不论这一结果的变化有多么突然？"但是我们所说的时间是什么意思呢？在实际科学中，无论是在物理学还是心理学中，时间都是通过我们认为"在时间中"发生的现象来测量的，例如地球的自转、沙子的流动、钟摆的振动、思想的传递、紧张和放松的感觉。同步性、之前和之后、时间长度，这些词语的工作含义都是基于日常生活中的科学事实。因此，我们可以说，把时间视为由以这些方式相关联的所有现象构成的，这在方法论上就足够了。[2]

因此，现象 y 在时间上的相对非连续性意味着，如果我们把平

---

① 在实际操作中，一个连续统的单纯连续性可以被表达为函数 $x' = x$，见第一章，第 9 页。

② 相对论会影响此类讨论的进一步细化，但不会对总体上的具体观点产生影响。

常的时间测量结果 t 放在 y 上,那么在 y 出现一个确定的差异时,测量现象的 t 却没有任何明显的差异。因此,当伽利略打开提灯的护罩时,光线"立刻"照在几英里外的山丘上。但是,斐索(Fizeau)用齿轮代替手动的灯罩,揭示出一种现象,它的变化率与光的变化率相比并非几乎为零[①]。因此,通过对问题的重新表述,把相对非连续性变成了相对连续性。

另一方面,关于前面讲到的,时间概念在哲学上的问题还将继续存在:是否有任何现象的变化具有如此大的数量级,以至于以任何有限单位测量的其他已知或未知的变化现象都无法与之对抗,因此,对应于足够小的测量差异,所讨论的现象的差异就应该是有限的吗?但是以这种形式来表述,这个问题唯一可能的含义也就变得毫无意义了。因为,如果这个问题的答案是肯定的,那么我们的科学实践只是把这种现象从时间顺序中排除出去,并称之为同时存在的不同事物,而不是同一事物的非连续变化。例如,为了便于论证,假设引力是即时的,那么我们应该直接说存在一个这样那样强度的力场,存在于这样那样的点上;而不是说即时传播的波或辐射。因此,我们可以说,根据已经发现为最合用的时间定义:自然是时间的连续函数。于是,自然的连续性就不再是一个哲学结论,而是在围绕科学优势这个球体进行的一个很大的循环之中。

---

① 译者注:斐索实验是法国实验物理学家斐索(A. H. L. Fizeau)1851 年进行的一项实验,测定了光在运动的水中的相对速度。为了确定介质运动对光速的影响,斐索使用了一台特制的干涉仪。

第八章　结论和进一步的问题

1. 结论概要

如果问题、方法和结论是"平行"联系在一起的，那么表述整个研究结论的最佳方式就是指着各个单独的章节说："瞧!"问题的陈述本身和程序的方法本身都是结论的组成部分，并且它们的有效性和显著性可能会受到批评和争议。但是，为了便于参考，下面给出各章结论的概要[①]：

Ⅰ问题。——连续性的概念，在不同程度的数学准确性的意义上，作为方法论研究的指导线索，被认为是值得进行的。

Ⅱ方法。——一般来说，方法被视为杠杆。通过它，人们从一些现实开始，可以获得更多的现实。

这项研究的典型方法是深入到具体的事物中，找到它们的层级和顺序，根据标尺检查向外和向内的不同功能的案例，并随时把我们的观点转换为我们认为合适的观点。

Ⅲ分级概念。——当绝对地接受一些概念时，试着去看看把它们分级能够有多大的意义。有些特别的结论是：例子、类比、比喻、文字游戏等，都是构成概念定义的不同层级的元素。

在数学中，变量和常量之间有不同的参数阶段。

限制在一条线上的数学函数是限制在一根管或一条带的一个分级的数值。当其他因素的变化对现象没有"明显"的影响时，这一个因素就是现象的"唯一"原因。

Ⅳ系列排序——任何两件事物都可以按照任意定义的系列顺

---

①　这一概要跟我们可能在读论文之前看的，或者不读论文只看它的那个正式的"摘要"是不同的。

序进行比较。序列之间的可比性是一个程度问题。

人们对于一个序列顺序能陈述的事实越多,就越有证据表明对它的定义是好的。

只要应用过程中的波动和科学上的偶然失误在一个相关的阈值之下,我们对序列顺序的陈述就不用同义重复,这样我们就能够用一件事的定义之外的某个事物来称呼它。

V 极限点。——极限案例至少在是作为案例这一点上跟其他案例具有同一性,并且在作为极限案例这方面具有特殊性。

数学的精神是下限的精神,哲学的精神是上限的精神。科学和生活处于中间地位。但通过转换的方法,在某些方面会出现极限。

相比于形式上的空无一物,有限事物中的实际、范畴、事实等等,具有无限的性质。

在特定的问题中,上限阈值和下限阈值会代替极限。因此,建议对阈值构成的极限进行重新定义。这似乎符合数学上的用法。在这个意义上,我们说,真理就是真实的极限,意义或定义就是标准的极限,道德准则就是实际道德的极限,等等。

奥卡姆剃刀的这种应用与它通常的应用不同的一个重要方面是,例如,当物体被"简化"为一类有限的感知数据时,我只把它当成一种"把一部分现实跟另一部分现实进行的对抗",在这种对抗中,某些人或某些问题可能会获得"机械增益[①]"。但是,从循环的角度来看,在事物的当中引发出问题,很可能需要在另外的问题上,把定义扭转过来;例如,一位每天都工作的物理学家或生理学家会发现,感知数据远非终极数据,他们更愿意把它"简化"为其他人刚刚试图用来简化为感知数据的术语。

VI 连续性中的同一性。——显著的同一性总是有差异性为背景。连续性的概念有助于看到同一性,前提是明智地选择变量 x,其

---

① 机械增益,表示机械增力的程度,是机械中载荷与驱动力的比值。大于 1 就是省力,如杠杆;小于 1 则是费力。

中的事物在某个有意义的方面被看作是合并的。而连续性的概念就是在发现同一性过程中的一种辅助。

差异性背景可能是一些特别感兴趣的点，如零点、大的程度差异或小的程度差异。看到一个人目前立足的案例与其他案例的同一性也很重要。

一种对数学的特殊兴趣带来的偶然成果是"连续数学归纳法"定理，这是从楔形的细端开始论证的要点。这个论点的强度，就像所有论点一样，是建立在它的前提的强度之上的。

Ⅶ　连续性中的差异性。——显著的差异总是存在于同一性的背景下。差异不仅仅是差异，而是指划分类别、事件的不同问题、概念或感觉的差异以及行动过程的决策。

一种差异可能是来自 x 的幅度变化或是陡峭的曲线，这些曲线以奇点为标志，特别是以稳定的和不稳定的平衡点为标志。

一个奇点可能只因为它本身的奇特意义而跟其他点不同。当一个量的正负符号发生改变时，一个奇点可能因为它本身具有的意义而跟其他点不同。当一个量的正负符号发生改变时，它改变符号的地方可能会增加疑点，或者可以作为一种测量方法。

值得更突出强调的一种论证方法，是通过案例的连续性进行推理，这一方法可以用来检查有疑问的差异点。

2.　一般结论：它们的循环性

程度差异和种类差异之间的界限是什么？从"观点"的观点来看，我回答，这要看情况。

大自然是连续的吗？这也要看情况。

但是，基于一种和解的性情和一种混合的（如果不是混乱的）智慧，我倾向于看到事物相互融合，而不是把它们分隔开的障碍、界线和点。因此我会说大自然在原则上是连续的，并且称这篇论文为"连续性"。本着同样的精神，我也承认，如果某个头脑感觉到在知识世界中有更多的非连续性的需要和成果，它也可以用心思考这些章节的相同基础,并称这个研究为"非连续性"。

本着"某些性"(someness)的精神,我进一步得出结论,除了重言命题之外,没有任何普遍命题是真的,除了循环推理之外,没有任何理由是充分的。特别是数学和精确科学中,只要是精确的,就一定是循环的。

对于所有这些一般结论的一个明显反对意见是,这种一概而论的断言将是对所断言的事物的简化和归谬。面对这一攻击,人们很容易寻求在罗素和怀特海①的层级结构的庇护下来逃脱,并自称是作为一种"更高层次"的哲学来讲话的。但是我却宁愿在自己的领地上战斗或撤退,也就是说,用一种内部方法,我直接回答说:正是因为这些结论本身是循环的,所以它们是安全的。

然而,有些循环并不是恶性的。希望这些同样的一般结论,已经在上面这些章节中长时间应用实例法以后,现在已经获得了足够的意义,可以正式宣布这些结论的重要性;如果这些结论在引言中陈述的话,也会为无用的形式主义提供例子。从中可以很容易地看出,这些结论并不是这项研究的"终点",除非是在时间的意义上。它们也没有给出"连续性问题的解决方案",只是对连续性中各种研究问题的精简告知单,而"连续性问题"最终也必须由这些问题的研究来组成。

3. 进一步的问题

在引言中,我说过这项研究只是方法论中一般函数理论的一部分。为了进行这样一项系统性的研究,有必要对其中的变量和函数的类型进行调查。变量调查将是对物理单元维度的研究总结。从逻辑上讲,变量可以是一个连续体、一个密集序列、一个函数等等;从数学上讲,它可以是一个实数、一个几何点、一个角度、一个下标等等;而在更具体的应用中,它可能是时间、风险、强度、良好意愿、

---

① 译者注:怀特海(Alfred North Whitehead, 1861—1947),英国数学家、哲学家,"过程哲学"的创始人。

电荷、难度等问题。

　　数学中的函数只是抽象地进行"定义"。但在应用中，这个函数可能有不同的"模式"，可以说，设定 $y = f(x)$ 可以依据定义、分类、陈述、问题、假定、实验假设、估计、猜测、习惯性概念或误解、断言、一般法律、历史记录、观察、发现、感觉、义务、立法、命令或行动的方式提出。所有这些都需要很好地整理和研究。

　　值得特别注意的一种函数关系是包含一些动态因素的函数关系。例如，价格是供求关系的函数，但是，时间滞后的存在使得函数复杂化。这是一个具有普遍重要性的问题。

　　奇点仅在同一性和差异性下进行处理。但它们的重要性足以让人对它们单独处理。最大值和最小值问题在经济问题中尤为重要。在道德问题中，"黄金均值"可以概括为最佳点，或最佳路线的概念，这是属于最大值的一个问题。不同类型的平衡，只在"差异"下进行研究，也值得进行系统性的调查。

　　方法论中的函数理论也可以被视为一种具体数学，其中的数学概念，例如极限的概念，都作了具体解释，具体程度超出了数学物理学中的解释范围。本研究中没有涉及的一些抽象可能性是循环的或周期的序列，如年份、复数、有 n 个变量的 n 维函数、广义坐标、抽象几何中的投影关系以及"群"的特性。同样，具体数学只是一种方法，而不是一种学说，除了实际发现的解释之外，任何更多的解释都不要采纳。

4. 应用

　　有人说，当一个问题成为重要的中心主题时，我们会把这些研究应用于这个问题，而不管是使用什么方法或按照什么顺序。但在这两者之间"无法划清界限"，尤其是因为这整篇论文都是在讲方法和主题，我们也把反思的方法自由地用到这两个问题上。

　　正如通常理解的那样，在逻辑中存在着分类问题，可以从同一性和差异性的角度通过连续性来处理，也可以从跨维度的多维原则的角度来处理。

从逻辑平衡的阈值和稳定中心的角度来看,概念、定义、法则、理论的连续性和弹性本身就可以形成一个研究。(参见第四章第三节,第51页及以后;第七章第104页及以后。)

正如本文所给出的,相关性的含义和极限,特别是关于阈值的概念,值得给予比隐性处理更多的关注。

术语的原则问题与概念、定义等的研究密切相关。诸如用法、优雅、简洁、对称、系统、词源、色彩、中性等等,哪个因素的功能可以用来测量术语的合适程度呢?

谈到更多的哲学问题,机械论和活力论的问题,或是决定论和自由意志的定义,都可以从平衡的角度来研究,这不是什么新颖的任务。

解释绝对和无限的问题是人们最感兴趣的问题之一。把相对和有限作为参照是在解释说明还是敷衍搪塞? 目的论的道德或进化论的道德是道德的具体化,还是对真正道德的抛弃? 某些形式的宗教是对宗教的真正解释,还是仅仅是宗教的替代品?

在道德的特殊问题中,存在着保守主义和自由主义之间的调整问题,这涉及最佳(*par excellence*)连续性问题。

做某件事情的合法程度和不合法程度之间的界限问题,无论是肯定的方式还是否定的方式,都可以借助于连续数学归纳法进行处理。

司法问题也可能涉及许多变量的函数。[①]

有人说,一个人(或一个国家)只有在他所能够负担得起的范围内才是好的。这是一个重言式还是一个令人不安的事实? 你和我能负担得起多少? 这是一个问题,而不是事实。

涉及宪法、普通法、公平、先例、自行决定权的法律问题,属于"如有疑问"的问题。在这个领域,我只能用一种廉价的方式说,只有受过内部训练的人才知道如何处理那些方法论的杠杆。

在实验心理学中,对错觉的测量方法已经得到了一定的解释(第七章第114—116页)。

---

① 见 F. Y. Edgworth, *Mathematical Psychios*,第95页。

　　根据精确科学中发现的象征主义的优雅、相关性和丰富性的标准，很多通常的色彩似乎还是需要通过色彩金字塔来表现。值得一试的是，一个人能在多大程度上发展出"色彩解析几何"①。

　　这些方法的应用显然也延伸到工业和个人效率（最大值和最小值）的问题。在教育心理学中，训练运动技能的方法将涉及中间环节、特定位置、夹挤等因素的考虑。正如第七章（第 106 页）所提出的，一个值得发展的实用学科是通过解析知识的智力杠杆进行的"徒手几何绘图"系统。

　　在声学、音乐、声音的心理学以及实验语音学的边境领域，在这些学科的代表之间有大量意见相悖的讨论需要厘清。变量的定义和分类将会是这种研究中第一重要的步骤。

　　在音乐自身中，如音高（循环的和线性的序列顺序）、音程、韵律、节拍、力度、力度变化等元素，是方法论中函数理论的突出主题。

　　最后，让我来透露一个事实，我在文中的示例主要来自我在写作时碰巧参与的主题。无论是骑自行车、演讲、统计数据还是双色电影，每次我遇到新的事物，我都会发现更多的"示例"，而这些示例反过来又对我的一般问题产生了反应，并可能导致它们的解决（solution）、终结（resolution）或解除（dissolution）。

　　因此，"最终"，作为正式论文的结尾，目前所在的位置仅仅是在形式意义上的奇点。通过抽象概括和"资格无效"，我未来的所有活动，包括可能会发生的否定目前得出的大多数结论（由于在很长一段时间内的变化），都"没有理由"不看作是对于连续性进行连续写作的一篇连续的论文的连续。

---

① 　这一问题来自亨德森（Henderson）教授的建议。

I 参考文献

页码

9	Hobson, E. W.	*Theory of Functions of a Real Variable*, pp. 222 – 223.
13		*Scientific American*, Oct. 20, 1917.
16	Russell, B.	*The Philosophy of Leibniz*, 1900, pp. 64 – 65.
18	Aristotle	*The Nichomachean Ethics*, Chapter IX, Bk. II, (p. 56 in J. E. C. Welldon's tr).
20	Crothers, S. M.	*The Pardoner's Wallet*, 1905 (first essay).
22	Galilei, Galileo	*Dialogues Concerning Two New Sciences*, Eng. Tr. By H. Crew and A. De Salvic, 1914, p. 122.
27	Ruskin, J.	*Sesame and Lilies*, 1864, section 32 (Harvard Classics, vol. 28, p. 121).
32	Hollingworht, H. L.	" The Psychophysical Continuum ", *Journal of Philos. Psy. , and Sci. Meth.* , XIII, 1916, No. 7, pp. 182ff.
34	Bosanquet, B.	*Logic*, 2nd ed. , 1911, II, p. 141.
41	Pearson, K.	*The Grammar of Science*, 3rd ed. , 1911, Part I, chapter on Cause.
45	Huntington, E. V.	*The Continuum*, 1917.
48	Lewis Carroll Dodgson, C. L.	*The Adventures of Alice in Wonderland*, "A Mad Tea-party".

页码

50　　Franklin, B.　　　*Autobiography*, virtue No. 3 （Harvard Classics, vol. 1, p. 83）.

56　　Huntington, E. V.　*American Mathematically Monthly.* Jan. , 1918.

67　　Lewis Carroll　　　"What the Tortoise Said to Achilles", *Mind* , 1895, p. 278.

71　　Russell, B.　　　　*Our Knowledge of the External World* as a Field of Scientific Method in Philosophy, 1914, p. 42.

76　　Wood, R. W.　　　*Animal Analogues* , 1908, p. 1.

83　　Poynting, J. H. and Thomson, J. J.　　*Text-Book of Physics: Heat.* 3rd ed. , 1908, p. 116, foot-note.

95　　Galileo Galilei①　*Dialogues Concerning Two New Sciences* , Eng. Tr. By H. Crew and A. De Salvic, 1914, p. 72.

100　Weininger, O.　　*Sex and Character.*

106　Bayliss, W. M.　　*Principles of General Physiology* , 1914, p. 383.

107　Pierpont, J.　　　*Theory of Functions of Real Variables* , 1905, 1, pp. 202ff.

110　Leibniz　　　　　Letter to Pierre Bayle, 1687, in *Philosophical Works of Leibniz* , tr. by G. M. Duncan, 1890, pp. 33 – 34.

110　Galileo②　　　　*Dialogues Concerning Two New Sciences* , Eng. Tr. By H. Crew and A. De Salvic, 1914, p. 72.

114　Galileo　　　　　*Ibid.* , p. 141.

125　Edgworth, F. Y.　*Mathematical Psychios* , 1881, p. 95.

Ⅱ 其他相关文献

	Biometrica, 1901 to date, esp. articles by Karl Pearson.
Boussineso, J. M.	Conciliation du Véritable Determinisme Mechnicue avec L'Existence de la Vie et de la Liberté Morale, 1878.
Mach, E.	Die Principien der Warmelehre, 1899.
Mach, E.	The Science of Mechanics, 1883. Eng. tr. by T. I. Mc Cormick, 1902.
Meyerson, E.	Identité, et Féalité, 1907.
Moore, E. H.	General Analysis.
Petzoldt, J.	Mathematik und Cekonomie, in Vierteljahrschrift für Wissneschaftliche Philosophie.
Poincaré, F.	Foundations of Science, Eng. tr. by C. B. Halsted, 1913.
Poincare, F.	Dernierés Pensées, 1913.

补注①:"连续数学归纳法"的 笔记

1. 特殊案例。——令函数 $f(x)$ 定义在实变量 x 的某个区间内。

假设 1 令区间内存在点 a 使得 $f(a)=0$.

假设 2 令区间有常数 Δ,使得对于任意 $0<\delta\leqslant\Delta$, 有 $f(x)=0$ 隐含 $f(x+\delta)=0$.

则对于区间内的任意 b,当 $b>a$, $f(b)=0$.

证明。—— I. 若 $b-a\leqslant\Delta$, 则由假设 2 有以下结论。

II. 若 $b-a>\Delta$, 则首先应用阿基米德假说,也就是存在整数 n 和分数 $\theta(0\leqslant\theta\leqslant1)$ 使得 $b-a=(n+\theta)\Delta$, 或 $b=(a+\theta\Delta)+n\Delta$.

接着,应用一般数学归纳法。则:由假设 1 与 2,鉴于 $\theta\Delta<\Delta$.

∴ $f(a+\theta\Delta)=0$.

因此,基于 2,又有

(1)　　　　　$f[(a+\theta\Delta)+1\cdot\Delta]=0$.

由 2,若 $f[(a+\theta\Delta)+m\cdot\Delta]=0$, 则

(2)　　　　$f[(a+\theta\Delta)+(m+1)\cdot\Delta]=0$.

因此,联立(1)与(2),

$f(a+\theta\Delta+n\Delta)=0$.

---

① 译者注:原文载 *Bulletin of the American Mathematical Society*, vol. 26, p. 17 - 18. Oct. 1919. 作者于 1919 年 4 月 5 日在美国数学学会旧金山分会宣读。我们把赵元任首次提出并证明"连续数学归纳法"的这份原创记录文件作为附注,是出自两个考虑: (1) 这最早是出现在赵元任博士论文中,为全文的论述奠定了严密科学的数学基础; (2) 在此后的一百多年中,又有不同的作者研究和证明"连续数学归纳法",只有少数后来者引证了这篇原创性文章。

即

$f(b) = 0.$

2. 一般案例。——令 $\varphi(x)$ 为定义在一实变量 x 的某个区间内的任意命题函数。

假设 1 令区间内存在点 a 使得 $\varphi(a)$ 为真。

假设 2 令区间有常数 Δ,使得对于任意 $0 < \delta \leqslant \Delta$, 有 $\varphi(x)$ 隐含 $\varphi(x + \delta)$.

则对于区间内的任意使得 $b \gtreqless a$ 的 b, $\varphi(b)$ 分别为真。

除了显而易见的用词和符号的变化之外,证明与特殊案例相同。

说明。——这一定理基本上是建立在阿基米德公设和普通数学归纳法的基础上,但从把它作为一个特例的意义来看,它不是后者的推广。因为它涉及实变量 x,所以它不是数理逻辑中的定理。但它比处理等式的普通定理更通用,因为 $\varphi(x)$ 可能是关于连续性、收敛性、可积等性等的陈述,不能用 $f(x) = 0$ 这样的简单形式表示。

这一定理是对来自"楔形的细端"或"骆驼的鼻子"中同样的常见论点的数学公式化:

假设 1: 允许喝半杯啤酒。

假设 2: 如果任何数量 x 的啤酒都是允许的,那么只要 δ 不超过某个无法察觉的数量 Δ,那么就没有理由不允许 $x + \delta x$.

因此,任何数量都是可以允许的。

就像所有的数学定理一样,这个结论并不比它的假设前提更可靠。在这种例子中,如果论证失败了,通常是因为第二个假设中所需的常量 Δ 不存在。就拿楔子本身来说:如果用一个不变的力把楔子推进到被弹性力压在一起的两侧之间,那么在这个楔子受到的力被不断增加的阻力因素平衡抵消时,它将停止不动。在这种情况下,可以说,增加 δ 以使 $\varphi(x + \delta)$ 继续保持推进楔子的 Δ 可能将不是"在区间内不变的",而是会随着 x 接近危险点而变得越来越小,在超过这个危险点之后,结论就不再成立。

CONTINUITY
A Study in Methodology[*]

Yuen Ren Chao
Cambridge, Mass.,
April 13, 1918

---

* 译者说明：赵元任博士论文英文原稿是请美国布朗大学焦立为博士扫描哈佛大学保存的博士论文原件，校正了《赵元任全集》第 14 卷所收英文稿中个别单词拼写的误印。其中参阅本文的页码改为本书的页码。

SUMMARY

Problem and Method

Chapters I and II. —This study, as presented in the form of a thesis, is a stage in several growing lines of thought on certain forms of arguments, methods of discovery, methods of doing things, and on certain practical dilemmas. At the present stage, it is best described by the term "continuity", ranging in meaning from the vaguest connotations to as high degrees of mathematical rigor as its applications can bear.

The very methods studied are used as the methods of studying them, attempt being made to show that circles are not always vicious. Method, in general, is regarded as playing one part of reality, against another, in order to secure a methodological leverage, mechanical, intellectual, or moral.

The typical method (or methods) of continuity studied and used consists in the following stages: Method of (1) Concrete cases, (2) Gradations, (3) Serial order, (4) Extremes, (5) Explicit location, (6) Intermediates, (7) "Pinching", (8) Transformations.

Abstractly speaking, this whole study may be regarded as a methodological theory of functions of one continuous variable. It fails to be a mathematical study in being concerned with the links between the premises and their interpretation, application, or illustration, and in the neglect of making links of rigor any stronger than the weakest.

Results of Special Chapters

Chapter III. —Graded Ideas. —When we find ideas taken absolutely, it is well to ask how significantly they also admit of degrees, stages, shades, or grades. Some particular applications are:

Examples, illustrations, analogy, metaphor, etc., are different grades of elements which *constitute* the concrete definition of ideas.

A parameter, in mathematics, admits of grades or orders of variability, of which a variable and a constant are extreme cases. The order is often a matter of experimental convenience.

A mathematical function, as represented by a curve, is but a high degree of restriction of values to a region, a band, or a tube. A factor is "the" cause of a phenomenon when variations in other factors make no difference in the phenomenon that is appreciable for that problem.

Chapter IV Serial Order. —Any two things may be compared in a serial order defined at will. Serial comparability of concrete things is not a matter of yes or no, but a question of more or less.

We are able to make non-tautological statements about serial order whenever the fluctuations of usage and "accidental" errors of science are below a threshold of relevance, so that we can call one thing by something other than its mere definition.

Chapter V Limiting Points. —"Reasoning by continuity", one can always conclude that a limiting case is at least also a case. But a limiting case is at least peculiar in being a *limiting* case. The answer to each specific problem therefore depends upon further considerations.

The spirit of mathematics is to call a lower limit also a case. The spirit or philosophy is to follow out cases of usual things to their upper limit. Science and life occupy intermediate positions. But by the method of transformations, it is shown in what respects those extremes meet. The actual, the categorical, the factual, etc. , infinite things has the nature of the infinite compared with formal nothingness. It is actual talent, good will, capital, energy, etc. , that makes circles non-vicious.

In particular problems, upper and lower thresholds ("M" and "ε") will do in place of limits. It is therefore proposed to reinterpret limits as *constituted* by those very cases of thresholds that are relevant in actual problems. This is shown to tally with the *correspondence* definition of limits, now used in rigorous mathematics. *In this sense*, we say, meaning or definition is the limit of criteria, truth is the limit of truths, morality is the limit of morals, etc.

An important respect in which this procedure differs from "Occam's razor" is that it claims no finality or exclusiveness. Objects may be "reduced" to a limiting class of sense-data for certain purposes or for certain persons. But from a circular point of view, we have equal respect and sympathy for a physicist or a physiologist who finds it illuminating to "reduce" sense-data to terms that others were trying to reduce to them.

Chapters VI and VII Identity and Difference Thru Continuity. — The problem of identity and difference is one of discriminating the respects relevant to each problem.

The idea of continuity is an aid to see identities, provided that a judicious choice of a variable x is made, in which things are seen to merge in some nontrivial respect.

A background of difference that tends to hide identities may be a singular point of some sort, e. g. , a zero point, it may be a wide difference of degree, a small difference of degree, of the exaggerated importance of one's present standpoint over other points.

An incidental result of special mathematical interest is a theorem of "continuous mathematical induction", which is a mathematical formulation of the familiar argument from the thin end of the wedge. Its formal proof is based on (1) Archimedes Postulate, and (2) ordinary mathematical induction. But the actual strength of this argument, as of all arguments, depends upon the strength of its premises.

Difference is not mere difference, but means classification, alternate issues of events, difference of conception or feeling, decision on courses of action, etc.

A difference may result from a wide change of the variable x, or a steep curve. or marked by singular points, especially by points of stable and unstable equilibrium.

A point may be different from other points in being of interest on its own account, such as cases of balance of primary factors and entrance of secondary factors into relevancy. The idea of the continuity of cases (the usual definition of a continuous function) is very useful in this connection. The intermediate property that if $f(a)<0$ and $f(b)>0$, then there exists ε between a and b, such that $f(\varepsilon)=0$ also finds applications, especially in physical and psychological measurements.

Chapter VII Conclusion and Further Problems. —Is nature continuous? It depends. Both discontinuity and continuity are useful and applicable conceptions in science and life with varying degrees of mathematical accuracy and methodological effectiveness. Continuity of nature as a function of time probably consists in our relative success in so moulding our scientific conception of time as to make temporal functions continuous. It is another case of a non-vicious circle, subject to revision.

Further problems are the working out of a general theory of functions in methodology, with a survey of the concrete interpretations of variables and of functionality. From another point of view, this will constitute a kind of "concrete mathematics". Special applications, which have only been touched upon, but which deserve further study on their own account, are problems of equilibrium, the optimum point or a generalized golden mean, thresholds of relevance, principles of terminology, drawing the line in moral and legal questions, efficiency, methods of motor skill, musical technique, and all the rest of reality in so far as playing with such conceptions will lead to a magnification and not a reduction of our powers.

Yuen Ren Chao
Cambridge, Mass.
May, 1918

TABLE OF CONTENTS

CHAPTER I   INTRODUCTION

1. The Problem: Intermediate

A frog is resting on a rock, on the edge of a pond. Suddenly, nature makes a leap, and before the rings of ripples have spread very far, the frog has already reached the bottom. Yet is it not evident that sometime and somewhere, the frog must have been just beginning to break the surface of the water? I have been told that every year I am to grow two inches taller. Wouldn't it be fun, if I were permitted to stay up some New Year's Eve, to find out exactly when I gain those two inches, and just how the change would feel? But growth, they say, is a *growth*. If you want to be good, for example, you must get started in acquiring good habits right now. If you say, "I can take things easy now, of course I'll be serious and responsible when I become of age," then you will not become of age when you become of age. But are advices ever of any use? Those who will follow them don't need them, those who won't can't use them. It seems that I the mediocre' am perhaps just bad enough to need plenty of advices and good enough to follow some of them. But then, do we always find mediocre between things? My seat seems rather unsatisfactory for a dollar and half, and the people just behind me are certainly getting more than their dollar's worth. Too bad that these seats are not sold for a dollar and quarter. There is a man who lives near a watershed, and complains of lack of fresh fish and navigation facilities. When it rains, the water flows either into the Yangtze or the Yellow

River. Strange there is no valley between two adjacent valleys! Perhaps it is well that some things do come so. What if a trombone player should execute *legatissimo* between every note and the next? What if drops and cupfuls of quicksilver were used for money in place of coins? At times, however, I find it decidedly annoying or embarrassing that I have to decide on things, or to make choices before I have time to decide. "Cigarettes, chewing gum, ice cream cones, and evening papers," shouts the boy at the station. I wonder which is the *best* to take. but how can they be compared as to excellence. being such *heterogeneous* things? There upon the train answers. "Toot! Toot!" and carries me off, together with my meditations. Perhaps I am fortunate to have let the ice cream go. I have heard the advice: "Don't eat between meals unless hungry. In case of doubt, *don't* ," and that was a case of doubt. But sometimes it is doubtful whether it is a case of doubt. To be safe, let me call this a case of doubt. But what if it is doubtful whether it is a case of being doubtful whether it is a case of doubt? And so it goes. At any rate, surely, it is good to have let the cigarettes pass. If I commit one more last offense, there is no reason why I should not commit one more. Of course every offense is a last offense. Remember. to make one puff is identical in kind with smoking a whole box. But is inhaling somebody else's smoky atmosphere different in degree or in kind from smoking oneself? What, in the end, is a difference of degree or a difference of kind? Is the difference between a difference of degree and a difference of kind itself a difference of degree or a difference of kind, or both? How dot these different things come to sprawl all over these pages? Are they identical in kind? What has a last offense to do with an innocent amphibian making a dive?

This, then, is a somewhat unscholarly, nevertheless lengthy, " definition " of the problem with which this study is concerned. It is stated in this manner in preference to the alternative, which would begin with saying in general that it is a philosophical fault to begin with saying things in general when one has a number of things in particular to say, and would then proceed with giving the general reasons why this is the case. This miscellaneous way of introducing the subject is a reflective application of the "method of concrete cases". Certain lines of thought seem to converge to some problem vaguely felt, or better, seem to be connected in meshes of a set of possible problems. Irrespective of unity of principle or principles, more " cases " are looked for, which seem to have something to do with it, tho what "it" is is a very vague thing.

While this is obviously not a rationalistic method, which makes all things depend on, that is, hang on, one or a few pegs, it is also different from the kind of empiricism that stands on a few legs, like sense-data or feelings of relation. It is contented with beginning in the midst of things, things like color mixing, the periodic law, hunger on a train, or distribution of crowds.

The mere rambling among things, however, will not result in the formulation of one problem. If no limit were set to the subject matter treated, questions raised, methods adopted, and conclusions drawn. , this would cover the whole of philosophy and more, and there is no "theoretical" reason why one should not follow where one is led to. A naive pragmatism has it, however, that chunks of reality shall be marked out that may be conveniently managed within the precincts of a single institution, presented in three hours on the stage, exposited between the two covers of a book, or, in particular, written up as an academic dissertation, and further divisions into sub-problems marked out for treatment in separate chapters. Perhaps all problems arise and are defined in terms of action. But it is not the express intention of this thesis to defend philosophical pragmatism.

To apply the method of gradations and serial order (Chapters III, p. 180, and IV, p. 197), it may be suggested that problems may be arranged in the order of generality, ranging from dentistry and cooking cabbage to Boolean algebra and general analysis. It will appear then that such points as are illustrated in the opening paragraph occupy intermediate positions. To locate the problem more definitely, it seems to be, or I intend it to be, more general than sciences like physics or psychology, and less general than mathematical analysis.

Two objections, however, have to be met in justification of thus placing the problem. First, "do we always find mediocres between things?" There may not be any natural convergence of problems toward a stable unity in the neighborhood of such an intermediate generality (Cf. Chapter VII, pp. 265ff.). But for the tolerance and liberality of the Faculty at Harvard University, such a conglomeration of things in particular would perhaps never be allowed to pass as one study, being too shallow for philosophy and too inexact for science. The answer is that the mere absence of an intermediate kind of study may argue just as well for the need of taking it up as for a natural untenability of the position. The actual execution of the study, will therefore justify its undertaking more *or* less. Besides, it corresponds in point of generality approximately to the historical field of inductive logic and methodology, by which this study is called.

The second objection is that generality is not the only principle according to which problems may be divided, and that the position of philosophy itself would be doubtful unless I should he willing to concede to its identification with formal logic. In the spirit of this study, I acquiesce in the objection by saying that the selection of generality as a variable, x, is only a matter of judgment, made on one's own responsibility, for the purpose of locating the position of the problem. But there is no reason why we should not use the "method of transformations" of variables if questions arise where it will be better to consider problems with regard to their difficulty, human appeal, saleability, laughability, or what not.

In fact, more considerations than generality are needed to limit this study as a study of *continuity*, as relatively distinguished from other problems of methodology. Now that illustrative materials have been furnished in the opening section, it is less dangerous to attempt a formal statement of the problem. Using the "method of lower limit", I shall begin with nothing. But, "out of nothing, nothing comes." So I have to start with vague something. The problem will then be: What about it? That is, how can I understand it, appreciate it, or treat it rightly? To take a step beyond this vagueness, some features or respects about the thing may happen to be noticed and become interesting or seem to be important; and when we look at the world at large, we find other things that seem be different from or like the first thing in those respects. In epistemological language, we have as given *that* and then define it as a *what* by comparison with the *other*. In mathematical language, we have a certain term, then look for independent variables, and as the variables change, we find a corresponding function of which that term is one of the values. A systematic study of problems from this point of view might then be called the Theory of Functions in Methodology, which will cut across all arts and sciences in regard to subject matter, and will draw on the results of all mathematical theories of functions in so far as they bear sufficiently on the problems.

The present study, however, is much narrower than this. First, it only concerns itself chiefly with one-valued functions of one variable x, which is sufficiently near a continuum to be treated so in the problem concerned. Secondly, chief emphasis has been laid only on such questions as continuity of gradations (Chapter III), comparison of serial order (IV), examination of limiting cases (V), identity thru continuity and discontinuity (VI, VII). Problems of functions of multiple variables, and problems of maxima and minima, statistical variables, etc. , are not considered on their own account, But owing to the elasticity and length of the antennas of continuity as a method, some of those questions do come into our limited point of view, so that the study is not as narrow as it might seem.

2. Method: Internal

As the problem starts in the midst of things, so the method adopted is largely internal, or reflective, as illustrated in the preceding section. When a distinction is made, say between continuity and discontinuity, I would inquire whether they do not merge into each other, whether they are not limiting cases of each other. When a continuity is seen, as between this study and all other studies, I would ask, or at least others will ask me, where do I draw the line? To borrow the language of electricity problem, method, and solution do not follow "in series" here, but are connected "in parallel". If we dislike the paradox of their mutual *pre*supposition, we might choose the barbarism of their mutual *con*supposition. There is method in the problem started, there is problem in starting the right method, and there is solution in "Well begun is half done". This is like going in a circle, or pulling oneself up by one's boot straps. But, as will be shown in Chapter II on Methods (pp. 159 – 160), some circles are not vicious, and some ways of pulling one's boot straps are not futile.

The methods and results of ordinary mathematics will be used freely in this study. But their use is tempered by a spirit of "someness". To say that some things are so, means both of two things: Firstly, that there *are* such things, -this is the empirical motive, which calls attention to concrete cases; secondly, there may be things that are not so, -this is the analytic motive, which calls attention to abstract possibilities. Mathematics says that *if* A then B, and is perfectly safe in laying down universal propositions. But this study, being also concerned with the question whether things come under this or that hypothesis in the concrete, does not enjoy this security. Hence mathematical theorems are used to a much smaller extent than mathematical conceptions, and are never "proved" except in one instance of "continuous mathematical induction" (Chapter VI, pp. 251 – 252), which is original, so far as the writer's narrow acquaintance with rnathenlatical literature goes. A mathematical proof refers one hypothesis to another, and if the latter lends itself less readily to direct support from experience, the mathematical proof may be a methodological loss.

The validity of a method or a set of methods that claim to have no limit to the scope cf their application seems to need to be defended. (1) To begin with, I shall concede everything by saying that the idea of continuity in any aspect is applicable only in so far as it is applicable. How far, only the futile as well as the fertile applications (if any) in the body of the thesis can show. Some idealists and pragmatists speak of reality as indeterminate or flexible. It is a much better figure to speak of it as being elastic. Things like the shape of a silk thread or of water are flexible that do not resist, but yield to any force. Things like steel or steam are elastic that both resist and yield, to an extent depending upon the force applied. There are degrees of freedom of arbitrariness of thought. But when we apply any method to any problem, we do that on our own responsibility. When the applicability shades off into subliminal significance, like bending an iron bar by sighing on it, we are said to be applying the wrong method. The recognition of the limitation of a method, then, amounts to providing for a safety valve. Wherever elastic reality is too much to be confined in my small methodological boiler, it is allowed to leak out without dogmatic harm being done.

(2) Secondly, this view of looking at things as functions of one variable with continuities and discontinuities is only one of a possible number of views of things. It is natural, and perhaps desirable, that with an intellectual saw, one should "try it on the piano", on the door, on all other furniture that one bumps into, and even dream of sawing saws. But it does not follow that all things must then be defined exclusively with regard to their sawability. Going beyond the limitations of this metaphor, I might plead that the method of transformations would include all new considerations that are necessary in dealing with any problem. But this is simply a case of trying to be infinitely general and therefore safe, at the expense of emptiness (see Chapter V). A much safer attitude is to hope that whoever has an intellectual temperament

and training similar to the writer's will find the treatment highly suggestive on highly provoking, and to recognize at the same time the existential legitimacy of minds that find in this study a mere succession of formalism and far-fetchedness.

3. Terminology: Mixed

In reading thru the following chapters, one may get the impression of a lack of consistency in jargon except perhaps in the frequent occurrence of certain pet expressions of a pragmatic turn. Such consistency has been avoided on principle. On the other hand, figures of language are very freely used, and sometimes mixed. It has in fact been suggested that the whole study is an application of analogy of mathematical to non-mathematical or semi-mathematical subjects. This is true, except that this study is not peculiarly a method of analogy in a sense in which all methodology might not be regarded as analogy. As will be shown in Chapter III (p. 186), actual cases, "genuine" analogy, and metaphors differ only in degree. To use many kinds of jargon, varied figures, and illustrations has therefore the function of actually giving a constitutive definition of the idea. In fact, considering the nature of language as one fact among other facts, one activity having to do with other activities, it is questionable if any language can be completely literal and definite except by way of formal tautology. Wherever, therefore, differences of shades of meaning are not relevant to the question concerned. I shall have no scruple in stringing together a number of words as synonyms. Thus, "the absolute, the unconditioned, the infinite, the concrete, the categorical," need not be distinguished in one context, tho they may have important differences in other respects.

Certain terms have been avoided or used very sparingly, "Theoretically" and "practically" rarely occur in these discussions, as some word or other will be found to be more satisfactory whenever there is occasion to use one of those qualifications. The terms "subjective" and "objective" will hardly appear again after this mentioning, not that they are regarded as invalid ideas, but simply because it happens that they have not entered into these problems. "Truth" and "falsehood" have not played as important parts as their universal applicability seem to justify. Perhaps an interpretation (or a misinterpretation) is usually given instead, whenever there is an occasion to mention them. Frequently, "utility", "fruitfulness", "effectiveness", "significance", and "artificiality", "barrenness", "futility", "triviality", suffice to describe the situation in question.

An attempt has been made to let words explain themselves by trying to be idiomatic, or even colloquial, and letting the center of gravity of their rich associations in the context determine possible ambiguities. But where this does not suffice, explanations or definitions will be given.

A few terms of frequent occurrence may be explained in this connection:

Thing is nearly always taken in as wide a sense as in the word *something*. It seems to be just as good a word as *entity*, *term*, *objective*, and in many discussions (not necessarily philosophical), it actually connotes something more general.

Point, when used in a context of formal discussions, does not necessarily refer to a geometrical point, but any element in a series, that is, anything. Thus. in Chapter V, the whole opening maxim is a limiting "point", or in Chapter VI (p, 257), a whole athletic contest is a "point".

Idea, *notion*, *concept*, *conception*, are not discriminated except with regard to the idiom and context.

Threshold, *limen* are used interchangeably, ε is used for a lower threshold and M for an upper threshold.

A *singular point* is taken in the wide sense of any point peculiar interest. It is denoted by ξ.

Universe of discourse means something well marked out, and *context* suggests something vaguely associated. But where the two shade into each other and the distinction does not matter, the expressions will be used interchangeably.

Infinity, as discust in Chapter V. is only used in the sense of a variable, as used in mathematical analysis. The conception of completed, static infinities, or the transfinite numbers have not been applied in this study.

A *value* of a *function*, in a mathematical context, means nothing but a constant determination that the function has when a constant is assigned to the variable x. Thus, the value of the function $f(x) = x^2 + 17$ is 26 when $x = 3$. It is very difficult to avoid this firmly established mathematical usage. But this being a borderland study, it is especially important to make explicit that there need not be anything valuable in the constant 26, or anything teleological in the relation $f(x) = x^2 + 17$. In a different context, of course, one is at liberty to speak of the vital value of the function of respiration, or the political value of state functions or social functions.

Last and most, the term *continuity* needs an explanation. The two mathematical meanings of the continuity of a series and the continuity of a function will both be used in this study. Since the applicability is a matter of degree, the terms will be used for cases where things are only approximately continuous. Careful mathematicians will insist that the two meanings of continuity have nothing to do with each other, that there may be a continuous function of a variable which is merely dense, and not at all continuous. [1] But by a sophisticated innocence, we may perhaps make a confusion between the two. A continuum will then be regarded as a special case of a continuous function $x' = x$. A continuum has two properties, the so-called Dedekind property of closure, which amounts to filling up every limiting point, and the property of denseness, by which intervals can be subdivided indefinitely. Now let us confuse the former with the property of a continuous function that it passes thru all intermediate value[2] and the latter with the property that as the difference in the variable approaches zero, the difference in the function will approach zero. Then we shall be able to speak of continuity in general. This stolen analogy does not of course claim to stand the test of mathematical rigor. For instance, in one case, the two properties are independent, while in the other case they are not. But analogies are partial identities among partial differences, and to what serious or subliminal extent the neglect of these mathematical differences in the indiscriminate use of the words "continuity" and "continuous" has invalidated or muddled the methodological results, only the actual cases will determine.

---

[1]   E. W. Hobson, *Theory of Functions of a Real Variable*, pp. 222 – 223.

[2]   That this is usually proved by the method of pinching is highly suspicious. See Chapter II, top of p. 169.

4. Sources: Miscellaneous

If research consists in a systematic and exhaustive survey of all that has been said on a subject, and saying a little more, then this study will not deserve the same of research. For the *typical* source of material is like watching a frog, quitting cigarettes, getting into practical dilemmas, collecting plays on words, and perverting mathematics. This is a search of some sort, but hardly research.

Another source of material is from training in sciences, chiefly in physics and mathematics. This accounts for the preponderance of examples in physical over those in natural sciences, and of examples in science over those in other fields. It is easy to say that the same *principles* may hold for all other subjects. But in view of the belief that illustrations are constitutive of principles, it is more than likely that the general plan will be much transformed if, say biological subjects have been more freely drawn upon. (Cf. the concluding paragraph. p. 297).

Historically, reasoning by continuity has appeared here and there, Leibniz and Galileo being important examples. But Leibniz makes it a philosophical principle, and Galileo uses it only as it occasionally enters in other problems. A systematic study of continuity as a method, therefore, has not been seen. To be sure, many, and probably most of the ideas that are presented here without ceremony are either imperfect restatements of ideas that have been previously better and more fully stated by others, or simply unrecognized reminiscences of ideas instilled is from previous readings. The failure of sufficient acknowledgment is therefore a mark not of arrogance, but of ignorance.

In many cases, however, explicit reference is avoided on

purpose. Some general statement is made in as good king's English as possible, then a few illustrations are drawn from out of the way to give it meaning, and a certain line of thought is thus presented. But if some one calls out, "Why, this is a camouflage of Descartes' analytic geometry," or, "That is simply Hegel's thesis. antithesis, synthesis over again," then one who is historically well-grounded will at once switch over all ones associations of these authors' stock illustrations to their well-established sub-divisions. Now if illustrations constitute ideas, then new illustrations of old ideas will not likely converge quite to what the old ideas were meant to be; and since the new illustrations, like the water between two valleys, are not in stable equilibrium, they will flow into established courses, unless they are given a chance to gather in small hill side pools and carve out new streams. (Cf. Chapter VII, pp. 265ff. on equilibrium). There is therefore, in the loss due to ignorance, both real and pretended, the possibility of a gain in freshness.

A list of references, so far as they have been made, is given at the end of the thesis (pp, 299 – 301). But it seems to be conducive to intellectual honesty also to give the names of works which have not been used a tall or not to any considerable extent, but which might, if more carefully examined, have improved or greatly modified the working out of this study.

Finally, conversations, correspondence, and discussions have shaped this study even to a greater extent than readings. Special acknowledgments are due to Prof. I. J. Henderson, who has kept my scientific interests alive by the "method of concrete cases", particularly in directing my attention to the methods used by Galileo; to Prof. E. V. Huntington, who has opened my eyes to many mathematical possibilities, and made many corrections of detailed points; and to Dr. H. M. Sheffer, who has helped me in the general planning of the thesis, and in setting up high standards of clearness and accuracy. For if clearness is only a matter of degree, depending upon the requirements of each problem, it must at least be high enough to pass the threshold of the degree required. Other acknowledgments cannot be made in full. But, as already referred to above, it is the scientific liberalism of the Department of Philosophy and Psychology at Harvard University, as has been inherited from the tradition of Prof. Royce, that has made possible the undertaking of such a study in the borderlands among different fields of knowledge.

CHAPTER II   METHODS

1. Method: Leverage

Method, in its broad aspect, may be regarded as playing one part of reality against another. It may be variously described as being something mediate, indirect, discursive, formal, artificial. , mechanical; as contrasted with the immediate, direct, intuitive, material, natural, spontaneous. A crow had no immediate access to the water in a tall pitcher. It picked pebbles, threw them into the pitcher, and the level of the water rose to within its reach. This was method. Man is a helpless creature amidst the elemental forces of nature. He lengthens and strengthens his arms by science and technology and makes servants of those forces. This is method.

Method, then, may be regarded as leverage. Given a limited force ε, which I have at my disposal. Required that a greater force M be overcome. The method will consist in finding a leverage n, such that $n \times \varepsilon$ shall exceed M. Method, again, may be compared with trigger action. I cannot throw a ball beyond 200 feet. I can make gun and powder and pull a trigger, and thus send a ball miles away.

In method, there is something like pulling oneself up by one's bootstraps. Attach the boot straps over a pulley and pull down. The whole weight will be raised by one half the force. [1] This is

---

[1]   See *Scientific American*, Oct. 20, 1917.

what science has been doing all along. A few observations of the planetoid Ceres determined such and such an orbit. Therefore some "star" previously recorded must have been Ceres. If this was Ceres, then the orbit must be, more exactly, *such and such*, and not as it was first determined. Thus, we go around invalid circles by obtaining a *purchase* on reality.

But method is not just method, it is also a problem. A man weighing 300 pounds is not likely to have a strength of 150 pounds at his disposal. Hence he will have to solve the *problem of applying* the method. Perhaps he puts in another pulley, so that a given force of 75 pounds will now suffice. Or he might wind his boot straps on a motor and turn on a switch which needs only a few ounces of strength. Francis Bacon seems to think that a scientific methodology, once perfected, can be applied by anybody. But a method is a method only when its wise choice and effective execution is within the genius of its applier. To arrange a few small business items in the order of importance is an affair simple enough. So we call it the method *of* serial order *for* the problem of dispatching business. But when it comes to rating the qualifications of men for certain positions, we resort to further methods of weighing factors for the *problem* of serial order. Hence to every method, there may be a problem, Every *method of* admits of, and may need a *method for*.

A mere regress of methods, however, will not result in its application. Levers may be lengthened, triggers may be made more delicate, but some finite force will be needed to start them. Bacon's conception of method and Descartes's trigger argument for free will both rest on the assumption that by multiplying zero by *n*, we can get some finite result *M*. A man who has hanged himself by his boot straps cannot raise himself, because he has no strength left. Without reality to start with, circles are vicious.

The function of method is therefore not to *replace* intuition, direct experience, judgment, or any such categorical term, but only to link it to the solution of a problem. The more imagination, talent, skill, experience one has in a field, the more discriminately and effectively one will use formal methods. If method is playing one part of reality against another, it is not playing nothing against nothing, and the more reality one has, the better.

2. Methods

So much for method in general. Now as to methods in particular. The methods studied here cover but a small corner of the field of methodology. But there need be no limitation as to the subject matter to which they may apply. This applicability shades off into nothing as we reach problems that do not lend themselves to an effective treatment by the idea of continuity in any sense.

(1) *Method of Concrete Cases.* —A problem is not clearly defined unless we have sufficient and fair samples of its materials, We cannot tell what samples are sufficient and fair unless the problem is defined. But the factual existence of problems in science and life helps us out of this circle. Altho we are not yet sure of the definition of our problem, we have a vague feeling, from the historical development of the problem, of what we are about. Hence we can look into the world for gathering "cases", tho as yet we do not know cases of what.

Thus, we have the problem of mind and matter, the mental and the physical. etc. The method of concrete cases will then consist in finding examples, such as anger, panic. wealth, constitution. musical comedy, meteorite, noise.

If I feel some pessimism about things, I may look for cases of things like scientific achievements, war, a slip on an orange peel, children's noises, philosophy, sound sleeps, bad dinners, singing in tune and out of tune, etc.

This method is of course only a preliminary step and does not usually define a problem, not to say solve it. It tells one to dip into the thick of things, look for wild illustrations, and avoid premature settling into ruts of problems and systems. As one progresses, one may find reason to sub-divide a previous problem, or combine it with others, or even to dismiss the problem.

(2) *Method of Gradations*. —The looking for concrete cases is a part of any method in general that claims to be empirical. The notion of continuity enters when we look for concrete cases as stages, degrees, or gradations of an idea that is otherwise taken absolutely. This is what Leibniz[1] calls the continuity of forms, which says that between different kinds of things there will always be intermediate things. As a philosophy, it says that the intermediate forms *exist* in some sense or other. But as a method, we can content ourselves with saying that it is profitable to imagine and try to see whether ideas admit of degrees. As this method will be developed further in Chapter III, I shall not enlarge upon it here.

(3) *Method of Serial Order*. —The method of gradations becomes that of serial order when we define a scale x, such that cases can be compared as to precedence in some sense. The most important applications are found when x is approximately a mathematical continuum, tho the method applies also to other

---

① 　Bertrand Rursel, The Philosophy of Leibniz 1900, pp. 64 – 65.

series, such as integers. To the objection that one must not too readily take things quantitatively, I give the usual answer that applicability shades off in various cases and that the serial comparison of any two or more things may come up as a valid problem in unexpected situations, and applied as a valid method. The fuller treatment of this subject will be given in Chapter IV.

(4) *Method of Extremes.* —When we have conceived a problem in the form of a result y as depending on the condition x, it is often a fruitful method to vary x to wild extreme values. An extreme consideration often brings out facts that are in other cases not determinate or evident. Thus in serial comparison, it is difficult to define exactly what human excellence or what general health is, but in extreme cases, it is evident that an imbecile is inferior to a genius, or an athlete is more healthy than an epileptic.

An empirical caution, however, must be taken in saying that the result is "obviously" thus and so. For instance, one might suppose that in the extreme case of cashing only two dollars, it would be "absurd" if a bank clerk should turn over the two bills, wet his fingers, and count them in the regular way. But the fact is that he does, and that for the disciplinary value of that habit. A *reductio ad absurdum*, therefore, need not disprove anything.

Universal propositions are often asserted on the basis of a small number of cases, or a scientific law is laid down by extrapolation from a small range of facts. Then it will be well to test the result by the method of extremes. The acceleration of gravity was found by Galileo to be constant. But taking extreme distances, like that of the moon, Newton found that it decreased with the square of distance from the earth. Ptolemy and Alhazen experimented on refraction and found certain approximate relations

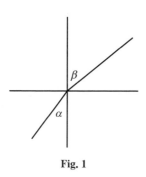

Fig. 1

between the angle of incidence and the angle of refraction. Tho they did not discover the law of sines, yet since they found that $\angle\beta$ is always greater than $\angle\alpha$ (Fig. 1), it was within their possible imagination to apply the method of extremes, by increasing the angle $\angle\alpha$ from the denser medium to extreme values, in order to see what might happen. But this was not done until Kepler, who thus discovered the phenomenon of total reflection, which appears when $\angle\alpha$ exceeds that which would make $\angle\beta = 90°$.

Again, oxygen is found to be a "non-magnetic" substance under ordinary conditions, but at extremely low temperatures, when it liquifies, it is highly magnetic. The realization of extremely low temperatures has indeed opened a wide vista of new physical phenomena, and the most prominent work done at the University of Leyden has been one great application of the method of extremes in this field.

The definition of functions is always a tentative and *more* or *less* accurate affair, and its validity depends upon the progress and outcome of the problem. (Cf. Chapter III p. 190ff. on function). Not only may the method of extremes lead to modifications of a formula of a function, it may lead to transformation of the functionality to quite different variables; that is, in extreme cases, the function may break down and otherwise secondary factors become prominent. Thus, in a problem of electricity in a small wire, the phenomenon may be sufficiently described by a comparatively simple formula. But in the extreme case of a long

Atlantic cable, the formula breaks down because such factors as capacity and inductance become prominent.

The method of extremes may be used as a preliminary step to the method of pinching, as will be described later. "You cannot be too this, or too that", is often a false advice. But going to an extreme, one often steps on the other side of the mean. After this, one is prepared to come back to the mean when the pendulum swings back.

Thus, a freshman using a chemical balance starts with a weight too little, adds one gram, finds it still too little, adds 500 milligrams, adds another centigram, and so on, and never finds the weight. The correct way is of course to proceed with large weights until it is obviously too much, and then come down to finer units.

Many persons have the fault of playing a pseudo-arpeggio on a piano by striking with the left hand a little before the right. An effective corrective is to err consciously in the other direction, in order to realize how it feels to strike the right hand too soon; then striking with both hands together will be more easily learned. This goes as far back as Aristotle, who compares the idea with straightening a bent stick. [1]

The method of extremes need not of course be applied in a physical sense. It may be done by way of postulation, imagination, in order to see what might follow, as well by actual experimentation for getting an emprical result. A medical investigator would not try an overdose of chloroform to insure its

[1] *Nichomachean Ethics*, Book II, Chapter IX (p. 56 in J. E. C. Welldon's translation).

effect, or an economic student invest a million on a square foot to verify the law of diminishing returns.

The extreme form of the method of extremes is the method of limits, by which we inquire what becomes of a result as the measure of a condition approaches a lower limit or increases indefinitely. For example, a null class is also called a class by generalization. The formula

$$\int_a^b ydx + \int_a^b zdx = \int_a^b (y+z)dx$$

may also hold good when b becomes infinite. The method of limits is used to obtain generality, symmetry, and simplicity of statement or of psychological conception, or to discover conditions under which something becomes different. Further elaboration of the idea will be carried out in Chapter V.

(5) *Method of Explicit Location*. —It is a truism that for a full understanding of anything, we must appreciate its place among various other things. In this study, we shall be concerned with the position of a thing among other things on a scale, as it has been defined by the method of gradations and serial order.

A nation, for example, may have no definite conception of the health of its people. Examinations may discover that the average is very low among nations. In general, the instrument of statistics is very useful in making explicit positions that have been either neglected or wrongly conceived.

Explicit location is a preliminary to the finding of the golden mean. I have seen two plays in eight months. Is this near the mean? If not, on which side of the mean is it? The method brings to light many cases of hidden zeroes. A person may have been doing zero amount of exercise, carrying zero amount of personal correspondence, working zero amount of time in a laboratory, playing with zero number of children, quarreling zero number of times a year. contributing zero money to any cause, speaking zero number of foreign languages. drinking zero amount of alcohol. From the mixed nature of the examples, it is evident that zero is not *necessarily* a defect or an excess. The point is that the method of explicit location stirs up things and ask, is it? To be sure, many questions are trivial enough to be dropt, or better never raised at all. This must rest upon common sense or Aristotle's "practical wisdom", As was shown above, a method does not tell itself when it should best be applied. [1]

(6) *Method of Intermediates.* —The method of extremes tries to extend the domain of our function beyond what we started with. The method of intermediates looks inward for interesting cases between known cases. The two methods correspond to extrapolation and interpolation, but are more general than these in that they do not necessarily say, "The same thing will be true outside or inside", as in the case of extrapolation and interpolation, but simply asks *what* will be true in unexamined parts of the scale.

More exactly, the method of intermediates is based on the property of a continuous function, briefly exprest as the property of taking on all intermediate values. This method is therefore a development of the method of gradations.

Thus, when a shot is in the cannon at one moment and miles away at another, then at some time it must be just one foot in front of the muzzle. It is hardly imaginable, but a rapid exposure

----

[1]   Cf. Samuel M. Crothers, *The Pardoner's Wallet* (first essay).

photograph will catch the intermediate cases.

We often take intermediate cases for granted, tho we may have only a wrong conception of them. In the ancient history of motion pictures, when E. Muybridge made a series of photographs of a horse, running thru strings attached to cameras, interesting and surprizing facts were brought to light as to the actual forms of intermediate positions of animals in motion. With the perfection, of modern photography, it is possible to apply the method of intermediates also to flying birds.

In the exploration of intermediates, a judicicus choice of points often saves unfruitful trials. If the mathematical function is cleverly defined for the problem, then points that are singular in some mathematical respect are likely to be of significance also in the concrete. Examples of points are $-\infty$, 0, 1/2, $+\infty$, 100%, middle point between known points, arithmetical and other kinds of mean between points, habitual points, points of natural inclination, points given in the statement of the problem. etc. It will be seen that this list include also cases for the method of extremes.

(7) *Method of Pinching*. — When our interest is not merely in inter-mediates in general, but turns to some peculiar case in particular, then we use what might by called, for want of a more elegant name, the method of pinching. In one case we have one result. in another, then let the cases approach, and inquire what happens in the critical situation, as the difference of cases approaches zero. This, as can be seen, can be reduced to a particular case of the method of limits, but its special importance calls for a separate treatment.

The mathematical form of the method is exprest in the

theorem that in the interval (a, b),

If (1) $a \leqslant a_1 \leqslant b_1 \leqslant b$,

$\qquad a_1 \leqslant a_2 \leqslant b_2 \leqslant b_1$,

$\qquad a_2 \leqslant a_3 \leqslant b_3 \leqslant b_2$,

$\qquad \cdots\cdots$

Fig. 2

and (2) $\lim_{n \to \infty} (b_n - a_n) = 0$,

then there is a point ξ, such that

$$\lim_{n \to \infty} a_n = \lim_{n \to \infty} b_n = \xi.$$

This is in fact the method by which the intermediate property of a continuous function is proved (or by which a lemma is proved by which that property is in turn proved).

The finding of the golden mean may take the form of a pinching process. In focusing a microscope, we start with a position of the eyepiece that is too high. Then we use the method of extremes and turn it down until the objective barely fails to crush the object or the slide, so as to be sure that we have passed the mean. Then we come back and try finer and finer variations of position, until we get the best focus we can.

The estimation of a quantity is often done by the method of pinching with a result more accurate than by direct intuition. A mechanic once said from experience that when he wanted to design, say a rod for some purpose, and could not guess at the right dimensions, he would first draw (on paper) a ridiculously thin wire and then a ridiculously stout cylinder; next, he would draw a rod not quite so wiry, tho still too thin, and another not quite so heavy, but still too stout. Thus, he went on narrowing down the differences between a_n and b_n more and more, until they became of doubtful weight. Then he took the arithmetical mean and called it his ξ. the mean. This method proved to work well when applied.

The finding of the golden mean by the method of pinching can therefore be compared with the vibrations of a damped pendulum. The fact that man always errs in extremes on one or the other side of the mean, and that history always swings in pendulums need not discourage us, if we find that some pendulums are being damped.

Galileo makes use, in certain reasonings, of the method of pinching. It is asserted that a long rope is weaker than a short one. Now suppose that the rope breaks at D under weight C (Fig. 3). Then it will also break at D if the suspension is at F, a little above D. Again, there is no reason why it should not break at D if the weight below a certain point, say E, is fastened at that point, a little below D. Hence the rope will be just as strong as its weakest part, whether it is a short piece FE, or a long piece AB[①].

Fig. 3

While this method plays an important part in the proof of theorems about continuous function in mathematics, it cannot be taken as favoring continuity in any problem. For if there is a discontinuity, the method will locate it just as well as other points of interest. Fuller treatment of singular points will be deferred to Chapters VI and VII on Identity and Difference.

3. (8) Method of Transformations

So far I have treated developments of methods that do not go beyond a certain variable and a certain function. But since there is

① Galileo, *Dialogues Concerning Two New Sciences*. Eng. *Trans*. by H. Crew & A. De Salvio, p. 122.

no absolute reason why we should remain within the point of view that we start with in conceiving a problem, we may have recourse to the method of transformations, if a change seems to be advisable. For instance. in the problem of sharpness of view as a function of the position of the eyepiece of the microscope, when we reach the critical situation of near focus, we find that there is no "the focus", but only focuses for different planes of the object. Thus a new x is introduced into the problem.

For the sake of generality of statement and conception, we may regard the very method of gradations as a lower limit of transformations. So is the act of defining a function $y = f(x)$ in the first instance. It is in fact idiomatic mathematics, to speak, for example, of the "linear transformation"

$$w = Az + B,$$

Which is simply a way of saying that w is a linear function of z. If, therefore, we were to go toward the upper limit of completeness in treating transformations, we should cover the whole extent of this thesis, and even more. Necessity has it then that only a sketchy account of transformations can be given in this section.

First, as to the purposes of transformations. Formally. some of the purposes for which a transformation is made are: to secure

  1) continuity of a function
  2) discontinuity of a function
  3) flatness of a curve
  4) steepness of a curve
  5) linearity of a function
  6) finitude of quantities.

But it is very easy for a non-mathematical person to see that these cannot be more than proximate ends, having only instrumental value. The *scientific* purposes for which transformations are made can be felt more as "purposes". To enumerate some of the most important ones, transformations may be made for

1) more adequacy towards defining the originally vague intention which raised the problem.

2) ease of comprehension.

3) convenience of mathematical or logical "manipulation".

4) convenience of literal manipulation.

5) increasing accuracy of result (leverage *par excellence*).

6) general purposes of finding new factors and new results.

Coming to the transformations themselves, we can divide them into changes of the variable x and changes in the function y. In many cases, they overlap; for example, to multiply x by n is equivalent to dividing y by n. The difference, then, is one of emphasis.

Changes of x. —Following is a list of the most important forms of changes of x:

Description	*General Form*	*Particular Forms*
1) Multiplication	ax	$nx,\ x/n,\ -x$
2) Addition	$x+a$	$x+a,\ x-a$
3) Power	x^a	$x^n \cdot \sqrt{x},\ 1/x$
4) Exponential	a^x	e^x
5) Trigonometric		
6) Others		$x'=x_1/(x_1+x_2),$
		$x'=x/\sqrt{x^2+1}$
7) New factors		

To illustrate some of these forms, we find a case of multiplication, when Galileo uses an inclined plane instead of free falling bodies, thereby changing

$$v = gt$$

into

$$v' = g(sin\ \alpha)\ t'$$

(α being the angle of the plane), that is, he lengthens the time in order to flatten the curve for ease of (literal) manipulation, and for increased accuracy of judging just when the ball is where, in its slow movement.

3) Taking a reciprocal is a particular case of the power x^a, when $a = -1$. For instance, instead of saying that current varies inversely as resistance, which would give an unmanageable hyperbola, it is sometimes better to say that current varies directly as conductivity, which gives a straight line.

7) The introduction of new factors is especially important, as the method of extremes and the method of pinching often lead to such a step. The examples of capacity and inductance in an Atlantic cable. and the difference of levels in focusing a microscope have already been mentioned. Further, a discontinuity at a point for a certain function, may be transformed into a continuity for another function, as will be fully illustrated in a later chapter (Chapter VII, pp. 276 ff.).

Changes of y. —Changes of y may be divided into constant operations on y itself. and compositions of different functions, the latter being the counterpart of the method of new factors.

Constant Operations. —

Description	*General Form*	*Particular Forms*
1) Multiplication	$af(x)$	$nf(x)$, $f(x)/n$, $-f(x)$
2) Addition	$f(x)+a$	$f(x)+a$, $f(x)-a$
3) Powe	$[f(x)]^a$	$1/f(x)$
4) Exponential	$a^f(x)$	
5) Logarithm	$\log f(x)$	
6) Trigonometric		
7) Signum, or sign	$\operatorname{sgn} f(x)$	
8) Derivatives	$f^{(n)}(x)$	$f'(x)$, $f''(x)$
9) Steps		$E[f(x)]$

5) For example, in plotting correlation curves in statistics, logarithms are taken so that the curves will be straight.

7) Sgn $f(x)$ means simply the sign of $f(x)$. It may be used to mark differences, as will be more fully treated in Chapter VII. p. 272.

8) As examples of derivatives, we may consider the valuing of the accuracy of a time piece. The most naive view, which a child or an ignorant person may have, is that

a) A clock is not good if it does not read right. That is, if we let $f(t)$ be its reading, as a function of time, the clock is judged bad in so far as $f(t)$ deviates from t itself.

b) But a more intelligent man says, a clock that reads wrong can be set, or the error allowed for, the important thing is that it shall run at a correct rate, neither too fast nor too slow. In other words, he considers $f'(t)$, and is not satisfied unless

$$f'(t) = 0.$$

c) But a man who has handled accurate clocks would say that if the rate is wrong, it can be regulated or allowed for, the important thing is that it shall be constant, in other words, the rate of the change of rate shall be zero, or

$$f''(t) = 0.$$

The real defect of most time pieces, then, is that the second derivatives of motion is not zero.

9) The taking of discontinuous steps may [be] regarded as a generalized form of transforming a function into two values by sgn y. In plotting statistical curves, for instance, instead of drawing continuous curves, for which data are too few, we group figures together and call, for instance, $5' 3 /4$ and $5' 6'' 1 /4$ both as belonging to the five feet and half class, and thus transform a smooth curve into a histogram, which is a curve with square tops, as in Fig. 4.

Fig. 4

Compositions of Functions.

Description	General Form	Particular Forms
1) Multiplication	$f_1(x) f_2(x)$	
Multiplication by x		$xf(x)$
Multiplication to reduce discontinuity		$(x - a)f(x)$
Dividing by x		$f(x)/x$
2) Addition	$f_1(x) + f_2(x)$	
Addition proper		$f_1(x) + f_2(x)$

Subtraction of x　　　　　　　　　$f(x) - x.$

1) A function y is often multiplied by x in order to secure linearity.

Thus, if we have

$$xy = a + bx,$$

then, putting

$$y' = xy,$$

we get

$$y' = a + bx$$

2) To illustrate dividing by x, let us recall Fuskin's saying that if a book is worth reading, it is worth buying[①], or the trite advice that if a thing is worth doing, it is worth doing well. Now the question is not whether more benefit comes from more time, energy, money, etc., but whether the yield is more or less than proportional. In other words, instead of considering the function $f(x)$ that occurs to us in the first instance, it is the transformed function $f(x)/x$ that matters. Thus, in general, a course that is worth working thru is worth taking a final examination in, because giving one tenth extra time yields more than one tenth added benefit from getting a bird's-eye survey of the subject. Fig. 5 represents the relation in a general way, where

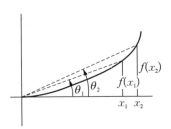

Fig. 5

---

① *Sesame and Lilies*, section 32 (Harvard Classics, vol, 28, p. 121).

$$\frac{f(x_2)}{x_2} > \frac{f(x_1)}{x_1}. \quad (Since \ tan \ \theta_2 > tan \ \theta_1)$$

But a newspaper is very worth reading the first few minutes, and as we come down to "brain foods" and bargain sales, the effect of the law of diminishing returns being to tell. In such cases, for $x_1 < x_2$ we have

$$\frac{f(x_2)}{x_2} < \frac{f(x_1)}{x_1}.$$

as shown in Fig. 6.

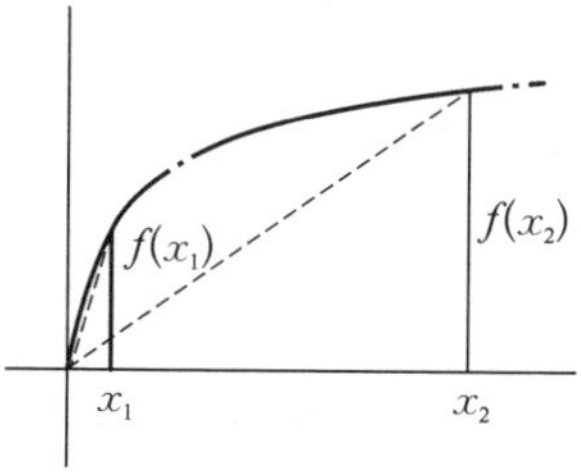

Fig. 6

Many things are worth doing that are *not* worth doing thoroly.

2) Composition by addition is often in the form where the function added is a neglected consequence, which would be called a subtraction from a natural point of view. Thus, by enlarging a plant. one should not only think of the increase of total earnings, but also subtract from it the increase of operating expenses. Visionary reformers tend to dwell on the advantages that would result if the reform were accomplished now. But conservatives call their attention to the necessity of subtracting from the advantages the wastes, risks, and dangers in overcoming tradition, habit and in jeopardizing real values that have been conserved by association with otherwise irrational institutions.

In the whole study of methodology, one may raise the objection that the generalized expense in rigging up intellectual scaffolding for increasing accuracy, certainty, etc. , for discovering the best courses of action, may involve such wastes. risks, and extraneous processes, that the discounted result would give a

fractional instead of a magnifying leverage. The answer to this
objection is to assent to it. By the method of lower limit, we may
regard no method also as a method, which may be called the
method of inspection, intuition, or direct judgment (see Chapter
IV, p. 204). A sound methodology does not advise running a
steam-driven crane to pick up a pebble, or reading up Aristotle's
Ethics in one's sleep before deciding what is the best time to stop
sleeping and wake up.

4. Methods as Stages

Such, then, are the outlines of methods, which will be
developed in part in the following chapters. Taken together, they
may be regarded as natural stages of one method of continuity,
which gradually evolves as the problem evolves. We start with
concrete cases, find in them, gradations arrange them in serial
order, explore outward into extreme cases and inward in
intermediate cases, and here and there concentrate our attention on
points of special interest. When these steps seem to be
insufficient, were formulate our problem by the method of
transformations, which, again, is a class name for sub-methods of
unlimited possibilities.

This, however, only by way of formal statement. In actual
application, one or another of the stages may be of primary interest
and importance, and then we are said to be employing this or that
sub-method.

Again, the problem may be such as to need application of the
methods in different orders, or a repeated application of the same
method. This is not strange, as we can transform our point of view
at any time we see fit, and attach the problem afresh, or, since we

cannot even be sure of speaking of "*the* problem", we might be attacking fresh problems altogether.

The different stage, tho having a natural sequence, have no claim to rigor of logical succession. It may well be that one stage has a good purchase on reality altho in some aspects it is very loose and farfetched. Thus, the method of serial arrangement of things in order of importance is a fairly effective and definite process, even tho the variable x, the measure of importance, is an extremely vague thing. Or, again, the method of pinching, whose mathematical proof applies only to a mathematical continuum x, may be very illuminating, even tho we have to do with a series that are not even "dense" from a more refined point of view. In short, if method is conceived as an effective aid to get at things with reference to one problem, it does not matter if it is insufficient for another problem. There are of course methods of greater rigor, exhaustiveness, accuracy and comprehensiveness, which will be needed in more and more exact fields. These fields, be they canons and fugues, or celestial mechanics, are still always prescribed from definite points of view. But if we should raise the question of *the* true or valid method at large, we should be going outside the scope within which this thesis is intended to be delimited.

CHAPTER III   GRADED IDEAS

1. Graded Ideas and Serial Order

By a graded idea, I mean something which admits of gradations, degree, shades, or stages. The study of graded ideas differs from that of serial order in that the latter starts from two or more terms and a scale; while the former starts with some given idea, and inquires whether we can find possible or actual gradations of the idea that may be of interest. To draw two illustrations from the same material, "Is A taller than B?" is a question of serial order, while "Is A a tall man? He is tall to such and such an extent", will be an application of graded ideas. An exact mathematical definition of a scale is often important for a problem in serial arrangement, as will be treated in the next chapter. But when our interest is in the graded ideas themselves, their exact formal relation is not always of special concern. Thus, one does not have to have a numerical scale of crediting inventions in order to appreciate the gradual nature of the development of the steam engine. The gradation we shall study, then, may be approximately a continuum or a dense series, or simply a row of discrete terms, or even a series of terms which have no clearly defined individuality.

2. Problem and Method of Gradations

If we are asked to grade an idea, the most, obvious way is to open our mind's eye and body's eye and look for concrete cases of gradations ("method of concrete cases"). As a guide, we can select some aspect x in the given idea, such that when x varies, different gradations will result. In general. it is a simple matter to find some sort of gradations of an idea, but whether the result is trivial or not is a further question.

It does not, however, often happen that one is called upon to find gradations of an idea, which has already been snugly pigeonholed in people's minds as A or not A. To grade an idea is not so much a problem as a method which we try on problems. We might call it an aggressive problem. What are some possible consequences of such a trial?

(1) First, the finding of concrete cases may serve to discover unknown things or to call attention to neglected things. When people are talking about mind and matter, it is well for one to mention "anger, panic, plague, beauty, wealth, strike, war,"[1] to disturb the dualistic peace.

(2) Gradation may be a preliminary step for "explicit location (Chapter II, p. 165), that is, the position of an idea that we start with is often better appreciated when seen in a graded series. A man has graduated from a course in French and thinks he "has learned French". But if he considers the gradations: "learning to read a menu, to read science, to read a novel, to speak, to listen to lectures, to write, to chat with children, to quarrel, to dream or multiply in French, to understand a French vaudeville", he may be surprized to discover that his position is not what the phrase "having learned French" would suggest.

---

[1]   Cf, H. I. Hollingworth, "The Psychophysical Continuum", *Journal of Philos. , Psy. , and Sci. Method* ,XIII7, 182ff.

(3) Definitions may have to be made more precise. Revised, or may even have to be abandoned, in the light of gradations of the idea defined. "Intelligent behavior" is sometimes defined as behavior that can deal with new situations. The association of red with food is called mere association, while the ability to recognize "the second door from the left" is called intelligence. But if we consider the possible gradations of complexity and generality by arranging the elements of color, shape, size, positions, order, condition of door, etc., then it is evident that the definition of "new" or "not new" needs to be further explicated. Here the method of gradations simply raises a problem without promising to solve it by itself.

(4) A common sense idea, especially when wrapped up in a word, may be pierced thru and drawn out with advantage. For a word tends to gather around itself associations which are not intended for it in the context in which it is used, and thus lead to errors. If we express the fact that a man is a member of a church by saying that he is a Christian, then everything Christian tends to be entered on his account. But if we consider gradations of men's Christianity both outside and inside the church, on seven days of the week, we may gain a different conception of the man in question.

Similarly, we may grade such dichotomies as important, not important; very interesting, not very interesting; recent, not recent; necessary, superfluous; conservative, liberal; etc. These terms are well used if the context shows the implicit qualifications unmistakably and ill-used if they mislead one to wrong associations.

(5) Statements of decision of legislation are subject to the

same uncertainty of definitions, since to state them involves definition. Thus, by the method of gradations. we shall see the inadequacy in the bare statement of such rules as: "All intelligent beings shall have rights to humane treatment", "Do not speak unless it is necessary", "Read only important books. "

(6) From the above, it will be seen that grading an idea may be a preparatory step for the method of pinching[1], that is, of starting with two different results under two different conditions and letting the two conditions approach so as to examine where and how the change of result is made or is to be made.

(7) Arguing from the camel's nose (Chapter VI, p. 253) may also be prepared for by grading an idea. Thus, if one says that we cannot see the movement of molecules, we can say that if we can "see a chair, thru the crystalline lens of the eye, there is no reason why we cannot "see" a distant tree thru spectacles, so we can "see" the singer thru a pair of opera "see" a cell thru a compound microscope, "see" a flower blossom glasses in a few seconds in a stop picture, "see" the earth turn under a Foucqult pendulum, "see" thru a telescope a 12th magnitude star that was in that direction a few years ago, "see" the movement of molecules in the Brownion movement. Of course the mere possibility of grading the idea is no sufficient argument. In all such arguments, the mere *form* of the camel's nose is of no consequence without the camel's *material* strength back of it.

(8) Some aspect of identity of things can often be brought out by gradations. Thus in a later section (p. 185), I shall try to show that illustration, analogy, metaphor, etc. are actually constitutive

---

[1]   For illustrations see Chapter II, pp. 169 – 170.

of some widened conception, and in that respect, all are instances. Again, if we find examples of degrees of interference of nature, varying from making a chemical compound thru grafting flowers to watching a meteor, we may find that experiment and observation are identical except in regard to the degree of human interference. ①
But the full treatment of identity thru continuity is the subject of Chapter VI.

(9) Grading an idea may take the form of generalizing from a case by treating some constant feature of it (e.g., 0 or 1) as a variable, or from another point of view, by treating the case as one in a series when a certain variable takes on some particular value. Thus the treatment of regional restriction (p. 190) amounts to generalizing from the case of a strict function where the correlation is 1 to cases where it is not 1. Or, in the last example, Bosanquet might define observation as a case of generalized experiment when the degree of human control is zero, if he condescended to use my jargon.

(10) I have so far dwelt on the continuous aspect of gradations. But precisely because ideas are graded, why shouldn't they have graded consequences? Identity in some respects does not exclude difference in others. To reduce observation to a degree of experiment where some variable is zero does not prevent us from putting a certain class of experiments whose degrees of control is less than a certain e under the name "observation" and giving them a special logical, methodological, academic, or financial treatment.

All criminals are alike in being criminals, yet society has found it best to grade the punishments in accordance with grades of

---

① Cf. Bosanquet, *Logic*, *2nd ed*, II. P. 141.

crimes. All students who pass, but educational practise has it that they shall pass with grades A, B, C, etc., sometimes with difference in practical consequences. As a trivial example, I may mention further that in practising early rising, it is more effective to keep a record of the different grades of lateness and promptitude, than merely marking a cross every morning one rises behind time. Grading the laziness will deter one from making the worst of it because one failed to make the best of it anyway. For a methodology of graded treatment one will need an exact working definition of the scale of gradations, in other words, of the serial order. Thus we pass outside the mere method of gradations as considered in this chapter. Like any other method, the method of gradations starts somewhere in a problem, brings it a step forward if it bears on it, never solves the final problem of life and the universe, and often does not solve the limited problem to the extent intended, This concludes the general discussion on graded ideas. In the following sections, a few cases of special interest will be discust, viz. , logical generality; variable, parameter, and constant; mathematical function and regional restriction; and intellectual progress.

3. Graded Logical Generality

We are familiar with such series of graded logical generality as "being, animal, man, Greek, Socrates". Yet one often forgets that a general idea and an example are only two relative terms in this kind of series. If n terms are arranged in the order of generality, as a_1, a_2, $\cdots\cdots a_n$, we can take any two a_i two a_j, and say "a_i, for example, a_j", where a_i precedes a_j. Thus, in the series: an event, a past event, a scientific discovery, the discovery of a physical law, Newton's discovery of the law of cooling, we can say "a past event, for example, the discovery of a physical law".

Some persons seem to have a style of illustrating their ideas by vague examples. They say "an event, e.g., a historical event", "a scientific discovery, e.g., one in chemistry". "a theorem, e.g., some theorem in mathematics". The vagueness lies in that the grade of the illustrating idea is not very different from that of the illustrated idea. One should not therefore be misled into satisfaction with the expression "for example", or the like, since it is an idea admitting of gradations, and its grade may be too low to pass the required threshold in the question concerned.

Another graded series similar to the one just mentioned is the series; instance, or case, or example, illustration, analogy, metaphor. play of words. The relation between the earth and the sun is a case, or instance, or example of gravitation. Cavendish's experiment repeated in a modern classroom would be called an illustration of gravitation, not being an in-stance that is important on its own account, but serving to make the idea concrete. Comparison of gravitation with sound, light and heat would be analogy. The Empedoclean idea of love would be a metaphor. And I might reach beyond my wit's end for a good play of words on gravitation to finish the series. Here I propose to regard the gradations as an ascending series of logical generality. Thus gravitation, light, sound, heat, etc., fail under the same conception of inverse square intensity. A metaphor, if it is a good one, ought to have other points of identity besides the apparent aspect from which it is made. If so, there will be so much actually in common that will put gravitation and love under the same class. And with good play of words, there is usually a logical as well as a philological identity. The conclusion is that we should not unqualifiedly draw a line, and say that what comes before "illustration" is all essence and look down upon the rest of the series as accidents. All are essences *to a degree*, they are *constitutive* of ideas.

In the light of graded generality, one can perhaps see a relation between a formal implication and a material implication. A formal implication holds between two statements which are not propositions, but propositional functions, owing to their containing, either explicitly or implicitly, variable terms; and according as these are more or less specified, the implication may be called less or more "formal" D①, so to speak. But when all terms are specified so that we have two propositions, i. e., significant statements, then we reach a limit which is a material implication. An example follows:

1) "x is a," implies "x is not non-a". (very formal)

2) "x is in one place" implies "x is not in another".

3) "A man is in one place" implies "a man is not in another".

4) "A man is in England" implies "a man is not in America".

5) "Bertrand Russell is in England" implies "Bertrand Russell is not in America", (with implicit variable time)

6) "Bertrand Russell is in England April 1, 1918" implies "Bertrand Russell is not in America April 1, 1918". (material implication)

---

① Since "formality" has not been used in a graded sense, there is no terminological objection to letting it mean the variability of values in a formal implication. The question as to how or whether this variability can be measured in terms of the number of explicit and implicit variables and possible range of values for each variable is perhaps an important one, but is not essential to the point discust here.

This point is only one aspect of the problem of implication. It does not tell what difference the fact of the variability being zero will make, e.g., whether material implication would be a useful conception. (Cf, Chapter V, p. 222).

4. Variable, Parameter, Constant

It is usually with some difficulty that a student of elementary mathematics is introduced to the notions of a constant and a variable. Until familiarity kills curiosity, he does not see why C is a more definite number than x, any more than 丙 is a more definite number than 天. The notion of a parameter is still more of a paradox. It is a constant and yet a variable. Even teachers of mathematics sometimes speak of a parameter as a freakish thing. In the following, however, I shall try to show that a parameter is the rule rather than the exception in the field of mathematics.

In being introduced to the use of letters, we are told that each letter will represent the same number thruout the same "discussion" (or the same universe of discourse). But what constitutes one discussion? There are evidently all grades of inclusiveness from a part of a single expression to the whole of mathematics. Now consider the expression $x + x = 2x$. Why don't we write $x + x = 2y$? Because x is supposed to remain constant in the very short discussion "$x + x = 2x$". But in the wider discussion "'$x + x = 2x$' is true for every x'', then x may have different values each time we have finished the discussion '$x + x = 2x$'. Thus it becomes a variable. There is therefore something parametric even about a variable x. It is the constant aspect of variables that probably explains the puzzling self-identity of different variables x, y, z, etc. They are called variables because their constant aspect is taken for granted and their variable aspect is emphasized.

On the other hand, a constant R in the equation of the circle $x^2+y^2=R^2$ is a constant in the discussion where we keep it fixt as x and y vary. But if we widen our discussion and consider circles of different numerical radii, then R becomes a parameter with respect to which a radius, say 2, would be a constant. But in a discussion about radii of numerical values, say 2, we would not measure two inches in one direction and two centimeters in another, but assume that the unit to be constant, which would be variable in a wider discussion. Hence even "2" may be regarded as a parameter, being a shorter way of writing "2 units".

Hence we can say that in the whole field of mathematics, all terms dealt with are potentially parameters. By a parameter so-called, with respect to a discussion, we shall mean a term which is constant while some other terms may vary, but which may itself vary in the whole discussion. A term during whose constancy no other term varies will be a variable. and a term which does not vary with respect to any term in the discussion will be a constant. Between these two, there may be any number of graded parameters. The essence of this view is certainly nothing new to anyone who has worked with mathematical problems; but it is useful to keep clear in the back of one's head the degrees of variability or parametricity in teaching elementary analysis, and in studying such problems as uniformity of continuity of convergence, integration and differentiation of series, and other cases of double limits, which it would be too much a field to illustrate here in full.

While there is a sense in which all our universes of discourse are arbitrary, yet in our actual theoretical life, there is a naturalness of problems that fosters in us certain habits or prejudices. Thus x looks to us like a variable, x would be a fairly good letter to be a parameter, while K and C are usually the constants of a problem. There is no logical difference between $x^2 + y^2 = R^2$ and $K^2 + y^2 = \rho^2$. Yet the latter equation at once arouses in us an impulse to vary the radius and the ordinate, keeping the abscissa K constant, and then consider different vertical lines as K takes on different values in the wider discussion.

In physical problems. there is often a "natural naturalness" in the order of variability. In the equation for a pendulum,

$$x = A\cos(2\pi\sqrt{l/gt})$$

x and t are the most variable quantities, because the pendulum moves as time goes on, while the amplitude A and the period are unchanged. After this, A is naturally a more variable parameter than l. for we can easily change the amplitude by pulling the pendulum to a different position or giving it a different push, and prefer to keep other things undisturbed thruout a series of experiments with different amplitudes. Finally, g is naturally a still more constant parameter than l, for one would certainly prefer to finish a series of experiments with different lengths before packing up one's apparatus and traveling to a different latitude to experiments on a different g. But if a man is sufficiently rich, leisurely, and foolish, he might travel back and forth to keep A and l constant, while g varies, and then vary his A and l after completing the world's tour. Thus the variability of parameters is not even in a fixt serial order, but may change with the problem proposed.

5. Mathematical Function and Regional Restriction

If we take at random any two variables[1] x and y, in the universe, it is not likely that one is a mathematical function of the other, For instance, the color of a crannied wall will not be determined by the number of branches in the root of the flower that grows on it. But very often, a variable x may put certain restrictions on the variation of y. Thus, tho the pitch and the intensity of a flute note are in general independent, yet it is impossible to play low C *fortissimo* or a very high note *piano*. Graphically speaking (Fig. 1), let x represent the pitch and y the loudness of a note, then the possible combinations, while they are not in strict one — one functional correspondence, as would be represented by a curve, such as AB, yet are confined within a band, or region (the unshaded part in Fig. 1). So that for a low note, the variation is restricted within the range LL, never reaching up to a *forts*, and for a high note, the variation is restricted within the range HH, never reaching down to a *piano*.

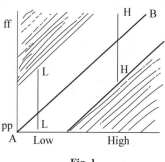

Fig. 1

Again, while virtue and knowledge are not strictly correlated, yet with too little knowledge, one can be neither a saint nor a great villain.

---

[1]   Two variables are considered here for simplicity. The whole discussion may be easily generalized for n variables by calling a band an n-dimensional tube, and making other corresponding changes.

Hence the kind of restriction as represented in Fig. 2. Near 0, we have the state of an idiot, who can be neither very good nor very bad.

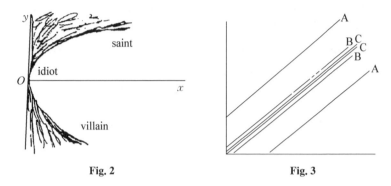

Fig. 2　　　　　　　　　　Fig. 3

Again, taking over the example of temperature discust in Chapter IV on Serial Order (p. 211), we have successively restricted regions of variation between temperature and its various physical interpretations (Fig. 3).

Finally, in all statistical correlations between two variables x and y, the instances do not lie on a single curve, but are scattered more or less broadly according as x and y have a smaller or a greater correlation coefficient (Fig. 4). Cases of very accurate measurements of a "single" magnitude are simply correlations where the points lie within a very narrow region on account of one factor being dominant, and "accidental" or "irrelevant" factors being minimized. [1]

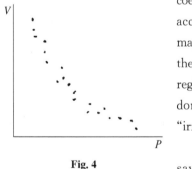

Fig. 4

From these examples, we can say that if we take two variables x

[1]　See K. Pearson, *Grammar of Science*, 3rd ed. , Chapter on Cause.

and y at random, it is as likely as not that they have some degree of regional restriction. At the lower limit, we have complete independence (if any). At the upper limit, we have strict functional relation (if any). Between these extremes, we can raise the methodological problem of inventing either a general definition of a coefficient of regional restriction or coefficient of generalized functionality, or special definitions of such coefficients, as have been worked out with statistical correlations. For each problem, we can decide as to how close a restriction is demanded before we call it practically a function.

Note. —An obvious comment one may make on this loose-collared view of a function is that the looseness comes from the fact that there is an unspecified " concealed coordinate" or "hidden factor". For instance, with a given electric conductor, the current I passing thru it is approximately proportional to the voltage V applied to it. That the relation is not a curve, but a band, is because we did not specify the third factor temperature, the variation of which makes the current vary somewhat for the same constant voltage. To this, I may say that what results from specifying the important factor of temperature is simply a much higher *degree* of restriction or generalized functionality. For who can tell that a Hall will not come once every quarter of a century to discover a new factor, such as the influence of a magnetic field on a current? Consequently, Ohm's law, in so far as it is a significant assertion specifying a finite number of factors, will be only a degree of regional restriction, and in so far as it is a mere definition of resistance as the ratio V/I, under which are lumped all possible factors, known and unknown, becomes thereby a strict mathematical function only at the expense of being a tautology (cf, concluding section of Chapter IV on Serial Order).

6. Intellectual Progress

It is legitimate to ask, "Who invented the first steam engine?" "Did Descartes know the third law of motion?" "Who first used the term function?" "Was Beethoven an original composer?" But when we forget the qualifications which are usually implied in the answers to such questions, then it is well to bring out the idea of the stages as against the notion that before a certain discovery there was nothing, and since that everything.

(1) *Inventions*. —The conversion of steam heat into mechanical power went as far back as Hero of Alexandria; Shortly before Watt, there were the engines of marquis of Worcester and Newcomen, etc.; and in our own day, the invention of the steam turbine by Hon. C. A. Parsons is no small stride. If Messrs. Hero, Worcester, Newcomen, Watt, and Parsons should stand in a row, and Mr. Watt should be nominated as the official inventor of the steam engine, there is no objection to that if his title is to remind one of the over-towering importance of such and such improvements that he made, and is not to imply or suggest that he created everything out of nothing.

(2) *Knowledge of a Truth*. —The question whether or not a certain truth or idea "was known" to a person or an age is often better resolved to one of degrees of knowledge. Newton's third law of motion was understood to a very practical extent as early as men knew how to propel boats with a push pole. Descartes' doctrine of the conservation of motion was only an algebraic step from the conservation of momentum, which is the essence of the third law of motion. And now that our ideas of mass and inertia are being

developed, our knowledge of the law is still undergoing corresponding modifications.

(3) *First Mentioning and Idea.* —The act of first naming an idea is often important in that it reacts on the future progress of the idea named, But when, for example, Leibniz first named a certain relation a "function", he was preceded by studies in such things as polynomials and trigonometric variables, and followed by such generalized notions of functions as those invented by Fourier and Weierstrass, which he would hardly recognize as his legitimate intellectual offspring. In fact, having merely mentioned or noted down an idea is often of little significance. An objector to a system is rightly unsatisfied if its builder tells him that an idea that would answer him is mentioned once somewhere in his system. Similarly, if one starts with a private museum of occasional thoughts, one may simply note them down briefly for occasional reference. But as they grow to an unwieldy bulk, the museum tends to become a cemetery. We should then either have to enter a thought systematically under many cross references, or elaborate it on the spot to a high grade of explicitness. or else it will be lost. For merely having entered it in a thick scrapbook would be as comforting as the knowledge that having finally dropt my frequently mislaid watch in the sea, I at least know now where it is.

(4) *Originality.* —The standard of originality may be marked outwith respect to specific problems, as in classifying copies from originals in an art collection. A doctor's thesis, e. g. , may be rejected with perfect logical legitimacy as being "not original". But in general, originality may vary from absolute creation thru new ideas of combination, new treatment or interpretations of old ideas

that are not fully shaped, commentaries, imitations, and finally to plagiarism and mechanical copying. To take a musical example, a person cannot be absolutely original in the sense of having a new psychophysical organism. It would be too exacting, too, to demand for originality the creation of a new musical mode; even Debussy's whole tone scale is made of combinations of known elements. If we analyze all Beethoven's works into short motives, it is probable that everyone had occurred to some previous composer. So that if one wants to be hyper-critical, nothing is original in music unless indeed one goes to some such thing as "color symphony". On the other hand, there is a degree of originality that is individual even to a child that plays the five finger exercises, and so on up the scale. And by this musical example. I mean to intimate that all originality in intellectual progress may be graded between two hypothetical extremes, with whose existence we are not primarily concerned in this connection. (Cf. Chapter V.)

CHAPTER IV   SERIAL ORDER

When we ask the question: "Is A x-er than B or B x-er than A?", we have a question of serial order. The same idea may be variously called " comparison of magnitude ", " order of precedence", "arrangement in a linear scale", or any other term that involves a connective, transitive. and asymmetrical relation. The formal logic of serial order has been well developed, as in Huntington's book on *The continuum* (1917). The present chapter is concerned primarily with the methodological applications of the idea. First, I shall try to explicate the meaning of serial order, then treat some common fallacies in serial order. Next, methods will be considered by which serial order is established, and then serial order will be treated as a method to be applied to further problems. In a concluding section, the meaning of serial order will be further developed from the point of view of the threshold idea.

1. Meaning of Serial Order: What it is

Dichotomic View. —When we ask: "Is A x-er than B or B x-er than A?", we often hear the reply: "Are A and B, *as a matter of fact*, comparable with respect to x? We can ask: 'Is London more populous than Paris?' but not 'Is missing a train more pleasant than smelling sulphur dioxide?'" According to this view, then, two things are either comparable or are not comparable in one dimension x.

Continuous View. —Including and transcending this view, the following gradations of cases are presented for consideration:

(1) If we are asked which is the heavier of two persons, it is a question of a very definite meaning and admits of a simple answer. Weight, then, has a simple definite meaning.

(2) To the question which is the greater of two fractions m/n and q/p, the answer is not so simple, since a fraction has two elements to be considered. One way of *defining* the relative magnitude of a fraction is to say that m/n is greater or less than q/p according as mp is greater or less than qn. This is in fact the definition universally agreed upon for various justifying reasons. Thus, magnitude of fractions has been well defined.

(3) Now, as to the question which of two vocations is the more "fitting" for a certain person to follow, we *feel* that the question ought to have a meaning and an answer. Yet we must first define a standard of fitness. What weights should we give to natural aptitude, interest, available educational facilities, present attainment, need of the community, etc., etc.? Here, altho no satisfactory definition of fitness has been agreed upon, we still believe that there is such a thing as degree of fitness. Thus vocational fitness is granted to be *something*, but something still to be defined, standardized.

(4) If now we are asked whether English pronunciation or German pronunciation is more difficult for a Chinese, then we can give the always correct answer: "It depends." In the sense of difficulty of making the sounds, German is much more difficult; in the sense of difficulty of recognizing the correct sound from the spelling, English of course surpasses most languages. Thus there is no "pronunciation difficulty" as such, but only difficulty qualified in specific senses.

(5) Again, we may be asked: "Who was the prior discoverer of Neptune, Adams or Leverrier?" Suppose that on being asked whether priority is taken in the sense of earlier working out or prior publication, or first having had an influence on the intellectual world, one says: "Take the three kinds of priority exprest in years, months, days, etc. , add them up, divide by three, and call the result priority as such. " On this procedure, we would naturally remark that there is no "logical" objection against it, but it would be a purely "arbitrary", or "trivial" definition of priority.

(6) Finally, when one's mind absents itself from the dinner table in order to consider kinds of serial order, the question is heard: "Would you rather have ice cream or plum pudding?" Without giving theoretically adequate consideration to the matter, one may simply echo "plum pudding" without actually feeling any greater inclination toward it. I choose it not because I prefer it in any significant sense, but I am said to prefer it merely in the sense of happening to take it[1]. Here the order of preference is simply defined *ad hoc*, *i. e.*, tautologically.

To sum up, we may compare things with respect to a magnitude which is (1) well-known, or (2) well-defined, or (3) supposed to be definable, but not yet well-defined, or (4) definite only when specifically qualified, or (5) an arbitrary thing, or (6) defined tautologically. Serial comparability is therefore not a question of yes and no, but a question of more or less.

The classification of six degrees of significance, however, is not important. In fact, even the standard of weight in case (1)

---

[1]   Cf. the behavioristic meaning of pleasantness and unpleasantness.

may have occasion to come into dispute. While in most dealings with weight, slight variations of meaning and measurement do not matter, there may be cases where two things differ so little that the secondary factors become prominent. Thus A may be heavier than B at noon, but B, being a heartier eater, may be heavier than A at 2 PM. If for any reason a finer comparison is needed, we shall have to refine and redefine weight, say, as the average weight of six week days taken at stated hours. Thus, we are now in danger of stepping on the grade of artificiality. On the other hand, if we take extreme cases, then small differences will make no chief difference. Thus, the Chinese may be said to have discovered the magnetic declination prior to the Europeans in any of the class of slightly incompatible senses of priority. These two points give a new twist of meaning to the truism that the $\begin{cases} \text{less} \\ \text{more} \end{cases}$ thing differ, the $\begin{cases} \text{harder} \\ \text{easier} \end{cases}$ it is to tell them apart.

2. Fallacies in Serial Order: What it is not

Here, as elsewhere, fallacy or not is a matter of degree. At one extreme, we may compare things indiscriminately and fall into confusions; at the other extreme, we may deny all comparison and throw up our hands before the bewildering concreteness of multiple-dimensional reality. It is however our natural tendency to make all kinds of comparisons, and a useful one, if followed cautiously.

(1) *Fallacy of One Dimension.* —But when one is asked: "Who is your best friend?" one may be at a loss to choose between one's daily companion, one's moral benefactor, or one's lifelong

teacher, and so on. As long as one does not have to make a choice, what is the point of arranging them in a scale of friendship, which is such a many-sided affair? Similarly, we find questions like, which is stronger, a healthy little girl or a very sick athlete? Which knows more music, one that plays "grade IV" badly or one that plays "grade II" perfectly? Is 90° difference in longitude greater or smaller than 30° difference in latitude? Is a raven more like a writing desk or a tea tray?[1]

In each of these questions,

1) We have two things which *prima facie* differ in several respects. Latitude and longitude, for instance, are in different geographical dimensions.

2) The respect x is one which is not understood to be well-defined.

3) To no intent or purpose does there seem to be any use of defining a standard of comparison. So the question can be dismist on the charge of "Fallacy of One Dimension". (Seclusically this amounts to the failure of the terms to satisfy the postulate of connexity.)

(2) *Confusion of Standards.* —Against that charge, however, one might plead that to ask any question out of a concrete context is likely to appear foolish or meaningless. If we have been talking about weather, and the foregoing geographical question is asked, then 30° latitude is likely to be a greater difference than 90° longitude. In other words, the *context* gives the qualification required to make the comparison significant. (In the upper extreme case of "perfectly definite" questions, such as

---

[1]   Lewis Carroll, *The Adventures of Alice wonderland* , "A Mad Tea-party".

concern fractions, the context is the whole field of mathematics or some other large field, as the ease may be.) But in as much as the context is usually implied and often very vague, there is a danger of a confusion of standards of comparison, when we carry the verbal result of a comparison into a different context.

Thus if I am grinding a lens for a telescope, spherical and chromatic aberrations are more serious than curvature of the field. So I measure the "goodness" of my lens chiefly by its freedom from the first two kinds of aberrations. As my vocation or avocation in my grinding shop is sufficient context for me, I don't have to qualify "goodness" of the lens by the adjective "telescopic" or "chromatic". But as "goodness" is a term which has many associations in other contexts, it may happen that I forget the qualification and still call a lens good or bad thru my habit of "colored" judgment when I am in my neighbor's shop, where *photographic* lenses are made and where goodness depends to a much greater extent upon the flatness of the field of image. And unless we make our qualified standards explicit, we shall never end our dispute. Here, then, we have an instance of confusion of one standard with another.

The lesson to draw from this is not that we should always qualify things explicitly, which is neither necessary, nor always possible, nor again desirable, but that we should be aware of the possibility of such confusions whenever difficulties arise.

(3) *Irrelevant Irradiation*[①]. —Again, there are cases where a comparison made on the basis of number of factors is unconsciously applied only to one of them, or even applied to

---

① Cf. "Fallacies of Composition and Division."

something quite irrelevant. Thus if nation A is on the whole greater than nation B. as judged by the achievement of their great men, it need not follow that the greatest man of A is greater than the greatest man of B. In other words. the greatest of the greatest need not be the greatest. Again, if Franklin[1] is, on the whole, more virtuous than you and I, it does not follow, let us hope, that you and I are inferior to him in the matter of order. If a man is great in factory management, it does not follow that his judgment is always sound in international affair.

Arguments about importance often fall into this fallacy. Since on the whole, patriotism is above art, if one had to make an exclusive choice, people would argue that anything loosely connected with patriotism, such as the hackneying of a certain tune, should take precedence over the existence of a great artistic organization. Similarly, a truant might make an excuse for going down town to buy a pencil rather than practising piano lessons, because, he argues, writing is more important than music.

Just as we cannot argue from whole to part, we cannot always argue backwards, either. Thus, if I have decided on my life work on a number of considerations, I should not waver because, occasionally, I find parts of other work more attractive than parts of my work in hand.

In these cases of fallacy of irradiation, which shade into confusion of standards, it is again neither necessary, nor possible, nor desirable always to demand an exact qualification of the meaning "on the whole", because that would tend to lead to barrenness. Recalling the last remarks in section 1 on extreme

---

[1] *Autobiography*, virtue no. 3(Harvard Classics, vol. 1, p. 83).

cases, we may say, if a man attains eminence, say in physics, it is fairly certain that he is high in the scale of mathematical ability. It is reasonable to presume that he uses his language fairly well. It is unlikely that he is a moral imbecile, altho once in a great while, we find a man like Giorlamo Cardan. In fact, we have here a descending list of statistical correlation coefficients. The golden mean attitude to take toward such fallacies is to be aware or the possibility of unsafe or irrelevant irradiation of conceptual "interference fringes", while at the same time we might make interpretations of standards freely and fruitfully, and in proportion perilously.

(4) *Denying Comparisons*. —The fault opposite to that of one dimension is the fallacy of denying the comparability of anything in any magnitude (general), or of denying a comparison when there ought to be one made (particular). Since students differ in aptitude, application and accomplishment, therefore the teacher refuses to arrange them on a scale of marks. In fact, all cases of indecision consist in the failure to make a choice of preferance between "qualitatively" different things. The philosophy of the fallacy consists in asserting that since all concrete things differ in many respects and all standards of serial comparison contain some degree of arbitrariness and artificiality, therefore all such comparisons are artificial and should never be made. As well say that anything short of infinity must be zero!

3. Method for Serial Order: where it is from

In the chapter on method, I have tried to show that (for) every *method of*, there is a *method for*. So before treating the application or use of the method of serial arrangement, I shall inquire how serial order is established.

Inspection. —Sometimes the question: "Is A x-er than B?" is so clear and the answer is so obvious that we can answer at a glance without any "method". Skyblue is lighter than a new serge suit, ambition is better than despair, an aeroplane is heavier than air. This may be called the method of inspection or intuition, which is the zero, or lower limit of method. The significance of this method lies in that no matter how many steps of complicated methodological machinery may join the answer to the problem, somewhere this aspect of inspection, or intuition, or direct appeal to experience, must come in to *apply* the method. (Cf. Chapter II pp. 176 – 177).

Defining x. —If the scale x cannot be judged so easily, then we have to find criteria of comparing x, in other words, to make the meaning of x more explicit. To ask whether gold is heavier than silver is to mean how the two compare in weight for the same volume, or what is found out to be equivalent, what part of weight they lose in water. So we weigh them in water to find out the answer. Thus the intervention of a method puts off the act of inspection to the reading of scales, thereby increasing the leverage of accuracy.

Choice of x. —But very often the question is put in such a way that we cannot argue definitely about the meaning that is worth considering in the context in which the question occurs, then it may be left unanswered, i. e., we call it a name, "fallacy of one dimension". On the other hand, usage and utility of the x-conception may tell us that we *can* make something out of the question which is x-er. The question now is, what and how?

Extremes. — One way is to try the method of extremes

(Chapter II, p. 162). By doing so, either actually or hypothetically (if necessary for safety), we bring out cases for judgment by inspection and make explicit what factors may have to be considered in cases where they are not so prominent.

Weighing Factors. — Next we have to combine these factors and ask what we mean by the resultant x. An example is the rating of intelligence by considering a number of standard tests and taking a resultant number of points by combining the figures in a certain way. Here we had some idea of degrees of intelligence x, but only when we have established scale, do we have a workably definite meaning x. For the range of variations of meaning of "intelligence" is too wide to be satisfactory in scientific psychology of its applications.

Usage. —What is the guide for the standard of comparison? The answer to this question, as in definition in general, is usage and utility. "Usage" is a rather infavorable term among theorists. "What's in a name?" But unless the question is too trivial to be considered, there must be some rough idea conveyed by the ill-defined question. The question: "Is A or B the better lens?" is ambiguous within a certain range. But the range is not infinite. Usage of "goodness" limits it to a (perhaps ill-defined) domain, with a limited extent of elasticity. We cannot define the goodness of a lens as the abundance of scratches on its surface, without stretching the term beyond the "limit of perfect elasticity". It is usage, there, that first tells us what we are about and sets us going.

Stability. —If usage is too indefinite, inconsistent, to satisfy our purpose, the consideration of utility comes in to decide. For our problem, what is the most significant or least arbitrary way of defining our x? If utility is deemed an objectionable term, we may call it logical stability. What way of standardizing the serial order x is likely to occur often in the course of actual affairs, in experimentation, or in the formulation of true laws? It usually turns out that a scientifically very stable or useful definition of x does not come anywhere near an average meaning of x in usage. If it is very far, then out of respect to usage, we may use technical qualifications or choose some other term, or simply let the fact that the term occurs between the two covers of a scientific treatise be sufficient qualifying context. Thus, the scale of hotness and coldness had a general meaning in usage. Later, it was defined by the expansion of liquids, still later, by expansion of gases, and finally in terms of thermodynamic relations, which is the most "stable" definition of temperature for physics. If we find a spoon at 60℃ hotter than a cup at 61℃, then we may qualify it and say that this is only psychological warmth and coldness and not physical temperature.

In general, then, we may say that usage may start a problem, but utility points where to go. If we find reason to go far, then let us say so, make it explicit. Else we might confuse standards and call good bad and bad good.

4. Method of Serial Order: What it is for

Serial order is a method in so far as it is itself supposed to be carried out and thereby serves some further purpose.

(1) *Precedence.* —In the choice of courses of action, of things, or of persons, we must compare the alternative on a scale of preference. Very often, the mere ordering is important as a method. Such is the case when a hasty decision is better than no decision. If one feels confused by a number of sundry things to do and does not know where to begin, a way out to reality is simply to put them down in an arbitrary order of precedence, and despatch them item by item. In the practise of "lining up", the order is less arbitrary. For here the order of "serving" is defined as the order of "coming".

(2) *Location*. —Serial arrangement may also help one to locate something on a scale. One way of marking a very large class of students is to arrange them in the order of merit, and then assign marks A, B, C, etc., according as the student is in the first, say 3% of the class, or the next 21%, or the next 45%, etc. While there is a "subjective" element in the first arrangement by inspection, the result of such a procedure, for a large class, is more "objective" than merely trying to call an examination paper a B-paper or a D-paper. Another example is the practice of arranging things in alphabetic order, as the words in a dictionary, or in numerical order, as the pages in a book. This is too obvious to need discussion.

Definitions. —In terms of serial order, certain vague ideas may be defined. Economy, for instance, need not mean saving this or denying that, but might well be defined to mean that we should arrange out possible expenses by common sense, or by further method in a "reasonable" order or importance, and reaching down the scale up to a point where the total expense is still within one's means.

"Possibility", in the practical sense, can also be considered with respect to a scale. "I cannot possibly do it by tomorrow", will then mean that if I arrange my business in the order of urgency, the total time it takes me to finish the things preceding the "it" will extend beyond tomorrow.

Truths. —But the most important application of serial order lies in the meaning of serial order itself, as illustrated in the first three sections. In so far as a serial order is significantly defined, there will be *truths* about it: we can recite *theorems* about x: we can play *tunes* on the scale now. If A is heavier than B, he falls with greater impact. It takes more energy for him to move about, he leaves his tailor a narrower margin of profit, he is less safe skating on thin ice, and a host of other truths about weight. To common sense, there seems to be more sense in "lining up" than in all such scientific devices in mental measurements or the more abstract theorizing on probability and entropy. Such conceptions, however, are of service in science, precisely because they are more than mere *definitums*, of which nothing is true besides their *definiens*. Far from being artificial, they enter into interrelated laws and true propositions which give them as much concrete meaning as the fat man's understanding is the significance of fatness.

5. Conclusion: Threshold[1]

It is a platitude that Life and Science are approximate affairs. In the concrete, "a=b" means that if any finer comparison should bring out a difference between a and b, it will be less than concerns us. If ε is the threshold of minimum relevancy in a problem, then "a=b" means that $|a-b|<\varepsilon$. From this point of view, "confusion of standards" is as often a virtue as it is a fault. The three kinds of temperatures defined by mercury, gas, and

---

[1]   Cf. Chapter V esp. 34, pp. 227ff.

energy may be regarded indiscriminately as "temperature" *without adding corrections*, and this is allowable for all the multitudes of purposes when the slight discrepancies make no difference. The gain from this lies in that we can thus freely say that (within certain margins) gas expands in proportion to temperature, etc.

The inconsistencies of usage, too, are often subliminal, and if so, we can profitably let them live in peace under the same term. "Human excellence" certainly has shades of inconsistent meanings in usage, and yet in many connections, we do not want a dry and lengthy strict definition, which limits its sphere of applicability.

These are pleas not for carelessness, but for the conservation of fruits, I would not lose the truth that high temperature is warm, out of the scruple that high temperature is not sensation. Within a certain ϵ, they are members of the same class. Disputes and paradoxes occur only when subrelevant inconsistencies become relevant without warning, i.e., pass the threshold by a change of point of view, or shift of ground. So that the way to avoid them is to know the range of one's ground. The carelessness I advocate, or seem to advocate is therefore not of the naive kind, but of the sophisticated kind, like the artificial naturalness of art.

Now a man of a mathematical turn of mind may suggest that the remedy of paradoxes lies in exact definition. For if data are approximations, then the question naturally raises itself, approximations to *what*? Why not find out this *what* and make *it* the standard? Very well, abhorring the inconsistencies of unscientific notions of temperature, let us adopt the thermodynamic definition of temperature used in theoretical physics. Then the simple gas law $PV=RT$ will be true only of an "ideal gas". But no gas is ideal. Hence the sad result that no gas obeys the gas law and no gas is fit for measuring temperature. But, one will urge, if you refine your theory and experiments, you will find a *true* law of gas in terms of *real* temperature, such as exprest in Van der Waal's equation

$$\left(P + \frac{a}{V}a\right)(V - b) = RT$$

which takes into consideration that molecules are not perfectly elastic and are not geometrical points. But is this not simply a higher degree of refinement, a diminution of ε? It has been found out that Van der Waal, too, has not been able to enforce strict legislation over actual gases. Hence, if we adhere to a strict definition of *temperature-in-itself*, we can say nothing true about it except its definition. Measurement of energy relations is subject to accidental errors; Van der Waal's equation is inexact; the simple gas law is false; sensation of heat and cold are illusory. Consequently, all the great amount of researches made with thermometers and all that sort of thing before the advent of Lord Kelvin's thermodynamic standard of temperature would be unscientific or had nothing to do with temperature as such, not even after then. Similarly, since in current discussions of the conceptions of mass, no final definition has been agreed upon, all our conception of mass would really have nothing to do with mass. When Prof. E. V. Huntington[1] interpreted mass in terms of force and other concrete relations he was rebuked by some, saying that "mass is just *mass*." So in the name of logic, T is T, and T is not non-T. *Q. E. D.*

---

[1]   American Math, Monthly, Jan., 1918.

But as soon as a margin of approximation is allowed, then we can say that T is not T, perhaps in a Hegelian sense, that is, we can then say something of something. In most contexts of common sense, the threshold is wider than in science. But in science, too, it is never zero, and the progressive refinement of science in comparing things in a series does not consist in arriving at barren exactness by declaring $\varepsilon = O$, and at the same time reducing the number of truths to nil, but in securing fruitful accuracy by trying to narrow down ε and yet have many true laws within that ε.

Perhaps it will be clearer to many minds if the idea is put in a few diagrams than in pages of rhetoric. Let T represent abstract temperature. Then we have the tautology $T = T$, which can be represented by the straight line $y = x$ (Fig. 1). Next, let T' represent the result of measurement based upon physical laws. Since laws and measurements are only approximate, the same temperature may have different readings and the same reading different temperatures, so that T and T' are really multiple-valued functions of each other, and the $T < T'$ graph will not be a curve, but a band (Fig. 2) (cf. Fig. 1, p. 191). Thirdly, let T' represent the rough guesses of our skin, which is subject to more disturbing influences than a thermometer. Then the judgment of temperature will be still rougher and the representation will be a much broader band. (Fig. 3. Of course the band need not have sharp, straight

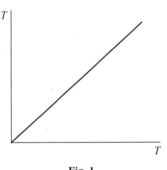

Fig. 1

boundaries.) Take a spoon at 60℃ and a cup at 61℃. Our first thermometer will give readings a′, b′, and since its variations are within a small fraction of a degree, it will show that the cup is hotter. But our lips, which are subject to the influences of conduction, may estimate the spoon at a″ and the cup at b″, so that its result is inconsistent with that of the thermometer. [1]

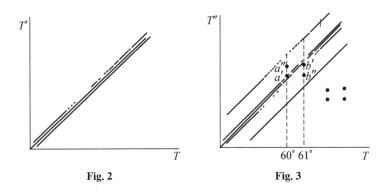

Fig. 2   **Fig. 3**

Now the point is this. In extreme cases, even the skin will always be right. On the other hand, in critical cases of small difference, even a good thermometer will look indifferent. The difference between the skin and the thermometer can therefore be regarded as one of degree. Every band is in a degree practically a curve. Within its width, all discrepancies are irrelevant, sub-liminal. Truths about magnitudes, then, consist in that several small bands lie within the same "band of discourse", so to speak. In Fig. 4, let the simple gas law be true within the broad band AA, then it means that the fine hands, representing empirical observation of actual gases, (marked solid black) lie within the band. Now as a

---

[1]   Cf. Chapter II p. 190 – 191, on function and regional restriction.

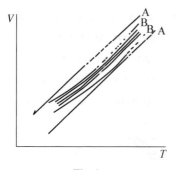

Fig. 4

further degree of approximation, the Law is refined to a narrowed band *BB*, say by Van der Waal's equation, it still includes the fine bands. This consititues progress. But if we make a limiting standard of temperature by drawing a line instead of a band, then obviously it will not include any of the empirically plotted hands. What science wants is to find a band that shall at once be narrow and yet contain many other bands, a narrow inclusive band, as against a linear exclusive curve. These are the graphical translations of "fruitful accuracy" as against "barren exactness". If we measure utility or logical stability of standard of serial order by some such notion as n/ε, the number of included bands n divided by the width of the band ε, then fruitful accuracy will mean a large n over a small ε, but barren exactness, which by putting $\varepsilon = 0$, makes n zero, would result in the nonsense $0/0$, which is far removed from logical stability.

CHAPTER V   LIMITING POINTS

1. The General Nature of Limiting Points

"If you cannot have what you like, then like what you have."
But if I do like what I have, haven't I then what I like? In other
words, by reducing my claim upon life to a lower limiting point,
its satisfaction is automatically raised to an upper limiting point of
one hundred per cent. This reasoning is not intended to reduce
stoicism either to absurdity or to rationality. but to illustrate the
two-sided nature of a limiting point, as it is conceived in this
study. The formal nature of a limiting point may be represented by
such terms as C, 1, or ∞, or any other term that may be
conveniently regarded as the limit of a scale. The notion of a lower
limit may be represented by 0, as "zero claim", or by 1, as,
"Thought is conversation with oneself". The notion of an upper
limit may be represented by 1 or 100%, as "the whole universe of
discourse", or by ∞, as "the totality of relevant factors". To go a
step beyond than the stoic example, we can apply the simple
mathematical trick of transforming any interval (a, b) of a scale
into any other interval (ϵ', b'), in particular, into $(0, \infty)$, by
setting up any one-one correspondence in such a way that a shall
correspond to 0 and b to ∞, or reversely. Thus, from a
professor's point of view, a freshman may have a certain finite
degree of intelligence a, and after four years, a slightly higher
degree of intelligence b; but in the transforming eyes of a senior, a
freshman represents the upper limit of ignorance and stupidity,

which in four years is supposed to vanish to nothing, in other words, a goes to ∞, and b goes to 0.

This feature of transformability makes the study of a limiting point more general than the special symbols may suggest. For instance, all cases of equality of two things may be regarded as a lower limit of their differences. It is in fact a familiar mathematical technique, especially in dealing with complex variables, to deal with $a-b=0$, rather than $a=b$.

In many cases, however, there is a natural preference in the choice of points of view, whose elasticity cannot be overcome except at some undue expense of methodological force. Thus, in a world of strivings and achievements, we naturally look at tlle stoic position as one of zero ideal, and do not find much significance in the fact of its perfect attainment. So we call it a case of lower limit. A characteristic expression for a lower limit is "to say the least". Everybody can have *some* attainable ideal, namely zero, to say the least.

Now take a man of common sense, he is not conscious of the absence of schedules and schemes, i. e., of his being at the lower limit of method, but simply knows that he gets things done, that is, he is at the upper limit of intuition, which starts apparently from nothing and jumps to reality "1". A characteristic expression for an upper limit is "in the end". Thus, in the end, whether method or no method, one must have some actual will power with which to execute an act, some intuition to get at reality.

Whether it is a case of an upper limit or a lower limit, the central problem of a limiting point is the question of identity and difference. In what ways is a limit just like the rest of the series? In what ways is it different? These I shall treat in order in the following sections.

2. Identity in Limiting Points

To have merely called things limiting points and to stop at that seems indeed to be a lower limit of the utility of definitions. So it is reasonable to demand with what further significance these empty notions are to be filled.

(1) *Formal Generality*. —The first reply is, "None". I extend a scale to include out-of-the-way things and put them at the zero and infinity of my scale, just as an experiment on generality, to gain simplicity or symmetry of statements, to save my logical face. This, in fact, is the spirit of formal logic and mathematics. Since we are not always sure that S is P, we can at least say that A is A, to make sure. A null class is simply a class of which the number of members is zero. If the finite disjunction that A is either B or C is not certain, we can at least make the infinite disjunction that A is either B or C or *neither*. If we make our universe of discursus wide *enough*, we can say virtue is not square, or in any case, A is not non-A, to say the least. Same cause, same effect, *under the some total conditions*. Aliens, insane persons, etc. , who registered on June 5, 1917 in the United States are in one of the five classes registered for military service. In every "specific" problem, you must take into account all the "concrete", "material" considerations. Remember always, " it depends ". Everything real is unique. One coin fresh from the mint is not another coin, to say the least. In other words, the policy consists in gaining a logical bird's-eye view, by including as much as I can, not caring for the moment how little I can say.

An interesting class of cases is where we prefer to complete a universe by jumping over a chasm. Instead of saying that expenditure minus receipts equals deficit, we say that receipts plus deficit meets the expenditure. Similarly, let F_e and F_w be sums of forces acting east and west respectively, a acceleration toward the east, m the mass acted on; then instead of saying that $F_e - F_w = ma$, i. e., the forces differ by an amount ma, d'Alembert would write, according to his principle. $F_e - F_w - ma = 0$, i. e., the sum of all forces balance each other, which is in a (not very serious) sense begging the question. Again, instead of leaving in the air items not belonging to any of my categories, I may surely complete the universe by putting the unclassified into the unclassified class. Thus the "miscellaneous" heading can always supplement finitude and fill up the rest of infinity; or, to transform my statement, I may say that if we look for compensation *on* principle, we shall always find compensation *in* principle.

A formal generalization is no crime if it is taken for what it is worth. But if one tries to eat one's cake and have it too, it would be committing a fallacy. It is well to remind one that one should work hard but not too hard; that one can attain any *reasonable* ideal if one takes it seriously *enough*. The golden rule and Kant's universal moral law are applicable to persons *under the same circumstances*, or, since the circumstances are never absolutely the same, under the same *relevant* circumstances, in other words, under the circumstances under which they are applicable. Thus by the time a statement is securely qualified, its significance is also nullified.

(2) *Significant Generalization*. —But perhaps the significance of what I can say is not quite zero. A generalization that is nominal to start with is often more than nominal in effect. We find certain

things true in certain cases. They may also be true in the limiting case. If so, then the generalization will not be nominal.

Thus, if two triangles in space make certain solid figures and have certain properties, they may retain these properties in the limiting case when the solid figures "degenerate", i. e. , are flattened down into a plane. This was in fact the way in which the famous Desargues' theorem was first proved.

If we disregard the actual history of mathematics, we may logically say that our whole system of numbers is a repeated application of lower limits. A complex number $a + b^i$ "degenerates" into a real number when $b = P$, and so on, until finally, we have a positive rational fraction with denominator 1, "degenerating" into a positive integer, which is the lower limit of the series of lower limits in the process of arithmetization of modern analysis. Here we know that many things true of the higher cases are also true of the lower cases.

Many theorems in mathematics for certain finite terms hold good when they become infinite. Thus there are theorems about integrals with finite limits which hold good for the cases of so-called improper integrals when one or both limits become infinite, or when at some points the integrand becomes infinite. As we saw, an upper limit is from another point of view a lower limit. $\int_{a}^{1/a} f(x)dx$ may just as well be regarded as $\int_{1/a}^{a} g(y)dy$, where $y = 1/x$.

In studying stereographical mapping by complex variables, we are often annoyed that theorems true for all points, including the north pole, cannot be stated and proved in one breath, because the north pole, being at infinity, is an analytic outlaw. But by a simple transformation, the north pole is as good a point as the south pole.

The law of parallelogram of forces says that the resultant of two forces is represented by the diagonal of the parallelogram if the forces represent its sides. But when we have a parallelogram of area zero, i. e. , when the forces are at $0°$ or $180°$, the law still holds good. In view of such traits of continued identity in the limit, it seems therefore somewhat unfair for mathematicians to talk of a parallelogram "degenerating'" into a segment of a straight line. For a limit is not always such an utter degenerate that it has lost all its ancestral traits.

(3) *Psychological Extension.* —It is in fact doubtful whether any nominal extension can ever remain nominal. By pretending to stand at zero, we often wedge into something by a psychological trick. If I could succeed in assuming an attitude of always giving and never claiming, then I might be pleasantly surprised by the modicum of blessings that I have and don't see that I deserved. When a child refuses to observe bed-time, the mother says, "Then stay up, for I must be obeyed anyway. " By thus saving her logical face in using a zero command, she has better chance next time to make her child "stay up, but be a little more quiet, please. "

In trying to lead a perfectly rational life, one is often confronted by opportunities and excusable temptations (if there are ever such things), which would break one's rules and plans to pieces and which may not after all be worth the disciplinary cost paid. In such cases, one may use the trick of a formal recognition of system breaking and call it a part of the system, however outrageous it seems. Thus, in the midst of busy work, it is safer to schedule in black and white the preposterous proposition of a fifteen mile hike followed by a three hour gossip and going to work or bed, as the case may be, than to lounge a single quarter-hour and wink at the schedule, which says, "This is your business hour".

(4) *Limit as an Ideal.* —In the case of an upper limit. We can often set it up as an ideal, and tho we do not attain it, we may yet attain something in its direction. Thus, we may define why as an upper limit of degrees of *how*. In asking questions, we can just as well ask "how is it that" as "why". But if we keep in mind a feeling of the ideal *why*, it may stimulate one's search for further *how's*, e. g. , a further explanation of the law of gravitation.

Again, in practical affairs, we have only limited optimum points to consider. But it is a useful ideal to look up to a synthesis of all optimum points, with the right algebraic signs, into one optimum point, because it broadens our realms of values. (Cf. Chapter VIII, p. 294 on the optimum point)

In general, it seems to be the spirit of metaphysics, whether in the person of philosopher or a scientist, to entertain ideals in the forms of upper limits, by prefixing the unique article *the* to such notions as true, good, and beautiful, which are only exemplified in the finite and relative.

By this, however, I do not mean to imply that no ideal is attainable. By standing at one limit and looking toward another, one may often find a sufficient number of steps for getting across. Plato's analytic method, applicable both to geometrical construction and to the proof of theorems, is an examplē of this. Given point A and circle with center at O. To draw a tangent from A to the circle. Plato would start with saying, "Assume that the tangent AB is drawn. " This is merely begging the solution, the zero of the analysis. But we do not remain in this cave of zero

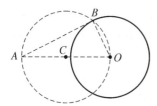

light. We can go a little way further and say, *OB* perpendicular to *AB*. Therefore △*AOB* can be inscribed in a circle with *AO* as diameter. Therefore the mid-point *C* between *A* and *O* is the center of this circle. Hence if we start with bisecting *AO*, all the rest can be done. Thus, out of nothing we get something by some intermediate things.

In general, the mathematical spirit of securing maximum generality at the risk of minimum significance serves sometimes to call attention to cases of slightly less generality and more significance, which the man of a concrete temper fails to notice because he clings to an habitual minimum significance and is afraid to venture further. Thus, mathematical logic has been criticized as empty, but its detailed working out is far from being the zero of significance.

3. Difference of Limiting Points

(1) *Lower Limits*. —So far I have dwelt on the aspect of identity of a limit with other cases. But a limit is unique as a limit, to say the least, and we have seen that the least is not always the most we can say. In general, a limiting point has more than a nominal peculiarity as well as identity.

In ordinary mathematical analysis, 0 is a number having many of the properties of other numbers. But it is peculiar in being the only constant whose absolute value is less than any value of a vanishing variable ε, in having no reciprocal, in having, only one value for its nth root, and in many other respects.

It often happens in mathematics that what holds for a variable may not hold for a limiting case. Thus, tan x is a continuous function of x between $\pi/2$ and π, but when $x = \pi/2$, tan x, whatever value is assigned to it, is discontinuous. Such cases, however, are nothing new. It takes but a simple transformation to see that they are but the peculiarity of zero over again.

Propositions, if you like, may be generalized into propositional functions of which it is a lower limit of ambiguity of meaning. But it has the peculiarity of being true or false, and, when standing in a relation of implication to another proposition, of making the implication difficult to understand. (Cf. Chapter III on Graded Ideas, p. 187)

To be alone, as a lower limit, is simply a monalic social relation. It is, to be sure, worth while to point out that one converses with oneself when thinking, can talk aloud with oneself, can really hate oneself, love oneself, play tricks on oneself, offer pretexts to oneself, etc. , etc. , and yet in many respects how important the obvious difference.

(2) *Upper Limits.* —A class of limits which are preeminently cases of unique upper limits is exprest by antitheses like the absolute vs. the relative, the unconditioned vs. the conditioned, the infinite vs. the finite, the concrete vs. the abstract, the *that* vs. the *what*, the individual vs. the universal, the categorical vs. the hypothetical, etc. Thus, no matter how many stitches a sewing machine may make in order to make the first stitch secure, it would be an infinite progression unless somewhere the end of the thread is pulled thru the loop to take care of the remainder of the infinite series. No matter how long Achilles and the tortoise quibble over the rule to draw a conclusion when the premise says that the conclusion be drawn, no piling up of rule upon rule will

draw the conclusion without somebody actually to do it. ①

No matter how elaborate a methodology a scientist may have, it takes some element of intuition and skill to apply it in the laboratory. No matter how much foresight law-makers may have in defining all possible cases, there must be some judge to interpret the law for each particular case. No matter how minutely a system of casuistry may be worked out, it takes some intelligent conscience to apply it and apply it right. No matter how long a chain of resolutions one may make, it takes some will power to start the easiest one going. No matter how complete a mnemonic system one may devise, it takes some degree of native retention to remember the substitutes. No matter how many out of an infinite number of theorems in a postulate system may turn out to be consistent, it takes some concrete exemplification to verify that all the theorems will be consistent. In fine, no matter, how great a leverage N one may have, it takes some actual force ε greater than zero to verify "Archimedes postulate", that $N \times \varepsilon$ shall be sufficient to move the earth.

A similarity will be noticed between the cases like the deficit meeting expenditure discust under formal generality, cases of upper limits as ideals, and these cases of unique limits. In fact, if the first is looking across the chasm of the Grand Canyon, the second would be making a telescopic study of the opposite shore, and the third would be actually flying across and landing on solid ground.

(3) *Lower Thresholds*. —In studying a part of a universe of discourse, one is often led to the conclusion that the whole is like

---

① Lewis Carroll, "What the Tortoise Said to Achilles", *Mind*, 1895, p. 278.

that part. In experimenting on conductors and non-conductors, Charles Dufay found that all bodies conduct electricity to some extent, that there is no such thing as a non-conductor, or in our jargon, that the lower limit of conductivity and the upper limit of resistance do not exist. Yet the distinction had arisen and has always stood in special problems in which conductivity below a certain threshold, relevant to each problem, is regarded as practically zero. Hence even if a unique limit does not exist, there will be a unique neighborhood, or threshold of the limit, such that cases coming under it call for a different treatment.

Philosophical insight often stumbles over these thresholds without having noticed them. All thought is action. Yet below a certain degree (relative to some problem) of overtness and promptitude of decisiveness, an " action " is better treated as a thought. All experience is contemplation. Yet above a certain degree of conflict and striving, the spectacle is contemplated in a rather noncontemplative way. Everything is unique, no two things are alike. Yet in most problems, one coin is as good as another, that is, of the same denomination. All pain is imaginary, says the Christian Scientist. Yet, granting that, there will be imaginary imaginary pains below a certain threshold, and real imaginary pains above that threshold of organic lesion. Everything real is concrete, like an organism, not like a heap of sand. Yet below a certain threshold of practical or theoretical importance, things may be treated as disorganized. It is safe, in most of our universe of discourse, at least to treat a heap of sand as a heap of sand.

A man is often counseled that he can always make the best of a situation however bad it may be, that he can always choose his best effective environment out of his potential environment, that even if his hands and feet were bound, he could still *think* what he likes, in a word, that there is no such thing as zero degree of freedom. Yet when this degree falls to a negligible ε, then making the best of it will not be much better than making the worst of it. If I am laid up with an acute illness, I may excusably ignore the advice to make the most of my opportunities for studying continuity.

In Chapter VII (p. 268ff), I shall try to show that all physical systems are either in stable equilibrium or in no equilibrium, that unstable equilibrium, as a lower limit of stable equilibrium when the (generalized) base of stability is zero, does not exist. Yet if the stability is lower than a certain threshold, we call it a case of unstable equilibrium, especially if there is a steep toboggan slide beyond the little platform at the top. Thus a super-cooled solution or supersaturated air is said to be in unstable equilibrium because the introduction of minute particles to throw the equilibrium out of its base is so insignificant compared with the enormous change that results. Now why wouldn't a single electron start the whole change? Because its antics would not push the system out of its small base of stability, altho this base is subliminal from our usual point of view.

(4) *Upper Thresholds*. —I have so far spoken of threshold as if it were always a small interval near zero. But from the point of view of the upper limit, a neighborhood within an ε would consist of cases beyond a certain upper threshold M. Thus, to say, "A body with less conductivity than a certain ε is practically a non-conductor," is the same as saying, "A body with greater resistance, say, than that of dry air, has practically infinite resistance." Zero conductivity, one hundred per cent insulation, and infinite resistance are synonymous terms.

In the general problem of a phenomenon y as a function of an unlimited number of possible factors, we can say that we can take into account only some of them, that there is no such thing as having considered all factors influencing the phenomenon y, that we could never write

$$y = f(x_1, x_2, x_3, \cdots)$$

completely. Yet for each problem, it is sufficient to consider a finite number of factors M, and say that the total effect in our problem of disregarding

$$\frac{\partial f}{\partial x_{M+1}}, \frac{\partial f}{\partial x_{M+2}}, \cdots$$

is negligible, that is, when the number of factors considered is greater than M, it is as good as infinity. And practical infinity need not be a large number, either. A practical electrician need only know the length, thickness, material, and voltage of a wire in order to know the current, so that his infinity is equal to four. In a more refined physical problem, one may have to know the temperature and the magnetica field, which make only six.

4. Concrete Meaning of Limits

(1) *Limit as a Class.* —The distinction has been hinted above (pp. 217 and 220), that formal logic and mathematics deal with lower limits while philosophy deals with upper limits. In view of the transformability of the points of view, we can say that the two extremes meet. Now we found that in specific problems (excepting cases of a finite number of discrete elements), we can substitute, in place of zero and infinity, terms less than a lower or greater than

an upper threshold, determined for those problems. Then shall we discard the exact limiting points and disparage metaphysics and mathematics? No, we should then perhaps be the terminological loser.

Let us apply Occam's razor, or more specifically, Russell's principle of abstraction, Since we do not need strict zero or finity, and their meaning is undefined, we can simply proceed to define zero as the class of all finite ε's, and infinity as the class of all finite M's, that occur in our limited problems (dimension of physical or other units being of course properly regarded). Thus, the principle of abstraction might be called the principle of concretion[①].

Applying this treatment to various cases of limits, we can then say that $y = x^2$, for example, is the class of all problems in which the band or tube of x is narrower than the ε that is assigned in each case (Cf. Chapter III, p. 192). Thus, instead of saying, "From a mathematical point of view, a jet of water is practically a parabola," we can now say, "From a concrete point of view, a jet of water is a member of the class parabola, that is, simply is a parabola." The technical sense of the verb to be or "$\in$" in the symbolism "$J \in P$" is thus interpreted in the ordinary sense. Again, instead of saying that various phenomena *measure* temperature (Chapter IV, p. 210ff.), we can say that temperature is the class of those phenomena of gases, liquids, changes of state, change of radiation frequencies, heat and cold sensations, correlated in certain ways.

(2) *Methodological Interpretation of the Mathematical Definition of Limit.* —This sounds like loose talk on zero and

---

① Cf. B. Russell, *Our Knowledge of the External World*, p. 42.

infinity and limit, in total disregard of mathematical usage. Now I must come to close quarters with the standard definition of a limit. The text book says, "L is the limit of $f(x)$ as x approaches 0", shall mean. For any preassigned ε, there corresponds a δ, such that

$$| f(x) - L | < \varepsilon, \text{ whenever } | x | < \delta. \text{ ①}$$

Now the language in the first clause of the definition is rather quasi-dramatic. It pictures x and $f(x)$ as going thru a Heraclitean process. But in actual mathematical study, a more *workable* meaning of a limit is that of the logical correspondence of a δ to a preassigned ε (or an N to a preassigned M, etc. , as the cases may be), and in any single instance of correspondence, neither ε nor δ need be small, from an average point of view. What I have done, or meant to do, then, is simply to interpret this logical mathematical correspondence into a methodological correspondence. The mathematician says "for any preassigned ε", and stops at that. I ask, who is it that comes uninvited to preassign the ε? The mathematician does not care, he is willing to let the question pass. Now methodologically, and probably also historically, is it not the actual problems that preassign certain thresholds, such that if differences fall below them, then they will "make no difference"? In the same subject matter, e.g., equilibrium, there will be an indefinite number of various problems with various thresholds of relevancy. The fact that we have not actually proposed an infinite number of problems is no objection, since in the correspondence definition of a mathematical limit, we need not

---

① The following remarks apply equally well to other cases of limits with obvious changes in wording.

have all the ε's specified and written on paper. A much more serious objection is that the class of ε's arranged in order of magnitude may not converge to zero, but to some positive limit, something greater than zero. The answer is that this is possible only if we take some ε's and leave out others. For the lower bound of ε's in all finite problems is just what we *mean* by the methodological zero. The objection, which would stand in a mere mathematical cases where only ε's in a special universe of discourse are concerned, would involve a contradiction in terms in the general case. It seems therefore that this extra-mathematical interpretation of the mathematical definition of a limit is after all not such an unmathematical step that one need feel for it any pang of mathematical conscience.

(3) *Philosophical Application.* —Now apply this view to the ideal of philosophy mentioned in section 2, p. 343, in which the question of its validity was rather left in the air. 1) Philosophy, it was said, aims at the "absolute" (or any of the variations played on it). 2) Let us do away with this absolute and say that our finite intellectual inquiries above a certain upper threshold M of comprehensiveness and depth shall be called philosophy. 3) Now that the absolute is no longer needed, we are free to *define* it as the class of those inquiries and results called philosophical. 4) Thus we get our philosophical absolute back in the concrete. The true, the good, the beautiful, if stated in humanistic and temporal terms, may therefore mean the actual course of the evolution of standards of knowledge, morality, and art, such that at each stage, judging from the progress attained so far, plus whatever power of vision into the future one may be endowed with, one can say practically, that is, categorically, whether

anything, in the concrete, is or is not true, or good, or beautiful. This is certainly saying much. But I should take this philosophical point less seriously than the examples of limiting points themselves, or which a theory of limiting points must, in the last resort, be based, or of which it must consist. For after going thru these "concrete cases", one should not be surprized that by saying "saying much", I must have meant to say "saying little".

CHAPTER VI   IDENTITY THRU
CONTINUITY

Identity and Difference. —In philosophical discussions of identity and difference, difference of degree and difference of kind, continuity and discontinuity, change of quantity and change of quality, uniformity or consistency and variety, one and many, constancy and variability, permanence and change, habit and intelligence, etc., etc., we are constantly reminded that there is no identity without difference and no difference without identity, no permanence without change and no change without permanence, etc. Lest this reminder-at-large should make us forget the meaning of the idea, it will be well to inquire just what kinds of identities and differences do or do not go together in our everyday conduct of intelligence.

As a method of study, to be justified by its results, if any, I shall chiefly treat the things in question as if they lay on a serial scale x for which ground has already been prepared in Chapters. III and IV on Graded Ideas and on Serial Order. Given two things to be compared. Find a scale of gradations, whether discrete or practically continuous. As we run thru the gradations, ask. What aspects remain identical? This is the subject of the present chapter. And what aspects become different, and if different, where and how? This is the subject of the following chapter.

Being a method and not a dogma, this procedure is neither true nor false, but may be good or bad, effective or trivial. Where it has no firm hold on its working substance, the latter simply leaks out of its safety valve. Thus, take a cabbage and a king, and consider gradations of forms from one to the other. We gain thereby an insight that they are identical in belonging to the same serial class, which, unfortunately, is constructed *ad hoc*. In general, I can formally put any two things A, B into a class K, look away for a moment, and ho! Now A and B are identical in belonging to the same class K. On the other hand, take an Egyptian pyramid at 10:16 A. M., April 13, 1918 and at 10:18 A. M., April 13, 1918. As time passes, the pyramid changes from an ante-17-minute pyramid to a post-17-minute pyramid, which is a decided difference. In general, I can always say that everything must be different from everything else, and that however A and B are alike, A is not B, to say the least. Between these extremes we find things of interest, on which the method has a bearing.

Identity. —To come to the subject of this chapter, we shall speak of the identity of A with B in a respect K thru continuity of x over a point of difference ε or an interval of difference x, which underlies the identity, the various prepositions being chosen with a view to avoid ambiguity rather than to conform to idiom. Thus we have identity of white with black in neutrality of hue, thru the continuity of grays over the point of middle gray or the interval of intermediate grays.

A and B are the things to start with. By "putting them on a scale x" is meant that some serial order x is considered so that corresponding to a point x_1 we have A, and corresponding to x_2 we have B. In other words, we define a function $f(x)$, such that $f(x_1) = A$ and $f(x_2) = B$, and the method of gradations by imagination or observation or practical instalment, consists in

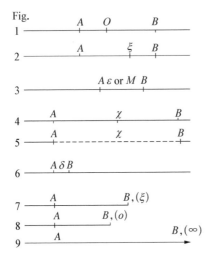

defining $f(x)$ for values of x between x_1 and x_2.

The choice of the series is both free and restricted. In the example of gradations of a U-tube to a tube in a bowl (p. 241), it is obvious that there is a wide range of multiple-dimensioned variations thru which one shape can pass to the other. But, within limits, one series of variation is as good as any other series for the purpose of showing the identity of the hydrostatic relations. Very often, a series of a few discrete terms serves the purpose of suggesting the identity, so that x need not even be an approximate continuum. This is freedom. On the other hand, if we take a bee and a beetle, and instead of showing the biological identity thru the intermediates that we believe actually existed in evolution, we should draw pictures grading from bee thru a beet to a beetle[1], the choice of the dimension of x, in prosaic biology at least, would be an impertinent one. This is restriction.

The background of difference which underlies an identity will be the principle according to which the chapter is divided. This difference may be over the zero point of a scale, over which the identity runs from A to B (Fig. 1). It may be over a point ξ, which is peculiar or singular in some respect (Fig. 2). Or it may be a

① R. W. Wood, *Animal Analogues*, p. 1.

threshold of difference ε or M (Fig. 3), which differs from a point in being not very sharply defined. (For instance. the lower threshold of tone audition is a statistical affair.) Again, the background may be a whole stretch of x, either actual or hypothetical (Fig. 4, 5), which is long enough to make things on opposite sides of it appear different, altho there is no point of special interest in between. If this interval is small in some respect, then it gives rise to situations which deserve special treatment (Fig. 6). Finally, the mark of difference itself may be identical with other points of the series in a respect to be revealed thru continuity, and this point may be a general point ξ, or 0, or ∞ (Figs. 7, 8, 9)[①].

Since now identity is always identity in some respect, it will not be a transitive relation except in the same respect. Thus if black and neutral gray are identical in hue and neutral gray and a certain violet are identical in brightness, it does not follow that black and violet are identical in either. Things identical to the same thing are therefore not always identical with each other.

1. Identity over Zero: Change of Sign

The difference of sign on opposite sides of a zero point is one that very easily hides an identity, and according as this zero is more or less arbitrary, the difference of positive and negative sign will be less or more significant. Thus, all temperatures are alike in belonging to one continuous scale. $+1°F$ and $-1°F$ are somewhat different, but no more so than, say 14°F and 16°F. The difference between $+1°C$ and $-1°C$ is more significant in that it corresponds

---

① On the mutual transformability among points, see Chapter V pp. 215 and 226.

to a change of state of the most important liquid, but it makes no difference to the state of many other substances.

Fig. 10

Identity over a change of sign is sometimes called in mathematics "the principle of continuity". Thus, in ordinary language we say that if two lines intersect inside a circle, their angle is equal to half the sum of the intercepted arcs, and that if they intersect outside the circle, their angle will be measured by half the difference of the intercepted arcs. Now suppose that we consider the sum of the arcs measured from one of the line to the other, and take into account the directions. Then we find that in changing from the one to the other case, one arc has changed from a positive sign thru zero to a negative sign, but that the same law holds for all cases, namely, that the angle is equal to half the *algebraic* sum of the arcs.

Since identity is always qualified, we need not have any psychological scruple in seeing in red and verdigris an identity of a linear scale, extending from saturated red thru gray to saturated verdigris. Red, then, is negative verdigris and verdigris negative red. Granting that this is not the whole story, we at least gain a point of view which is very helpful in dealing with color mixing, adaptation, after-images, etc. The same identity applies of course to other pairs of complementary colors.

In making records, plans, rules, etc., one often changes a principle when there is a change of sign. I may, for example, set out to practice promptitude and record accurately how many minutes I am behind time, but only make a check each time I am on time or ahead of time. To be sure, before time and behind time are not the same thing. But we can also measure promptitude on the same scale extending on two sides of the standard. The question is not whether I should *a priori* act on a principle of consistency rather than of variety, but whether I make the difference merely by accidentally blundering into it, or make it on some grounds.

Physics is full of cases of identity thru change of sign, of which the aspect of difference is often quite misleading. We naturally imagine a head-on collision between two automobiles to be more violent than a collision from behind. Now the violence of the collision depends entirely upon the algebraic difference between the speeds. If the collided car is going ahead, its speed is subtracted, if it is coming against the colliding car, its speed is added. Therefore the shock from 30 miles an hour overtaking 10 miles an hour is the same as 12 miles an hour against 8 miles an hour (i.e., $12 - (-8) = 12 + 8$). It is well therefore for a fast driver to remember the identity of the law which runs thru the differences of sign in the speed of his prospective victims.

The Cartesian conception of the conservation of motion is also a case of seeing a difference thru a change of sign, where identity persists. The Cartesian theory of impact of elastic bodies says: Let mass m_1 collide with mass m_2, with velocities v and $-v$ respectively. If $m_1 > m_2$, then both bodies will move with velocity

v after the collision. If $m_1 = m_2$, each body reverses its velocity. If $m_1 < m_2$, both will move with velocity $-v$. Now if we talk in the non-Cartesian language of algebraic momentums, the momentum before the collision is $vm_1 - vm_2$, or $v(m_1 - m_2)$. After the collision, according to the theory, it will be

$$v(m_1 + m_2), \text{ if } m_1 > m_2,$$
$$v(m_1 - m_2), \text{ if } m_1 = m_2,$$
$$-v(m_1 + m_2), \text{ if } m_1 < m_2,.$$

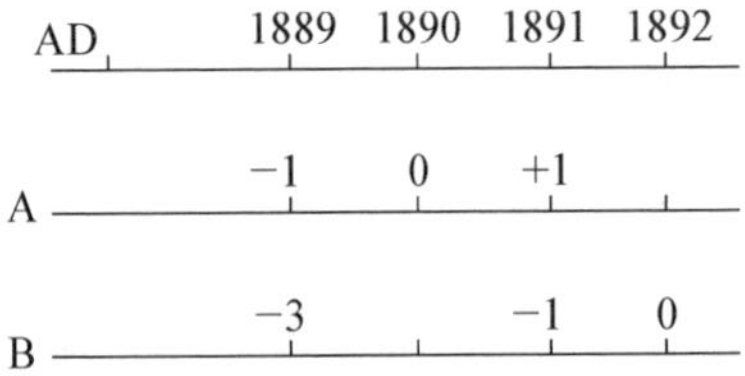

Fig. 11

Without using the Leibnizian argument of continuity of cases (see p. 129), it suffices to say, so far as our point is concerned, that Descartes associates (by implication if not consciously) a difference of law, with a difference of the sign of $m_1 - m_2$, whereas the fact is that the total momentum of the two bodies in question will always be identically $v(m_1 - m_2)$, irrespectively of the sign of $m_1 - m_2$.

A similar case is found in the identity of the relation between the atmosphere and an aeroplane. I believe it is a fact that an aeroplane can either fly forwards, stand still, or fly backwards, with respect to the earth. But don't aviators say that a machine cannot rise without a minimum speed of about 40 miles an hour? Yes, but this speed is the speed of aeroplane on the surrounding air. While it is among the clouds, all earthly things are irrelevant, at least in the aerodynamic sense, if not in a military or esthetic sense. Hence, if it is flying at 40 miles an hour against a wind of 40 miles an hour, it will stand still; and if the wind is 50 miles instead of 40, the machine will appear to spectators to be flying backwards with a speed of 10 miles an hour. Yet this difference of sign of its terrestrial speed has nothing to do with the lifting power of the air under its wings.

Finally, to take a trivial but clear example, let A be born in 1890 and B in 1892. The years 1889 and 1891 are different for A in that he had no experience of 1889 but some experience of 1891; but his zero point of conscious time is irrelevant to B, from whose point of view 1889 and 1891 are identical in both being negative points of his conscious time.

2. Identity over Singular Point §

Having treated identities on different sides of zero, I come to identities on opposite sides of some peculiar or singular point different from zero, for instance, the identity of the chemical composition of water at 30. 2°F and at 33. 8°F over the point 32°F, peculiar in that water has different states on opposite sides of it. One moment! Did I not use this same freezing point as an example of zero? Yes, this exactly brings up the next point, namely, that altho zero looks like a special case of singular points, it is always possible to shift our scale so that the point in question shall be called zero. In other words, instead of regarding zero as a special case of singular points, all singular points can be regarded as special cases of zeroes on a properly transformed scale of reference. However, there is a *raison detre* of a separate treatment of singular points, that is, some points are by habit or for methodological convenience not regarded as zero and yet as being peculiar.

Thus there is a geometrical theorem that the area of the

curved part of a spherical segment is equal to πR^2, where R is the distance from the apex A to the circumference of the segment. If the segment is very flat, as in Fig. 12a, it looks reasonable that the curved area must be about that of a circle of radius R. But with a segment as in Fig. 12b, it looks as if it were a different situation. The method of continuity will then consist in inventing a gradation of segments, measured by, say the altitude x from A to the base of the segment (Fig. 13), and as it changes from AB to AC, we find that there is a peculiar point where x is equal to the radius of the sphere and the segment is a hemisphere. But on further analysis, we find that this peculiarity is irrelevant to the proof of the formula in question. Hence the formula remains identical thru this singular point.

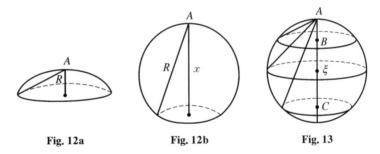

Fig. 12a　　　　**Fig. 12b**　　　　**Fig. 13**

Again, we hear the law that the weight of a body above the surface of the earth varies inversely as the square of its distance x from the center of the earth, but also the other law that the weight of a body underground, e.g., in the shaft of a mine, varies directly as its distance from the center of the earth.[1] Is there then a difference of law thru this singular point at the surface of the

---

[1]　Neglecting changes of density of rocks in different concentric shells of the earth.

earth? In one sense, of course there is. But if we consider the relation between the body and every part of the earth's mass, of course the law of universal gravitation holds whether it is inside or outside the earth.

Topological relations, that is, relations of position irrespective of shape of things, often remain identical in one respect over a singular point in some other respect. Thus two vessels as shown in Fig. 14 may be regarded as being identical in that they are both pairs of communicating

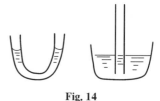

Fig. 14

vessels. Many teachers fail to make plausible Torricelli's argument that air pressure on the surface of the mercury in the outer vessel will somehow, mysteriously, turn upwards and push the liquid up the tube when its upper end is sealed and empty. To the student, the argument does not *feel* solid enough, and his imagination (which once was mine) balks at comparison of the tube and vessel with the easily understood case of a U-tube. To bring out the identity, one way is to imagine a series of intermediate cases as shown in two projections in Figs. 15 – 20. In 15, we have a plain U-tube. In 16, one end is flattened and curved around, which is topologically and hydrostatically identical with 15. In 17, the curved part is still more curved around the other tube. In 18, the two corners of the curved mouth are joined from end up, so as to form a ring. From above, there appear now three rings. In 19, the space between the inner and the second ring is filled with solid glass, so as to form one solid ring or tube. This of course has no effect on the liquid. Finally, this tube is made thinner, as in 20, which gives us the tube and bowl. And this whole series may be made as gradual as we like by inserting more intermediate forms. But continuity does not mean identity. An important topological change does occur between cases 17 and 18, where a simply bounded surface of the liquid changes into a ring surface. This is important enough to be called *the* singular point of our problem. However, it does not take much physical knowledge or imagination to see that it does not affect the pressure relation. Hence cases 15 and 20 are to be regarded as identical so far as that is concerned.

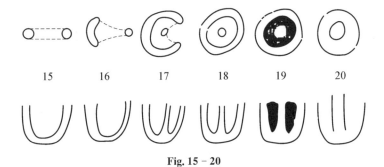

Fig. 15 – 20

The boundary between a human body and its environment is certainly singular in many important respects. But we can easily find problems where the two merge into each other. Thus, when one sings from a stage, the reflecting wall behind the singer, the floor, and the singer's vocal organs are identical, in so far as they belong to one continuous resonant system; and if both the physical and the physiological parts of the system are under his control, he will not be completely excusable for choosing a bad hall to sing in, any more than for choosing to sing with a cold.

When the variable is time, a singularity will mean a sudden change of something, over which the question of identity is raised. The identity of matter thru its various transformations is an instance of importance. But this importance is often so exaggerated that it is regarded as identity *as such*. When hydrogen and oxygen change into water, the identity simply consists in the conservation of the mechanical property called mass and in the limitation of the number of ways in which the chemical properties can vary. But hydrogen and oxygen are different from water none the less. Systems in dynamic equilibrium, like the Niagara Falls, or any organism, have aspects of identity just as important as matter. It is the unjustified unique emphasis laid on the identity of matter that begets such paradoxes as the identity of the darned stocking that contains none of the material that was once bought.

Identity of energy is another case in question. Poynting and Thomson remarked in their *Text-Book on Heat* (foot-note, p. 116) that the identity of energy is a harmless metaphysical notion and is used for simplicity of statement, and that strictly we should have to say, for instance, that when a definite amount of kinetic energy disappears, a certain amount of heat energy appears. Now, since significant identity is always qualified identity, why not bring metaphysics down to earth and say that the constancy of the rates of exchange among measures of different phenomena and the consequent possibility of a common measure is just what we *mean* by the identity of energy, which we can therefore talk about freely now. Simplicity of statement then becomes a scientific method instead of a scientific excuse.

A singular point of time that easily overshadows continuity and identity is a symbolic mark of some stage of accomplishment. (Cf. Intellectual Progress, Chapter Ⅲ p. 193ff) A diploma of graduation, a marriage cerimony, or a revolution for democracy may mark a stage of progress of something at a somewhat general trend of speed. If the progress is something like curve (1) in Fig. 21, the psychological effect of marking a point ξ is to give the impression that the progress is like curve (2) and by way of psychological reaction, the future progress may actually take a course like curve (3), as is often met with. To mistake identity for difference in one direction may therefore lead to a difference in an opposite direction.

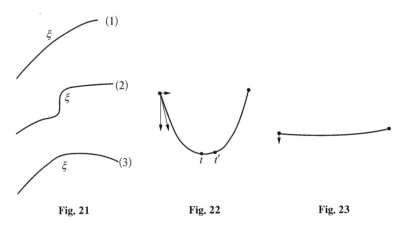

Fig. 21　　　　　Fig. 22　　　　　Fig. 23

3. Identity over Threshold ξ or M

By a threshold, I mean a singular point on a scale, which need not be exactly located, but which nevertheless marks a distinction in some respect. It may, for example, mark a distinction between the finite and the practically infinite or the practically zero. (Cf. Chapter V p. 224). In experimenting on the velocity of sound, the velocity of light signal is beyond the threshold of practical infinity. Yet over this threshold, there is the identity of both sound and light in having a finite velocity, and this finitude becomes relevant in the phenomenon of aberration of stars.

It is said in mechanics that a flexible chain "hanging loose" is a catenary, whose equation is

$$y = a \left[\cosh\left(\frac{x}{a}\right) - 1 \right],$$

and whose shape is like Fig. 22. The question comes up, "What is the shape of the chain when it is pulled 'taut'?" Once I actually suspected that "tautness" must involve a radical difference of law. But by imagining Fig. 23 as Fig. 22 pulled out, or as being similar to a part of Fig. 22 marked tt', it is easy to see that the two cases differ simply in the ratio between vertical and horizontal components of tension at the point of support, as indicated by the vectors in the figures. For any particular problem, we may set a threshold of the ratio, such that on one side of it we shall call the chain loose and on the other side taut. But such a threshold will have no geometrical peculiarity, and looseness and tautness are simply gradations of a parameter of the same formula for a catenary.

In explaining how a glass globe with vacuum inside can withstand pressure, the usual way is to consider a small portion of the globe as shown in section at *ab* in Fig. 24. This little disc receives pressure towards its center from the adjacent glass all around, but since it is curved, there will be just enough resultant unneutralized component to push the disc out against the atmospheric pressure. Unfortunately, this proof, convincing as it is as to the necessity of the fact, often fails to pursuade a person of its intuitive reasonableness. To bridge over the imagination, let us consider a solid glass globe. It is easy to imagine how *it* can resist air pressure. Next, imagine a tiny vacuum bubble in the middle of the globe (Fig. 25). Then it is still within the threshold of practical zero, so far as its withstanding pressure is concerned. Then let us imagine bubbles of various sizes, until we have the hollow globe that we started with. We shall then see vividly the identity of principle thru all these gradations.

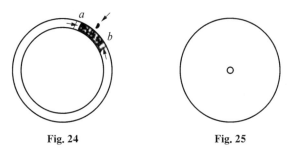

Fig. 24　　　　　　　**Fig. 25**

Very often, however, our psychological organism prescribes a threshold of conscious span, so that we can only understand an identity without having a more intuitive idea of it. Thus, it is not possible to *hear* an identity between the distinguishable flappings of the wings of an albatross and the continuous humming of a humming bird, or literally to *see* an identity between colors and the long waves sent out from a hot radiator.

From this, however, it does not follow that the identity is "imperfect", but it is all the more interesting to see. For instance, when two tones differ by a few vibrations per second, we hear beats, and if the beats come at a frequency greater than our lower threshold of tone audition, they will cause sympathetic vibrations of some part of the basilar membrane, and we hear a tone of corresponding frequency. From this, one might have predicted the existence of combination tones before their empirical discovery. Yet some psychologists strangely speak of combination tones as originating in the ear, as if it originated in the ear in a peculiar sense in which other tones do not originate in the ear.

The principle of a mechanical system often remains identical beyond a point where we feel a decided difference of conception. We are told that a motion picture film (1) remains at absolute rest for a while, (2) then it is covered by a shutter, (3) begins to move, (4) attains a maximum speed, (5) slows down, (6) stops, (7) is uncovered when the shutter has passed, and (1) remains at rest again for a while. Now it cannot take less than a few seconds to imagine this process. But what happens is that stage (1) occupies $2/3$ of $1/14$, or $1/21$ of a second, and the whole series of six stages from (2) to (7) occupies about $1/3$ of $1/14$, or $1/42$ of a second. The logic of the machine simply grinds out these sorites, leaving our imagination behind; and with the present stage of technological development, the rate can still be increased somewhat before the system breaks down, that is, before the threshold of mechanical workability is passed.

Similarly, a text book on internal combustion machines explains at length how one step follows another according to electrical, chemical, and mechanical reasons in making one complete cycle, and gives one the impression of the easy going motion of a reciprocating steam engine on an ocean liner. But when we hear the cycles merge into a continuous buzz, as in an aeroplane, our imagination fails to see how nature can go thru so many reasonings at such a frantic rate.

4. Identity over an Interval of x

It is idle to say in general that if a difference of degree is great enough, it will be a difference of kind. But this sort of statement gives an idea of the content of this heading. We have an obvious difference between A and B, tho we see no particular point on the scale to separate them. The logic of the case, then, is to see the identity, and not to make a point of distinction haphazardly or to take for granted the existence of a well-marked point of distinction.

Thus, in statistics, one often finds curves of the form shown in Fig. 26. The statistician calls the little ups and downs fluctuations and the larger sweeps the general trend. But suppose that we have a curve like Fig. 27, then there will be fluctuations of fluctuations and trend of trends, and apart from drawing a line between fluctuation and trend for any particular question, they are all alike in being variations of the data. Toward the latter part of Fig. 27, even the grades are not distinguishable.

Fig. 26

Fig. 27

The same question may be taken more generally from the point of view of smooth and rough curves. "What is the smoothest and most close-fitting curve for my data?" asks the plotter. This question, put bluntly, is a contradiction in terms. If curve 1 in Fig. 28 is the most close-fitting, it is the most ragged, and if curve 5 is the smoothest, it is the least close-fitting. The question therefore has no blanket answer apart from a threshold of compromised fitting-smoothness, depending upon the frequency of the abscissa, the accuracy of the ordinates, and the factors intended to be called relevant or accidental.

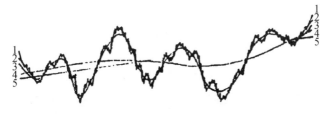

Fig. 28

In music, sometimes an identity is hidden by a difference of name or notation, but can be discovered thru intermediates between widely different cases. Grace notes, because they are written small, are often felt by the novice as something of an outlaw, and are to be executed "as quickly as possible", while large notes are supposed to occupy finite and definite lengths of time, however rapid the tempo. As a matter of fact, melodic figurations have all degrees of rapidity and are identical as such, whichever way they are written. The proof of it is that in intermediate cases, a listener cannot tell whether a certain motive is written as

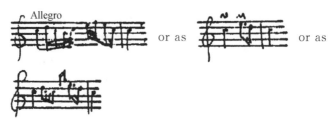

tho he can *prefer* one or the other notation as more convenient. The significance of this identity lies in that it will argue for an identity of treatment. If, for instance, ordinary notes can be played too fast, there is also such a thing as rendering grace notes too fast. Grace notes are not gratuitous notes.

Identity of harmony is also often hidden by a wide difference of some variable. A broken chord or arpeggio is as much a chord as a simultaneously sounding chord, and in intermediate cases, as at the end of a cadence, a listener cannot tell whether it is written as

Again, a passage like

as a succession of wildly jumping notes, is difficult to grasp, but it differs only in degree from

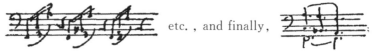

and the pedagogical way of grasping the first form is to try to *hear* its identity with the last form.

Sometimes, the stretch of the variable between x_1 and x_2 is unnoticed, not because of our lack of observation, but because the intermediates do not exist in a sense in which we understand existence in our problem, that is, $f(x)$ has no values for those values of x. In this case, $f(x)$ may be defined for the gap by imagination, hypothesis, or actual creation.

Thus, we find animals differ in species abruptly. But in the probable previous existence of missing links, we find an evidence and gain a comprehension of the continuity[①] of evolution and the identity of origin of the whole animal kingdom.

The popular notion of the difference between animals and plants is that animals move and react to stimuli, while plants do not. Now aside from some lower plants and the sensitive plants, all plants do react to stimuli too. A strong light thrown sidewise on a plant will make it turn toward it in a short time. But this short time is a matter of hours, while the reaction time of animals is a matter of a second; and the difference is striking because we do not find many organisms with reaction time of the order of a minute. But, bridging over this gap by purely imaginary reaction time, whose statistical ordinates are zeroes, we gain a conception of the identity of the two, so far as the fact of reaction is concerned.

We find that the shortest waves in ultra-violet radiations are about 500×10^{-8} cm. , while the longest waves of $X-$ rays are about 20×10^{-8} cm. What the electromagnetic wave theory of both kinds of radiations does is to see an identity of the two kinds of waves in important respects over the gap of intermediate wave lengths.

---

① Taken in a sense wide enough to include mutation.

5. Identity over Small Increments δ: " Continuous Mathematical Induction"

The mathematics and psychology of identity over a small increment δ are of special interest. Suppose we have two stimuli x_1 and x_2, where $x_2 - x_1 = \delta$ is less than the difference limen of sensation ε. Then x_1 and x_2 are identical in that they give the same sensation. If now we take $x_3 = x_2 + \delta$, then x_2 and x_3 are again identical in giving the same sensation. But if $2\delta > \varepsilon$, then x_1 and x_3 will not give the same sensation. Here, then, is a case where qualified identity is not a transitive relation.

This is only one side of the question. The other side is that when a similar logical situation is applied to cases where there is no such limitation of an ε which automatically calls out "different", then the force of inertia, cumulative habit, consistency of principle, and the like will be able to wedge in thru imperceptible increments until no differences amount to a difference before we know it. (Cf. last section)

The mathematics of this I might formulate in a theorem which I shall call for want of a better name "continuous mathematical induction". The statement follows:

1) Let the propositional function $\varphi(x)$ be true for $x = a$;

2) Let there be a limen Δ for the interval concerned, such that $\varphi(x')$ implies $\varphi(x + \delta)$ for any δ between 0 and Δ, inclusive.

3) Then $\varphi(x')$ is true for any value of x in the interval concerned beyond the point a.

Proof. —Let b be any value of x greater than a. If it exceeds a by not more than Δ, then, by 2), the conclusion follows.

If it does, then *apply Archimedes' Postulate*, namely, that the difference $b-a$ can be covered by a sufficient number of Δ's plus a fraction $\theta\Delta$ (Fig. 29), i.e., there is an integer n and a proper fraction θ, such that

$$b - a = (n + \theta)\Delta$$

or, $$b = (a + \theta\Delta) + n\Delta.$$

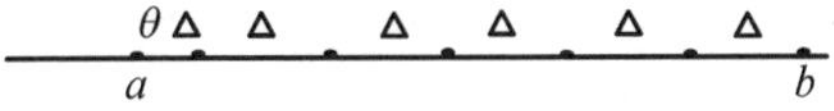

Fig. 29

Next, *apply ordinary mathematical induction*:

Ⅰ. By hypotheses 1) and 2), $\varphi(a + \theta\Delta)$ will be true.

∴ by 2) again, $\varphi(a + \theta\Delta + 1 \cdot \Delta)$ is true.

(The minor premise is established for $n=1$.)

Ⅱ. By 2), if $\varphi(a + \theta\Delta + r \cdot \Delta)$ is true, where r is an integer, then it will be true for $r+1$. (The major premise)

Ⅲ. Therefore, according to ordinary mathematical induction, $\varphi(a + \theta\Delta + n\Delta)$ is true, that is, $\varphi(b)$ is true Q. E. D.

The rigor and generality[①] of the theorem could easily be increased at the expense of brevity and perspective. But it suffices to say here that the strength and weakness of it lies in the second hypothesis, which will not be fulfilled in negative cases like the difference limen ε being exceeded. Now to come back to applications:

We let in the camel's nose thru the opening of the tent. This hardly differs from not letting him in. Yet, once the first part is admitted, he asserts the second hypothesis that there is no reason

---

① This theorem stated in terms of a propositional function is already more general than if it were treated from the point of view of the continuity of cases. (Cf. p. 275)

why he should not be admitted a little more, and more, and more, until his entire identity steps inside over the threshold.

A piece of bamboo may be hard to split. But if the thin end of a wedge is once driven in, the thick end follows, whence the Chinese expression, "with the impetus of splitting bamboo".

Drinking half a glass of beer is harmless and allowable. After the first half glass, there [is] no reason why I should not take another sip, and another, and another ... As the δ's multiply, it is easier and easier to attain any number b of glasses by means of Archimedes' postulate.

Using a public one cent stamp for private correspondence seems to be trivial enough. But then I might as well use two, or use a public penny that comes handy, and so on; and the burden is on me to prove my ability to dam up my fall toward corruption after the dam is once broken.

We smile at white lies. But are there white lies so pure but are tainted with some grade of grayness? From exaggerating an incident for the altruistic purpose of pleasing somebody, thru saying a literal truth with the effect of misleading, to a plain black lie, there can be a finite number of finite Δ's, each of which makes no difference, but the sum of which does make a difference, over which the identity of indiscriminating habit runs with great momentum.

In beginning something, such as breaking a habit, starting a work, or trying to make the best of everything, one often says, I shall begin to-morrow, or in the near future. To be sure, the effect of a delay of a short time may be below the threshold of importance. But we live in a world where one to-morrow begets another to-morrow and one future another future. The peculiar thing is that to-day's to-day is to-day, but to-morrow's to-morrow is not to-morrow; now's now is now, but near future's near future is not near future. Hence, the safest attitude to take is to *see* a continuity and *suspect* an identity between to-morrow and the positive half of eternity.

In all these examples, *A* and *B* have such an obvious *difference of result*, that it seems that intelligent discrimination ought to be able to find a limen ε beyond which δ's shall not be multiplied. Yet our psychological inertia, habit, etc. , tends to make the second hypothesis of the continuous induction come true, so that an *identity of practise* tends to be realized. Hence it is safer and easier to treat *A* just the same as *B*. To the general question as to when the advantage of intelligent discrimination overweighs the consideration of safety or *vice versa* , one can only give the general answer: "It depends". Hypotheses are not verified by mathematics.

6. Identity of Singular Point ξ

Having treated identities over different parts of a scale, we shall consider cases where the interest is in the identity of a point itself with other points, as the identity of a parabola with ellipses and hyperbolas in those properties that are common to all conic sections. In such a problem, we may simply take this point and one side of the scale. Then the point appears to be at the end of the new scale, and it can be transformed so that it is the unity or infinity or zero of the scale to suit our convenience. We have therefore the problem of identity and difference of limiting points, which was treated in Chapter V. The respects in which a limiting point may be identical with the rest of the series was treated in section 2 (pp. 216ff), especially paragraph (2) on significant generalization. Not to repeat things, I shall treat here only a few new cases.

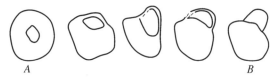

Fig. 30

Topological relations, again, often remain identical in limiting cases. Thus, a ring region of complex variables can be gradually varied as in Fig. 30, until finally we have a simple region with a mere filament added to it. And it can be shown, but it cannot be taken for granted without being shown, that certain theorems about complex variables true for A remain true for B.

This kind of reasoning by continuity to a limiting point is often used by Galileo in his mechanics. He finds that a ball rolling down an inclined plane from a certain height will roll up another plane to the same height, therefore the less steep the second plane the farther the ball will go before it stops. In the limits, so reasons Galileo, if the plane is horizontal, the ball will go on forever except for the resistance from frictions. He is therefore implicitly announcing here Newton's law of inertia.

Now since friction is an annoyance, he experimented with falling bodies in different media, and finding that the difference of speed becomes less and less with rarer and rarer medium, he concluded cautiously that "We are justified in believing it highly probable that in a vacuum all bodies would fall with the same speed."[1]

---

[1]　Galileo, *Dialogue Concerning Two New Sciences*, Eng. Transl. , p. 72.

A point in a series often appears to be singular because it happens to be our standpoint for the moment. But it may not be singular in any other respect. So it is a good policy to be very scrupulous about inferring other singularities from this subjective standpoint, and to try instead to see identities thru it.

Thus the present seems to be peculiar because I am now at present, but is it peculiar in any sense over and above the mere peculiarity of my being in it now?

If events have taken a certain course, one tends to find this event different from all previous ones. Yes, of course, but different in what sense and to what extent? Take a uniformly accelerated falling body. After falling thru a distance, at point A in the distance-time curve (Fig. 31), let us

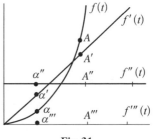

Fig. 31

suppose that it becomes interested in its own affairs, and says, "Now my condition is different from all previous ones so far. I have traveled more distance than ever before, and my speed is greater than ever before. " So far, so good. But from this it has no right to infer that the force acting on it now is any different from what it was before. As a matter of fact, it is the same force all the time. And as to the *change* of force, it has always been zero. Thus in Fig. 31, distance A is singular in being greater than all previous α's, in that its first derivative A' (velocity) is greater than all the α'' s, but it is *identical* with previous conditions in that $A'' = \alpha''$, and $A''' = \alpha''' = 0$. In short, this is saying nothing more than repeating the familiar equations of falling bodies:

$$f(t) = 1/2at^2$$
$$f'(t) = at$$
$$f''(t) = a$$
$$f'''(t) = 0.$$

In considering historical series, one also tends to forget where difference ceases and identity begins. "Our age is the age of high cost of living." "Our age is the age of science." Every age says, "Our age is at the zenith of enlightenment." How can any progress of any great account be made when we have accomplished so much now? "The question is," To which n^{th} derivative is our enlightenment more enlightened than all previous enlightenments?

Newspapers make a specialty of insinuating a singularity of things where singularity has ceased. "Such and such athletes have broken all previous records. Moreover, more records were broken at this contest than at any previous contest." But such a report might be repeated from year to year. Every time I take a step, I break my record of my lifelong distance walk.

If a person has made many friends, there might be a time when one would say, "I love *her* (or *him*) more than anyone else so far." But is it methodologically sufficient to conclude as to any significant singularity of the point on no further than this mere formal ground?

If one has had a certain trend of progress in some undertaking, one often tends to consider that after "the present", there will be a radical change of luck. But this change, the possible, is not to be waited for, but to be worked for. If I have been paying my correspondence debts at the rate of three out to every four in, the burden of practical proof is on me to expect to clear up my debts within a finite length of time from to-day on.

The argument by continuous mathematical induction may also take the form of urging an identity under a singularity of standpoint. The present temptation seems to be especially excusable. "This will be my last offense, and there can be only one last offense. " But I have to show that this is the last in a sense in which it is not identical with future offenses as just one of a series of lasts.

"This will be my last illness," says the chronic pessimist. Maybe. But in what ways is it any different from previous illnesses?

"This will be the last war," say we optimists. Maybe. But not on the ground that this has been the last war so far, which every war must be when it is waged. If we find singularities in further respects, such as the development of humanitarian ideals, facilities of communication and increased understanding among peoples, progress of world organization, self-consciousness of history, if any, etc. , such that their resultant effect will bring the world over the threshold of war prevention, then well and good. If not, not.

But one qualification must be added. If we set up a problem outside of ourselves, such as watching a stone falling from a safe distance, and asking whether the acceleration of its downfall is changed or not, we can stop with saying, "If not, not". That is where the singularity ends and identity begins, and I accept it as a fact. But if I have been falling from a wrecked aeroplane and find that I am having a constant acceleration, or at least a constant high velocity (owing to air resistance), then l am *inside* the problem, and if identity exists where I want a singularity, I may create one from now on. If I am prepared, I may open a parachute, so that from now on my speed shall be greatly changed. And this parachute may be made of an extra effort to have no more last offenses, or made of a league to enforce peace, or what not, as well as of cloth. Here, then is a new meaning of making a difference thru continuity ad hoc, or by mere fiat. A logical fiat is only a tautology, but the fiats of nature and man will make non-tautological differences over intervals of identity and furnish materials for the next chapter.

CHAPTER VII   DIFFERENCE THRU CONTINUITY

Corresponding to the general statement of identity thru continuity, we shall now speak of the difference of A from B with reference to a dividing point ξ, or an interval x, thru the continuity of x, within an identity K, which underlies the difference. Thus, we have difference of white from black with reference to the dividing point of middle gray or the intermediate grays, thru continuity of the gray series, within the identity of the neutrality of hue.

If a treatment of difference parallel to that of identity were adopted, the whole chapter might be disposed of by a repetition of the same headings and the same examples as in the last chapter. Thus,

1. Zero. —The legal status of two colliding automobiles will be different according as the speed of one automobile is on one or the other side of zero.

2. Singular Point. —Water and ice are different on different sides of 32°F.

3. Threshold. —Tones are not beats.

4. Interval. —Man is not ape.

5. Continuous induction. —An appointment for to-morrow is different from an appointment for never.

6. Of Singular Point. —The present is unique as present for all that. However, in order not to force the matter to suit the form

for the sake of uniformity, the previous headings will be subdivided, combined, cut across, and reordered in this chapter.

To state difference thru continuity as a *problem*, we are given two things that may pass insensibly into each other when a certain variable, such as time, length, speed, temperature, varies. It is asked, in what interesting respects, for what purpose, and where should we draw the line of distinction? As will be illustrated in all the following cases, such an act of drawing a line of distinction consists in a transformation of A and B as function of x into a new function of two values, of which A has one and B has the other, whereas in the last chapter the situation was to put A and B into one class K.

1. Interval of Difference, *x*

To begin with obvious cases, let us consider differences arising from a wide difference of degree, where, owing to a lack of foresight, intentional limitation of problem, or factual gap, the question of "drawing a line" in the intermediates is not raised. More strictly, I should say that here the question of marking a point is not raised. For is not a difference thru an interval a difference that is made by drawing a line (lengthwise)?

An important class of cases is where small fluctuations of a curve are distinguished from larger sweeps. Thus, the annual fluctuation of health due to seasonal changes are easily distinguishable from the general trend of improved health due to consistent care, or of impaired health due to persistent wear. The general question of identity of fluctuations and trend as raised in the last chapter (p. 248, Fig. 27) is not raised here, because intermediate kinds of variation do not occur in this health problem.

Similarly, the rotation of the earth is distinguishable from its precession. Individual accents in a musical passage are recognizable over and above a general *crescendo* or a *diminuendo*, Little ripples are seen riding on large swells (Cf. p. 272). It has been asked, "Since the Chinese language makes inflections of pitch a philological part of the words themselves, how can it use variations of pitch for purposes of expression?" The answer is that a Chinese orator can let his voice roll up and down in waves, at the same time that the individual syllables make ripples, whichever part of the wave their average pitch happens to fall on.

As examples of a statistical gap, the differences between the reaction times of plants and animals, between waves lengths of light and X-rays, and between different species, have been mentioned in the last chapter. Whatever ethical grounds we have for using animal labor and consuming meat, the problem is certainly much simplified by the gap between man and beast. What rights should the missing links be entitled to if they should all live to-day? The question, if not unanswerable, would then have to be answered.

Since the choice of the scale x is a matter of intellectual discretion, and the functionality of A and B with respect to x is a matter of approximation (see Chapter III on Graded Ideas, p. 190ff), it may turn out that the point on the scale x does not determine the function sufficiently. For instance, corresponding to a length of 200 words, we may have an anecdote or a short story. But if we see a statistical distribution with two maxima, then it will suggest a distinction, even tho there is no gap between the maxima. The problem can then be studied with reference to other variables. Thus, by reconsidering our variable, we may, for instance, conclude that an anecdote has only one point to make, while a short story has several conflicting elements to work out. Again, in experiments on the so-called natural simple reaction in psychology, it is found that there are two maxima in the distribution of reaction times, which on further examination prove to correspond to muscular and sensory reactions.

In his book on *Sex and Character*, O. Weininger says that the male and female differ simply in the ratio of two kinds of characters which exist both in the so-called males and females. His point, however, would be exaggerated if one were to forget that in the statistical distribution of the ratio, the normal individuals are either predominantly one or the other.

2. Steep Curves

In the preceding section, we have a region of doubt that does not enter into the limited problem. If this region is narrow enough to be negligible with respect to a problem, then we have a practical discontinuity. Thus, if we mix hydrogen and oxygen in a flask, pass a spark in it, we shall find water immediately afterwards, if we live to examine it. The flask, being made of elastic substance, is of course first strained by degrees until the breaking point is reached, when the pieces begin to separate from each other gradually. But, for many purposes, this gradualness is so steep that we call it a discontinuous jump, which marks a point of distinction between a flask and broken piece of glass.

If we throw up a chair at a drop lamp, there is a range of velocities where the chair will touch the lamp lightly, but not break it. This can be verified by carrying the chair to the height of the lamp and knocking it gently against it. But this safety range is so small compared with the variations uncontrollable that throwing is capable of, that we can practically say that a chair either does not touch the lamp, or will break it if it touches it at all.

In the last chapter (p. 240), the surface of the earth is considered as a singular point, marking a difference between the law of direct-distance inside and the law of inverse-square outside. But if we actually bore a hole of finite size with a body falling from above to below, the change of the force, that is, of the second derivative, will be gradual, altho it looks like a jump if we draw it on a scale of a lunar distance to the foot.

From this point of view, we also find a relative justification for the use of the term "discontinuity" in speaking of adolescence, which marks apart periods of one's life by a very steep curve. The phenomenon of biological mutation was spoken of as part of the continuity of evolution (footnote, p. 251, Chapter VI). But talking in another order of magnitude, mutation is steep enough to be called a jump.

3. Stable Equilibrium

Why, it may be asked, are things separated by intervals or by steep variations? Perhaps some light may be had by a study of a generalized conception of equilibriun 1, in so far as it bears on the problem of difference. To put it schematically, we may let x represent a generalized variable (which need not be spatial), and y a generalized "potential", which tends (physically, socially, etc.) to be a minimum. The rate of variation, or the slope of the $y - x$ curve, will then represent the generalized "force", which measures the tendency to go down hill.

In Fig. 1, of balls on hills, A is in "stable equilibrium", in

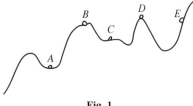

Fig. 1

that if it is slightly displaced, it will return to the valley. *B* is also in stable equilibrium, tho the "base" within which it may be displaced and return is small. *C* is in "neutral equilibrium", in that it is not urged forward or brought back, by any force, but remains neutral. *D* is in "unstable equilibrium", in that if it is displaced, however slightly, the displacement will be favored by a force, so that it will tumble down hill. *E* is not in equilibrium, as there is a force urging it to move down. So much, then, for what is familiar ground.

If now a shower falls on these hills, is it not evident that the drops will be automatically classified by the valleys into which they tumble. separated by the water-sheds? Centers of stable equilibrium, then, furnish the unity or identity of a class, separated from the other classes.

In chemical reactions, there are hypothetically many intermediate kinds of compounds, and in radio-activity, there are also hypothetical elements formed. But only those compounds and elements that are in stable equilibrium are identified and named. Hence we find the distinct kinds of substances, that do not merge into each other. The sharply marked characteristics of crystals, and biological phenomena like the regularity of phyllotaxis come under the same idea on higher planes of complexity.

In the production of tones from brass or wood wind instruments, or in fact of any "stationary waves" in physical phenomena, there are only certain definite frequencies, differing from each other by discontinuous steps, that can be kept up. A horn player may try to "coax" his instrument to produce a slight displacement of the pitch, but he cannot perpetrate the sort of *legato* effect that a trombone clown is capable of. But how does a serious trombone player, or a violinist, or a singer produce exactly those diatonic or chromatic notes? It is sometimes said that musicians of this class have an infinitely more difficult task than musicians of keyed instruments, because, out of an infinitely number of wrong notes, they have to hit the only one that is right. But from the point of view of stable equilibrium, they are not so badly of or so admirable as they seem. The singer acquires by training certain centers of equilibrium of relative pitch from which he deviates slightly in actual singing, but if he has learned accurate intonation, the deviation will not go beyond a base of equilibrium beyond which the singer will feel a need of readjustment or the listener will feel a need of correction. We think the Javese *equally* divided pentatonic scale to be unthinkable, because the Javese are trained to distinguish and center around notes which are unstable for those differently trained.

Similarly, continuous gradations of phonetic sounds can be produced by continuous gradations of the positions of the speech organs. But in any given language, there are a small number of centers of habitual equilibrium from which a native speaker does not deviate beyond a limit. If he wants to learn a foreign language with good accent, he will have to acquire new centers of stable equilibrium, just as a European ear trying to learn the Javese scale. If the new centers are near his native ones, it will be very difficult to acquire. To pronounce "sir" as "soeur", or "parlez-vous français?" as "parley voo frongsay?" simply amounts to using the nearest old centers of equilibrium as substitutes for new centers, whence the phenomenon of foreign accent. A polyglotte is one who has acquired many centers of equilibrium which he can keep stable and distinct.

A stable center may also be established in nonhabitual matters by discretion. The drawing of a line as between a lawful and an unlawful act, or a moral and an immoral act in many instances may not be consistent. But if a person is bent on being lawful or moral, he will not deviate far from a stable average of judgment.

As a general example, we might say that ideas or conceptions get settled by their logical or methological stability. Here we may regard variations of their definition as displacements, and the unnaturalness or cumbersomeness as the potential. Thus, the conception of "friend" is fairly stable, let us hope; but if I define my friends as the class of my friends as ordinarily understood plus my pet dog, then this deviation will result in the frequency of use of such expressions as "my friends except my dog" and the relative infrequency of the expression "my friends". In this condition of a logical strain, there is a logical force tending back toward the point of stable equilibrium. Perhaps the finding of centers of logical stable equilibrium is an aspect of all problems of definitions. (Cf. Chapter IV. pp. 204ff.).

4. Unstable Equilibrium

(1) If things gather around centers of stable equilibrium, what about things in unstable or neutral equilibrium? If a hail stone is lodged on the ridge of a water-shed or a level slab, which valley does it belong to? Here let us apply the method of gradations and limiting points. In Fig. 2, A is evidently in stable equilibrium. So is B. C has a very small base of stability. For instance, the hail

stone might be lodged in a small shallow crack in a rock. In the limit, when the base approaches zero, we have D in unstable equilibrium. Now it is only by abstraction for any concrete problem that we call a certain potential y as a function of x. In Chapter IV, p. 209, I tried to show that a function is only an ideal limit in which one factor (or a very few) is predominant, and all the rest that cause slight variations are considered irrelevant. And the same remarks apply to neutral equilibrium. If, now, a hail stone rests on a smooth convex ridge of a mountain range, or on a smooth slab on the ridge, the primary factors of gravity become practically zero, and the so-called secondary · factors become primary. A gust of wind, for instance, may blow it over to one side or the other. Hence the thing in unstable or neutral equilibrium is really not in equilibriun 1 at all, but on the *slope* of a curve, that is, under a force, which is too small to push its base when it is in primary stable equilibrium, or to show any additional effect when it is on a primary slope, but does make a difference when the primary factor is balanced.

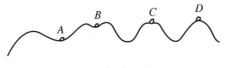

Fig. 2

On the other hand, if the air is still and the earth is not whirling too violently, the molecular roughness of the smooth stone and the smooth hail stone may still be sufficient to keep the latter unmoved. But then this is only a stable equilibrium over again, only with a very small base of stability.

Hence, in general, we can say that a thing is either in stable equilibrium or not in equilibrium at all. Following the distinction of unique thresholds (pp. 223 – 226) we can say that a stable equilibrium on top of a hill which can be upset by factors regarded as accidental or irrelevant from the point of view of a problem will be called an unstable equilibrium in that problem.

The application of this result to making differences is this. We can reformulate our problem by admitting new factors, and this refinement can be carried on indefinitely. But if we think that it has been carried far enough for our problem and yet a seeming case of unstable equilibrium arises. we can say that a toss of a coin will be good enough to decide the case. A decision, whether of action or bringing up a decimal, is therefore always possible, unless we make the limiting demand that an infinite number of possible factors should exactly balance, which we need never make in any finite problem.

Thus, a ball player between two bases will run one way or the other and will not rest there because the chances of getting caught at either base seem to be equal. A walker looking for a trolley car will not tarry slowly between two stops because the chance of missing a car at one is the same as at the other. Buridan's ass between the hay and the water may be equally hungry and thirsty, if such a case were possible, but a gentle breeze from the side of the hay will attract him slightly to one side and then the unstable equilibrium ceases to be an equilibrium. An infinite number of factors can exactly balance only in a scholastic universe of discourse.

(2) In the spirit of continuity, one might say that every little counts, but more carefully, one should say that every little *may* count, but need not count, unless it is enough to cross a ridge, or

threshold of difference. In physiology, there is the principle of "all or nothing"[①], according to which if the nerve of a muscle is stimulated, the muscle will not respond at all until the intensity attains a minimum threshold beyond which it will respond with full force. Similarly, to light a candle for a plant kept indoors is of absolutely no help to its metabolism. For, below 1/100 part of the normal light that a plant receives, any light is as good as no light. Again, slowly oozing water will not fall until the weight of the water exceeds the hold of its surface tension, when the whole drop comes off. Electric charge gather relatively continuously from the combs of a static machine, but will discharge by units across the knobs. According to the quantum theory of radiation, energy is continuously absorbed, but when gathered to a degree which its carrier cannot hold, it will be radiated as a unit.

(3) A point of unstable equilibrium may be crossed by the multiplication of a secondary factor connected with the primary factor by a sort of trigger or lever action. Thus, to describe slowly the mechanism in a cycle of the motion picture or the gas engine amounts to reducing the speed from without to within our conscious span. Similarly, our ability of doing things may be multiplied from below a required threshold to above it. I cannot raise a stone, but I can use a lever to multiply my force. I cannot draw accurately an angle of 30°, but by first drawing (freehand) an equilateral triangle and then bisecting it, I get a resulting 30° which is much more accurate than a direct estimation. It is in fact a study worth carrying out to develop a technique of "freehand geometrical drawing" by using analytic leverage, so to speak. Again, the result

---

① See W. M. Bayliss, *Principles of General Physiology*, 1914, p. 383.

of one's will power may be increased by establishing trigger connections. I cannot stop playing on the piano once I have started, I cannot easily refrain from starting to play with the piano open before me. But it may be within my will power to lock up the piano and give the key to a friend. Then the unattainable result is attained by a sort of moral leverage.

In general, all *method* can be regarded as leverage, as shown in Chapter II. Given a required standard S (Fig. 3) and a finite trigger A to work with, be it judgment, skill, will, force, good intentions, or what not. The problem of method will then consist in establishing such connections that A shall be multiplied to point B beyond S, or, in analytic language, A shall be transformed into B. This same point was raised in the chapter on Limiting Points (p. 222) where the emphasis was on the

Fig. 3

difference of A from zero, that is, of something from nothing, compared with which it seems to be infinite. Here, the emphasis is on the difference of A from B with respect to the Standard S, that is, of the given from the elaborated.

5. Difference with Respect to Singular Points

Singular points in general need not be points of unstable equilibrium except in a formal sense. Thus, take any series x, take any point point a. We may by a mere formal fiat, call it a singular point, having the properties of an unstable equilibrium, tho there may not be any dynamic character in the kind of variables involved. Let us take the function

$$f(x) = \frac{2}{\pi} \tan^{-1} [n(x-a)]$$

where $\tan^{-1}$ is taken in the first quardrant, and n is a large number relative to the problem. Then a point $a - \eta$, a little to the left of a, will result in A, nearly equal to -1, and a point $a + \eta$, a little to the right of a, will result in B, nearly equal to $+1$. In the limit,

$$f(x) = \frac{2}{\pi} \lim_{n=\infty} \tan^{-1}[n(x - a)]$$

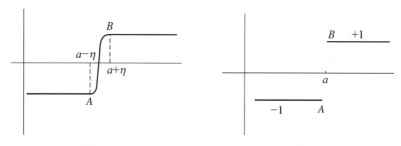

Fig. 4   Fig. 5

which is the signum function sgn $(x - a)$[1], as shown in Fig. 5, where any point to the left of a slides right into -1, and point to the right of a slides into $+1$, no matter how small a trigger $-\eta$ or $+\eta$ we start with. This is an analytic way of saying, in plainer language, that we can arbitrarily take any point as a dividing point, so that anything on one side of it, however near, we put in one class, and anything on the other side we put in the other class. This is the lower limit of the significance of difference (see last chapter p. 233 on the Egyptian pyramid). In cases of unstable equilibrium, significant dynamic factors enter as variables. In this section, other cases of significant differences will be considered.

We see some things called waves and others called ripples,

---

[1]   See Pierpont, *Theory of Function of Real Variables*, vol. I, p. 202.

differing most strikingly in their lengths, as already discust in section 1 of this chapter. On further investigation, we find all intermediate lengths. We notice next that waves travel at different speeds, small ripples overtaking large ones. Further, we find that waves are propagated both by surface tension and by weight and inertia, and that above a certain length (about 1.6cm. for water) of minimum speed, the longer the wave the faster it travels, and below the point, the opposite is true. We thus propose to make this point a neutral point, and call all disturbances longer than this "waves" and those shorter than this "ripples". The algebraic sign of the change of speed on each side of the dividing point serves therefore as the trigger in the logical unstable equilibrium, and this difference of classification *may* lead to finite differences of action or happening.

Again in going thru a continuous spectrum from red thru yellow to green, we pass a point in the yellow, when there is a change in the "direction" of the shading, as represented by a corner in the color pyramid. This singular point, therefore, marks a significant difference between two parts of a series.

In the last chapter, red and verdigris were said to be identical tho different. Here, then, the point is simply that red and verdigris, tho identical, are different with respect to the dividing point of zero saturation. If we are sorting yarns into two baskets, a slight tinge of one or the other hue will lead to a finite difference of the fate of the yarn.

The defense of formal differences is that they may cover significant differences in many respects. But by a psychological or legal action, an arbitrary distinction *is* a distinction of fact the moment it is made. In the situation of a continuous induction, emphasis was laid on the identity of a with b, the second hypothesis says, "There is no reason why I should not do this another to-morrow rather than this next to-morrow." But I can say, "I call the seventeenth to-morrow a singular day and will make it singular by actually starting that work on that day." And of course singular it *will* be if my will is strong enough to carry it out in fact. In general, since every point is peculiar in some respect, it is possible to defeat the second hypothesis by either seizing every opportunity to stop a dreaded induction, or by fearing a hitch that might invalidate a desired induction. To "There is no reason why not." answer, "There is no reason why."

Convention and law can also make a material distinction out of a formal one. A few decades ago. line was drawn near the 180° meridian, such that at any point in its east neighborhood, the time shall read 24 hours less than any point in its west neighborhood. There is no geographical mark that an explorer can discover on the international date line, but when questions of schedules, dates, telegraphic communications are concerned, there will be actual finite differences. We have also a case of factual distinction in name when we change from daylight time to daylight-saving time. The setting of a clock from 2 A. M. to 3 A. M. on a certain day is of course only a case of a steep curve in the motion of the clock hands, but this continuity is not relevant to the legal significance of the singular point.

6. Limitations of Differences

A significant difference is more than what it is merely called to be, but less than what it is not. It is therefore important to look at the other side of the question again for a moment.

(1) *Continuity of Cases*. —In testing the validity of a proposed distinction, one should keep in mind the open possibility that by examining intermediate cases, there may or may not be a discontinuity as the problem stands without transformation. Unless a clear mark is shown, it is well to apply the continuity of cases. Thus, in the example of the Cartesian theory of impact discust in the last chapter, a singular point at zero is proposed, such that a slight trigger difference of the masses in one or the other direction makes the whole thing move one way or the other with a finite difference of velocity of $2v$. If speed or momentum is a continuous function of the mass differences, it ought to have a small change for small difference of cases. This is in fact Leibniz's argument[1] against the Cartesian theory. Philosophically, Leibniz says that nature is continuous, that therefore Descartes is wrong. But methodologically, one may be contented with saying that a function in a prescribed problem *may* be continuous, and (*if* so) Descartes *may* be wrong, which he is, on further factual grounds in mechanics.

In arguing[2] against the Aristotelian theory that heavier bodies fall faster, Galileo supposed that two bodies of different weights are joined together, and reasoned that since body a moves with speed A and the heavier body b moves with a greater speed B, the two will move with a speed between A and B, and not greater than B, as the Aristotelian theory would require, from its own premises. To pose as an Aristotelian, I might answer that two

---

[1]　Letter to Pierre Bayle, 1687, in *Philosophical works of Leibniz*, tr. by G. M. Duncan 1890, pp. 33 – 34.

[2]　Galileo, *Dialogues Concerning Two New Sciences*, Eng. Trans. , p. 63.

bodies joined as one really act as one and the reasoning applied to the compromising effect between the two parts do not hold. And an up-to-date Aristotelian might cite the fact that we cannot reason about the electric action of two separate conductors in the same way as when they are joined together by the least contact. The weight of Galileo's argument is felt only when we ask what is the difference between being joined and not being joined, and show that as two balls are joined in different cases by a single filament of a cobweb, a string, a chain, a crossbar, by soldering, the mechanical difference of result, will be, as a matter of fact, gradual and not like that of electric connections. This *reductio ad absur dum* therefore rests on a suggested continuity of cases confirmed by fact, as against the existence of a singularity, which is implied by the Aristotelian theory, but which does not exist.

It is stated in aerodynamics that air resistance to an aeroplane below 100 miles an hour is proportional to the square of the velocity, and above 100 miles, to the cube of the velocity. This is a valid difference of formulas within certain limits, but by the continuity of cases, we find that the 100 miles velocity is a singular point only by technological convention and not singular according refined physical measurement. For the variation of resistance with speed around 100 miles an hour is not an abrupt or even a steep change, but the exponent y in

$$\text{Resistance} = Cv^y$$

is already greater than 2 when v is nearly 100, and not quite 3 when v

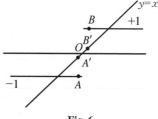

Fig. 6

has just passed 100.

(2) *New Variable*. —A difference may be limited by the fact that a clear distinction with reference to one set of variables may merge continuously or become constant when other variables are considered. Thus, analytically, in

$$y = sgn\, x$$

A and B are clearly marked by the dividing point 0 (Fig. 6). But in

$$y = (sgn\, x) \cdot |\, x\, |,$$

which amounts to

$$y = x,$$

A' and B' are less and less different near 0. This is simply referring finite differences back to their triggers. Another simple transformation, and we have identity over again.

A loss of singularity may also come from a transformation of the independent variable x. Thus, the freezing point of water marks the difference between water and ice. Below it, we have no water and 100% ice, above it we have no ice and 100% water (Fig. 7). But if we consider the heat instead of the temperature as the x, then, as heat is added to the ice, there will be intermediate proportions as shown in Fig. 8, so that the singular point is stretched out into a continuous curve by introducing another variable. Again, in a chemical change from one substance into another, if we pass a point spatially from a mass of one to a mass of the other substance, we find no intermediate, but a distinct change in crossing the boundary. But if we consider the *time* it takes one quantity to change into the other, we shall find that the change is a continuous function.

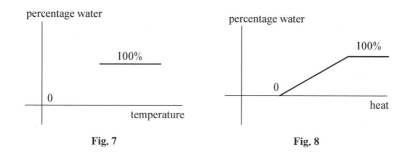

Fig. 7   Fig. 8

7. Difference of Singular Points

We shall now come back to the question as to where the singular point itself belongs, partly answered under the treatment of unstable equilibriums.

(1) *"In Case of Doubt"*. —We often hear decisions like these:

Vessels sailing in the same channel shall pass on port side of each other, but vessels may pass on their starboard if they are far apart. In case of doubt, pass on the port side.

Don't eat between meals unless really hungry. In case of doubt, don't.

Don't cross if the automobile is near, cross if far. In case of doubt, don't.

I shall buy a stop watch or a gold watch according as which is cheaper. "Other things being equal", I prefer a stop watch.

Nominally, we have settled the singular point. But what if it is doubtful whether it is a case of doubt? Call this doubtful? Then what if it is doubtful whether it is doubtful to the second degree? This doubt is evidently endless. More concretely, suppose we judge contestants in an oration by the material alone. In case of equality, the better language counts. In case of further equality, the better delivery counts. In case of further equality, the better drest counts, and so on. In other words, we have the situation of secondary factors becoming primary thru balance of the primary factors, as described above under unstable equilibrium, and the practical conclusion was that we can either settle it by introducing a few more factors, or if doubt, still continues, decide by discretion or chance, trusting the safety of the statistical average of the results. Thus a tongue that has not been addicted to candy and ice cream will have a safe average interpretation of "doubt" in not eating between meals in cases of doubtful hunger.

(2) *Zero of Functions.* —In the last section, the point considered is in a kind of unstable equilibrium, where the point must tumble down one way or the other, however trivial the trigger. Two vessels heading toward each other passing neither on the port nor on the starboard will simply collide, which is again a case of unstable equilibrium, tho in terms of another set of variables. But if we have a situation with formal analogy to a stable equilibrium, where a slight deviation one side or the other of a point makes a difference small enough to be called zero, then we can single out this singular point as a class by itself. (Cf. above on stable equilibrium as a center of classification). This is especially amenable to treatment by the property of a continuous function that it passes thru all intermediate values. If a function $f(x)$ is continuous, and

$$f(a) < 0, \ and \ f(b) > 0,$$

then somewhere between a and b, there is a point ξ, such that

$$f(\xi) = 0$$

where ξ may be a singular point of interest by itself (Fig. 9).

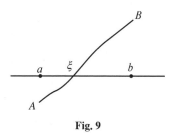

Fig. 9

Thus, a pair of opera glasses magnifies distant things and reduces things near at hand. Therefore there must be a distance where things will appear just as large as they are thru the opera glasses.

Under a bridge, I see tide rushing down stream one part of the day and up stream another part of the day. There must then be some time when the water is still.

In hitting a base ball, if the ball comes near the hand, the bat will give a jar toward the hand; if it comes near the end of the bat, the latter will give a jar away from the hand. There must therefore be a point ξ on the bat where a ball will not jar the hand at all. This proves to be the center of percussion of the swinging bat center (Fig. 10).

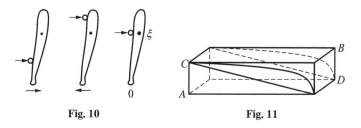

Fig. 10   Fig. 11

If we have a rectangular beam AB held at the end A (Fig. 11), its strength will weaken toward the supported end. If by a diagonal saw-cut, only the portion CD is left, the strength will increase toward the point of support. "This being so," says Galileo, "it would seem not merely reasonable, but inevitable, that there exists a line of section such that, when the superfluous material has been removed, there will remain a solid of such figure that it will offer the same resistance at all points"[1], that is, a figure in which the variation of strength will be zero. This he proves to be a parabolic section.

(3) *Zero Applied to Measurement*. —Since in many cases it is easier to judge by inspection a zero than to judge a quantity, we often use it as a method of measurement. Thus, on a rolling ship on the ocean, it is impossible to measure the angle between the horizon and the sun in a straightforward way. But here comes a sextant, which, by reflection and direct lighting, brings the sun and the horizon near together. With one adjustment, their distance is of one sign, with another adjustment another sign. Therefore, there is an adjustment where they will just touch, which can be judged by inspection with considerable accuracy.

If certain quantities have not been defined, they can be defined by being canceled by a known quantity. Thus, pb and $p'b'$, being equal in length, pb appears to be longer. How much longer? But first, what does it mean to ask how much longer? One way of defining the measure of the illusion is this: Take a point a so near p that pa appears obviously shorter than $p'b'$. Therefore there must be a point ξ such that $p\xi$ appears equal to $p'b'$. $b\xi$, then, will be the measure of the illusion. This is in fact familiar ground in psychology. (In actual experimentation, the points a, ξ, b should not appear on the same line, as in Fig. 12, which is only for a diagramatic purpose.)

---

① *Ibid*. p. 141.

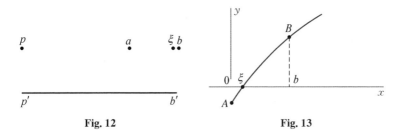

Fig. 12   Fig. 13

Again, treating yellow as minus blue, color contrast may thus be measured. Take a thin strip in a constant blue background. Let x be the blueness of the strip as seen normally, and y its blueness as seen against the background. If we take a gray strip (—its blueness $x=0$), then by contrast, it appears yellow ($y=a$ minus blue).

Hence we have the point A (Fig. 13[1]). If we take a decidedly blue strip, it will appear blue too, so we have the point B, whose y is greater than zero. If now y is a continuous function of x, there ought to be a strip of some intermediate tinge of blue, such that when it is placed in the strong blue background, it will appear gray, that is, there will be a ξ, such that

$$y = f(\xi) = 0.$$

This is in fact the method used by H. Pretori and M. Sachs[2], in color contrast, and by C. Hess and H. Pretori in brightness contrast. [3]

A general caution about such singular points which is implied in all this study, is that we must never take $y = f(x)$ in simple

① Cf. Chapter I on the diving frog.

② *Pfluger's Archiv* (*Physiol.*), vol. 60, 1895, 71ff.

③ *Archiv f. Ophthalmologie*, vol. 50, No. 4, 1894, 50ff.

strictness under all circumstances. As was said before, when the effect of primary factors become negligible, that of secondary factors will not be negligible. Thus, if a strip is not narrow enough, then near the critical point, we may have a blue strip with yellowish borders. With a pair of cheap opera glasses, there will be some critical distances where some parts of the field will be magnified and other parts reduced. There is then no clean-out zero even in a relative sense, unless we make sure that on concrete considerations, the other factors may be called by such adjectives as accidental, irrelevant, or negligible.

(4) *Limiting Points.* —The last chapter advised caution in inferring singularity in a limiting point. So this chapter should bring out the possibility of the difference of a limiting point from other points. Again, since this is treated in Chapter V, there is no need of further elaboration besides making use of some material studied thereafter.

In the argument by continuous induction in the last chapter, the motive for saying that "a little" is as bad as "much" is that "not at all" is decidedly different from "a little". "Now" is unique. "Do it now" is decidedly different from "just a second". Total abstinence is decidedly different from occasional idulgence, however moderate. To be sure, it is impossible not to take any particle of alcohol, as thru fruits, or not to inhale a particle of smoke, as at certain club meetings. But conventionally, the absence of contact with a glass or a pipe makes an absolute zero in principle.

From the point of view of equilibrium, we can gain some light as to how a singular limiting point can exist. After breaking the glass, one is in stable equilibrium at zero. But if a single sip is taken out of a glass, there will be a force pushing one down hill. We often hear that we can never be sure that water is absolutely pure, that there might be minute quantities of anything in it. Yet, if there be any particles of free sodium, for instance, it will not be in equilibrium at all, but will at once be changed into its hydroxide. So that we can be sure that a zero amount of free (uncharged) sodium in water is a singular point, which alone is one of stable equilibrium.

Certain biological or sociological forces always rush to a limiting point as the only point of stable equilibrium. A high water mark, is not merely singular in being the upper limit of water level, but it can be measured by plant growth. If plants grow above the level, they will spread down, if they grow below it, they will be killed before they have a chance to grow up. Hence they will push as far as they can.

In making rules or laws, it is always well to look out for limiting points toward which things will rush, If a public sale of a commodity in shortage is opened, the points of time are not all alike, but a crowd will rush toward that singular limit of time, which is the moment of opening.

In railroad transportation of freight, the cost of maintenance is so great that the extra expense of operation is negligible. If, therefore, two parallel line compete unlimitedly, there will be a cut-throat competition, approaching charging nothing for handling freight as a stable limit. From another point of view, say concerning the further existence of the lines, of course the point may not be one of stable equilibrium, as illustrated in the history of railroads.

8. Continuity of Nature

After going thru these actual cases of specific identities and differences, by using transformations of continuities and discontinuities into each other, one may still be tempted to ask, whether, in the last resort, nature is continuous or not. One answer is that methodology does not resort to the last. Continuity is significant, accurately or approximately, only when we have chosen our variables and function. Water-slate and temperature relation is discontinuous. Water-ice proportion and heat relation is continuous. Whether simply water and ice relation at large is continuous or discontinuous is meaningless, pending further definition. So in general, nature is neither continuous nor discontinuous. For only a function can be continuous[①], and nature as nature is not a function. We can make an aspect of nature continuous or discontinuous at liberty and at our risk by proper transformations; and the result is illuminating and useful if we succeed in laying hold of the long end of a methodological lever, and artificial and wasteful if we happen to grasp the wrong end of the lever.

The question of continuity of nature, however, is not yet dismist if we look kindly into its motives and try to make it significant by a proper statement. The most important motive is in fact concerned with continuity in time as the independent variable. To ask, "Is nature continuous?" usually means. "By going to sufficient refinements, is it always possible to express a

---

① In application, the simple continuity of one continuum may be regarded as the function $x'=x$. See Chapter I , p. 155.

measurement of any phenomenon, however, suddenly it changes, as a continuous function of time?" But what do we mean by time? In actual science, whether in physics or in psychology, time is measured by phenomena that are said to occur "in time", as rotation of the earth, flowing of sand, vibrations of a pendulum, passing of ideas, feelings of tension and relaxation. The *working* meaning of simultaneity, before and after, length of time, are all based on everyday facts of science. We can therefore say that it is methodologically sufficient to regard time as constituted by all the phenomena that have been correlated in these ways. ①

Relative discontinuity of a phenomenon y in time, then, means that if we lay an ordinary measurement t of time on y, there will be a decided difference of y without there being any appreciable difference in the measuring phenomenon t. Thus, as Galileo opened a shutter of a lantern, the light "instantly" fell on the opposite hill miles away. But by replacing the hand-operated shutter by a toothed wheel, Fizeau laid on light a phenomenon whose rate of change is not practically zero compared with that of light, hence the relative discontinuity become a relative continuity thru a reformulation of the problem.

On the other hand, the philosophical question, on the foregoing conception of time, will run: Is there any phenomenon whose change is of such an order of magnitude that no other phenomenon of change, known *or yet to be known*, measured in terms of any finite unit, could be laid against it so that for a sufficiently small difference on the measure, the corresponding

---

① The theory of relativity will affect the further elaboration of these discussions, but not the general concrete point of view.

difference in the phenomenon in question shall be made finite? But stated in this form, the only possible meaning of the question becomes meaningless. For, if the question is answered in the affirmative, our scientific practise simply excommunicates that phenomenon from the temporal order, and calls it simultaneous existence of different things, and not a discontinuous change of the same thing. Thus, assume for argument's sake that gravitaion is instantaneous, then we should simply say that there is a field of force of such and such intensities, existing at such and such points, rather than speaking of a wave or radiation as being communicated instantly. We can therefore say that nature is a continuous function of time by the very definition of time that has been found to be most serviceable. The continuity of nature, then, is not a philosophical conclusion, but arguing in a great circle around the sphere of scientific advantages.

CHAPTER VIII   CONCLUSIONS AND
FURTHER PROBLEMS

1. Summary of Results

If problem, method, and conclusion are connected "in parallel", then the best way to state the conclusions of this whole study is to point to the separate chapters and say, "Voila!" For the very statement of the problem and the very methods of procedure are part and parcel of the conclusion, and can be criticized and disputed as to validity and significance. But, for the convenience of reference, a summary will be given of the results of the chapters, as follows[①]:

I The Problem. —The idea of continuity, taken in senses with varying degrees of mathematical accuracy, is used as a guiding thread along which a methodological study is deemed to be worth undertaking.

II Methods. —Method, in general, is regarded as leverage, by which one gets more reality by starting with some reality.

The typical method in this study is to dip into the midst of concrete things, find gradations and serial order in them, examine different cases of functions outward and inward on the scale, and transform our point of view whenever we see fit.

III Graded Ideas. —When ideas are taken absolutely, try to

---

① This summary is different from the official "Summary", which may he read before or without reading the thesis.

see how significantly they also admit of degrees. Some particular conclusions are:

Example, analogy, metaphor, play of words, etc. are different grades of elements that constitute a definition of ideas.

Between a variable and a constant in mathematics, there are different stages of parameters.

A mathematical function restricted to a line is a degree of restriction of values to a tube or a band. A factor is "the" cause of a phenomenon when variations in other factors make no "appreciable" difference in the phenomenon.

IV Serial Order. —Any two things may be compared in a serial order defined at will. Serial comparability is a matter of degree.

The more truths one can state about a serial order, the more evidence it is that it has been well defined.

We are able to make non-tautological statements about serial order whenever the fluctuations of usage and accidental errors of science are below a threshold of relevance, so that we can call one thing by something other than its mere definition.

V Limiting Points. —A limiting case is at least identical in being a case, and at least different in being a *limiting* case.

The spirit of mathematics is that of the lower limit, the spirit of philosophy is that of the upper limit. Science and life occupy intermediate positions. But by the method of transformations, there are respects in which extremes meet.

The actual, the categorical, the factual, etc. in finite things has the nature of the infinite in comparison with formal nothingness.

In particular problems, upper and lower thresholds will do in

place of limits. It is therefore proposed to redefine limits as
constituted by those thresholds. This seems to be in accord with
mathematical usage. In this sense, we say, truth is the limit of
truths, meaning or definition is the limit of criteria, morality is the
limit of actual morals, etc.

An important respect in which this application of Occam's
razor differs from its usual application is that, when, for example,
objects are "reduced" to a limiting class of sense-data, I simply
take it a "playing of one part of reality against another", in which a
"mechanical advantage" may be found for certain persons or certain
problems; but that from a circular point of view, which starts
problems in the midst of things, it may very well be that in some
other problem, the definition should be turned around; for
instance, a work-a-day physicist or physiologist would find sense-
data far from being ultimate and would prefer to "reduce" them to
terms that others have just tried to reduce to sense-data.

VI Identity Thru Continuity. —Significant identity always has
a background of differences. The idea of continuity is an aid to
seeing identities, provided that a judicious choice of a variable x is
made in which things are seen to merge in some non-trivial
respect.

The background of difference may be some point of peculiar
interest, as a zero point, a wide difference of degree, or a small
difference of degree. It is also important to see the identity of the
case of one's present standpoint with other cases.

An incidental result of special mathematical interest is a
theorem of "continuous mathematical induction", which is the gist
of the argument from the thin end of the wedge. The strength of
this argument, as if all arguments, depends upon the strength of

its premises.

VII Difference Thru Continuity. —Significant difference is always within a background of identity. Difference is not mere difference, but means classification, alternate issues of events, difference of conception or feeling, and decision on courses of action.

A difference may result from a wide change of x or a steep curve, marked by singular points, especially by points of stable and unstable equilibrium.

A singular point may be different from other points in being of interest on its own account. When a quantity changes sign, the place where it does change sign may raise points of doubt, or serve as a method of measurement.

A method of reasoning that deserves more prominent emphasis is reasoning by the continuity of cases, which may be used to examine points of questionable difference.

2. General Conclusions: Their Circularity

What is the line between a difference of degree and a difference of kind? From the "point-of-view" point of view, I answer, It depends.

Is nature continuous? It also depends.

But by a conciliatory temperament and a muddling, if not muddled, intellect, I tend to see things merge into each other more than the barriers, lines and points separating them. Hence I say nature is continuous on principle, and call this thesis "Continuity". In the *same* spirit, I also grant that if a mind feels the need and fruitfulness of having more discontinuities in the intellectual world, it may go over the same ground of these chapters and call the study "Discontinuity".

In the spirit of "someness", I conclude further that no universal proposition is true except a tautological one, and that no reason is sufficient except one that is circular, that, in particular, mathematics and the exact sciences are circles in so far as they are exact.

An obvious objection to all these general conclusions is that such sweeping assertions would be a *reductio ad absurdum* of the very things asserted. From this attack, it would be easy to escape by seeking refuge under Russell and Whitehead's hierarchy of types, and say that I am speaking as a philosophy of a "higher order". But prefering to fight or retreat on my own ground, that is, to use an internal method, I simply answer that these conclusions are safe, precisely in so far as they are themselves circular.

Some circles, however, are not vicious. And it is hoped that these same general conclusions, which, if stated in the introduction, would have furnished examples of futile formalism, have, after a long application of the method of concrete cases thru these chapters, now acquired sufficient meaning to make their formal announcement on non-trivial. It is easy to see from this that these conclusions are not the "end" of this study except in a temporal sense, nor do they give "the solution of the problem of continuity", but are simply condensed reminders of various studies of problems in continuity, of which "the problem of continuity", must, in the last resort, consist.

3. Further Problems

In the introduction, I stated that this study is only a part of a general theory of functions in methodology. To undertake such a systematic study, it will be necessary to make a survey of the kinds of variables and functionality there are. The survey of variables will be a generalization of the study of dimensions of physical units. Logically, the variable may be a continuum, a dense series, a function, etc. ; mathematically, it may be a real number, a geometrical point, an angle, a subscrpit, etc. ; and in more concrete applications, it may be time, risk, intensity, good will, electric charge, difficulty, etc.

A function in mathematics is simply abstractly "defined". But in application, this functionality may have different "modes", so to speak. $y = f(x)$ may be posited by way of definition, classification, statement, question, postulate, trial hypothesis, estimation, guess, habitual conception or misconception, claim, general law, historical record, observation, discovery, feeling, obligation, legislation, command, or action. All these need to be well sorted out and looked into.

A functional relation that deserves special attention is one where some dynamic factor enters. For instance, price is a function of supply and demand, but, there is a time lag which complicates the functionality. This is a point of quite general importance.

Singular points have been treated only under identity and difference. But they are important enough to be treated on their own account. Problems of maxima and minima are especially important in economic problems. In moral problems, the "golden mean" can be generalized into a conception of the optimum point. or the optimum course, which is a problem in maxima. Different kinds of equilibra, which have only been studied under "Difference", also deserve a systematic survey.

The theory of functions in methodology may also be regarded as a kind of concrete mathematics, in which mathematical conceptions, for instance, that of a limit, are interpreted in the concrete, beyond the extent to which this has been done in mathematical physics. Some abstract possibilities which have not been touched in this study are cyclic or periodic series, like the year, complex numbers, n-dimensional functions of n variables, generalized coordinates, projective relations in abstract geometry, and properties of "groups". Concrete mathematics, again, is only a method and not a doctrine, and no more interpretation is to be taken for granted than is actually found.

4. Applications

We are said to apply these studies to a problem when the subject matter of the problem is of central interest, irrespective of what methods are used or in what order. But "no sharp line can be drawn" between the two, especially as this whole thesis has been at once method and subject matter, to which reflective methods have been applied at liberty.

In logic, as ordinarily understood, there is the problem of classification, which may be treated from the point of view of identity and difference thru continuity, and of multiple-dimensional principles of cross divisions.

The continuity and elasticity of concepts, definitions, laws, theories, from the point of view of thresholds and centers of stability of logical equilibrium, may form a study in itself. (Cf. the terms of § 3. Chapter IV, pp. $204ff$, also Chapter VII pp. 267)

The meaning and limits of relevance, especially with respect to the idea of threshold, deserve more than implicit treatment, as given in this thesis.

Closely related to the study of concepts, definitions, etc. , there is the problem of the principles of terminology. What function of such factors as usage, elegance, brevity, symmetry, system, etymology, coloring, neutrality, etc. , shall be taken as the measure of fitness?

Coming to more philosophical problems, the question of mechanism and vitalism, or the definition of determinism and free will may be studied from the point view of equilibrium, which is no novel undertaking.

The problem of explaining the absolute and the infinite is one of central interest. Does reference to the relative and finite explain or explain away? Is a teleological or an evolutionistic ethic a concretion of ethics, or a doing away with true ethics? Do some forms of religion give the real interpretation of religion, or only substitutes for religion?

Among special problems of ethics, there is the question of the adjustment between conservatism and liberalism, which involves problems in continuity *par excellence.*

Questions of the line between what is a legitimate extent of doing something and what is not will lend themselves to treatment by continuous mathematical induction, both in an affirmative and in a negative way.

Problems of justice may also involve functions of many variables. [1]

It is said that a man (or a nation) is good only to the extent he

---

[1]　See F. Y. Edgworth, *Mathematical Psychios*, p. 95.

can afford to. Is this a tautology or a disconcerting truth? *How much* can you and I afford? It is a problem and not a fact.

Legal questions involving constitutionality, common law, equity, precedence, discretion, are questions of "in case of doubt". In this field, I can only say in a cheap way that only the inside trained know how to handle the methodological levers.

In experimental psychology, the measure of illusions has been explained at some length (Chapter VII, pp. 282 – 283).

According to the standards of elegance, relevancy, and fertility of symbolism that one finds in exact sciences, much seems still to be desired in the usual representation of colors by the color pyramid. It is worthwhile to see how far one can develop an "analytic geometry of colors". ①

Applications evidently extend also to problems of industrial and personal efficiency (maxima and minima). In educational psychology, methods of training motor skills will involve such considerations as intermediates, explicit location, pinching, etc. A useful discipline which deserves development, as has been proposed in Chapter VII (p. 271), is a system of "freehand geometrical drawing" by means of intellectual levers of analytic knowledge.

The borderland field in acoustics, music, psychology of sound, and experimental phonetics, among whose representives there has been much talking at cross purposes seems to deserve clearing up. The classification and definition of variables will be the first important step in such a study.

In music itself, such elements as pitch (cyclic as well as linear

---

① This problem was suggested by Prof. Henderson.

serial order), intervals, rhythm, tempo, force, change of force, etc. are preeminently subject matter for a theory of functions in methodology.

Finally, let me disclose the fact that my illustrations have been drawn chiefly from the subjects which I happened to be occupied with at the time of writing, and each time 1 met with something new, be it bicycle riding, elocution, statistics, or two-color motion pictures, there I found some more "illustrations", which, in turn, reacted on my general problems, and might lead to their solution, resolution, or dissolution.

Thus, "in the end", the present standpoint is singular merely in the formal sense of being the end of a formal thesis; and by way of abstract generality, and "nullification by qualification", "there is no reason why" all my future activities, including the possible repudiation (due to change thru a wide interval of time) of most of the results arrived at so far, may not be regarded as a continuation, thru continuity, of the continual writing out of a continuous thesis.

APPENDIX

I WORKS USED

Page

154 Hobson, E. W.   *Theory of Functions of a Real Variable*, pp. 222 – 223.

159   *Scientific American*, Oct. 20, 1917.

161 Russell, B.   *The Philosophy of Leibniz*, 1900, pp. 64 – 65.

165 Aristotle   *The Nichomachean Ethics*, Chapter. IX, Bk, II, (p. 56 in J. E. C. Welldon's tr.).

166 Crothers, S. M. *The Pardoner's Wallet*, 1905 (first essay).

170 Galilei, Galileo *Dialogues Concerning Two New Sciences*. Eng. Tr. by H. Crew and A. De Salvic, 1914, p. 122.

175 Ruskin, J.   *Sesame and Lilies*, 1864, section 32 (Harvard Classics, vol. 28, p. 121).

181 Hollingworht,   " The Psychophysical Continuum ".
     H. L.   *Journal of Philos. , Psy. , and Sci. Meth. ,* XII, 1916, No. 7, pp. 182ff.

183 Bosanquet, B.   *Logic*, 2nd ed. , 1911, II, p. 141.

192 Pearson, K.   *The Grammar of Science*, 3rd ed. , 1911, Part I, chapter on Cause.

197　Huntington,　　*The Continuum* , 1917.
　　　E. V.

200　Lewis Carroll　　*The　Adventures　of　Alice　in*
　　　(Dodgson, C. L.)　*Wonderland* ,
　　　　　　　　　　　　"A Mad Tea-party".

202　Franklin, B.　　*Autobiography*, virtue No. 3 (Harvard
　　　　　　　　　　　Classics, vol. 1, p. 83).

211　Huntington, E. V.　*American　Mathematically　Monthly* ,
　　　　　　　　　　　　Jan. , 1918.

223　Lewis Carroll　　"What the Tortoise Said to Achilles".
　　　　　　　　　　　Mind , 1895, p. 278.

228　Russell, B.　　*Our　Knowledge　of　the　External*
　　　　　　　　　　World as a Field for Scientific Method
　　　　　　　　　　in Philosophy, 1914, p. 42.

234　Wood, R. W.　　*Animal Analogues* , 1908, p. 1.

242　Poynting, J. H.　*Text-Book　of　Physics:　Heat* ,　3rd
　　　and Thomson, J.　ed. , 1908, p. 116, foot-note.
　　　J.

256　Galileo Galilei　　*Dialogue　Concerning　Two　New*
　　　　　　　　　　　Sciences , Eng. Tr. by H. Crew and
　　　　　　　　　　　A. De Salris, 1914, p. 72.

263　Weininger, O.　　*Sex and Character* .

269　Bayliss, W. M.　　*Principles　of　General　Physiology* ,
　　　　　　　　　　　1914, p. 383.

272　Pierpont, J.　　*Theory　of　Functions　of　Real*
　　　　　　　　　　Variables , 1905, I, pp. 202ff.

276　Leibniz　　　　Letter　to　Pierre　Bayle,　1687,　in
　　　　　　　　　　Philosophical Works of Leibniz , tr.
　　　　　　　　　　by G. M. Duncan, 1890, pp. 33 – 34.

276   Galileo   *Dialogue Concerning Two New Sciences*, Eng. Tr. by H. Crew and A. De Salris, 1914, p. 63.

280   Galileo   *Ibid.* , p. 141.

295   Edgworth, F. Y.   *Mathematical Psychios*, 1881, p. 95.

II SOME OTHER RELEVANT WORKS

	Biometrica, 1901 to date, esp. articles by Karl Pearson.
Boussineso, J. M.	Conciliation du Véritable Determinisme Mechnicue avec l' Existence de la Vie et de la Liberté Morale, 1878.
Mach, E.	Die Principien der Wärmelehre, 1899.
Mach, E.	The Science of Mechanics, 1883. Eng. tr. by T. J. Mc Cormick, 1902.
Meyerson, E.	Identité et Féalité, 1907.
Moore, E. H.	General Analysis.
Petzoldt, J.	Mathematik und Cekonomie, in Vierteljahrschrift für Wissneschaftliche Philosophie.
Poincaré, F.	Foundations of Science, Eng. tr. by C. B. Halsted, 1913.
Poincaré, F.	Dernierés Pensées, 1913.

A NOTE ON "CONTINUOUS MATHEMATICAL INDUCTION." [1]

1. *Special case.* —Let the function $f(x)$ be defined in some interval of a real variable x.

Hyp. 1. let there be a point a in the interval such that $f(a)=0$.

Hyp. 2. Let there be a constant Δ for the interval, such that $f(x)=0$ implies $f(x+\delta)=0$, whenever $0<\delta\leqslant\Delta$.

Then for any b in the interval, where $b>a$, $f(b)=0$.

Proof. — I. If $b-a\leqslant\Delta$, then by Hyp. 2 the conclusion follows.

II. If $b-a>\Delta$, then first apply Archimedes' postulate, that is there will be an integer n and a fraction $\theta(0\leqslant\theta\leqslant1)$ such that

$$b-a=(n+\theta)\Delta, \text{ or } b=(a+\theta\Delta)+n\Delta.$$

Next, apply ordinary mathematical induction, thus: By Hyp. 1 and 2, since $\theta\Delta<\Delta$.

$$\therefore f(a+\theta\Delta)=0$$

Therefore, by 2, again,

(1) $$f[(a+\theta\Delta)+1\cdot\Delta]=0.$$

By 2, if $f[(a+\theta\Delta)+m\cdot\Delta]=0$, then

① 原文载 *Bulletin of the American Mathematical Society*, vol. 26 p. 17 – 18, Oct. 1919. (Read before the San Francisco Section of the American Mathematical Society April 5, 1919.)

(2) $\qquad f[(a+\theta\Delta)+(m+1)\Delta]=0.$

Hence, combining (1) and (2),

$$f(a+\theta\Delta+n\Delta)=0,$$

that is,

$$f(b)=0.$$

2. *General case*. —Let $\varphi(x)$ be any propositional function, defined in some interval of a real variable x.

Hyp. 1. Let there be a point a in the interval such that $\varphi(a)$ is true.

Hyp. 2. Let there be a constant Δ for the interval such that $\varphi(x)$ implies $\varphi(x\pm\delta)$, whenever $0<\delta\leqslant\Delta$.

Then for any b in the interval such that b $\gtreqless a$, respectively, $\varphi(b)$ is true.

The proof will be the same as for the special case, except for obvious changes of wording or sign.

Remarks. —The theorem rests essentially on Archimedes' postulate and on ordinary mathematical induction, but it is not a generalization of the latter, in the sense of including it as a special case. It is not a theorem in mathematical logic, since it is concerned with a real variable x. But it is more general than ordinary theorems dealing with equalities, in that $\varphi(x)$ may be a statement about continuity, convergence, integrability, etc. , that cannot be put in the simple form of $f(x)=0$.

The theorem is a mathematical formulation of the familiar argument from " the thin end of the wedge ", or again, the argument from "the camel's nose":

Hyp. 1. Let it be granted that the drinking of half a glass of beer be allowable.

Hyp. 2. If any quantity, x, of beer is allowable, there is no reason why $x + \delta$ is not allowable, so long as δ does not exceed an imperceptible amount Δ.

Therefore any quantity is allowable.

Like all mathematical theorems, the conclusion is no surer than its hypothesis. In this case, if the argument fails, it is usually because a *constant* Δ required in the second hypothesis does not exist. Take the very wedge itself. If a wedge is driven with a constant force between two sides which are pushed together by elastic forces, it will be stopped when balanced by the component of the increasing resistance. In this case the Δ within which δ may increase for $\varphi(x + \delta)$ to continue to hold will not be "uniform for the interval", so to speak, but will become smaller and smaller as x approaches the dangerous point, beyond which the conclusion ceases to be true.

附录　ChatGPT 译文

连续性：
一项方法论研究*

赵元任
马萨诸塞州剑桥市
1918 年 4 月 13 日

---

　　*　译者说明：赵元任博士论文的 ChatGPT 译稿是在美国麻省理工学院陈彤老师、美国布朗大学焦立为老师和美国明德大学中文学校周凌菲硕士帮助下，用 ChatGPT3.5 完成的。译文都是依据经过译者校改过的英文原稿，分章节输入电脑，得到中文对译内容，再合起来组成全文。其中参阅本文的页码改为本书英文原稿的页码。有兴趣的读者可以跟我们前面的译文相互对照。为保持对译原貌，其中有一些误译的词句都没有做出修改。特此说明。

概　　要

问题和方法

第一章和第二章。——本研究以论文形式呈现，是关于某些形式的论证、发现方法、做事方法和某些实际困境的思考逐渐发展的其中一个阶段。在目前的阶段，它最好用"连续性"这个术语来描述，其意义从模糊的联想到能够承载应用的高度数学严谨性的范围内。

所研究的方法即被用作研究它们的方法，试图表明圆并非总是错误的。一般来说，方法被看作是在现实中起一部分作用，通过将一种方法对抗另一种方法来获得一种方法论杠杆，机械的、智力的或道德的。

研究和使用的典型连续性方法（或方法）包括以下阶段：(1) 具体案例方法，(2) 分级方法，(3) 序列方法，(4) 极端方法，(5) 显式位置方法，(6) 中介方法，(7) "夹紧"方法，(8) 变换方法。

抽象地说，这整个研究可以看作是一个关于一元连续变量函数的方法论理论。它在关注前提条件及其解释、应用或阐述之间的联系，以及忽视使严谨的联系比最弱的联系更强这一点上，未能成为一项数学研究。

特定章节的结果

第三章—分级思想——当我们发现某些思想绝对地被采用时，我们需要问一下它们是否也具有程度、阶段、层次或等级的显著性。一些特定的应用包括：例子、插图、类比、隐喻等是构成思想具体定义的不同等级的元素。

在数学中，参数可以具有不同等级或变化程度，其中变量和常量是极端情况。变化程度通常是实验上方便的问题。

在数学中，由曲线表示的数学函数仅是将值高度限制在一个区域、一个带状区域或一个管道中。当其他因素的变化对于该问题可感知的现象没有影响时，某个因素是该现象的"原因"。

第四章　序列排序——任何两件事情都可以按照自己定义的序列顺序进行比较。具体事物的序列可比性并不是二元的问题，而是一个更或少的问题。

只要使用的波动和科学中的"偶然"误差低于相关性的阈值，我们就能够对序列顺序做出非自反式的陈述，以便我们可以用除了它的纯定义以外的东西来称呼一件事情。

第五章　极限点——"通过连续性推理"，我们总是可以得出极限情况至少也是一种情况的结论。但是，极限情况至少在成为极限情况方面是独特的。因此，每个具体问题的答案取决于进一步的考虑。

数学的精神是把下限也称为一种情况。哲学的精神是将通常事物的情况一直追溯到它们的上限。科学和生活则处于中间位置。但是通过转化方法，可以展示这些极端在哪些方面相遇。实际的、范畴的、事实的等无限的事物与形式上的虚无相比具有无限的性质。实际的才能、善意、资本、能量等才使得圆形不会无限扩散。

在特定的问题中，上限和下限（"M"和"ε"）可以代替极限。因此，建议将极限重新解释为实际问题中相关的那些阈值情况所构成的。这被证明与现在在严格数学中使用的对应定义的极限相符。在这个意义上，我们说，意义或定义是标准的极限，真理是真理的极限，道德是道德的极限，等等。

这种方法与"奥卡姆剃刀"不同的一个重要方面是它没有声称具有终极性或排他性。某些特定的目的或某些人可能会将对象"简化"为一类有限的感官数据。但是从一个循环的观点来看，我们同样尊重和理解一个物理学家或生理学家，他们将感官数据"简化"为其他人试图将其简化为它们的术语。

　　第六和第七章　　相同与不同的连续性。——相同和不同的问题在于区分与每个问题相关的方面。

　　连续性的概念可以帮助我们看到同一性,前提是要明智地选择一个变量x,通过这个变量,我们可以看到某些方面上的事物融合在一起。

　　差异的背景可能会掩盖同一性,这背景可能是某种奇异点,例如零点,可能是度的广泛差异,小的度差异,或者是将现在的观点过分强调,而忽略其他观点。

　　一个特殊而有数学兴趣的附带结果是"连续数学归纳"的定理,它是熟知的楔子论证的数学形式化。它的正式证明基于(1)阿基米德公设,和(2)普通数学归纳。但这个论证的实际强度,就像所有论证一样,取决于其前提的强度。

　　差异不仅仅是差异,而是分类、事件交替出现、概念或感受上的不同、行动方针的决策等。

　　一个差异可能来自变量x的广泛变化、陡峭的曲线,或者是显著的奇点,特别是稳定和不稳定平衡点。

　　一个点可能因为它本身有趣而不同于其他点,比如主要因素的平衡和次要因素的相关性的进入。连续性概念(连续函数的通常定义)在这方面非常有用。中间值定理,即如果$f(a) < 0$且$f(b) > 0$,则存在介于a和b之间的ε,使得$f(\varepsilon) = 0$,也被广泛应用于物理和心理测量等方面。

　　第七章　　结论与进一步问题。——自然是连续的吗? 这要看情况。在科学和生活中,不连续和连续都是有用和适用的概念,具有不同程度的数学准确性和方法论效果。自然的连续性可能在于我们相对成功地塑造了时间的科学概念,使时间函数连续。这是另一种非恶性循环的情况,可以进行修订。进一步的问题是在方法论中制定函数的一般理论,并对变量和功能的具体解释进行调查。从另一个角度来看,这将构成一种"具体数学"。仅是略作涉及,但应就其本身进行进一步研究的特殊应用包括平衡问题、最优点或广义黄金分割点、相关阈值、术语原则、道德和法律问题的界定、效率、运动技巧、音乐技术以及其他所有现实，只要玩弄这些概念将导致我们能力的扩大而非缩小。

赵元任

马萨诸塞州剑桥市

1918 年 5 月

目　　录

第一章 引 言

1. 问题：中间态

　　一只青蛙正躺在池塘边的一块岩石上休息。突然，大自然跃动，涟漪的波纹还没有扩散很远，青蛙已经到达了池塘的底部。然而，显而易见，青蛙肯定在某个时间和地点刚开始打破水面，对吗？有人告诉我每年我会长高两英寸。如果我被允许在某个新年前夜保持清醒，找出我何时长了那两英寸，感受一下这种变化会不会很有趣呢？但是，他们说，成长是一个过程。例如，如果你想变得优秀，你必须从现在开始养成良好的习惯。如果你说："现在我可以轻松一些，当我成年时我肯定会认真负责的"，那么当你成年时你就不会成年。但是，建议真的有用吗？那些愿意遵循的人不需要它们，而那些不愿意遵循的人则无法使用它们。似乎我这个平庸之人也许正巧足够糟糕以需要大量的建议，同时又足够优秀以遵循其中一部分。但是，我们总是在事物之间找到平庸吗？我的座位似乎对一美元五角的价格而言相当不理想，而我身后的人肯定比他们支付的票价得到更多。可惜这些座位不是以一美元二角五分的价格出售。有个住在分水岭附近的人抱怨缺乏新鲜鱼和航行设施。下雨时，水流要么流入长江，要么流入黄河。两个相邻山谷之间没有峡谷，这很奇怪！也许有些事情就是这样比较好。如果长号演奏家在每个音符和下一个音符之间都演奏得很连贯会怎样呢？如果用水银的滴和满满一杯来代替硬币作为货币，那会怎么样呢？然而，有时候，我发现在我有时间决定之前，不得不在事情上做出决定或做出选择，确实令人恼火或尴尬。"香烟、口香糖、冰淇淋和晚间报纸"，车站的男孩大声喊着。我想知道哪个是最好的选择，但是如何比较它们的优劣，因为它们是如此不同的东西呢？于是火车发出"嘟嘟"的声音,带着我和我的沉思离开了。也许我很幸运没有吃冰淇淋。我听说过这样的建议："除非饿了,否则不要在饭间吃东西。如果有疑问,就不要吃。"那时我有些犹豫。但有时候,是否有疑问本身就是个问题。为了安全起见,让我称之为有疑问的情况。但如果是否有疑问本身是否有疑问,那又该怎么办呢?事情就这样发展下去。无论如何,不吸烟肯定是好的。如果我再犯一次,那就没有理由不再犯第二次了。当然,每一次犯错都是最后一次。记住,吸一口烟与抽一整盒是同一种性质的事情。但是,吸入别人的烟雾环境与自己吸烟在程度上或者性质上有区别吗?到底程度上的差异和性质上的差异有什么区别?程度上的差异和性质上的差异之间的差异本身是程度上的差异还是性质上的差异,还是两者都有?这些不同的事物如何扩散到这些页面上?它们在性质上是相同的吗?最后犯错与无辜的两栖动物潜水有什么关系呢?

这样,对于这项研究所关注的问题,这可以说是一种有些不太学术但又冗长的"定义"。之所以以这种方式陈述,是因为相较于另一种方式,后者通常从一般性地陈述开始,即当有许多具体问题要表达时,从一般性地陈述开始是一种哲学上的错误,随后再进一步给出为什么这样做的一般性原因。这种杂乱的方式来引入主题是对"具体案例法"的一种反思性应用。某些思路似乎汇聚到一些模糊感受的问题上,或者更好地说,似乎与一组可能的问题网状地相互关联。不考虑原则或原则的统一性,需要寻找更多似乎与之相关的"案例",尽管"它"是一个非常模糊的概念。

虽然这显然不是一种理性主义的方法,它使一切事物依赖于一个或几个支点,但它也不同于那种只依赖于一些支柱(如感官数据或关系感受)的经验主义。它满足于从事物的中间开始,例如颜色混合、周期定律、火车上的饥饿或人群分布等事物。

然而,仅仅在事物之间漫无目的地游荡,并不会导致一个问题的形成。如果对所处理的主题、提出的问题、采用的方法和得出的结论不加限制,那将涵盖整个哲学甚至更多内容,没有"理论上"的理由阻止我们追随思绪的走向。然而,朴素的实用主义认为应该将现实世界划分为一块块可以在单个机构内方便管理的区域,可以在舞台上三小时内呈现,可以在一本书的两个封面之间阐述,或者特别地写成一篇学术论文,并对子问题进行进一步划分,以分别在各个章节中进行处理。也许所有问题都是以行动为基础产生和定义的。但本论文并不明确意图为哲学实用主义辩护。

为了应用分级和序列秩序的方法(第三章,第180页和第四章,第197页),可以建议将问题按照广泛性的顺序进行排列,范围从牙科和烹饪白菜到布尔代数和一般分析。然后可以发现,开篇段落中所阐述的观点占据了中间位置。为了更明确定位问题,它似乎比物理学或心理学等科学更一般,但比数学分析更不一般。

然而,对于将问题放置在这样的位置,有两个反对意见需要应对。首先,"我们是否总是在事物之间找到平庸之处?"在这种中间广泛性的附近,问题可能没有自然的汇聚趋向稳定的统一(参见第七章,第265页以下)。但如果没有哈佛大学教职员的宽容和宽大,这样一种特定事物的混合可能永远不会被允许作为一个研究通过,因为它对于哲学来说过于肤浅,对于科学来说过于不精确。回答是,中间类型的研究的缺失本身可能同样有助于对其进行探索,正如对该立场的自然不可持续性的论证一样。因此,对于这项研究的实际执行将在一定程度上证明其可行性。此外,就广泛性而言,它大致对应于归纳逻辑和方法论的历史领域,而本研究正是在这个领域中进行的。

第二个反对意见是,广泛性并不是唯一可以根据其划分问题的原则,而且如果我不愿意将其与形式逻辑等同起来,哲学本身的位置可能是可疑的。在本研究的精神中,我同意这个反对意见,通过说选择广泛性作为变量 x 仅仅是一种判断,是自己负责做出的,目的是为了确定问题的位置。但我们没有理由不使用"变量转换的方法"来处理问题,如果出现了需要从困难性、人类吸引力、销售性、可笑性或其他方面考虑问题的情况,使用这种方法会更好。

事实上，为了将这项研究限定为连续性的研究，相对于方法论的其他问题，需要考虑的因素不仅仅是广泛性。现在，由于在开头部分提供了说明材料，因此尝试对问题进行正式陈述就不那么危险了。使用"下限方法"，我将从零开始。但是，"无中生有"。因此，我必须从模糊的某种东西开始。问题将是：它是怎么回事？也就是说，我如何理解它、欣赏它或正确对待它？在超越这种模糊性的同时，我们可能会注意到关于这个事物的一些特征或方面，并且这些特征或方面可能变得有趣或似乎很重要；当我们观察整个世界时，我们会发现其他事物在这些方面似乎与第一件事物不同或相似。用认识论的语言来说，我们已经给出了那个东西，并通过与其他事物的比较来定义它是一个什么。在数学语言中，我们有一个确定的术语，然后寻找独立变量，随着变量的改变，我们找到一个相应的函数，其中该术语是其中之一的值。从这个观点对问题进行系统研究，可以称之为方法论中的函数论，它将涉及到所有艺术和科学的主题，并将利用所有数学函数理论的结果，只要它们与问题足够相关。

然而，目前的研究比这要窄得多。首先，它主要关注的是一个变量 x 的一值函数，该变量足够接近连续性，以便在所涉及的问题中进行处理。其次，重点仅放在连续性的渐变（第三章）、顺序比较（第四章）、极限情况的检验（第五章）、通过连续性和不连续性的恒等性（第六、七章）等问题上。多个变量的函数问题、最大值和最小值问题、统计变量等问题并未单独考虑。但由于连续性作为一种方法具有弹性和广泛性，其中的一些问题确实进入了我们有限的视角，因此这项研究并不像它看起来那样狭窄。

2. 方法：内部

由于/问题起源于事物的中间，所以采用的方法主要是内部的或反思的，正如前面一节所示。/当进行区分，例如连续性和不连续性之间的区别时，我会询问它们是否不是相互融合，它们是否不是彼此的极限情况。当看到一种连续性，比如这项研究与所有其他研究之间的连续性时，我会问，在哪里划定界限？借用电学问题的语言，方法、问题和解决方案在这里不是"串联"的，而是"并联"的。如果我们不喜欢它们相互前提的悖论，我们可以选择它们相互共同前提的野蛮性。在问题的开始中有方法，在开始正确的方法中有问题，在"好的开端是成功的一半"中有解决方案。这就像在一个圈子里转圈，或者用自己的靴带把自己拉起来。但是，正如将在第二章"方法"（第 159—160 页）中展示的那样，有些循环并不恶性，有些拉靴带的方式并不是徒劳的。

在这项研究中，将自由地运用普通数学的方法和结果。但是它们的使用受到"几分"的精神的调控。说某些事情是这样的，意味着两件事：首先，存在这样的事情，这是经验动机，它关注具体情况；其次，可能存在不是这样的事情，这是分析动机，它关注抽象可能性。数学表明如果 A 成立，则 B 成立，并且可以放心地提出普遍命题。但是这项研究还涉及到具体情况下事物是否符合这个或那个假设的问题，因此并不享有这种安全性。因此，数学定理在这项研究中的应用要小得多，而且除了一种"连续数学归纳"的例子之外（第六章，第 251—252 页），从未被"证明"，在作者对数学文献的有限了解范围内，这是独创的。数学证明将一个假设与另一个假设联系起来，如果后者不太容易直接得到经验的支持，数学证明可能会带来方法论上的损失。

一个声称自己的方法或一套方法在应用范围上没有限制的有效性似乎需要进行辩护。（1）首先，我将通过说连续性在任何方面的观念只适用于它适用的范围内来做出一切让步。到底有多远，只有论文主体中的无用和有用的应用（如果有的话）才能说明。一些唯心主义者和实用主义者将现实称为不确定或灵活的。更好的表述是将其称为弹性。丝线或水的形状等灵活的东西不抵抗，而是顺从于任何力量。钢铁或蒸汽等有弹性的东西既有抵抗性又有顺应性，程度取决于施加的力量。思想具有任意性的自由度是有限度的。但是当我们将任何方法应用于任何问题时，我们是自负其责。
当适用性逐渐变得模糊不清，例如通过叹息使一根铁棒弯曲时，我
们说我们正在应用错误的方法。因此，对方法的局限性的认识相当
于提供了一个安全阀。无论何时弹性现实太过于无法在我这个小
小的方法论锅炉中局限，它都被允许泄漏出来，而不会造成教条主
义的伤害。

（2）其次，将事物视为具有连续性和不连续性的单一变量函数
的观点只是可能的众多观点之一。用一把智力之锯，将其用于钢琴
上，用于门上，用于所有其他不期而遇的家具，甚至梦想锯锯。但这
并不意味着所有事物都必须被单独定义为可锯性。超越这个隐喻
的限制，我可以辩称变量转换方法将包括在处理任何问题时所需的
所有新考虑。但这只是试图在无限广义和安全之间取得平衡的情
况下，以牺牲空虚为代价（见第五章）。更安全的态度是希望那些具
有与作者相似的智力气质和训练的人会发现这种处理方法极具启
发性和刺激性，同时认可将这个研究视为一系列形式主义和牵强附
会的思维的存在合法性。

3. 术语：混合

在阅读以下章节时，人们可能会对术语的一致性感到不一致，
除非在经常出现的某些实用主义转向的特定表达上。基于原则，已
经避免了这种一致性。另一方面，语言形式非常自由，有时还会混
合使用。实际上，有人建议整个研究是将数学与非数学或半数学主
题进行类比的应用。这是正确的，只是这项研究并不特别是类比的
一种方法，以某种方式，所有方法论都不应被视为类比。如第三章
（第186页）所示，实际案例、"真正"的类比和隐喻之间只有程度上
的差异。因此，使用多种术语、各种形式和插图的功能实际上是对
该思想进行构成性定义的方式。

实际上，考虑到语言的本质作为一种事实，与其他活动有关的
一种活动，任何语言是否可以完全字面和确定，除非通过形式上的

重复,这是值得质疑的。因此,只要词义的微妙差别与相关问题无关,我就不会有任何顾虑地将一系列词语串联在一起作为同义词。因此,"绝对、无条件、无限、具体、范畴性"在某种情境下无需区分,尽管在其他方面可能存在重要的差异。

在这些讨论中,某些术语被避免或者使用得很少。在涉及到这些限定性词语时,往往会发现其他更合适的词语。例如,"理论上"和"实际上"在这些讨论中很少出现,因为在使用这些限定性词语时通常会找到更满意的词语。在这之后,几乎不会再次出现"主观"和"客观"这两个术语,这并不是因为它们被视为无效的概念,而仅仅是因为它们没有涉及到这些问题。与它们的普遍适用性相比,"真实"和"虚假"并没有起到重要的作用。也许,在提及它们时通常会给出一种解释(或误解)。常常使用"实用性"、"富有成效性"、"有效性"、"重要性",以及"人为性"、"贫瘠性"、"无用性"、"琐碎性"等词语来描述相关情况已经足够。

尝试通过采用习惯用语甚至口语的方式,让词语自行解释,并让其在上下文中所携带的丰富联想的重心确定可能的歧义。但是,如果这样还不够,将给出解释或定义。

在这方面,可以解释一些经常出现的术语:在本文中,"thing"几乎总是被理解为与"something"相同的广义概念。它似乎是一个和"entity"、"term"、"objective"一样好的词,而且在许多讨论中(不一定是哲学性的),它实际上还蕴含着更加普遍的含义。

当在形式讨论的语境中使用"point"时,并不一定指代几何点,而是指系列中的任何元素,也就是任何事物。因此,在第五章中,整个开头的格言是一个"限定点",或者在第六章(第 374 页)中,整个运动竞赛是一个"点"。

"Idea"、"notion"、"concept"、"conception"在这里没有进行区分,仅依据习语和上下文来处理。

"Threshold"和"limen"在这里可以互换使用,ε 用于表示下限阈值,M 用于表示上限阈值。

　　"Singular point"在广义上指的是任何一个特别重要的点。它用符号 ξ 表示。

　　话题领域(universe of discourse)指的是明确定义的概念范围，而上下文则暗示着模糊相关的事物。但在二者交叉并且区分不重要的情况下，这两个表达将可以互换使用。

　　无穷大(Infinity)，正如第五章所讨论的，仅在数学分析中作为变量的概念使用。完整、静态的无穷大或可数无穷大数的概念并未应用于本研究。

　　在数学上，函数的值指的是当变量 x 被赋予常数时函数所具有的确定值。因此，函数 $f(x) = x2 + 17$ 在 $x = 3$ 时的值为 26。很难避免这种确定的数学用法。但由于这是一项边界研究，特别重要的是明确指出常数 26 可能没有任何价值，或者函数 $f(x) = x2 + 17$ 的关系可能没有任何目的性。当然，在不同的背景下，可以自由地谈论呼吸功能的重要值或国家功能或社会功能的政治价值。

　　最后，术语"连续性"需要解释。在本研究中，连续性的两个数学含义——数列连续性和函数连续性——都将被使用。由于适用性是一个程度问题，这些术语将用于仅近似连续的情况。谨慎的数学家会坚持认为连续性的两个含义互不相关，即可能存在一个连续的变量函数，它只是稠密而不连续①。但在一种复杂的无知中，或许我们可以混淆这两个概念。连续体将被视为连续函数 $x' = x$ 的特例。连续体具有两个特性，即所谓的 Dedekind 闭合性，它意味着填充每个极限点，以及稠密性属性，即通过将区间细分无限次来实现。现在让我们将前者与连续函数通过所有中间值②的特性混淆起来，将后者与当变量的差趋近于零时，函数的差趋近于零的特性混淆起来。然后我们就能够谈论连续性的一般概念。这种类比当然不能

---

　　①　E. W. Hobson,《实变函数论》，第 222—223 页。

　　②　通常情况下，这一点通常通过夹逼法来证明，但这种方法是非常可疑的。请参考第二章 169 页顶部。

通过数学严谨性的测试。例如，在某种情况下，这两个特性是独立的，而在另一种情况下则不是。但类比是部分差异中的部分相似，只有实际情况才能确定忽视这些数学差异在不加区分地使用"连续性"和"连续"这两个词时对方法论结果产生了多大程度的无效或混淆。

4. 来源：杂项

如果研究是对某一主题的系统而全面的调查，并多说一点，那么这项研究将不配称为研究。因为典型的资料来源涉及观察一只青蛙、戒烟、陷入实际困境、收集双关语和歪曲数学。这是某种形式的搜索，但几乎谈不上研究。

另一个资料来源是在科学中的培训，主要是物理学和数学。这解释了在自然科学中的例子超过其他领域的例子，并且在科学中的例子超过其他领域的例子的优势。可以轻易地说同样的原则可能适用于所有其他学科。但考虑到插图是原则的构成部分的信念，很可能一旦自由地运用生物学主题，总体计划将会发生很大的变化（参见结尾段落，第 297 页）。

从历史上看，连续性推理偶尔出现在这里和那里，莱布尼茨和伽利略就是重要的例子。但莱布尼茨将其作为哲学原则，而伽利略仅在其偶尔出现在其他问题中时使用。因此，连续性作为一种方法的系统研究尚未被观察到。确实，这里所提出的许多观点，可能大多数都是之前其他人更好、更完整地表述过的观点的不完美重述，或者仅仅是从之前阅读中潜意识地记起的想法。因此，不足的致谢并不代表傲慢，而是无知的标志。

然而，在许多情况下，故意避免明确引用。一般会以尽可能清晰的英语进行一些总体陈述，然后从不寻常的角度提供一些例子来赋予其意义，并以此展示一定的思路。但是，如果有人指出，"噢，这只是笛卡尔的解析几何的伪装"，或者，"那只是黑格尔的论点、反论点、综合再现"，那么一个有着历史背景的人会立即将这些作者的常见例子转化为它们的确立分支。现在，如果插图构成了观念，那么对旧观念的新插图很可能无法完全趋近于旧观念的原意；而且由于新插图，就像两个山谷之间的水，并没有处于稳定的平衡状态，它们会流入已经形成的水道，除非给予它们机会集结成小的山坡水池，并开辟新的水流。（参见第七章，第265页及以下有关平衡的内容）。因此，在由于无知而导致的损失中，无论是真实的还是假装的，都存在一种新鲜感的可能性。

参考文献的列表已经在论文末尾给出（第299—301页）。但为了保持学术诚实，也有必要提供未被使用或未被广泛使用但如果经过更仔细的审查可能会改进或极大改变本研究的作品名称。

最后，与他人的对话、通信和讨论对这项研究的影响甚至超过了阅读。特别感谢 I. J. 亨德森教授，他通过"具体案例法"使我的科学兴趣得以保持，并特别指导我关注了伽利略使用的方法；感谢 E. V. 亨廷顿教授，他让我看到了许多数学可能性，并对细节进行了许多修正；感谢 H. M. 谢弗博士，在论文的整体规划和确保清晰准确性方面给予了帮助。因为如果清晰度仅仅是一个程度问题，取决于每个问题的要求，那么它至少要足够高，以达到所需的程度门槛。其他致谢无法一一列举。但正如上面所提到的，正是哈佛大学哲学和心理学系的科学自由主义，继承自罗伊斯教授的传统，使得在不同知识领域的边界地带进行这样的研究成为可能。

第二章　方　　法

1. 方法：杠杆

方法从广义上来看,可以被看作是将现实的一部分对抗另一部分的过程。它可以被描述为中介、间接、推理、形式化、人工、机械等,与即时、直接、直观、物质、自然、自发相对应。乌鸦无法直接接触到高瓶中的水。它选择捡起小石子,投入瓶中,水位随之上升到它能够够到的位置。这就是方法。人类是在自然的基本力量中无助的生物。通过科学和技术,人类延长并加强自己的臂膀,并使这些力量成为自己的仆人。这就是方法。

因此,方法可以被看作是杠杆。假设我拥有一个有限的力量 ε。需要克服一个更大的力量 M。方法将在于找到一个杠杆 n,使得 $n \times \varepsilon$ 大于 M。方法也可以与扳机作用进行比较。我无法将球扔出200英尺之外。但我可以制造枪和火药,扣动扳机,将球发射数英里远。

在方法中,有一种像用靴带将自己拉起来的感觉。将靴带系在滑轮上,向下拉动。整个重量将会被一半的力量提起[1]。这正是科学一直在做的。对小行星谷神星的几次观测确定了特定的轨道。因此,之前记录的某颗"星星"必定是谷神星。如果这是谷神星,那么轨道必定是更准确的,而不是最初确定的轨道。因此,通过对现实的把握,我们在无效的循环中前行。

但方法不仅仅是方法,它也是一个问题。一个重300磅的人很可能没有150磅的力量可以支配。因此,他将不得不解决应用方法的问题。也许他安装了另一个滑轮,这样一个给定的75磅的力量

---

[1]　参见《科学美国人》,1917 年 10 月 20 日。

就足够了。或者他可以将靴带缠在电动机上，打开一个只需要几盎司力量的开关。弗朗西斯·培根似乎认为，一旦完善，科学方法论可以被任何人应用。但只有在应用者的智慧选择和有效执行之下，方法才能成为方法。将几个小事项按重要性排序是相当简单的事情。所以我们称之为处理业务问题的顺序方法。但当涉及评估人员在某些职位上的资格时，我们需要采用更多的方法来衡量顺序问题的因素。因此，对于每种方法，可能都存在一个问题，每种方法都需要一个方法。

然而，仅仅进行方法的回归并不会导致其应用。杠杆可以变长，扳机可以更加精细，但启动它们仍然需要一定的力量。培根对方法的理解和笛卡尔关于自由意志的扳机论证都基于这样一个假设，即通过将零乘以 n，我们可以得到一些有限的结果 M。一个用靴带上吊的人无法将自己抬起，因为他已经没有剩余的力量。没有现实作为起点，循环是恶性的。

因此，方法的作用并不是取代直觉、直接经验、判断或任何类似的范畴术语，而仅仅是将其与问题的解决联系起来。在某个领域拥有更多的想象力、才能、技巧和经验，一个人就能更有辨别力和效果地运用形式方法。如果方法是在将现实的一部分对抗另一部分，那么它并不是在将无物对抗无物，而是拥有更多现实的人会更好地运用方法。

2. 方法

所以，关于方法的一般性讨论就到此为止。现在我们来谈谈具体的方法。在这里研究的方法只涵盖方法论领域的一个小角落。但对于它们适用的主题并没有限制。然而，当我们遇到那些无法有效处理连续性概念的问题时，这种适用性会逐渐消失。

（1）具体案例法。——一个问题如果没有足够和公平的样本来定义，那么它就无法清晰地被定义。除非问题被定义，否则我们无法确定哪些样本是足够和公平的。但科学和生活中问题的实际存在帮助我们摆脱这个困境。虽然我们还不确定问题的定义,但从问题的历史发展中,我们对问题的大致了解。因此,我们可以去世界上寻找"案例",尽管我们还不知道这些案例是关于什么的。

　　因此,我们有了心灵和物质的问题,心理和生理等问题。具体案例法的方法就是找到一些例子,比如愤怒、恐慌、财富、宪法、音乐喜剧、陨石、噪音等。

　　如果我对事物感到一些悲观,我可以寻找一些事物的案例,比如科学成就、战争、在橘子皮上滑倒、孩子们的声音、哲学、安眠、糟糕的晚餐、音准和音痴等。

　　当然,这种方法只是一个初步的步骤,通常不能定义问题,更不用说解决问题了。它告诉我们要深入事物的核心,寻找生动的例证,并避免过早陷入问题和体系的老路。随着我们的进展,我们可能会发现有理由将一个以前的问题细分,或将其与其他问题结合,甚至将问题撤销。

　　(2)渐进法。——寻找具体案例是任何声称是经验主义的一般方法的一部分。当我们将具体案例视为一个绝对的观念的阶段、程度或层次时,连续性的概念就进入其中。这就是莱布尼兹所称的形式连续性,它表明在不同种类的事物之间总会存在中间事物。作为一种哲学观点,它说中间形式以某种方式存在。但作为一种方法,我们可以满足于说想象并尝试去看看观念是否允许有程度的存在是有益的。由于这种方法将在第三章中进一步发展,我在这里不再详述。

　　(3)序列顺序法。——当我们定义一个标度 x,使得案例可以在某种意义上按照优先顺序进行比较时,渐进法就变成了序列顺序法。最重要的应用是在 x 大致是一个数学连续体的情况下,尽管这种方法也适用于其他序列,比如整数。对于那些认为不能过于轻易地定量处理事物的反对意见,我通常的回答是适用性在不同情况下有所不同,任何两个或更多事物的序列比较可能成为在意想不到的情况下出现的有效问题,并被应用为有效方法。这个主题的更详细讨论将在第四章中给出。

（4）极端法。——当我们将一个问题构想成结果 y 依赖于条件 x 的形式时，经常使用的一个富有成果的方法是将 x 变化到极端值。极端考虑往往能够揭示在其他情况下不确定或不明显的事实。例如，在序列比较中，很难准确定义什么是人类的卓越或什么是普遍健康，但在极端情况下，很明显一个低能人比一个天才差，或者一个运动员比一个癫痫患者更健康。

然而，需要注意的是，在说结果"显然"是如此时要保持经验的谨慎。例如，有人可能认为在只兑换两美元的极端情况下，如果银行职员将两张钞票翻过来，弄湿手指，用正常的方式数钞票，这将是"荒谬"的。但事实是他确实这样做，这是因为这种习惯具有纪律性价值。因此，证明一个反面观点并不一定能够推翻任何东西。

通常基于少数案例来断定普遍命题，或者通过对有限事实范围的推断来制定科学定律。这时，使用极端法来测试结果是很有必要的。伽利略发现重力加速度是恒定的。但是当考虑到极端距离，如月球距离时，牛顿发现重力加速度随着距离的平方而减小。托勒密

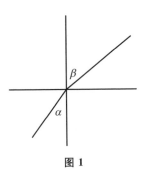

图 1

和阿尔哈真进行了折射实验，发现入射角和折射角之间存在某种近似关系。尽管他们没有发现正弦定律，但由于他们发现 $\angle\beta$ 始终大于 $\angle\alpha$（图 1），他们有可能想象运用极端法，通过增加从较密介质到极端值的角度 $\angle\alpha$，来观察可能发生的情况。但直到开普勒才真正进行了这样的实验，他从中发现了全反射现象，当 $\angle\alpha$ 超过使 $\angle\beta=90°$ 的角度时就会出现全反射。

同样地，氧气在普通条件下被认为是一种"非磁性"物质，但在极低温度下，当它液化时，它具有很高的磁性。实现极低温度确实开启了广阔的新物理现象视野，而莱顿大学所进行的最重要研究之一就是在这个领域中应用了极端法。

　　函数的定义总是一种暂时的、或多或少准确的事务,其有效性取决于问题的进展和结果。(参见第三章第 190 页及以下关于函数的内容)。极端法不仅可以导致对函数公式的修改,还可以将功能性转换为完全不同的变量;也就是说,在极端情况下,函数可能会失效,而其他次要因素则变得突出。因此,在一个关于一根小导线中的电问题中,现象可以用相对简单的公式来描述。但在大西洋长海底电缆的极端情况下,公式失效,因为电容和感应等因素变得突出。

　　极端法可以作为后续采用的"捏合法"(稍后将进行描述)的初步步骤。常常听到"你不能过于这个,或过于那个"的建议,但是当一个人走到极端时,往往就会跨越平均水平。在此之后,当钟摆摆回时,一个人就准备好回到平均水平。

　　因此,一个新生使用化学天平时开始时放置的重物太轻,添加了一克,发现仍然太轻,又加了 500 毫克,再加一厘克,如此往复,始终找不到合适的重量。当然,正确的做法是使用较大的重物进行称量,直到明显太重,然后逐渐减小单位。

　　许多人弹奏钢琴时会出现一个错误,就是左手比右手早敲击一点。有效的纠正方法是有意识地在另一个方向上出错,以体会到右手过早敲击的感觉;然后同时敲击两只手将更容易学会。这个方法可以追溯到亚里士多德,他将这个想法比作一根弯曲的棍子的校直[1]。

　　当然,极端法并不一定只适用于物理意义上的应用。它也可以通过假设、想象来进行,以了解可能发生的情况,也可以通过实际实验来获得经验性的结果。一个医学研究者不会试图过量使用氯仿来确保其效果,经济学学生也不会投资一百万美元来验证边际收益递减定律。

　　极端法的极端形式是极限法,通过该方法,我们可以探究随着

_____

　　[1]　《尼各马可伦理学》(Nichomachean Ethics)第二册,第九章(J. E. C. Welldon 翻译,第 56 页)。

条件的度量接近下限或无限增大时结果会如何变化。例如，一个空类也被称为一种概括的类。公式

$$\int_a^b ydx + \int_a^b zdx = \int_a^b (y+z)dx$$

同样的法则也可能在 b 趋向无穷时成立。极限法用于获得一般性、对称性和简明性的陈述或心理概念，或者发现使某些事物变得不同的条件。该思想的进一步阐述将在第五章中进行。

（5）明确位置法。众所周知，为了全面理解一件事物，我们必须将其放置在其他各种事物中的位置上。在这项研究中，我们将关注一件事物在经过分级和顺序排序方法定义的尺度上与其他事物的位置。

例如，一个国家可能对其人民的健康没有明确的概念。经过检查可能会发现，该国的平均水平在国际上非常低下。总的来说，统计工具在明确那些被忽视或错误理解的位置上非常有用。

明确位置法是寻找中庸的初步步骤。我在八个月内看了两场戏剧。这接近中庸吗？如果不是，它是在中庸的哪一侧？该方法揭示了许多隐藏的零值案例。一个人可能在锻炼方面零活动量，没有私人通信，没有在实验室工作，没有和孩子们玩耍，一年没有发生争吵，对任何事业没有捐款，不会说外语，不喝酒。从这些混合性的例子可以看出，零不一定是缺陷或过度。关键是明确位置法激起了思考，并问"是这样吗？"当然，许多问题足够琐碎，可以被忽略，或者最好根本不提出。这必须依靠常识或亚里士多德的"实践智慧"。正如上面所示，一种方法并不自我告诉何时最好应用[1]。

（6）中间法。极限法试图将我们的函数领域扩展到起始范围之外。中间法则在已知案例之间寻找有趣的案例。这两种方法对应于外推和内插，但它们比外推和内插更为普遍，因为它们并不一定

---

[1]　比照塞缪尔·克罗瑟斯(Samuel M. Crothers)，赦免者的钱包(第一篇文章)。

说："相同的事情在外部或内部也是真实的"，而只是简单地询问在未经考察的刻度部分中会发生什么。

更准确地说，中间法是基于连续函数的性质，简要表达为具有取得所有中间值的性质。因此，这种方法是渐变方法的发展。

例如，当一个炮弹在某一时刻在大炮里，而在另一时刻在几英里远的地方时，那么在某个时间点它必须刚好在炮口前一英尺处。虽然很难想象，但快速曝光的照片将捕捉到中间情况。

我们经常视中间情况为理所当然，尽管我们可能对它们有错误的概念。在电影的古老历史中，当 E·马伊布里奇拍摄了一系列通过连接到相机的绳子奔跑的马的照片时，有趣而令人惊讶的事实被揭示出来，关于动物在运动中的实际中间位置的形态。随着现代摄影技术的完善，中间法也可以应用于飞翔的鸟类。

在探索中间情况时，明智地选择点通常可以避免无结果的尝试。如果数学函数对问题进行了巧妙定义，那么在某些数学方面具有特殊性的点很可能在具体情况中也具有重要性。例如：$-\infty$，0，$1/2$，$+\infty$，100%，已知点之间的中点，点之间的算术和其他种类的平均值，习惯性点，自然倾向的点，问题陈述中给定的点等。可以看出，这个列表中还包括极限法的案例。

（7）夹逼法。——当我们的兴趣不仅仅是一般的中间情况，而是特别关注某种特殊情况时，我们使用了一种可以称为"夹逼法"的方法，尽管这个名称可能不够优雅。在一个案例中，我们得到一个结果，在另一个案例中，让这些案例逼近，并探究在临界情况下，当案例之间的差异趋近于零时会发生什么。可以看出，这可以归结为极限法的一个特殊情况，但其特殊重要性需要单独讨论。

该方法的数学形式表示为在区间 (a,b) 中的定理，

If　（1）$a \leqslant a_1 \leqslant b_1 \leqslant b$,

　　　　$a_1 \leqslant a_2 \leqslant b_2 \leqslant b_1$,

　　　　$a_2 \leqslant a_3 \leqslant b_3 \leqslant b_2$,

　　　　……

图 2

and　(2) $\lim_{n \to \infty}(b_n - a_n) = 0$,

then there is a point ξ, such that

$\lim_{n \to \infty} a_n = \lim_{n \to \infty} b_n = \xi$.

实际上，这就是证明连续函数的中间性质的方法（或通过引用引证的引理来证明该性质）。寻找黄金比例可以采用挤压的方法。在调焦显微镜时，我们从眼镜筒位置设置得过高开始。然后我们使用极端法，将其向下转动，直到目标物或载玻片几乎被压碎，以确保我们已经超过了平均位置。然后我们逐渐微调位置，直到获得最佳焦点。

估量一个数量通常可以通过挤压的方法得到比直觉更精确的结果。一位机械工程师曾经根据经验说，当他想设计某种杆材用于特定目的时，无法猜测出正确的尺寸，他会首先在纸上画出一个非常细的线材，然后是一个非常粗的圆柱体。接下来，他会画出一根稍微不那么细但仍然太细的杆材，以及一根稍微不那么重但仍然太重的杆材。他会一直逐渐缩小 an 和 bn 之间的差异，直到它们变得无法确定。然后他取算术平均值，并称其为他的 ξ，即平均值。这种方法在应用时证明效果很好。

通过挤压的方法找到黄金比例，可以类比于阻尼摆的振动。事实上，人们在平均值的两个极端之间总是犯错，而历史总是像摆钟一样摆动，如果我们发现某些摆钟正在被阻尼，这并不应使我们感到沮丧。

在某些推理中，伽利略使用了挤压的方法。有人声称长绳比短绳更脆弱。现在假设绳子在重量 C 下在点 D 处断裂（图 3）。那么如果悬挂点在稍高于 D 的点 F 处，绳子也会在 D 处断裂。同样，如果将在某一点（例如 E）以下的重量固定在稍低于 D 的点上，也没有理由它不会在 D 处断裂。因此，无论是短段 FE 还是长段 AB，绳子的强度都取决于最薄弱的部分[1]。

图 3

---

　　① 伽利略《关于两种新科学的对话》，亨利·克鲁（Henry Crew）和阿方索·德萨尔维奥（Alfonso De Salvio）翻译版，第 122 页。

虽然这种方法在数学中连续函数的定理证明中起着重要作用，但不能认为它在任何问题中都支持连续性。因为如果存在不连续性，这种方法将能够准确地确定它以及其他感兴趣的点。对奇异点的详细处理将在第六章和第七章关于同一性和差异性中进行延迟讨论。

（8）变换方法。到目前为止，我已经讨论了不超出某个变量和某个函数的方法的发展。但由于在构思问题时没有绝对的理由使我们保持原始观点，如果变换似乎是可取的，我们可以借助变换方法。例如，在显微镜的目镜位置与视野清晰度之间的问题中，当我们达到近焦点的关键状态时，我们发现不存在"the focus"，只有不同物体平面的焦点。因此，在问题中引入了一个新的变量 x。

为了保证陈述和概念的普遍性，我们可以将渐进法视为变换的下限。同样，定义一个函数 $y=f(x)$ 也是如此。事实上，将"线性变换"$w=Az+B$，看作是 w 关于 z 的线性函数的方式。因此，如果我们要在处理变换时追求完整性的上限，我们应该涵盖整个论文的范围，甚至更多。然而，由于必要性，本节只能对变换进行粗略的介绍。

首先，谈到变换的目的。从形式上来说，进行变换的目的包括：

1. 确保函数的连续性

2. 确保函数的不连续性

3. 使曲线变得平坦

4. 使曲线变得陡峭

5. 使函数呈线性

6. 使数量有限。

但非数学专业的人很容易看出，这些目的不过是近似的目标，只具有工具性的价值。进行变换的科学目的可以更深刻地感受到作为"目的"的存在。以下是其中一些最重要的目的，可以进行变换以实现：

1. 更准确地定义最初模糊的问题意图。

2. 更容易理解。

3. 数学或逻辑"操作"的方便性。

4. 文字处理的便利性。

5. 提高结果的精确度（最佳杠杆效应）。

6. 寻找新的因素和新的结果的一般目的。

谈到变换本身，我们可以将其分为变量 x 的变化和函数 y 的变化。在许多情况下，它们是重叠的；例如，将 x 乘以 n 等效于将 y 除以 y。因此，区别在于强调的方面。

描述	一般形式	具体形式
1）乘法	ax	nx, x/n, $-x$
2）加法	$x+a$	$x+a$, $x-a$
3）幂次方	x^a	$x^n \cdot \sqrt{x}$, $1/x$
4）指数函数	a^x	e^x
5）三角函数		
6）其他		$x' = x_1/(x_1+x_2)$, $x' = x/\sqrt{x^2+1}$

7）新的因素

为了说明其中一些形式，我们发现乘法的一个例子，当伽利略使用斜面而不是自由下落的物体时，从而改变了

$$v = gt$$

变成了

$$v' = g(\sin \alpha)\, t'$$

（其中 α 是斜面的角度），也就是说，他延长了时间以便于（字面）操作，提高了判断球在慢速运动中的位置时的准确性。

3）取倒数是幂函数 xa 的特例，其中 $a=-1$。例如，与其说电流与电阻成反比，这将得到一个难以处理的双曲线，有时候更好的做法是说电流与导电性成正比，这将得到一条直线。

7）引入新因素尤为重要，因为极值法和夹逼法通常会导致这一步骤。已经提到了大西洋电缆的电容和电感以及聚焦显微镜的焦平面差异的例子。此外，对于某个函数的某一点的不连续性可以通过转化为另一个函数的连续性来实现，这将在后面的章节中详细说明（第七章，第276页及以下）。

y 的变化。一 y 的变化可以分为对 y 本身的常数操作和不同函数的组合，后者是新因素方法的对应方法。

常数操作。一

描述	一般形式	具体形式
1）乘法	$af(x)$	$nf(x)$，$f(x)/n$，$-f(x)$
2）加法	$f(x)+a$	$f(x)+a$，$f(x)-a$
3）幂函数	$[f(x)]^a$	$1/f(x)$
4）指数函数	$a^f(x)$	
5）对数函数	$\log f(x)$	
6）三角函数		
7）符号函数或符号	$\operatorname{sgn} f(x)$	
8）导数	$f^{(n)}(x)$	$f'(x)$，$f''(x)$
9）阶跃函数		$\mathrm{E}[f(x)]$

5）例如，在统计学中绘制相关曲线时，取对数使得曲线是直线。

7）$\operatorname{sgn} f(x)$ 简单地表示 $f(x)$ 的符号。它可以用于标记差异，这将在第七章中更详细地讨论（第272页）。

8）作为导数的示例，我们可以考虑对时间设备准确性的评估。最天真的观点，可能是一个孩子或一个无知的人会持有的观点，是：

a）一个时钟如果读数不准就不好。也就是说，如果我们将 $f(t)$ 作为其读数随时间变化的函数，那么时钟被判断为不好，只要 $f(t)$ 与 t 本身存在偏差。

b）但是，一个更聪明的人会说，一个读数错误的时钟可以调整或允许误差，重要的是它的运行速率是否正确，既不快也不慢。换句话说，他关注的是 $f'(t)$，并且只有当 $f'(t)=0$ 时才感到满意。

c) 但是,一个处理过准确时钟的人会说,如果速率不正确,可以进行调节或允许误差,重要的是它必须是恒定的,换句话说,速率变化的速率应为零,即 $f''(t)=0$。因此,大多数时间设备的真正缺陷在于运动的二阶导数不为零。

9) 进行不连续步骤的采取可以被看作是通过 sgn y 将一个函数转化为两个值的广义形式。例如,在绘制统计曲线时,我们不再绘制连续曲线,因为数据量太少,而是将数字分组,例如,将 5'3/4 和 5'6"1/4 都归入五英尺半的类别,从而将平滑曲线转化为直方图,即具有方形峰值的曲线,如图 4 所示。

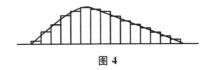

图 4

函数的复合。

描述		一般形式	特殊形式
1) 乘法	$f1(x) \cdot f2(x)$ 乘法	$x \cdot f(x)$ 乘以 x 乘法以减小	$(x-a) \cdot f(x)$ 不连续性除以 x $f(x)/x$
2) 加法	$f1(x)+f2(x)$ 加法	$f1(x)+f2(x)$ 减去	$xf(x)-x$

---

1) 为了确保线性,常常将一个函数 y 乘以 x。例如,如果我们有 $xy=a+bx$,然后令 $y'=xy$,我们得到 $y'=a+bx$。

2) 为了说明除以 x,让我们回忆一下福斯金的话:"如果一本书值得读,那就值得买。"[①]或者那句陈词滥调的建议,"如果一件事值得做,那就值得做好。"现在的问题不是更多的时间、精力、金钱等是否会带来更多的利益,而是收益是否超过了成本。换句话说,我们关注的不是我们最初想到的函数 $f(x)$,而是经过变换的函数 $f(x)/x$。因此,通常情况下,值得学习的课程也值得参加期末考

---

① 《芝麻与百合》,第 32 节(哈佛经典,第 28 卷,第 121 页)。

试，因为多花十分之一的时间所带来的收益比从一个鸟瞰课程主题的角度获取的十分之一的收益更多。图 5 以一般的方式表示了这种关系，其中

$(f(x\_2))/x\_2 > (f(x\_1))/x\_1$。（因为 $\tan \theta\_2 > \tan \theta\_1$）

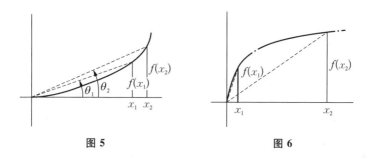

图 5　　　　　　　　　　　图 6

但是，读报纸头几分钟非常值得，而随着我们深入阅读"头脑食品"和特价促销，递减收益法则开始发挥作用。在这种情况下，对于 $x1 < x2$，我们有

$$\frac{f(x_2)}{x_2} > \frac{f(x_1)}{x_1}.$$

如图 6 所示。

有许多事情值得去做，但并不值得彻底去做。

2) 通过加法进行组合的形式经常涉及被忽视的结果，从自然角度来看这可以称为减法。因此，当扩大一家工厂时，我们不仅应考虑总收益的增加，还应扣除运营费用的增加。具有远见的改革者倾向于强调如果立即实施改革将产生的好处。但保守派则提醒他们需要从这些好处中扣除克服传统、习惯以及危及与否理性机构相关联的真实价值所涉及的浪费、风险和危险。

在整个方法论的研究中，人们可能会提出一种反对意见，即为了提高准确性、确定性等，为发现最佳行动方案而搭建智力脚手架的广义费用可能涉及浪费、风险和无关的过程，从而导致折扣后的

结果只能提供部分而不是放大的杠杆效应。对这个反对意见的答案是接受它。通过采用下限方法，我们可以将没有方法也视为一种方法，这可以称为检视、直觉或直接判断的方法（参见第四章，第329页）。一个合理的方法论并不建议用蒸汽驱动的起重机去捡起鹅卵石，或在睡觉时阅读亚里士多德的《伦理学》，然后决定最佳的醒来时间。

4. 方法作为阶段

　　这些，便是方法的概要，在接下来的章节中将会进行部分展开。综合起来，它们可以被看作是一个连续性方法的自然阶段，随着问题的发展逐渐演化。我们从具体案例开始，发现其中的层次差异，将它们按顺序排列，向外探索极端情况，向内研究中间情况，而且我们会把注意力集中在特别感兴趣的点上。当这些步骤似乎不够时，我们会通过转化的方法来阐明问题，而这又是无限可能性的子方法的统称。

　　然而，这仅仅是形式上的陈述。在实际应用中，其中一个阶段可能具有主要的兴趣和重要性，那么我们就说我们正在使用这个或那个子方法。此外，问题可能需要按不同的顺序应用这些方法，或者反复应用同一方法。这并不奇怪，因为我们可以随时根据需要改变观点，并重新考虑问题，或者，由于我们甚至不能确定"问题"的存在，我们可能完全面对新的问题。不同的阶段，虽然具有一种自然的顺序，但并不要求严格的逻辑连续性。尽管在某些方面它非常松散和牵强，但事实上，一个阶段对现实有很好的把握。因此，按重要性的顺序进行事物的串联排列是一种相当有效和明确的过程，即使重要性的度量变量 x 是一个极其模糊的概念。又或者，夹取的方法，其数学证明仅适用于数学连续体 x，但即使从更精细的角度来看，我们所处理的一系列事物并不"密集"，它仍然可以提供很多启示。简而言之，如果方法被构想为一种有效的辅助手段，用于解决一个问题，那么它对于另一个问题是否不够充分并不重要。当然，还有更加严谨、全面、准确和全面的方法，它们将在越来越精确的领域中得到应用。这些领域，无论是规范和赋格，还是天体力学，始终都是从明确的观点来规定的。但是，如果我们提出广义上的真正或有效的方法的问题，我们将超出这篇论文所限定的范围。

第三章 分 级 观 念

1. 分级观念与序列顺序

通过分级观念，我指的是某种可以分等级、程度、层次的东西。分级观念的研究与序列顺序的研究不同，后者从两个或更多的术语和一个刻度开始；而前者从一些给定的观念开始，并探究我们是否能够找到可能的或实际的分级，这可能是有兴趣的。从同样的材料中引用两个例子，"A 比 B 高吗？"是一个序列顺序的问题，而"A 是一个高个子吗？他在某种程度上是高个子"则是对分级观念的应用。对于序列排列问题，一个准确的数学刻度定义通常很重要，这将在下一章中讨论。但是，当我们对分级观念本身感兴趣时，它们的确切形式关系并不总是特别关注的。因此，人们不必为了欣赏蒸汽机的逐渐发展而拥有一个数字刻度来衡量发明的价值。我们将研究的分级可能是近似连续的或密集的系列，或者只是一系列离散的术语，甚至是一系列没有明确定义个体性的术语。

2. 分级问题和方法

如果我们被要求对一个观念进行分级，最明显的方法是打开我们的心灵之眼和身体之眼，寻找具体的分级案例（"具体案例法"）。作为指导，我们可以选择给定观念中的某个方面 x，当 x 变化时，将产生不同的分级。通常而言，找到某种形式的观念分级是很简单的，但结果是否平凡是另一个问题。

然而，很少有人被要求找到已经在人们心中被紧密归类为 A 或非 A 的观念的分级。对一个观念进行分级并不是一个问题，而更多地是一种我们尝试应用于问题的方法。我们可以称之为一种积极的问题。这种尝试可能会有哪些可能的后果呢？

（1）首先，找到具体案例可能有助于发现未知的事物或引起对被忽视事物的关注。当人们谈论心灵和物质时，有人提到"愤怒、恐慌、瘟疫、美丽、财富、罢工、战争"[1]，打破二元论的和平是很有益的。

（2）分级可能是"明确定位（第二章，第 165 页）的一个初步步骤，也就是说，当我们看到一个分级系列时，我们所开始的观念的位置通常更容易被欣赏。一个人已经完成了一门法语课程，认为自己"学会了法语"。但是，如果他考虑到不同的分级："学会读菜单，学会读科学文章，学会读小说，学会说话，学会听讲座，学会写作，学会与孩子们聊天，学会争吵，学会用法语做梦或做乘法，学会理解法语轻歌曲"，他可能会惊讶地发现自己的位置并不是"学会法语"这个短语所暗示的那样。

（3）在观念的分级中，定义可能需要更加精确，修订甚至可能需要被放弃。"智能行为"有时被定义为能够处理新情况的行为。将红色与食物的关联称为纯粹的联想，而能够识别"左边第二个门"的能力被称为智能。但是，如果我们考虑到颜色、形状、大小、位置、顺序、门的状况等要素的复杂性和普遍性的可能分级，那么很明显，"新"或"不新"的定义需要进一步阐明。在这里，分级方法只是提出了一个问题，但并不保证单独解决问题。

（4）一个常识的观念，特别是当它被用一个词来表达时，可能会受益于被穿透和深入挖掘。因为一个词倾向于吸引一些在使用它的上下文中并不适用于它的联想，从而导致错误。如果我们用"基督徒"来表示一个人是教会的成员，那么一切基督教的事情都倾向于与他联系起来。但是，如果我们考虑到基督教的分级，包括教会外和教会内的不同情况，每周七天，我们可能会对所讨论的人有不同的概念。

同样地，我们可以对一些二分法进行分级，比如重要、不重要；

---

[1]　参考：H. I. 霍林沃思，"心理物理连续体"，《哲学、心理学和科学方法杂志》，第 13 卷 7 期，第 182 页及以下。

非常有趣、不太有趣；最近、不太近；必要、多余；保守、自由等。如果上下文清楚地显示了隐含的修饰，那么这些术语就被正确使用；如果它们误导人产生错误的联想，那么就被误用了。

（5）决策或立法的陈述也受到定义的不确定性的影响，因为陈述本身就涉及到定义。因此，通过分级的方法，我们将看到这样的规则陈述的不足之处："所有有智能的生物都有受到人道对待的权利"、"不必要时不要说话"、"只阅读重要的书籍"。

（6）从上面可以看出，对一个观念进行分级可能是启动"挤压法"①的准备步骤，也就是说，在两种不同条件下产生两种不同结果，并让这两种条件逐渐接近，以便研究结果的变化是如何产生或将要产生的。

（7）通过对一个观念进行分级，也可以为"骆驼的鼻子"论证（第六章，第 253 页）做准备。例如，如果有人说我们无法看到分子的运动，我们可以说，如果我们可以通过眼睛的晶状体"看到"一把椅子，那么没有理由我们不能通过眼镜"看到"远处的树，所以我们可以通过歌剧望远镜"看到"歌手，可以通过复合显微镜"看到"一个细胞，可以在几秒钟内通过静止图像"看到"一朵花开，可以通过福科扁摆"看到"地球转动，可以通过望远镜"看到"一个几年前在那个方向的 12 星等星星，可以"看到"布朗运动中分子的运动。当然，仅仅分级这个观念的可能性并不能构成充分的论证。在所有这些论证中，如果没有坚实的论据支持，那么"骆驼的鼻子"的形式就没有任何意义。

（8）通过分级，我们常常可以彰显事物的某些身份特征。因此，在后面的一节中（第 312 页），我将试图展示举例、类比、隐喻等实际上构成了某种拓宽概念的要素，并在这方面，它们都是实例。此外，如果我们找到自然干涉的程度的不同示例，从制造化学化合物、嫁

---

① 　图示请参见第二章，第 169—170 页。

接花卉到观察流星,我们可能会发现实验和观察在人类干涉程度[1]方面是相同的,只是程度不同。但是,通过连续性对身份的完整处理是第六章的主题。

(9)分级思考一个思想可以采取从一个案例中推广的形式,即将其中某个恒定特征(例如0或1)视为一个变量,或从另一个角度,将该案例视为一系列案例中具有特定取值的案例。因此,区域限制的处理(第316页)相当于从相关性为1的严格函数的案例推广到相关性不为1的其他案例。或者,以最后一个例子而言,如果Banquet屈尊使用我的术语,他可能会将观察定义为当人类控制程度为零时的广义实验的一种情况。

(10)到目前为止,我一直强调分级的连续性方面。但正因为思想是分级的,为什么它们不能产生分级的后果呢?在某些方面的身份特征并不排除在其他方面的差异。将观察归纳为某个变量为零的实验程度并不妨碍我们将一定类别的实验(其控制程度低于某个e)归为"观察"并给予它们特殊的逻辑、方法论、学术或财务处理。

所有罪犯在作为罪犯这一点上都是相同的,然而社会发现最好根据犯罪程度来分级刑罚。所有及格的学生,但教育实践是他们应该以A、B、C等级及格,有时具有实际后果上的差异。作为一个微不足道的例子,我可以进一步提到,在实践早起的过程中,将迟到和准时的不同程度进行记录更为有效,而不仅仅是每天早上迟到一次打个叉。对懒散行为进行分级评估将阻止人们将其恶化,因为无论如何都没能做到最好。在分级处理的方法论中,需要对分级尺度进行精确的工作定义,换句话说,要对连续顺序进行确切的界定。因此,我们超越了本章中所考虑的纯粹的分级方法。像任何其他方法一样,分级方法从问题的某个地方开始,如果与之相关,则使其向前迈进一步,从不解决生活和宇宙的最终问题,而且通常不能按预期程度解决有限问题。这里结束了对分级思想的一般讨论。在接下

---

[1]　参考:博桑奎,《逻辑学》,第2版,第 II 章,第141页。

来的几节中，将讨论一些特别感兴趣的案例，即逻辑普遍性、变量、参数和常量、数学函数和区域限制以及知识进步。

3. 分级的逻辑普遍性

我们熟悉诸如"存在、动物、人、希腊、苏格拉底"之类的分级逻辑普遍性系列。然而，人们经常忘记在这类系列中，一般概念和示例只是相对的术语。如果将 n 个术语按照普遍性的顺序排列，如 $a1, a2, \cdots\cdots, an$，我们可以取任意两个 ai 和 aj，并说"ai，例如，aj"，其中 ai 在 aj 之前。因此，在以下系列中：一个事件，过去的事件，一个科学发现，一个物理定律的发现，牛顿对冷却定律的发现，我们可以说"过去的事件，例如，一个物理定律的发现"。

一些人似乎喜欢用模糊的例子来阐述他们的思想。他们说"一个事件，例如，一个历史事件"，"一个科学发现，例如，化学中的一个发现"，"一个定理，例如，数学中的某个定理"。模糊之处在于阐述思想的概念的等级与被阐述思想的等级没有太大的差异。因此，人们不应该被"例如"或类似的表达所误导，因为它是一个可以分级的概念，它的等级可能太低，无法通过相关问题所要求的门槛。

另一个类似于刚提到的分级系列是：实例、案例、例子、说明、类比、隐喻、文字游戏。地球和太阳之间的关系是万有引力的一个实例、案例或例子；在现代教室中重复进行卡文迪许的实验将被称为万有引力的一个说明，它不是一个重要的实例，而是用来使概念具体化的；将万有引力与声音、光和热进行比较将是类比。恩佩多克勒的爱的概念将是一个隐喻。我可能需要尽力来找到一个关于万有引力的巧妙文字游戏来完成这个系列。在这里，我建议将这些分级看作是逻辑普遍性的升序系列。因此，万有引力、光、声音、热等都不符合相同的反方向平方强度概念。一个隐喻，如果是一个好的隐喻，除了从中形成的显而易见的方面之外，还应该有其他的共同点。如果是这样，那么实际上将有很多共同之处，使万有引力和爱归于同一类。而且，在巧妙的文字游戏中，通常会有逻辑上的认同以及词源学上的认同。结论是,我们不应该毫无保留地划定一个界限,并说在"说明"之前的一切都是本质,看轻了系列中的其他部分作为偶然性。所有的部分在一定程度上都是本质,它们构成了思想的要素。

在分级概括的光线下,我们或许可以看到形式蕴涵和实质蕴涵之间的关系。形式蕴涵适用于两个不是命题而是命题函数的陈述之间,这是因为它们包含了变量项,无论是显式还是隐式的;根据这些变量项的具体化程度的不同,蕴涵可以被称为更"形式化"[①]或者更"实质化"。但是当所有的术语都被具体化,形成了两个命题,即有意义的陈述时,我们达到了一个极限,即实质蕴涵。以下是一个例子:

1)"x 是 a"蕴涵"x 不是非 a"。(非常形式化)

2)"x 在一个地方"蕴涵"x 不在另一个地方"。

3)"一个人在一个地方"蕴涵"一个人不在另一个地方"。

4)"一个人在英国"蕴涵"一个人不在美国"。

5)"伯特兰·罗素在英国"蕴涵"伯特兰·罗素不在美国"(隐含变量时间)。

6)"伯特兰·罗素在 1918 年 4 月 1 日在英国"蕴涵"伯特兰·罗素在 1918 年 4 月 1 日不在美国"。(实质蕴涵)

这个观点只是问题蕴涵问题的一个方面。它没有说明变量为零的事实将产生什么不同,例如实质蕴涵是否是一个有用的概念。(参见第五章,第 222 页)。

4. 变量、参数、常量

对于初学数学的学生来说,常数和变量的概念通常会引发一些困惑。直到熟悉程度压制了好奇心,他们才会明白为什么 C 是一个

---

①　由于"形式性"并未以分级的意义使用,因此在让其指代形式蕴涵中的值的可变性上并无术语上的异议。关于如何以及是否可以通过显式和隐式变量的数量以及每个变量可能的值范围来测量这种可变性的问题可能是重要的,但对于本文讨论的要点来说并非必要。

比 x 更具体的数，就像丙比天更具体一样。而参数的概念更具反常性。它既是常数又是变量。即使数学教师有时也会将参数视为一种奇怪的东西。然而，在接下来的内容中，我将试图展示参数在数学领域中是规则而不是例外。

在引入字母的使用时，我们被告知每个字母在同一个"讨论"（或者说同一个论域）中代表相同的数。但是，什么构成了一个讨论呢？显然，从一个表达式的一部分到整个数学的范围，包含各种程度的广泛性。现在考虑表达式 $x+x=2x$。为什么我们不写 $x+x=2y$ 呢？因为在非常短暂的" $x+x=2x$ "讨论中，x 被假定保持不变。但是在更广泛的讨论"' $x+x=2x$ '对于每个 x 都成立"中，每次我们完成" $x+x=2x$ "的讨论时，x 可能具有不同的值。因此，它成为一个变量。因此，即使是变量 x 也具有某种参数化的特征。正是变量的常数方面可能解释了不同变量 x、y、z 等之间令人困惑的自我一致性。它们被称为变量，是因为它们的常数方面被默认为存在，并强调了它们的变量方面。

另一方面，在圆的方程 $x^2+y^2=R^2$ 中，常数 R 在我们将 x 和 y 变化时被保持不变的讨论中是一个常数。但是，如果我们扩大讨论范围，并考虑不同数值半径的圆，则 R 成为一个参数，而半径 2 将成为相对于该参数的常数。但是，在关于数值半径（比如 2）的讨论中，我们不会在一个方向上测量两英寸，在另一个方向上测量两厘米，而是假定单位保持不变，在更广泛的讨论中单位会变量化。因此，甚至"2"也可以被视为一个参数，它是书写"2 个单位"的简便方式。

因此，我们可以说在整个数学领域中，所有处理的术语都潜在地具有参数的特性。所谓的参数是指在某个讨论中，某个术语在其他术语可能变化时保持不变，但在整个讨论中它本身可能变化的术语。在其稳定性期间没有其他术语变化的术语将是一个变量，而在讨论中与任何术语不变化的术语将是一个常数。在这两者之间，可能存在多个分级的参数。这种观点的实质对于任何从事数学问题的人来说肯定并不新鲜；但在教授基础分析和研究诸如连续性、收敛性、级数的积分与微分以及其他双重极限问题等问题时,清楚地了解可变性或参数性的程度是有益的。在这里,无法详细展示所有相关的例子。

虽然在某种意义上我们的论域都是任意的,但在我们实际的理论生活中,有一种问题的自然性会在我们中培养出一定的习惯或偏见。因此,对我们来说,x 看起来像一个变量,x 将是一个相当好的参数的字母,而 K 和 C 通常是一个问题的常数。在 $x^2+y^2=R^2$ 和 $K^2+y^2=\rho^2$ 这两个方程中并没有逻辑上的区别。然而,后一个方程立即引发我们在保持横坐标 K 不变的情况下变化半径和纵坐标,并在更广泛的讨论中考虑不同的垂直线,而 K 则取不同的值。

在物理问题中,变量的顺序通常有一种"自然的自然性"。在摆动方程中,

$$x = A\cos(2\pi\sqrt{l/gt}\,)$$

x 和 t 是最可变的量,因为随着时间的推移,摆动也在进行,而振幅 A 和周期则保持不变。在此之后,A 自然比 l 更可变,因为我们可以通过将摆动器拉到不同的位置或给它一个不同的推力来轻松改变振幅,并且在进行一系列具有不同振幅的实验时,我们更倾向于保持其他事物不受干扰。最后,g 比 l 自然更为恒定的参数,因为在将仪器打包并前往不同纬度进行关于不同 g 的实验之前,人们肯定更愿意完成一系列具有不同长度的实验。但是,如果一个人足够富有、从容不迫且愚蠢,他可能会来回旅行,保持 A 和 l 不变,而 g 则变化,然后在完成世界之旅后再改变他的 A 和 l。因此,参数的可变性甚至没有固定的序列顺序,而是可能随着提出的问题而改变。

5. 数学函数与区域限制

如果我们随机选择宇宙中的任意两个变量 x 和 y[①],它们不太

---

① 出于简单起见,在此考虑了两个变量。整个讨论可以通过将带状区域称为 n 维管道并进行相应的改变,轻松地推广至 n 个变量。

可能是彼此的数学函数。例如，墙上的颜色不会由于生长在上面的花根的分支数目而确定。但是很多时候，变量 x 可能对 y 的变化施加一定的限制。例如，尽管长笛音符的音高和音量通常是独立的，但是不可能以非常响亮的方式演奏低音 C 或以非常高的音调弹奏钢琴音符。从图形上来看（图 1），让 x 表示音高，y 表示音量，那么可能的组合虽然不是严格的一对一函数对应关系，如曲线 AB 所示，但它们被限制在一个带状区域内（图 1 中未阴影部分）。因此，对于低音符，变化被限制在 LL 的范围内，永远不会达到非常响亮的音量；而对于高音符，变化被限制在 HH 的范围内，永远不会达到非常低的音量（钢琴音）。

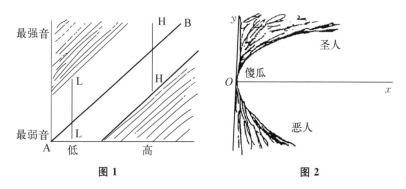

图 1　　　　　　　　　　　　图 2

同样，虽然德行和知识没有严格的相关性，但是缺乏知识的人既不能成为圣人，也不能成为大恶棍。因此，这种限制可以用图 2 来表示。在接近 0 的地方，我们有一个白痴的状态，既不能非常善良也不能非常邪恶。

再次，以第四章关于序列顺序的温度讨论为例（第 211 页），我们有温度与其各种物理解释之间连续的限制区域（图 3）。

最后，在所有关于两个变量 x 和 y 的统计相关性中，实例不会位于一条单一的曲线上，而是根据 x 和 y 的相关系数的大小而散布得多或少广泛（图 4）。非常精确测量一个"单一"数量的情况只是点在一个非常狭窄的区域内，这是因为一个因素占主导地位，而"偶

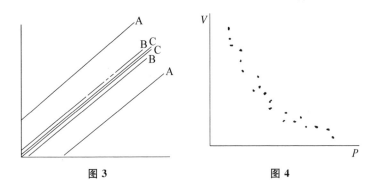

图3   图4

然"或"不相关"的因素被最小化。[1]

从这些例子中，我们可以说，如果我们随机选择两个变量 x 和 y，它们很可能具有一定程度的区域限制。在下限处，我们具有完全独立性（如果有的话）。在上限处，我们有严格的函数关系（如果有的话）。在这些极端之间，我们可以提出方法论问题，即发明区域限制系数或广义功能系数的一般定义，或者根据统计相关性的工作制定特定定义。对于每个问题，我们可以决定在称其为实际函数之前需要多么严格的限制。

注：对于这种宽松的函数观点，人们可能会提出一个明显的评论，即宽松性来自于未指定的"隐藏坐标"或"隐藏因素"。例如，对于给定的电导体，通过它的电流 I 大约与施加在它上面的电压 V 成比例。关系不是一个曲线而是一个带的原因是，我们没有指定第三个因素温度，对于相同的恒定电压，温度的变化会使电流略微变化。对此，我可以说，通过指定温度这个重要因素所得到的结果仅仅是更高程度的限制或广义功能。因为谁能说几十年才会有一个霍尔（Hall）来发现一个新的因素，比如磁场对电流的影响？因此，欧姆定律只是一个指定有限数量因素的区域限制程度，而在将电阻定义为

---

[1] 参见 K. 皮尔逊，《科学语法学》，第3版，有关原因的章节。

比值 V/I 的同时，将所有可能的已知和未知因素集合在一起，它才成为严格的数学函数，但这也以它成为一个同义反复（详见第四章关于序列顺序的结尾部分）为代价。

6. 知识进步

　　我们有权利问："谁发明了第一台蒸汽机？""笛卡尔是否知道第三运动定律？""谁最早使用了'函数'这个术语？""贝多芬是一位原创作曲家吗？"但当我们忽略了这些问题答案中通常隐含的限定条件时，引出阶段的概念对于摒弃"在某个发现之前什么都没有，而在那之后一切都有"的观念是很有意义的。

　　（1）发明。——将蒸汽热转化为机械动力可以追溯到亚历山大的赫罗。在瓦特之前，有伍斯特侯爵和纽科门等人的发动机；在我们现在的时代，查尔斯·A·帕森斯荣誉发明了蒸汽涡轮，这是一项巨大的进展。如果把赫罗先生、伍斯特侯爵、纽科门先生、瓦特先生和帕森斯先生排成一排，将瓦特先生指定为蒸汽机的正式发明者，并没有任何异议，前提是这个称号提醒人们他所做的某些改进的重要性，并不意味着或者暗示他是从无中创造了一切。

　　（2）知识的真相。——一个人或一个时代是否"知道"某个真理或思想的问题往往更好地解决为知识的程度问题。牛顿的第三运动定律在人们知道如何用推杆推动船只的早期阶段就被人们理解到了实际的程度。笛卡尔的动量守恒学说只是从动量守恒导出的一步代数推导，而动量守恒则是第三运动定律的核心。现在我们对质量和惯性的理解正在发展，我们对这个定律的认识仍在相应地进行修改。

　　（3）首次提及和思想。——第一次给一个思想命名的行为通常很重要，因为它对所命名的思想的未来进展产生影响。但是，例如，当莱布尼兹第一次将某种关系称为"函数"时，他之前已经有人研究了多项式和三角变量等内容，而后来出现的傅里叶和魏尔斯特拉斯等人发明的广义函数概念，他几乎无法认出它们是自己的合法智力产物。事实上,仅仅提及或记录一个思想通常意义不大。如果一个系统的建造者告诉一个对该系统提出异议的人,某个能回答他问题的思想在系统的某个地方只被提及过一次,那么这个人是有理由不满意的。同样,如果一个人开始有了一个零散的思想收藏馆,他可能只是简要地记录下来以备偶尔参考。但随着这些思想越来越多,收藏馆往往会变成一个墓地。我们要么必须在多个交叉引用下系统地记录一个思想,要么在当场对其进行详细阐述,要么它将会丢失。因为仅仅将其记录在一本厚厚的剪贴簿中并不能带来安慰,就像我终于把经常弄丢的手表掉进海里,至少我现在知道它在哪里一样。

（4）独创性。——独创性的标准可以根据特定问题进行划分,就像在艺术收藏中将复制品与原作区分开来一样。例如,一个博士论文可能因为"不具备独创性"而在逻辑上完全合理地被拒绝。但总体而言,独创性可以从绝对的创造,通过新的组合思想、对尚未完全形成的旧思想的新处理或解释、评论、模仿,最终到剽窃和机械复制等各种程度上存在。以音乐为例,一个人在心理物理学上不能完全原创,这意味着拥有一个全新的心理物理有机体是过于苛求的。要求创造一种全新的音乐模式也是过于苛求的;即使德布西的全音阶也是由已知元素的组合而成。如果我们将贝多芬的所有作品分解为短动机,很可能每一个动机都曾经在某个先前的作曲家的作品中出现过。因此,如果要过于挑剔的话,除非涉及一些类似于"色彩交响曲"之类的作品,否则音乐中没有什么是真正独创的。另一方面,即使是一个演奏五指练习的孩子,也有一定程度的个人独创性,这种独创性的程度可以逐渐提升。通过这个音乐的例子,我想表达的是在知识进展中,所有的独创性都可以在两个假设的极端之间进行分级,而这个存在与否并不是我们在这里主要关注的（参见第五章）。

第四章 序 列 顺 序

当我们提出问题:"A 是否比 B 更 x 一些,还是 B 比 A 更 x 一些?"时,我们涉及到序列顺序的问题。同一个概念可以以不同方式称之为"大小比较"、"优先顺序"、"线性刻度排列"或其他涉及到连结、传递和非对称关系的术语。关于序列顺序的形式逻辑已经得到了很好的发展,比如亨廷顿在他的《连续体》(1917 年)一书中。本章主要关注该概念的方法论应用。首先,我将尝试阐明序列顺序的含义,然后讨论一些序列顺序中常见的谬误。接下来,将考虑建立序列顺序的方法,然后将序列顺序作为一种方法应用于进一步的问题。在最后的部分,将从阈值概念的角度进一步发展序列顺序的含义。

1. 序列顺序的含义：它是什么

二分观点。——当我们问:"A 是否比 B 更 x 一些,还是 B 比 A 更 x 一些?"时,我们经常听到的回答是:"实际上,A 和 B 在 x 方面是否可比较? 我们可以问:'伦敦比巴黎人口更多吗?'但不能问'错过一趟火车比闻到二氧化硫更愉快吗?'"根据这种观点,两个事物在维度 x 上要么是可比较的,要么是不可比较的。

连续观点。——包括并超越这种观点,我们提出以下情况的分级供考虑:

(1) 如果我们被问到两个人中谁更重,这是一个非常明确的问题,可以得到一个简单的答案。因此,重量具有一个简单而明确的含义。

(2) 对于两个分数 m/n 和 q/p 中哪个更大的问题,答案就不那么简单,因为一个分数有两个要考虑的元素。定义分数的相对大小的一种方法是说,根据 mp 是否大于 qn,m/n 大于还是小于 q/p。这实际上是普遍认可的定义,有着多种合理的理由。因此,分数的大小已经得到了明确定义。

(3) 现在,对于两种职业中哪一种更适合某个人来从事的问题,我们觉得这个问题应该有一个含义和一个答案。然而,我们必须首先定义一个适应性的标准。我们应该给予自然才能、兴趣、可用的教育设施、当前的成就、社区的需求等等,什么样的权重? 在这里,尽管对适应性没有达成令人满意的定义,我们仍然相信适应性是存在的,但还需要定义和标准化。

(4) 如果我们现在被问到对于一个中国人来说,英语发音和德语发音哪个更难,那么我们可以给出始终正确的答案:"这取决于情况。"从发音的难度来看,德语要困难得多;从根据拼写辨认正确发音的难度来看,英语当然超过大多数语言。因此,并不存在所谓的"发音难度",只有在特定意义上有限定的难度。

(5) 再次,我们可能会被问到:"是亚当斯还是勒维里耶是海王星的先前发现者?"假设在被问及优先性时,是指较早的研究、先前的出版,还是首次对知识界产生影响,如果有人回答:"将年、月、日等三种优先性表达方式相加,除以三,将结果称为优先性本身。"对于这种做法,我们自然会指出,从"逻辑"上讲没有什么反对意见,但这将是一种纯粹"任意"的或者"琐碎"的优先性定义。

(6) 最后,当一个人的思绪离开餐桌以思考各种序列秩序时,会听到这样的问题:"你更愿意吃冰淇淋还是梅子布丁?"在没有对此事进行理论上充分的考虑的情况下,一个人可能只是机械地回答"梅子布丁",实际上并没有更强的偏好。我之所以选择它,并不是因为在任何重要的意义上我更喜欢它,而只是因为我碰巧拿了它①。在这里,偏好的顺序仅仅是临时定义的,即以同义反复的方式。

综上所述,我们可以根据以下几种情况来比较事物的大小:

---

① 参见愉快和不愉快的行为主义含义。

（1）已知的、（2）已定义的、（3）被认为是可定义的，但尚未明确定义的、（4）仅在特定条件下才具有明确性的、（5）任意的、或者（6）以同义反复方式定义的大小。因此，序列可比性不是一个是或否的问题，而是一个更多或更少的问题。

　　然而，对于六种程度的重要性进行分类并不重要。实际上，即使在情况（1）中的重量标准也可能引发争议。虽然在大多数重量的处理中，意义和测量的轻微变化并不重要，但也可能存在两个事物相差甚微以至于次要因素凸显的情况。例如，中午时刻 A 可能比 B 重，但由于 B 吃得更多，下午 2 点时 B 可能比 A 重。如果出于某种原因需要进行更精细的比较，我们将不得不对重量进行精细化和重新定义，例如将其定义为每周六天在特定时间段所测得的平均重量。这样，我们现在有可能陷入人为制造的境地。另一方面，如果我们考虑极端情况，那么小的差异将不会产生主要区别。例如，可以说在任何略微不兼容的优先级意义类别中，中国人在磁偏角的发现上比欧洲人更早。这两个观点赋予了一个新的含义转折，即事物之间差异越小，越难以区分它们。

2. 序列顺序中的谬误：什么不是序列顺序

　　在这里，与其他地方一样，谬误与否是一个程度问题。在一个极端，我们可能不加选择地比较事物，从而陷入混乱；在另一个极端，我们可能否定所有比较，在多维现实的错综复杂性面前束手无策。然而，我们自然倾向于进行各种比较，这是一个有用的倾向，但需要谨慎使用。

　　（1）一维谬误。——但当有人问："谁是你最好的朋友？"时，我们可能无法在我们的日常伴侣、道德恩人或终身导师之间做出选择，等等。只要我们不必做出选择，将它们按友谊的程度排列又有何意义，而友谊是如此多方面的事情呢？同样，我们会遇到一些问题，比如，一个健康的小女孩和一个非常虚弱的运动员，哪个更强壮？哪个更懂音乐，一个演奏"IV 级"不好的人还是一个演奏"II 级"

完美的人？经度的 90°差异与纬度的 30°差异哪个更大或更小？乌鸦更像写字台还是茶盘[①]？

在这些问题中：

1）我们有两个事物，从表面上看它们在几个方面有所不同。例如，纬度和经度位于不同的地理维度。

2）属性 x 是一个没有被理解为明确定义的属性。

3）看不出有任何目的或用途需要定义一个比较的标准。因此，可以认为这个问题存在"一维谬误"。（从逻辑上讲，这等于这些术语未能满足连贯性的假设。）

（2）标准混淆。——然而，对于这一指责，有人可能辩称，在没有具体背景的情况下提出任何问题可能会显得愚蠢或毫无意义。如果我们一直在谈论天气，并且提出了前面的地理问题，那么 30°纬度可能比 90°经度更大的差异。换句话说，上下文提供了使比较有意义的限定条件。（在"完全确定"的问题的极端情况下，例如与分数有关的问题，上下文是整个数学领域或其他大领域，视情况而定。）但是，由于上下文通常是暗示的，而且常常非常模糊，当我们将比较的言语结果带入不同的上下文时，有可能混淆比较的标准。

因此，如果我正在为望远镜研磨一个镜头，球面和色差畸变比视场曲率更严重。因此，我主要通过镜头在这两种畸变方面的自由程度来衡量它的"好坏"。由于我在研磨工作室从事的职业或爱好对我来说是足够的上下文，我不需要用形容词"望远"的或"色差"的来限定镜头的"好坏"。但是，由于"好坏"这个词在其他上下文中有很多联想，可能会发生我忘记限定，并且在我邻居的工作室中（那里制作摄影镜头），通过我"有色"的判断习惯仍然称呼一个镜头好或坏，而那里的好坏在很大程度上取决于图像的视场平坦度。除非我们明确表达我们限定的标准，否则我们永远无法结束争论。因此，在这里，我们有一个混淆一个标准与另一个标准的实例。

---

① 刘易斯·卡罗尔，《爱丽丝梦游仙境》，《疯狂茶会》。

　　从中可以得出的教训并不是我们应该始终明确限定事物，这既不是必要的，也不总是可能的，也不是可取的，而是我们应该意识到每当困难出现时可能发生这种混淆的可能性。

　　（3）不相关辐射①。同样，有些情况下，基于因素的数量进行的比较仅在无意识中应用于其中之一，甚至应用于与之完全不相关的事物。例如，如果国家 A 在其伟大人物的成就方面总体上超过国家 B，并不意味着国家 A 的最伟大的人物比国家 B 的最伟大的人物更伟大。换句话说，最伟大的人物未必是最伟大的。再例如，如果富兰克林②在整体上比你和我更有德行，这并不意味着，让我们希望如此，你和我在秩序方面就比他差。一个人在工厂管理方面很出色，并不意味着他在国际事务中的判断总是正确的。

　　关于重要性的论证经常陷入这种谬误。由于总体上来说，爱国主义高于艺术，如果必须做出独断性的选择，人们会争论任何与爱国主义有松散关联的事物，如某个音乐曲调的陈腐使用，应优先于存在一个伟大的艺术组织。同样，一个逃学者可能会找借口去市区买铅笔而不是练习钢琴课，因为他认为写作比音乐更重要。

　　正如我们不能从整体推导到部分，我们也不能总是逆向推理。因此，如果我基于多种考虑已经确定了我的终身事业，我不应该因为偶尔发现其他工作的某些部分比我手头的工作更有吸引力而动摇。

　　在这些辐射谬误的情况下，它们又与标准的混淆相交织，要求始终对"总体上"这一含义进行确切的限定既不是必要的，也不是可能的，也不是可取的，因为这可能导致贫瘠的结果。回顾第 1 节中的极端情况的最后一段话，我们可以说，如果一个人在物理学方面取得卓越成就，那么他在数学能力的评估中相当高。合理地推测他的语言运用也相当不错。虽然偶尔我们会发现像乔尔拉莫·卡尔

---

① 参见"整体与部分的谬误"。
② 自传，第 3 项德行（《哈佛经典丛书》第 1 卷，第 83 页）。

丹这样的人，但他不太可能是一个道德低能者。实际上，我们在这里有一个递减的统计相关系数列表。对于这些谬误，我们应采取的黄金中庸的态度是意识到概念"干涉条纹"可能存在不安全或不相关的辐射，同时我们可以自由而富有成效地解释标准，并相应地进行权衡。

（4）否认比较。与一维度的错误相反的错误是否认在任何程度上可以比较任何事物（普遍性），或者否认在应该进行比较的情况下进行比较（具体性）。因为学生在能力、应用和成就上有所不同，所以教师拒绝将他们按照分数排列。实际上，所有犹豫不决的情况都是由于无法在"质上"不同的事物之间做出优先选择。这种错误的哲学观点在于断言，由于所有具体事物在许多方面都不同，并且所有的串行比较标准都包含一定程度的任意性和人为性，因此所有这些比较都是人为的，不应该进行。这就像说除了无限大，其他一切都必须是零一样荒谬！

3. 序列排序的方法：方法的来源

在方法章节中，我试图表明对于每种方法，都有一种方法可以应用。因此，在讨论序列排列的应用或使用之前，我将探讨序列排序是如何建立起来的。

观察法。有时候问题："A比B更x吗？"非常明确，答案非常显而易见，我们可以一眼看出，不需要任何"方法"。天蓝色比新的细毛呢西装轻，抱负比绝望更好，飞机比空气重。这可以称为观察法或直觉法，它是方法的零点或下限。这种方法的意义在于，无论有多少复杂的方法论机制将答案与问题联系起来，在某个地方，观察、直觉或直接依据经验的方法必须介入应用该方法。（参见第二章第176—177页）。

定义 x。如果判断 x 的标度不那么容易，那么我们必须找到比较 x 的标准，换句话说，要使 x 的含义更加明确。询问黄金是否比银重意味着比较它们在相同体积下的重量，或者说它们在水中失去的重量的比例是多少。因此，我们在水中称重它们来找出答案。通过引入方法，将观察的行为推迟到读取刻度的行为，从而提高了准确性的影响力。

选择 x。但很多时候问题的提出方式使我们无法明确讨论在问题出现的上下文中值得考虑的含义，那么问题可能会得不到答案，即我们称之为"一维度的谬误"。另一方面，对 x 概念的使用和实用性可能告诉我们，我们可以从问题中得出某种 x-er 的东西。现在的问题是，是什么以及如何？

极端情况。一种方法是尝试极端情况的方法（第二章，第 162 页）。通过这样做，无论是实际地还是假设地（如果为了安全需要），我们可以通过观察引出判断的情况，并明确在这些情况下可能需要考虑哪些因素，即使这些因素并不那么突出。

权衡因素。接下来，我们需要结合这些因素，问问自己对于所得到的 x 我们指的是什么。一个例子是通过考虑一系列标准测试来评估智力，并通过某种方式组合这些数字得到一个综合得分。在这里，我们对智力 x 的程度有一些概念，但只有在建立了刻度之后，我们才有一个可以实际运用的明确含义 x。因为"智力"的意义变化范围太广，无法满足科学心理学在应用上的要求。

使用情况。对于比较的标准是什么？对于这个问题的答案，就像对于一般定义一样，是使用情况和实用性。"使用情况"在理论家中并不受欢迎。"一个名字有什么关系？"但除非问题太琐碎不值一提，否则模糊的问题必定传达了一些大致的概念。问题："A 或 B 哪个镜头更好？"在一定范围内是有歧义的。但是这个范围并不是无限的。"好"的使用将其限制在一个（可能不明确的）领域内，并具有有限的弹性范围。我们不能将镜头的好坏定义为其表面划痕的丰富程度，这样会超出"完全弹性的限制"。因此，正是使用情况首先告诉我们我们要做什么，并让我们开始行动起来。

稳定性。如果使用情况过于不明确、不一致，无法满足我们的目的，那么实用性的考虑就会介入决策。对于我们的问题，定义 x

的最重要或最不武断的方式是什么？如果实用性被认为是一个不可接受的术语，我们可以称之为逻辑稳定性。在实际事务、实验或真实定律的制定过程中，标准化序列顺序 x 的方式通常会经常出现。通常情况下，科学上非常稳定或有用的 x 的定义与使用中的平均意义几乎没有任何关系。如果它差异很大，那么出于对使用情况的尊重，我们可以使用技术上的限定或选择其他术语，或者简单地让术语出现在科学著作的封面之间就足够构成限定的背景。因此，热度和冷度的刻度在使用中具有一般含义。后来，它通过液体的膨胀被定义，再后来通过气体的膨胀被定义，最后以热力学关系的术语进行定义，这是物理学中最"稳定"的温度定义。如果我们发现 $60℃$ 时的勺子比 $61℃$ 时的杯子更热，那么我们可以进行限定，并说这只是心理上的温暖和寒冷，而不是物理温度。

总的来说，我们可以说使用情况可能引发一个问题，但实用性指引我们应该往何处去。如果我们有理由走得很远，那么让我们明确表达出来。否则，我们可能会混淆标准，将好的称为坏的，将坏的称为好的。

4. 串行排序方法：其作用

串行排序本身作为一种方法，因为其被执行并服务于一些进一步的目的而存在。

（1）优先级。——在选择行动、事物或人员时，我们必须将备选项按照优先级进行比较。往往，仅仅排序本身作为一种方法就非常重要。当匆忙做出决定比不做决定要好时，就是这种情况。如果一个人被一些琐碎的事情困扰，不知道从何开始，解决现实问题的一个方法就是将它们按照任意的优先顺序列出，并逐项处理。在"排队"的实践中，排序就不那么任意了。因为在这里，"服务"的顺序被定义为"到来"的顺序。

（2）定位。——串行排序也可以帮助我们在一个范围内定位某个事物。标记一个非常庞大的学生群体的一种方式是按照成绩的排名进行排序,然后根据学生在班级中的位置,例如前 3%、接下来的 21% 或者再下面的 45%,分配 A、B、C 等级。虽然第一种按照观察进行的排序存在一定的"主观"因素,但是对于一个庞大的班级来说,这种过程的结果比简单地将考试试卷称为 B 卷或 D 卷更加"客观"。另一个例子是按字母顺序排列事物,如字典中的单词,或按数字顺序排列,如书中的页码。这一点太明显,无需进一步讨论。

定义。——就串行排序而言,某些模糊的概念可以被定义。例如,经济并不一定意味着节省这个或否认那个,而可以被定义为我们应该按照常识或进一步的方法,按照"合理"的顺序或重要性安排可能的开支,并在达到一个总开支仍在自己承受范围内的点之前逐步减少。

从实际意义上讲,"可能性"也可以与某个尺度相结合来考虑。"我明天不可能做到这件事",这意味着如果我按照紧急程度的顺序安排我的工作,完成"这件事"之前所需的总时间将超过明天。

真理。——但串行排序最重要的应用在于串行排序本身的意义,正如前三节所示。只要串行排序被明确定义,关于它将存在一些真理:我们可以引述关于 x 的定理,我们可以按照这个尺度演奏曲调。如果 A 比 B 更重,他会带来更大的冲击力。他行动所需的能量更多,给他的裁缝留下的利润空间更小,他在薄冰上滑冰的安全性更低,以及其他关于重量的真理。对于常识来说,"排队"似乎比所有这些心理测量的科学设备或更抽象的概率和熵的理论更有意义。然而,这些概念在科学中是有用的,正是因为它们不仅仅是简单的定义,除了它们的定义之外没有任何真实内容。它们远非人为的,它们融入到相互关联的法则和真命题中,这些法则和真命题赋予它们与胖子的理解胖的意义一样具体的含义。

5. 结论：阈值[1]

生活和科学是近似的事务,这是一个陈词滥调。在具体情况

中，"$a = b$"意味着如果进行更精细的比较，a 和 b 之间的差异将小于我们所关心的阈值 ε。从这个观点来看，"标准的混淆"往往是一种优点，就像是一种缺点一样。由汞、气体和能量定义的三种温度可以 indiscriminately 地被视为"温度"，而不需要添加修正，而在轻微的差异不会产生影响的众多目的中，这是可以接受的。通过这种方式，我们可以自由地说，（在某些范围内）气体的膨胀与温度成比例等。

使用中的不一致性通常也是下意识的，如果是这样的话，我们可以让它们和平共处，属于同一术语下。"人类的卓越"在使用中肯定有不一致的含义，然而在许多情况下，我们不希望有一种干燥而冗长的严格定义，限制其适用范围。

这并不是对粗心的辩护，而是对成果保护的呼吁。我不想因为顾虑到高温不是感觉而失去高温是温暖的真理。在某个 ε 范围内，它们是同一类的成员。争论和悖论只会在下位相关的不一致性在没有警告的情况下变得相关，即通过改变观点或转换立场来超过阈值时出现。因此，避免它们的方法是了解自己的范围。我所提倡的粗心或看似提倡的粗心因此并非是天真的那种，而是像艺术的人为自然性一样复杂的那种。

现在，一个数学思维倾向的人可能会提出，悖论的解决之道在于精确定义。因为如果数据是近似值，那么自然会有一个问题出现，近似于什么？为什么不找出这个"什么"并将其作为标准？非常好，我们憎恶那些不科学的温度概念的不一致性，让我们采用理论物理学中使用的热力学温度定义。那么，简单的气体定律 PV＝RT 只对"理想气体"成立。但是没有气体是理想的。因此可悲的结果是没有气体遵守气体定律，也没有气体适用于温度测量。但是，有人会说，如果你完善你的理论和实验，你会找到一个真正的气体定律，以真实温度为基础，比如用范德瓦尔斯方程表示的真实温度：

$$\left(P + \frac{a}{V}a\right)(V - b) = RT$$

它考虑了分子不完全弹性和不是几何点的事实。但是，这不仅仅是更高程度的精细化，ε的减小吗？已经发现，范德瓦尔斯方程也无法严格适用于实际气体。因此，如果我们坚持对温度本身的严格定义，除了其定义之外，我们对它无法说出任何真实的信息。能量关系的测量容易受到偶然误差的影响；范德瓦尔斯方程是不精确的；简单的气体定律是错误的；热和冷的感觉是虚幻的。因此，热力学温度标准出现之前，使用温度计进行的所有大量研究以及在那之后的所有类似研究都是非科学的，或者与温度本身无关。同样地，在当前关于质量概念的讨论中，还没有达成最终的定义，所以我们对质量的所有概念实际上都与质量无关。当 E. V. 亨廷顿教授[①]用力和其他具体关系来解释质量时，有人斥责他说"质量只是质量而已"。因此，以逻辑的名义，T 就是 T，T 不是非 T。证毕。

但是一旦允许近似误差，我们就可以说 T 不是 T，或许从黑格尔的意义上说，也就是说，我们可以对某个东西说些什么。在大多数常识的背景下，阈值比在科学中要宽广。但是在科学中，阈值从来不是零，科学在比较一系列事物时的渐进精确性并不在于通过声明 ε＝0 来达到贫瘠的精确性，同时将真理的数量减少到零，而在于试图缩小 ε 的范围，但在这个 ε 范围内拥有许多真实的规律，从而实现有益的准确性。

也许用一些图表比用几页修辞更能清楚地表达这个想法，对许多人来说更容易理解。让 T 代表抽象的温度。然后我们有平凡等式 $T=T$，可以用直线 $y=x$ 来表示（图1）。接下来，让 T' 代表基于物理定律的测量结果。由于定律和测量只是近似的，同样的温度可能会有不同的读数，同样的读数可能对应不同的温度，因此 T 和 T' 实际上是彼此的多值函数，而 $T<T'$ 的图形将不是曲线，而是一个带状区域（图2）（参见第 317 页的图1）。第三，让 T' 代表我们皮肤的粗略猜测，皮肤受到的干扰影响比温度计要多。那么对温度的判

---

① 《美国数学月刊》，1918 年 1 月。

断将更加粗糙,表示将是一个更宽广
的带状区域。(图3。当然,该区域不
一定有尖锐、直线的边界。)拿一个温
度为60℃的勺子和一个温度为61℃
的杯子来说。我们的第一个温度计
将给出读数 a′,b′,由于其变化在几分
之一度的范围内,它将显示杯子更
热。但是我们的嘴唇受到传导影响,
可能估计勺子的温度为 a″,杯子的温

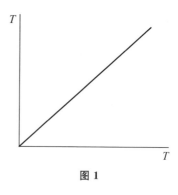

图 1

度为 b″,因此其结果与温度计的结果不一致。[①]

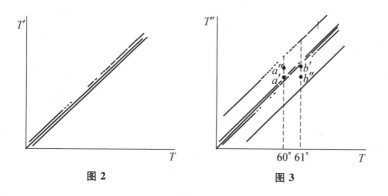

图 2　　　　　　　　　　图 3

现在问题是这样的。在极端情况下,即使是皮肤也总是正确
的。另一方面,在小差异的关键情况下,即使是一个好的温度计也
会显得漠不关心。因此,皮肤和温度计之间可以被视为程度上的差
异。从实际上讲,每个带状区域在程度上实际上是一个曲线。在其
宽度内,所有的差异都是无关紧要的、下意识的。关于大小的真理,
可以说是几个小带状区域位于同一个“论述带”之内。在图4中,假
设简单的气体定律在广泛的带状区域 AA 内是正确的,那么它意味

---

①　参见第二章,第190—191页,有关函数和区域限制的内容。

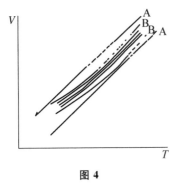

图 4

着表示实际气体的经验观察的细带（用实心黑色标记）位于该区域内。现在，当我们通过范德瓦尔方程将定律进一步精确到缩小的带状区域 BB 时，它仍然包含了细带。这构成了进步。但是，如果我们通过画一条线而不是一个带状区域来制定温度的限制标准，显然它将不包含任何经验上绘制的细带。科学希望找到一个既窄又包含许多其他带状区域的带状区域，一个窄而包容的带状区域，与线性的排外曲线相对。这些是"有益的准确性"与"贫瘠的精确性"之间的图形翻译。如果我们通过诸如 n/ε 这样的概念来衡量串行顺序标准的效用或逻辑稳定性，其中 n 表示包含的带状区域的数量，ε 表示带状区域的宽度，那么有益的准确性意味着 n 大于 ε 小，但是贫瘠的精确性通过将 ε 设为 0，使得 n 为零，会导致无意义的 0/0，这与逻辑稳定性相去甚远。

第五章　限　制　点

1. 限制点的一般性质

　　"如果你得不到你喜欢的,那就喜欢你所拥有的。"但是,如果我喜欢我所拥有的,那我不就得到了我喜欢的吗? 换句话说,通过将我对生活的要求降低到一个较低的限制点,它的满足度会自动提升到一个百分之百的上限。这种推理并不是为了把冷静主义归纳为荒谬或合理的一方面,而是为了说明限制点在这个研究中的概念是具有双重性质的。限制点的形式性质可以用 C、1 或 ∞ 这样的术语来表示,或者任何其他方便将其视为刻度的极限的术语。较低限制的概念可以用 0 来表示,比如"零要求",或用 1 来表示,比如"思想是与自己对话"。较高限制的概念可以用 1 或 100% 来表示,比如"话语的整个宇宙",或用 ∞ 来表示,比如"相关因素的整体性"。除了冷静主义的例子之外,我们可以应用简单的数学技巧,将刻度上的任何区间 (a,b) 转换为任何其他区间 (ε',b'),特别是转换为 $(0,\infty)$,通过建立任何一一对应的方式,使得 a 对应于 $0,b$ 对应于 ∞,或反之亦然。因此,从教授的角度来看,一名新生可能具有一定有限的智力程度 a,在四年后,会有稍高的智力程度 b;但在一位高年级学生眼中,一名新生代表着无知和愚蠢的上限,在四年中应该消失得无影无踪,换句话说,a 趋于 ∞,b 趋于 0。这种可转换性的特点使得对限制点的研究比特殊符号所暗示的更为普遍。例如,两个事物相等的所有情况都可以看作是它们差异的下限。事实上,这是一种熟悉的数学技术,特别是在处理复变量时,处理 $a-b=0$ 而不是 $a=b$。

　　在许多情况下,选择观点时存在一种自然的偏好,其弹性无法被克服,除非以某种不适当的方法论力量为代价。因此,在一个充满努力和成就的世界中,我们自然地将冷静主义立场视为零理想的一种，并且并不在其完美实现的事实中找到太多意义。因此，我们称之为一个下限的情况。一个下限的特征表达是"至少可以这样说"。每个人都可以有一些可实现的理想，至少是零。

现在来看一个常识人，他没有意识到时间表和计划的缺失，也就是说，他处于方法的下限，但他只知道他做事情有效，也就是说，他处于直觉的上限，直觉从表面上起初是无所依据的，然后跳跃到现实的"1"。一个上限的特征表达是"最终"。因此，最终，无论是否有方法，人们必须拥有一些实际的意志力来执行行动，一些直觉来接近现实。

无论是上限还是下限的情况，限制点的核心问题是身份和差异的问题。限制点与系列的其他部分有何相似之处？又有何不同之处？接下来，我将按顺序对这些问题进行阐述。

2. 限制点中的身份

仅仅称之为限制点并停止于此，似乎确实是对定义实用性的下限。因此，合理地要求对这些空洞概念有何进一步的意义。

（1）形式普遍性。——第一个回答是："没有"。我将一个刻度延伸到包括偏僻的事物，并将它们放在我的刻度的零和无穷处，只是作为一种普遍性的实验，为了获得简洁或陈述的对称性，为了保住我的逻辑立场。事实上，这正是形式逻辑和数学的精神所在。由于我们并不总是确定 S 是 P，我们至少可以说 A 就是 A，以确保。空类简单地是一个成员数量为零的类。如果有限的析取 A 是 B 或 C 不确定，我们至少可以进行无限的析取，即 A 是 B 或 C 或二者都不是。如果我们将我们的论述宇宙扩大到足够广，我们可以说美德不是正方形，或者无论如何，A 不是非—A，至少可以这样说。同样的原因，在相同的全部条件下，会有相同的效果。在美国，于 1917年 6 月 5 日注册的外国人、精神失常者等都属于五个为兵役登记的类别之一。在每个"具体"问题中，你必须考虑所有"具体的"、"实际的"因素。永远记住，"这取决于情况"。一切真实的东西都是独一无二的。刚从铸币厂出来的一枚硬币不会是另一枚硬币,至少可以这样说。换句话说,这种策略在于获得一个逻辑上的鸟瞰视角,尽可能地包含更多内容,不在乎此刻能说多少。

一类有趣的情况是我们更倾向于通过跳过一个鸿沟来完成一个宇宙。我们不是说支出减收入等于赤字,而是说收入加赤字满足支出。同样,设 Fe 和 Fw 分别为作用于东方和西方的力的总和,a 为向东的加速度,m 为受力物体的质量;那么,与其说 $Fe - Fw = ma$,即这些力的差额为 ma,d'Alembert 根据他的原理会写成 $Fe - Fw - ma = 0$,即所有力的总和互相平衡,这在某种意义上是在回避问题(虽然不是非常严肃)。再者,与其让一些不属于任何类别的事物悬空不置,我可以将这些未分类的事物放入未分类类别中,从而确保宇宙完备。因此,"杂项"标题始终可以补充有限性并填满其余的无限性;或者换个说法,我可以说,如果我们原则上寻求补偿,我们总能在原则上找到补偿。

如果一个形式的概括被理解其所值得的意义,那么这并不是错误。但是,如果一个人试图既吃蛋糕又保留蛋糕,那就会犯一个谬误。提醒自己要努力工作,但不要过度劳累;只要足够认真,就能实现任何合理的理想。黄金法则和康德的普遍道德法则适用于在相同情况下的人,或者说,在相同相关情况下适用于人们,换句话说,在它们适用的情况下。因此,当一个陈述被确定合格时,其意义也被抵消了。

(2)显著概括。——但也许我所能说的意义并不完全为零。一开始只是名义上的概括往往在效果上超过了名义。我们发现某些事情在某些情况下是真实的。它们在极限情况下也可能是真实的。如果是这样,那么这个概括就不是名义上的。

因此,如果空间中的两个三角形形成某些立体图形并具有某些性质,那么当这些立体图形"退化",即被扁平化成一个平面时,它们可能保留这些性质。事实上,这正是著名的德萨格尔定理最初被证明的方式。

　　如果我们忽略数学的实际历史，我们可以逻辑地说我们的整个数字系统是对较低限制的重复应用。当 $b=P$ 时，复数 $a+bi$ "退化"为实数，依此类推，直到最后，我们得到一个分母为 1 的正有理分数，"退化"为正整数，这是现代分析的算术化过程中较低限制系列的下限。在这里，我们知道许多在较高情况下成立的事物也适用于较低情况。

　　在数学中，许多定理在有限情况下成立时，在其变为无穷时同样成立。因此，对于有限限制下的积分定理，在某个或两个限制变为无穷时，或者在某些点上被积函数变为无穷时，这些定理同样适用于所谓的不定积分情况。正如我们所见，一个上限从另一个角度看是一个下限。$\int_a^{(1/a)} [f(x)dx]$ 同样可以看作是 $\int_{(1/a)}^a [g(y)dy]$，其中 $y=1/x$。

　　在通过复变量研究立体映射时，我们常常被困扰于真实于所有点，包括北极点的定理无法一脉相承地陈述和证明，因为北极点作为无穷远点是一个分析上的例外。但通过简单的变换，北极点就和南极点一样好用。

　　力的平行四边形定律指出，两个力的合力由平行四边形的对角线表示，如果这些力表示为其边。但当我们有一个面积为零的平行四边形，即力夹角为 0° 或 180° 时，这个定律仍然成立。考虑到极限中的持续同一性特征，因此数学家将一个平行四边形"退化"成直线段似乎有些不公平。因为极限并不总是如此彻底地退化，以至于失去了所有祖先的特征。

　　(3) 心理扩展。实际上，任何名义上的扩展是否能保持名义上的状态是值得怀疑的。通过假装处于零点，我们常常通过心理上的把戏陷入了某种情况。如果我能成功地保持一种总是给予而从不索取的态度，那么我可能会惊喜地发现我拥有的一点点幸福，并且没有意识到我应得到它们。当一个孩子拒绝按时上床睡觉时，母亲会说："那就不用睡觉，因为无论如何我必须被服从。"通过在使用零命令时保留她的逻辑立场,她下次更有机会让孩子"熬夜,但请再安静一些"。

在试图过一种完全理性的生活时,人们常常面临着机会和可原谅的诱惑(如果这种事情真的存在),这些诱惑会打破人们的规则和计划,而这些诱惑也许并不值得支付纪律成本。在这种情况下,人们可以使用一种正式承认破坏系统的技巧,并将其视为系统的一部分,无论它看起来多么令人愤慨。因此,在忙碌的工作中,将一个荒谬的命题(如进行一次 15 英里的徒步旅行,然后进行三个小时的闲聊,最后再工作或上床睡觉)明确地安排在黑白之中,比在一个季度的时间里闲逛并对着日程表眨眼睛更安全,而日程表上写着"这是你的工作时间"。

(4)极限作为理想。在上限的情况下,我们经常可以将其设定为一个理想,并且虽然我们无法达到它,但我们仍然可以朝着它的方向取得一些进展。因此,我们可以将为什么定义为对如何的程度的上限。在提问时,我们可以问"为什么"和"为什么是这样"的问题。但如果我们牢记理想的"为什么"的感觉,它可能会激发人们进一步追寻"如何"的动力,例如进一步解释万有引力定律。

再次,在实际事务中,我们只能考虑有限的最优点。但将所有最优点以正确的代数符号综合为一个最优点是一个有用的理想,因为它拓宽了我们的价值领域。(参见第八章第 294 页关于最优点的内容)

总的来说,无论是哲学家还是科学家,形而上学的精神似乎是持有以上限形式存在的理想。对于诸如真、善、美等概念,我们用唯一的冠词"the"作为前缀,这些概念只在有限的和相对的事物中得以体现。

然而,这并不意味着没有理想是可达到的。通过站在一个极限处,朝向另一个极限,我们经常可以找到足够的步骤来跨越其中的距离。柏拉图的分析方法,既适用于几何构造,也适用于定理的证明,就是一个例子。假设有点 A 和以 O 为圆心的圆。要从 A 点到圆上画一条切线。柏拉图会这样开始说:"假设已经画出了切线

AB。"这仅仅是在解决问题之前做一个假设，这是分析的零起点。但我们并不停留在这个零的洞穴里。我们可以进一步走一小段路，并说 OB 垂直于 AB。因此，$\triangle AOB$ 可以被内接于以 AO 为直径的圆。因此，A 和 O 之间的中点 C 就是这个圆的圆心。因此，如果我们从 AO 的中点开始，其他的事情就都能够完成。因此，我们通过一些中间的步骤，从无中获得了一些东西。

总的来说，追求最大广泛性而冒着最小意义的风险的数学精神有时会引起人们对略微不那么广泛但更有意义的情况的关注。一个重视具体事物的人可能会忽略这些情况，因为他固守着习惯中的最小意义，并害怕进一步冒险。因此，数学逻辑曾经受到了空洞的批评，但其详细的推导工作远非毫无意义。

3. 极限点的差异

（1）下限点。到目前为止，我一直强调了极限与其他情况的相同之处。但是极限作为极限是独特的，至少可以说，我们已经看到最少并不总是我们能说的最多的。一般来说，极限点除了具有名称上的特殊性之外，还具有更多的特殊性和身份。

在普通的数学分析中，0 是一个具有许多其他数的性质的数。但它在以下几个方面是特殊的：它是唯一一个绝对值小于任何一个趋近于零的变量 ε 的值的常数，它没有倒数，它只有一个值作为它的 n 次根，以及其他许多方面。

在数学中经常发生的情况是，对于一个变量成立的性质在极限情况下可能不成立。例如，$\tan x$ 是 x 在 $\pi/2$ 和 π 之间的连续函数，但当 $x = \pi/2$ 时，$\tan x$ 无论赋予它什么值，都是不连续的。然而，这样的情况并不新鲜。只需要进行简单的变换就可以看出，它们只是零的特殊性再次呈现出来而已。

命题，如果你愿意的话，可以被概括为命题函数，其中它是意义模糊的下限。但它有一个特殊之处，即它可以是真或假，并且当与另一个命题存在蕴含关系时，使蕴含难以理解。（参见第三章"分级思想”,第 187 页）作为一个下限,独处只是一种单一的社会关系。值得指出的是,当思考时人们会与自己对话,可以大声与自己说话,真正地厌恶自己、爱自己、戏弄自己、给自己找借口等等,在许多方面明显的差异是多么重要。

（2）上限。一类极具独特上限特点的限制被表达为对立概念,如绝对与相对、无条件与有条件、无限与有限、具体与抽象、具体对象与普遍概念、范畴与假设等等。因此,无论缝纫机在第一次缝制时需要进行多少次针脚以确保第一针的安全,除非在某处将线头拉穿环口以处理无限序列的剩余部分,否则这将是一个无限进程。无论阿基里斯和乌龟[①]在争论中堆砌多少条规则以便在前提要求下得出结论,没有人实际执行将无法得出结论。无论科学家的方法论多么精细,将其应用于实验室中都需要一些直觉和技巧。无论立法者在定义所有可能情况时多么具有远见,对于每个特定情况仍需要一些法官来解释法律。无论一个伦理学体系如何详尽,都需要一些有智慧的良心来应用并正确应用。无论一个人制定了多长的决议链,都需要一些意志力来开始最简单的决议。无论一个人设计了多完备的记忆系统,仍需要一定程度的天生记忆能力来记住替代物。无论在一个公设系统中有多少定理在无限数量的定理中保持一致,仍需要一些具体的例证来验证所有定理的一致性。总之,无论一个人拥有多大的杠杆作用力 N,都需要一些实际的力量 ε(大于零)来验证“阿基米德公设”,即 $N \times \varepsilon$ 足以移动地球。

在这些例子中,我们可以注意到一些相似之处,比如在正式的普遍性下讨论支出与收入的赤字,作为理想的上限的例子,以及这些独特限制的情况。实际上,如果第一个例子是在俯瞰大峡谷的深渊,第二个例子是对对岸进行望远镜观察,而第三个例子则是真正飞越并降落在实地。

（3）下限。在研究一个话语宇宙的一部分时,人们经常得出整

---

① 路易斯·卡罗尔,《乌龟对阿基里斯说的话》,《心灵》,1895 年,第 278 页。

体与该部分相似的结论。在对导体和非导体进行实验时，查尔斯·迪菲发现所有物体都在一定程度上导电，不存在所谓的非导体，或者用我们的术语来说，导电性的下限和电阻的上限是不存在的。然而，这种区别在特定问题中产生并一直存在，其中与每个问题相关的阈值以下的导电性被视为几乎为零。因此，即使不存在唯一的极限，也会存在一个唯一的邻域或极限的阈值，这样在其范围内的情况就需要采取不同的处理方法。

　　哲学洞察力常常在没有注意到它们的情况下跌倒在这些下限上。所有的思维都是行动。然而，在某种程度上（相对于某个问题而言），行动更适合被视为思考。所有的经验都是沉思。然而，在冲突和努力达到一定程度以上时，观察方式变得不那么沉思。一切都是独特的，没有两个东西是相同的。然而，在大多数问题中，一枚硬币和另一枚硬币是一样的，也就是说，它们的面额相同。基督科学家说，所有的痛苦都是虚构的。然而，即使承认这一点，在某个阈值以下会有虚构的虚构痛苦，而在有机损伤的阈值以上会有真实的虚构痛苦。一切真实的都是具体的，像一个有机体，而不是一堆沙子。然而，在实际或理论重要性的某个下限以下，事物可以被视为无组织的。至少在我们话语宇宙的大部分中，将一堆沙子视为一堆沙子是安全的。人们常常被告诫，无论情况有多糟糕，他总是能够充分利用局势，从潜在的环境中选择最好的有效环境，即使他的手脚被束缚，他仍然可以思考自己喜欢的东西，换句话说，不存在零自由度这样的事情。然而，当这个自由度降至可忽略的 ε 时，尽力而为也不会比尽量避免更好。如果我因患急性疾病而卧床不起，我可以原谅地忽略利用机会进行连续性研究的建议。

　　在第七章（第 268 页以下），我将试图展示所有物理系统要么处于稳定平衡，要么处于非平衡状态，当稳定性的（广义）基础为零时，不稳定平衡作为稳定平衡的下限是不存在的。然而，如果稳定性低于某个阈值，我们称之为不稳定平衡的情况，特别是如果在顶部的小平台之外有一个陡峭的滑坡。因此，所谓过冷溶液或过饱和空气处于不稳定平衡,是因为引入微小颗粒以扰乱平衡与其所产生的巨大变化相比非常微不足道。那么,为什么一个单独的电子不会引发整个变化呢? 因为它的行为不会将系统推出其较小的稳定基础,尽管从我们通常的观点来看,这个基础是下意识的。

(4) 上限阈值。迄今为止,我一直将阈值看作是靠近零的一个小区间。但从上限的角度来看,一个 ε 内的邻域包括了超过某个上限阈值 M 的情况。因此,说"电导率小于某个 ε 的物体实际上是非导体",等同于说"电阻大于例如干燥空气的电阻的物体实际上具有无穷大电阻"。零电导率、百分之百绝缘和无穷大电阻是同义词。在一个现象 y 作为无限多可能因素的函数的一般问题中,我们可以说我们只能考虑其中一部分,不存在考虑影响现象 y 的所有因素的情况,我们永远无法完全写出 $y = f(x1, x2, x3, \ldots)$ 然而,对于每个问题,只考虑有限数量的因素 M 就足够了,并且可以说在我们的问题中忽略 $\partial f/(\partial x\_(M+1))$, $\partial f/(\partial x\_(M+2))$, $\ldots$ 的总效应是可忽略的,也就是说,当考虑的因素数量大于 M 时,与无穷大一样好。实际的无穷大也不一定是一个很大的数字。一个实际的电工只需知道电线的长度、厚度、材料和电压,就能知道电流,所以他的无穷大等于四。在一个更精细的物理问题中,可能还需要知道温度和磁场,这只需要六个因素。

4. 限制的具体意义

(1) 类别中的限制。在上面的内容中(第 217 页和 220 页),我们提及到形式逻辑和数学处理的是下限,而哲学处理的是上限。考虑到观点的可转化性,我们可以说两个极端相遇。现在我们发现,在具体问题中(除了有限数量的离散元素的情况下),我们可以在零和无穷之间替代使用小于下限或大于上限的术语,这些术语在特定问题中确定。那么,我们是否应该丢弃确切的极限点,贬低形而上学和数学呢? 不,我们可能会在术语上失去一些东西。

让我们应用奥卡姆剃刀原则,或者更具体地说,罗素的抽象原则。由于我们不需要严格的零或无穷大，而且它们的含义是未定义的，我们可以简单地将零定义为在我们有限问题中出现的所有有限 ε 的类别，将无穷大定义为在我们有限问题中出现的所有有限 M 的类别（当然要正确考虑物理或其他单位的维度）。因此，抽象原则可以被称为具体化原则。[①]

将这种处理方法应用于各种限制的情况下，我们可以说例如 $y=x2$，它表示的是所有带有 x 的带或管的问题的类别，而这些带或管的宽度都小于在每个情况下分配的 ε（参见第三章，第 192 页）。因此，我们现在可以说，"从具体的角度来看，水柱从数学角度上说实际上是一个抛物线"，我们可以说，"从具体的角度来看，水柱是抛物线的一个成员，也就是说，它简单地就是一个抛物线"。在符号"$J \in P$"中，"$\in$"的技术意义也就被解释为普通意义上的"是"。再举一个例子，与其说各种现象测量温度（第四章，第 210 页），我们可以说温度是气体、液体、状态变化、辐射频率变化、热感和冷感在某种方式上相关联的现象的类别。

（2）数学定义的方法论解释。这听起来像是对零、无穷和极限的宽泛讨论，完全无视数学的用法。现在我必须与标准的极限定义进行密切接触。教科书上说，"当 x 趋近于 0 时，L 是 $f(x)$ 的极限"，这意味着对于任意预先确定的 ε，存在一个 δ，使得在 $|x|<\delta$ 时，

$$|f(x)-L|<\varepsilon。[②]$$

现在，定义的第一条语言相当戏剧化。它将 x 和 $f(x)$ 描绘成经历一种赫拉克利特式的过程。但在实际的数学研究中，极限更可操作的意义是逻辑上的 δ 与预先确定的 ε（或 N 与预先确定的 M，等等，视情况而定）之间的对应关系，而在任何单个对应实例中，从平均角度来看，ε 和 δ 都不需要很小。那么，我所做的，或者说我意图做的，只是将这种逻辑数学的对应关系解释为一种方法论的对应

关系。数学家说"对于任意预先确定的 ε"，然后就止步于此。我问，是谁不请自来地预先确定了 ε 呢？数学家并不在意，他愿意让这个问题过去。现在从方法论的角度来看，也许从历史的角度来看，难道不是实际的问题预先确定了某些阈值，如果差异低于这些阈值，那么它们就"没有差别"了吗？在同样的主题中，例如平衡，会有无数个不同的问题，具有不同的相关性阈值。我们实际上没有提出无限多的问题并不是一个反对意见，因为在数学极限的对应定义中，我们不需要将所有的 ε 都具体指定并写在纸上。一个更严重的反对意见是，按数量级排列的 ε 的类别可能不会收敛到零，而是收敛到某个正值，比零大。答案是，这只有在我们选择了一些 ε 而忽略了其他 ε 的情况下才可能发生。对于所有有限问题中 ε 的下界，正是我们所指的方法论零。这个反对意见，在仅涉及特定论域中的 ε 的纯数学情况下是成立的，而在一般情况下则涉及了一种术语上的矛盾。因此，这种对数学定义的非数学解释似乎并不是一种无数学良心的。

（3）哲学应用。现在将这种观点应用于第 2 节中提到的哲学理想，在那里对其有效性的问题被留在了空中。1）哲学被认为旨在追求"绝对"（或其变体）。2）让我们摒弃这个绝对，而是说我们有限的智力探究在某个上限阈值 M 之上的广度和深度将被称为哲学。3）现在，既然不再需要绝对，我们可以自由地将其定义为那些被称为哲学的探究和结果的类别。4）因此，我们将我们的哲学绝对重新具体化。真实、善良、美丽，如果用人文和时间的术语来表述，可以意味着知识、道德和艺术标准的实际演进过程，以便在每个阶段，从迄今为止所取得的进展出发，再加上一个人可能具备的对未来的洞察力，我们可以在实践上，也就是分类地，判断任何事物在具体情况下是真实的还是不真实的，是好的还是不好的，是美丽的还是不美丽的。这当然说了很多。但我对这一哲学观点的看法比对限制点的例子本身要不那么严肃，或者说限制点理论必须在最后基于这些例子，或者说限制点理论必须由这些例子组成。因为经历了这些"具体案例"之后，如果我说"说了很多"，那我一定是想说"说了很少"。

第六章　通过连续性建立身份

身份与差异。在关于身份和差异、程度差异和类型差异、连续性和不连续性、数量变化和质量变化、一致性和多样性、一和多、恒定性和可变性、持久性和变化性、习惯和智能等哲学讨论中，我们不断地被提醒，没有差异就没有身份，没有身份就没有差异，没有持久性就没有变化，没有变化就没有持久性，等等。为了不让这种普遍提醒使我们忘记这个概念的意义，我们需要探究在我们日常智能行为中哪些身份和差异是相互关联的。作为一种研究方法，如果能够得到合理的结果，我将主要将所讨论的事物视为位于一个已经在第三章和第四章中准备好的分级观念和连续序列的刻度 x 上的，两个待比较的事物。找到一个离散或实际连续的分级刻度。在我们逐渐过渡过程中，询问自己，哪些方面保持不变？这是本章的主题。以及哪些方面发生了不同，如果不同，是在哪里以及如何发生的？这是下一章的主题。

作为一种方法而非教条，这个过程既不真实也不虚假，但可能是好的或坏的，有效的或琐碎的。当它对其工作物质没有牢固控制时，后者就会从安全阀泄漏出来。因此，拿一个卷心菜和一个国王，考虑从一个到另一个的形式的渐变。通过这样做，我们可以认识到它们在属于同一连续类别上是相同的，不幸的是，这个类别是即兴构建的。一般来说，我可以正式将任何两个事物 A、B 放入一个类别 K 中，稍微转移目光，哦！现在 A 和 B 在属于同一类别 K 方面是相同的。另一方面，以 1918 年 4 月 13 日上午 10:16 为基准，再以 1918 年 4 月 13 日上午 10:18 为基准来看埃及金字塔。随着时间的流逝，金字塔从一个 17 分钟前的金字塔变成一个 17 分钟后的金字塔，这是一个明显的差异。一般来说，我总是可以说一切都必须与其他事物不同，无论 A 和 B 有多相似，至少 A 不是 B。在这些极端之间，我们发现了一些有趣的事物，这些事物与该方法相关。

身份。——让我们谈谈这一章的主题，我们将通过在差异点 ε 上或差异区间 x 上的 x 的连续性来讨论 A 与 B 在某一方面 K 上的身份，这个连续性构成了身份的基础，各种前置词的选择是为了避免歧义，而不是符合习惯用法。因此，我们在色调中的中性中有白色与黑色的身份，通过灰色在中灰色点或中间灰色区间上的连续性。

A 和 B 是起点的事物。通过"将它们放在一个刻度 x 上"，指的是考虑某种连续序列 x，使得与点 $x1$ 对应的是 A，与 $x2$ 对应的是 B。换句话说，我们定义一个函数 $f(x)$，使得 $f(x1)=A$ 和 $f(x2)=B$，并且通过想象、观察或实际安装的分级方法，我们定义了在 $x1$ 和 $x2$ 之间的 x 值上的 $f(x)$。

序列的选择既是自由的又是受限的。在 U 型管到碗中的管道的渐变示例中（第 241 页），显然存在着一个广泛的多维变化范围，通过这个范围，一个形状可以过渡到另一个形状。但是，在一定范围内，对于显示静水压关系的身份，一个变化系列和任何其他变化系列一样有效。很多时候，一系列离散的术语就足以暗示身份，因此 x 甚至不需要是一个近似连续的值。这是自由的。另一方面，如果我们拿一只蜜蜂和一只甲虫[1]，而不是通过我们认为在进化中实际存在的中间形态来展示生物身份，而是画出从蜜蜂到甲虫的分级图片，那么在散文性生物学中，选择 x 的维度将是不合适的。这是受限制的。

潜在身份之下的差异背景将是划分本章的原则。这种差异可以超过一个刻度的零点，从 A 到 B 的身份在其上运行（图1）。它可以超过一个在某方面具有独特或奇特的点 ξ（图2）。或者它可能是一个差异的阈值 ε 或 M（图3），与一个点不同之处在于它没有非常

---

[1]　R·W·伍德，《动物类比》，第 1 页。

明确的定义。（例如，音调听觉的下阈值是一个统计事件。）此外，背景可以是一段整体的 x，无论是实际存在的还是假设的（图4,5），它足够长，使得它两边的事物看起来不同，尽管之间没有特别的兴趣点。如果这个间隔在某种程度上很小，那么它会引起值得特别处理的情况（图6）。最后，差异标记本身可能在某个方面与系列中的其他点相同，这个点可以是一个一般点 ξ、0 或 ∞（图7,8,9）。[①]

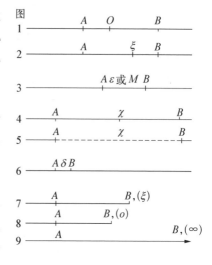

由于身份总是在某个方面上的身份，除了在相同的方面上，它不会是一个传递关系。因此，如果黑色和中性灰在色调上是相同的，中性灰和某个紫色在亮度上是相同的，就不能推断出黑色和紫色在任何方面上都是相同的。因此，与同一事物相同的事物并不总是彼此相同。

1. 零点上的身份：符号的变化

在零点两侧的符号差异很容易隐藏身份，根据这个零点是更随意还是更任意，正负符号的差异将更或更少具有重要意义。因此，所有温度都属于一个连续的刻度。+1℉和−1℉略有不同，但与14℉和16℉之间的差异并不大。+1℃和−1℃之间的差异更为重要，因为它对应着最重要液体的状态变化，但对许多其他物质的状态没有影响。

在数学中，符号变化上的身份有时被称为"连续性原理"。因

---

① 关于点之间的相互转化性，请参见第五章第215页和226页。

图 10

此,在普通语言中,我们说如果两条线在一个圆内相交,它们的夹角等于被截弧的和的一半;如果它们在圆外相交,它们的夹角将由被截弧的差的一半来衡量。现在假设我们考虑从一条线到另一条线的弧的总和,并考虑方向。然后我们发现,在从一个情况转变到另一个情况时,一个弧从正符号经过零变为负符号,但是对于所有情况,相同的规律成立,即夹角等于弧的代数和的一半。

由于身份总是有资格的,所以在红色和青铜绿中看到线性刻度的身份时,我们不必有任何心理上的顾虑,该刻度从饱和红色经过灰色到饱和青铜绿。因此,红色是负的青铜绿,青铜绿是负的红色。虽然这不是整个故事,但至少我们获得了一个非常有帮助的观点,用于处理颜色混合、适应、余象等。同样的身份当然也适用于其他互补色对。

在记录、计划、规则等方面,当符号发生变化时,人们经常会改变原则。例如,我可能打算按时行事,并准确记录我迟到了多少分钟,但只在我准时或提前到达时进行检查。确实,提前和迟到并不是同一回事。但我们也可以在同一个延伸于标准两侧的刻度上衡量准时性。问题不在于我是否应该从先验的一致性原则而不是多样性原则行动,而在于我是仅仅偶然犯错而造成差异,还是有一些理由来进行区分。

物理学中充满了通过符号变化而产生身份的案例,其中差异的方面经常具有误导性。我们自然会想象两辆汽车的正面碰撞比后面的碰撞更猛烈。现在，碰撞的猛烈程度完全取决于速度的代数差异。如果被碰撞的车辆前进，其速度被减去；如果它与撞车的车辆相向而行，它的速度被加上。因此，30 英里/小时追上 10 英里/小时的冲击与 12 英里/小时迎面相撞的冲击是相同的（即 12－（－8）＝12＋8）。因此，对于一个快速驾驶员来说，记住贯穿在他潜在受害者速度的符号差异中的法则的身份是很重要的。

笛卡尔对动量守恒的观念也是一个通过符号变化看到差异的例子，而身份保持不变。笛卡尔的弹性体撞击理论说：让质量为 $m1$ 的物体与质量为 $m2$ 的物体碰撞，它们的速度分别为 v 和 $-v$。如果 $m1>m2$，那么碰撞后两个物体都将以速度 v 移动。如果 $m1=m2$，每个物体都会反转速度。如果 $m1<m2$，两个物体都将以速度 $-v$ 移动。现在，如果我们用非笛卡尔语言的代数动量来讨论，碰撞前的动量为 $vm1-vm2$，或者 $v(m1-m2)$。根据该理论，碰撞后的动量将为：

$$v(m1+m2)，如果\ m1>m2，$$
$$v(m1-m2)，如果\ m1=m2，$$
$$-v(m1+m2)，如果\ m1<m2。$$

不使用莱布尼茨关于情况连续性的论证（见第 129 页），就我们的观点而言，可以简单地说，笛卡尔将（无论是暗示还是有意识地）一个不同的法则与 $m1-m2$ 的符号差异联系起来，而事实是，无论 $m1-m2$ 的符号如何，所涉及的两个物体的总动量总是恒等于 $v(m1-m2)$。

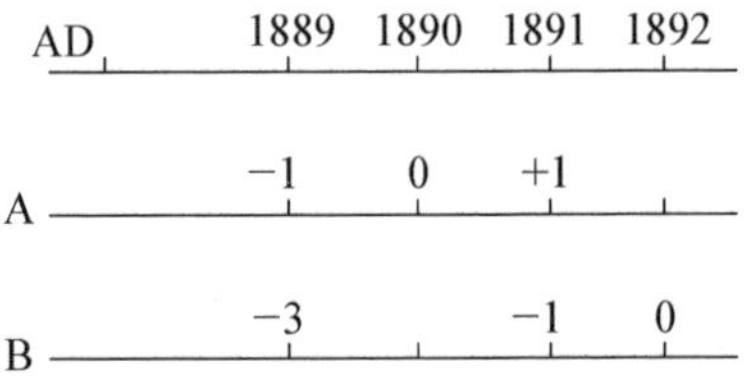

AD	1889	1890	1891	1892
A	-1	0	+1	
B	-3		-1	0

图 11

类似的情况也出现在大气和飞机之间的关系的身份中。我相信一个飞机可以相对于地球前进飞行、静止不动或者向后飞行。但飞行员不是说，飞机没有达到大约每小时 40 英里的最低速度就无法升空吗？是的，但这个速度是飞机在周围空气中的速度。当飞机在云层中时,所有地面上的事物都是无关紧要的,至少在空气动力学意义上是如此,即使在军事或美学意义上也是如此。因此,如果它以每小时40英里的速度逆风飞行40英里,它将保持静止;如果风速为50英里而不是40英里,飞机将会在观众眼中以每小时10英里的速度向后飞行。然而,它在地面速度上的这种符号差异与空气在其机翼下的承载力无关。最后,举一个琐碎但明确的例子,设A生于1890年,B生于1892年。对于A来说,1889年和1891年是不同的,因为他没有经历过1889年,但有一些1891年的经验;但是对于B来说,他的意识时间的零点与1889年和1891年无关,从B的角度来看,这两年都是负值。

2. 在奇异点 ζ 上的同一性

在处理零点两侧的同一性后,我们来讨论在某个特殊或奇异点上的同一性,例如,水在30.2℉和33.8℉时的化学组成,在奇异点32℉上呈现不同的状态。等一下!我不是将这个冰点作为零点的例子吗?是的,这正好引出了下一个观点,即尽管零点看起来像是奇异点的特例,但我们总是可以调整我们的刻度,使得该点被称为零点。换句话说,与其将零点视为奇异点的特例,我们可以将所有奇异点视为在适当转换的参考刻度上的零点的特例。然而,独立处理奇异点是有其存在的理由,因为某些点出于习惯或为了方法的方便性而不被视为零点,而是被视为特殊的。

因此,存在一个几何定理,即球面截痕的曲面积等于 πR^2,其中 R 是自顶点 A 到截痕圆周的距离。如果截痕非常扁平,如图12a所示,那么曲面积大约应该等于半径为 R 的圆的面积。但对于图12b所示的截痕,情况似乎不同。因此,连续性的方法将包括构造一系列的截痕,以高度 x(例如从 A 到截痕底部)进行测量,随着 x 从 AB 变化到 AC,我们发现存在一个奇异点,此时 x 等于球的半径,而截痕是一个半球体。但进一步的分析表明,这种特殊性与所讨论的公式的证明无关。因此,该公式在这个奇异点上仍然保持相同。

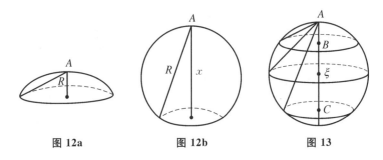

图 12a　　　　　　图 12b　　　　　　图 13

同样，我们听说过一个法则，即物体在地球表面以上的重量与其距离地球中心的平方成反比，但也有另一个法则，即物体在地下（例如矿井井筒中）的重量与其距离地球中心成正比。① 那么，在地球表面的这个奇异点上是否存在不同的法则呢？从某种意义上说，当然是存在的。但是，如果我们考虑物体与地球质量的每个部分之间的关系，当然普遍的引力法则无论是在地球内部还是外部都成立。

在某一方面上，无论事物的形状如何，拓扑关系，也就是位置关系，往往在其他方面上的奇异点上保持一致。因此，如图 14 所示的两个容器可以被认为是相同的，因为它们都是一对连通容器。许多教师未能使托里切利的论证变得有说服力，即外容器中汞表面上的气压在某种神秘的方式下会向上推动液体进入管子，当管子的上端被密封并且为空时。对学生来说，这个论证不够坚实，他们的想象力（我曾经也是如此）无法将管子和容器与易于理解的 U 型管进行比较。

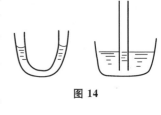

图 14

为了展示它们的相同之处，一种方法是想象一系列的中间情况，如图 15 - 20 中的两个投影所示。在第 15 图中，我们有一个普通

---

①　忽略地壳不同同心球层中岩石密度的变化。

的 U 型管。在第 16 图中，一端被压扁并围绕弯曲，从拓扑和静水学的角度来看与第 15 图相同。在第 17 图中，弯曲部分围绕另一个管子的曲度更大。在第 18 图中，弯曲口的两个角被连接起来，形成一个环。从上方看，现在出现了三个环。在第 19 图中，将内环和第二个环之间的空间填充固体玻璃，形成一个实心环或管子。当然，这对液体没有影响。最后，在第 20 图中，将该管子变得更薄，得到了管子和碗。这整个系列可以通过插入更多中间形式来使其变得更加逐渐。但是，连续性并不意味着相等。在第 17 和第 18 图之间发生了一个重要的拓扑变化，液体的简单有界表面变成了环面。这足够重要，被称为问题的奇异点。然而，不需要太多的物理知识或想象力就可以看出它不会影响压力关系。因此，在涉及到压力关系时，第 15 和第 20 图被视为相同的情况。

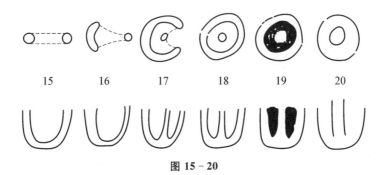

15　　　　16　　　　17　　　　18　　　　19　　　　20

图 15－20

　　人体与环境之间的边界在许多重要方面显然是奇异的。但我们很容易找到两者融合在一起的问题。例如，当一个人站在舞台上唱歌时，歌手背后的反射墙、地板和歌手的声带是相同的，因为它们属于一个连续的共鸣系统；如果他能够控制这个系统的物理部分和生理部分，那么他选择在一个糟糕的大厅中唱歌就没有完全的借口，就像选择感冒时唱歌一样。

　　当变量是时间时，奇异性意味着某种突然的改变，引发了对身份的问题。物质在其各种转化中的身份一致性就是一个重要的例子。但是，这种重要性常常被夸大到被视为身份本身。当氢和氧变成水时，身份的一致性仅仅在于保持了质量这个被称为质量的机械性质，并限制了化学性质可以变化的方式数量。但是，氢和氧与水仍然是不同的。处于动态平衡的系统，如尼亚加拉瀑布或任何有机体，其身份的方面与物质一样重要。正是对物质身份的不合理独特强调导致了一些悖论，例如含有一点也不属于曾经购买的材料的破洞袜子的身份一致性。能量的一致性是另一个问题。Poynting 和 Thomson 在他们的《热学教程》(脚注，第 116 页)中指出，能量的一致性是一个无害的形而上学概念，并用于简化陈述，严格来说，我们应该说，当一定量的动能消失时，一定量的热能出现。现在，由于显著的一致性总是有条件的一致性，为什么不将形而上学降到实际，并说相互联系的不同现象的测量之间的交换速率的恒定性以及由此产生的共同测量的可能性正是我们所说的能量的一致性，因此我们现在可以自由地谈论它。简化陈述成为一种科学方法而不是科学的借口。

　　时间的奇异点往往会在连续性和身份的背景下显得特别突出，它象征着某种成就的阶段。比如，毕业证书、婚礼仪式或民主革命可能标志着某种进步的阶段，以某种总体趋势的速度前进。如果这种进步类似于图 21 中的曲线(1)，标记时间点 ξ 的心理效应就是给人一种进步类似于曲线(2)的印象，由于心理反应的方式，未来的进展实际上可能会采取类似曲线(3)的路线，这种情况经常会遇到。因此，错误地将同一性误认为是不同性，可能导致相反方向的差异。

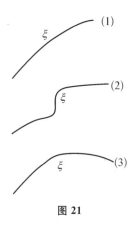

图 21

3. Identity over Threshold ξ or M(注：未译出来)

　　通过阈值，我指的是一个刻度上的奇异点，它不一定需要精确地定位，但它在某些方面标志着一个区别。例如，它可以标志有限和实际无限之间的区别,或者实际上的零和非零之间的区别。(参见第五章,第 224 页)。在研究声音速度时,光信号的速度超过了实际无限的阈值。然而,在这个阈值上,声音和光在具有有限速度方面是相同的,而这种有限性在星体偏差现象中变得相关。

在力学中,有一种说法是"松弛悬链线"是一种悬链线,其方程为 $y = a[\cosh(x/a) - 1]$,形状如图 22 所示。问题是,"当悬链线被拉紧时,它的形状是什么?"有一次,我实际上怀疑"拉紧"必定涉及一种根本不同的法则。但是通过将图 23 想象成拉开的图 22,或者将其类比为图 22 中标记为 tt' 的部分,很容易看出两种情况仅仅在于支撑点处的张力的垂直和水平分量之间的比率,如图中的矢量所示。对于任何特定问题,我们可以设定一个比率的阈值,以便在其一侧我们称之为松弛的,而在其另一侧我们称之为拉紧的。但是,这样的阈值在几何上并没有特殊之处,松弛和拉紧只是悬链线公式的一个参数的不同程度而已。

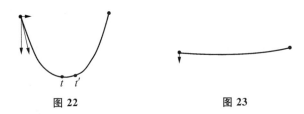

图 22　　　　　　　　　图 23

解释玻璃球内部真空如何承受压力的常用方法是将球体的一个小部分进行切割,如图 24 所示的截面 ab。这个小圆盘从周围的玻璃上方收到向其中心的压力,但由于它是弯曲的,将会有恰好足够的未被抵消的合力分量将圆盘向外推,抵抗大气压力。不幸的是,这个证明尽管对于该事实的必要性是令人信服的,但往往无法说服人们对其直观合理性的理解。为了弥合这种想象力的差距,让我们考虑一个实心玻璃球。很容易想象它如何抵抗大气压力。接下来,想象球体中间有一个微小的真空气泡(图 25)。从承受压力的角度来看,它仍然在实际零点的阈值内。然后,让我们想象各种大小的气泡，直到我们得到最初的空心球体。我们将清晰地看到通过所有这些渐变的原理的一致性。

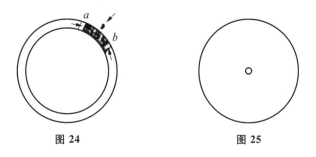

图 24　　　　　　　　　　　　　　　图 25

　　然而，很多时候，我们的心理机制会给意识范围设定一个阈值，以至于我们只能理解一个事物的一致性，而无法更直观地理解它。例如，我们无法听到信天翁翅膀的可区分的拍动和蜂鸟连续的嗡嗡声之间的一致性，也无法字面上地看到颜色与热辐射器发出的长波之间的一致性。

　　然而，由此并不意味着这种一致性是"不完美的"，反而更有趣。例如，当两个音调的频率相差几个振动每秒时，我们会听到拍音，如果拍音的频率超过我们对音调听觉的下限阈值，它们将引起基底膜的某部分产生共振，我们就会听到相应频率的音调。从这个观察中，人们可能会在实证发现之前就预测组合音的存在。然而，一些心理学家奇怪地将组合音视为起源于耳朵，仿佛它以一种特殊的方式在耳朵中产生，而其他音调则不是从耳朵中产生的。

　　在我们感到明显观念上的差异之后，一个机械系统的原理通常保持不变。我们被告知电影胶片（1）在静止状态一段时间，（2）然后被快门遮盖，（3）开始移动，（4）达到最大速度，（5）减速，（6）停止，（7）当快门通过时被揭开，然后（1）再次静止一段时间。现在，我们需要花费至少几秒钟的时间来想象这个过程。但实际上，第一阶段（1）只占据了 1/14 的 2/3，或者说 1/21 秒，而从（2）到（7）的整个过程大约占据了 1/14 的 1/3,或者说 1/42 秒。机器的逻辑简单地运算出这些连续的阶段,超过了我们的想象力;而在目前的技术发展阶段,系统仍然可以在破坏之前略微提高速率,也就是在机械可操作性的阈值之前。

　　类似地,一本关于内燃机的教科书详细解释了如何根据电学、化学和机械原因按照顺序完成一个完整的循环,并给人以轮船上往复式蒸汽机的平稳运行的印象。但当我们听到这些循环合并成连续的嗡嗡声,如同在一架飞机上时,我们的想象力无法理解自然如何能以如此疯狂的速度进行如此多的推理。

4. Identity over an Interval of *x*(注:未译出来)

　　在一般情况下,如果程度上的差异足够大,就会成为性质上的差异,这样的说法是无意义的。但这种说法可以给出这个标题的含义。我们在 A 和 B 之间有一个明显的差异,尽管我们在刻度上看不到特定的分界点。因此,情理的逻辑是看到它们的共同之处,而不是随意确定一个区别点或者默认存在一个明显的分界点。

　　因此,在统计学中经常会发现如图 26 所示的曲线形式。统计学家称小的起伏为波动,较大的扫过为总趋势。但是假设我们有一个类似于图 27 的曲线,那么就会有波动的波动和趋势的趋势,在为任何具体问题划定波动和趋势之间的界线之外,它们在本质上都是数据的变化。在图 27 的后半部分,甚至连趋势都无法区分。同样的问题可以从平滑曲线和粗糙曲线的角度更一般地来考虑。“对于我的数据,什么样的曲线最平滑且最贴合?”绘图者提问。这个问题直截了当地是自相矛盾的。如果图 28 中的曲线 1 是最贴合的,那么它也是最不平滑的;如果曲线 5 是最平滑的,那么它就是最不贴合的。因此,这个问题没有统一的答案,而是取决于横坐标的频率、纵坐标的准确性以及被认为相关或偶然的因素的平滑程度和贴合程度的折衷阈值。

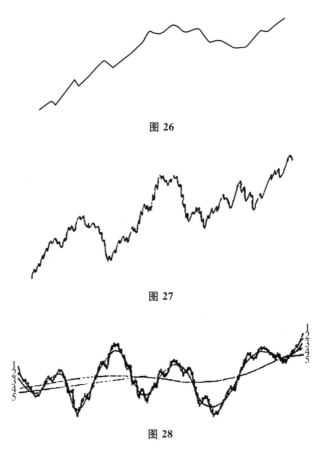

图 26

图 27

图 28

　　在音乐中，有时候一个身份被名称或符号的差异所隐藏，但可以通过不同案例之间的中间形式来发现。装饰音符由于其小写形式，常常让新手感觉它们有些特殊，需要"尽快"演奏，而大型音符被认为需要占据有限和明确的时间长度，无论速度多快。实际上，旋律构图可以以各种速度进行，而无论如何书写，它们在本质上是相同的。证明的方法是，在中间情况下，听众无法确定某个动机是如何书写的，尽管他们可以倾向于更方便的一种记谱方式。

这种身份的重要性在于它将为相同的处理方式辩护。例如,如果普通音符可以演奏得太快,那么装饰音符也可以演奏得太快。装饰音符并不是多余的音符。

和声的身份也经常被某个变量的广泛差异所隐藏。打断的琶音和同时发声的和弦一样,而在中间情况下,例如在一个终止音的结尾,听众无法确定它是如何书写的。

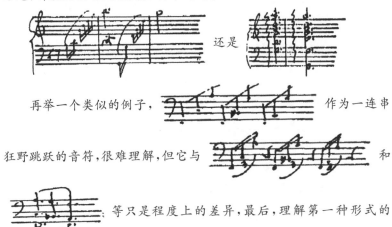

再举一个类似的例子,

狂野跳跃的音符,很难理解,但它与

等只是程度上的差异,最后,理解第一种形式的教学方法就是尝试听到最后一种形式的身份的相同之处。

有时候,我们并未注意到 $x1$ 和 $x2$ 之间的变量跨度,这不是因为我们观察不到,而是因为在我们问题中,这些中间值并不存在,也就是说,$f(x)$ 在那些 x 的值上没有取值。在这种情况下,我们可以通过想象、假设或实际创造来定义这个间隙的 $f(x)$。因此,我们发现动物的物种之间存在突变。但是在可能存在的缺失连接之前,我们发现了证据并理解了进化的连续性和整个动物王国的起源的身份。[1]关于动物

---

① 在广义上理解,包括突变。

和植物的普遍观念是动物会移动并对刺激做出反应,而植物则不会。现在,除了一些低级植物和敏感植物外,所有的植物也会对刺激做出反应。强烈的侧面光照射到植物上会使其在很短的时间内转向光源。但是,这个短时间是几个小时的事情,而动物的反应时间是几秒钟的事情;这个差异很明显,因为我们很少发现反应时间为几分钟量级的生物。但是,通过纯粹想象的反应时间,其统计坐标为零,我们对于反应这一事实的身份获得了一种理解。我们发现紫外辐射中的最短波长约为 $500 \times 10-8$ 厘米,而 X 射线的最长波长约为 $20 \times 10-8$ 厘米。无论在中间波长的间隙上,电磁波理论都能看到这两种辐射的波长在重要方面的身份的相同之处。

5. 小增量 δ 上的身份认同：连续数学归纳

对于小增量 δ 上的身份认同的数学和心理学问题非常有趣。假设我们有两个刺激 $x1$ 和 $x2$,其中 $x2-x1=\delta$ 小于感知的差异极限 ε。那么 $x1$ 和 $x2$ 在给出相同感觉方面是相同的。现在如果我们取 $x3=x2+\delta$,那么 $x2$ 和 $x3$ 在给出相同感觉方面又是相同的。但是如果 $2\delta > \varepsilon$,那么 $x1$ 和 $x3$ 将不会给出相同的感觉。在这种情况下,合格的身份认同不是一种传递关系。

这只是问题的一方面。另一方面是,当类似的逻辑情况应用于没有 ε 的限制自动引起"不同"的情况时,惯性力、累积习惯、原则的一致性等会通过不可察觉的增量逐渐渗入,直到我们意识到没有任何差异。(参见最后一节)

这个数学问题可以用一个定理来表达,我暂且称之为"连续数学归纳",因为没有更好的名称。陈述如下：1) 假设命题函数 $\varphi(x)$ 对于 $x=a$ 成立；2) 对于所涉及的区间,存在一个阈值 Δ,使得 $\varphi(x')$ 意味着对于 0 到 Δ 之间的任何 δ,$\varphi(x+\delta)$ 都成立；3) 那么对于区间内超过点 a 的任何 x 值,$\varphi(x')$ 都成立。

图 29

证明：设 b 是大于 a 的任意 x 值。如果它超过 a 不超过 Δ，那么根据 2)，结论成立。如果它超过 Δ，那么应用阿基米德的假设，即 $b-a$ 可以由足够多的 Δ 加上一个分数 $\theta\Delta$（图 29）来覆盖，即存在一个整数 n 和一个合适的分数 θ，使得 $b-a=(n+\theta)\Delta$ 或者，$b=(a+\theta\Delta)+n\Delta$。接下来，应用普通的数学归纳法：

Ⅰ. 根据假设 1)和 2)，$\varphi(a+\theta\Delta)$ 成立。∴再次根据 2)，$\varphi(a+\theta\Delta+1\cdot\Delta)$ 成立。（这个次要前提对于 $n=1$ 得到证实。）

Ⅱ. 根据 2)，如果 $\varphi(a+\theta\Delta+r\cdot\Delta)$ 成立，其中 r 是整数，那么它也成立于 $r+1$。（主要前提）

Ⅲ. 因此，根据普通的数学归纳法，$\varphi(a+\theta\Delta+n\Delta)$ 成立，也就是说，$\varphi(b)$ 成立。证毕。

该定理的严谨性和普遍性[①]可以通过牺牲简洁性和透视性来增加。但在这里，可以说它的优点和缺点在于第二个假设，该假设在负面情况下不会成立，例如差异极限 ε 被超过。现在回到应用的问题：我们通过帐篷的开口让骆驼的鼻子进来。这几乎没有与不让它进来有什么不同。然而，一旦第一部分被承认，它就断言第二个假设，即没有理由不让它再进来一点点，再多一点，直到它的整个身份跨过门槛进入内部。一根竹子可能很难分开。但是一旦把楔子的细端插进去，粗端就会跟随，因此有中国的说法，"顺势劈竹"。喝半杯啤酒是无害且可允许的。在喝完第一半杯之后，没有理由不再来一口，再来一口，再来一口……随着增量 δ 的增加，通过阿基米德的假设，更容易获得任意数量 b 的杯子。在私人信件中使用一分钱的邮票似乎微不足道。但然后我可能会使用两张，或者使用方便的一分钱的公共硬币，等等；在大坝一旦破裂后，我需要证明自己能够阻止腐败的溃堤之势。

我们对善意谎言微笑。但是否存在那种纯净无瑕的善意谎言

---

① 这个定理用命题函数的方式陈述已经比从情况连续性的角度处理更加普遍。（参见第 275 页）

却带有一些灰暗的成分？从为了讨好某人而夸大一个事件，到说出字面上的真相却误导他人，再到显而易见的彻头彻尾的谎言，存在有限数量的有限增量 Δ，每个增量都无关紧要，但它们的总和确实有所差别，而这种差别让不加区分的习惯的一致性以巨大的动力进行。

在开始某件事情时，比如改掉一种习惯，开始一项工作，或者尽力对待一切，人们常常说，我明天或者在不久的将来开始。当然，短暂延迟的影响可能低于重要性的阈值。但我们生活在一个明天衍生出另一个明天、未来衍生出另一个未来的世界中。奇特的是，今天的今天是今天，但明天的明天并非明天；现在的现在是现在，但近未来的近未来并非近未来。因此，最安全的态度是将明天和正面的永恒之半看作连续的，并怀疑它们之间的一致性。

在所有这些例子中，A 和 B 的结果有明显的差异，以至于似乎聪明的辨别能力应该能够找到一个阈值 ε，超过这个阈值，增量 δ 不应该再被增加。然而，我们的心理惯性、习惯等倾向于使连续归纳的第二个假设成为现实，以便实现一种实践的一致性。因此，将 A 与 B 同等对待更为安全和容易。对于智慧辨别力何时超过安全考虑或反之的一般问题，只能给出一般答案："这取决于情况"。假设不是通过数学来验证的。

6. 奇异点 ξ 的一致性

在处理尺度的不同部分上的一致性之后，我们将考虑兴趣在于点本身与其他点的一致性的情况，比如在所有锥曲线中，抛物线与椭圆和双曲线在共同特性上的一致性。在这样一个问题中，我们可以简单地取这个点和尺度的一侧。然后，这个点看起来位于新尺度的末端，并且可以进行变换，使其成为尺度的单位、无穷大或零，以适应我们的方便。因此，我们面临的是限制点的一致性和差异性问题，这在第五章中已经进行了处理。关于限制点与系列的其余部分可能一致的方面在第 2 节（第 339 页及以下）进行了讨论，特别是关于显著概括的第 2 点。为了不重复内容,我在这里只讨论几个新的情况。

拓扑关系在极限情况下通常保持一致。例如,复变量的环状区域可以逐渐变化,如图 30 所示,直到最后我们得到一个简单的区域,只是增加了一个细丝。可以证明,对于 A 真实的复变量定理对于 B 也是真实的,但不能不经证明就认为它是真实的。

图 30

这种通过连续性推理到极限点的方式在伽利略的力学中经常被使用。他发现,从一定高度下滚的球会向上滚到同样的高度的另一个斜面,因此第二个斜面越不陡峭,球在停止前走的距离越远。据此,伽利略推理,如果斜面是水平的,球将会永远滚下去,除非受到摩擦的阻力。因此,他在这里隐含地宣布了牛顿的惯性定律。

现在,由于摩擦是一种干扰,他在不同介质中进行了下落物体的实验,并发现速度差随着介质的稀薄而变得越来越小。他谨慎地得出结论:"我们有理由相信,在真空中,所有物体下落的速度是相同的。"[1]

在系列中,某一点通常因为它恰好是我们此刻的立场而显得独特。但它在其他方面可能并不独特。因此,对于从这个主观立场推断其他奇异性,我们应该非常谨慎,而是尝试通过它来看待一致性。

因此,现在似乎是特殊的,因为我此刻就在现在,但除了我此刻存在的这种独特性之外,它还有其他任何意义上的特殊之处吗?

如果事件按照一定的进程发展,人们往往会发现这个事件与之

---

① 伽利略,《关于两种新科学的对话》,英译本,第 72 页。

前的所有事件不同。是的，当然，但是在什么意义上和在多大程度上不同呢？以匀加速下落的物体为例。在下落一段距离后，在距离-时间曲线上的点 A（图 31）处，假设它对自己的情况产生了兴趣，并说："现在我的状态与迄今为止所有以前的状态都不同。我走过的距离比以前任何时候都要远，我的速度也比以前任何时候都要快。"这样说是没错的。但是它没有权利由此推断现在作用在它身上的力与以前有任何不同。事实上，一直都是同样的力在作用。至于力的变化，它一直是零。因此，在图 31 中，A 点的距离之所以与之前的所有 α 点不同，是因为它的一阶导数 A'（速度）比所有的 α'' 都要大，但在 A 点与之前的条件完全相同，即 $A''=\alpha''$，$A'''=\alpha'''=0$。简而言之，这只是在重复有关下落物体的熟知方程式而已：

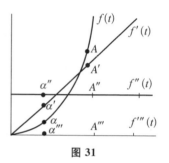

图 31

$$f(t) = 1/2at\hat{\ }2$$
$$f'(t) = at$$
$$f''(t) = a$$
$$f'''(t) = 0。$$

　　在考虑历史系列时，人们往往会忘记差异何时结束，一致性从何开始。"我们这个时代是高物价的时代。""我们这个时代是科学的时代。"每个时代都说："我们这个时代处于启蒙运动的巅峰。"当我们现在已经取得了如此多的成就时，如何能够取得任何重要的进展呢？"问题是"，我们的启蒙运动比以前的启蒙运动更加启蒙到第几个导数呢？

　　报纸专门暗示事物的独特性已经停止的独特性。"某些运动员打破了所有以前的纪录。而且，这场比赛打破的纪录比以往任何一场比赛都多。"但这样的报道可能一年又一年地重复。每当我迈出一步时，我都会打破我终生步行距离的纪录。

　　如果一个人交了很多朋友，可能会有一段时间他会说："我比迄今为止任何人都更爱她（或他）。"但是仅仅根据这个表面的理由就下结论，是否在方法上足够证明该点的显著独特性呢？

　　如果一个人在某个事业上有一定的进展趋势，他往往倾向于认为在"现在"之后将会有彻底的运气改变。但是这种改变，并不是等待，而是通过努力实现的。如果我一直以四进三出的速度偿还我的通信债务，那么从今天开始，我有责任证明我期望在有限的时间内偿清我的债务。

　　连续数学归纳法的论证也可以采取在一个特定的观点独特性下推崇一种一致性的形式。现在的诱惑似乎特别可以理解。"这将是我最后的过错，只能有一个最后的过错。"但我必须表明，这是在某种意义上的最后，它与未来的过错不同，只是最后一系列过错中的一个。

　　"这将是我最后的疾病，"慢性悲观主义者说。也许吧。但它有何不同于以前的疾病呢？

　　"这将是最后一场战争，"我们乐观主义者说。也许吧。但不是因为迄今为止这是最后一场战争，每场战争在发动时都是如此。如果我们在进一步的方面找到独特性，比如人道主义理念的发展、交流便利性和民族间的增加理解、世界组织的进展、历史的自我意识（如果有的话）等等，这些因素的综合作用将使世界超越战争预防的门槛，那就很好。如果没有，那就不是这样。

　　但是还必须添加一个条件。如果我们将问题设定在我们之外，比如观察一个从安全距离掉落的石头，然后问它的加速度是否发生了变化，我们可以用"如果没有，那就没有"来停止。这是奇异点的结束，身份的开始，我接受它作为一个事实。但是如果我从一架失事的飞机上坠落，并发现自己有一个恒定的加速度，或者至少是一个恒定的高速度（由于空气阻力），那么我就处在问题之中，如果身份存在于我想要的奇异点，我可以从现在开始创造一个奇异点。如果我有准备，我可以打开降落伞，这样从现在开始我的速度将发生很大的变化。这个降落伞可以是为了不再犯错而做出的额外努力，也可以是为了实施和平的联盟，或者其他什么，就像布一样。因此，在此处，通过连续性 ad hoc 或单纯的命令来产生差异的新含义出现了。逻辑上的命令只是一个重言式，但是自然和人的命令将在身份的间隔内产生非重言式的差异，并为下一章提供材料。

第七章　通过连续性的差异

与通过连续性的一般性陈述相对应,我们现在将讨论关于 A 和 B 之间的差异,其参考点为分界点 ξ 或间隔 x,通过 x 的连续性,在一个基础 K 的身份下,这个身份是差异的基础。因此,我们通过灰度系列的连续性,在色调中立的身份下,讨论白色和黑色相对于中灰色或中间灰色的分界点的差异。

如果采用与身份相平行的差异处理方法,整个章节可能通过重复上一章的相同标题和相同的例子来处理。因此,

1. 零点。根据一辆汽车的速度在零点的一侧或另一侧,两辆相撞汽车的法律地位将有所不同。

2. 奇点。在 32°F 的不同侧,水和冰是不同的。

3. 阈值。音调不是节拍。

4. 间隔。人不是猿。

5. 连续归纳。明天的约会与永远的约会不同。

6. 奇点。现在作为所有事情的当前是独特的。但是,为了不为了一致性而迫使事情适应形式,上述标题将在本章中进行细分、组合、交叉和重新排序。

为了将连续性中的差异陈述为一个问题,我们考虑到当某些变量如时间、长度、速度、温度等变化时,两个事物可能会不易察觉地转化为彼此。因此,我们需要问,在哪些有趣的方面、为了什么目的以及在何处应该划分界限。正如以下所有情况所示,划分一个界限的行为在将 A 和 B 作为 x 的函数转化为两个值的新函数时发生,其中 A 具有一个值,B 具有另一个值。而在上一章中,情况是将 A 和 B 放在同一个类别 K 中。

1. 差异区间, x

　　首先考虑一些明显的情况，即由于缺乏前瞻性、故意限制问题或事实空缺，中间状态的"划分"问题没有被提出，而是仅考虑宽度差异引起的差异。更准确地说，我应该说这里没有提出标记点的问题。因为差异区间不就是通过画一条线（沿长度方向）来制造差异的吗？

　　一个重要的案例类别是区分曲线的小波动和大波动。例如，由于季节变化而引起的健康年度波动可以很容易地区分出来，而由于持续关怀而产生的健康总体趋势或由于持续磨损而导致的健康恶化总体趋势也可以区分出来。上一章（第 248 页，图 27）提出的波动和趋势的身份问题在这里并没有提出，因为这个健康问题没有中间的变化。同样地，地球的自转可以区分出其岁差。音乐中个别的强调音可以在整体的强弱变化中被识别出来，小波浪可以看到在大浪头上起伏（参见第 272 页）。有人问，"既然汉语语言将语调的变化作为词本身的语言学部分，那么它如何使用语调的变化进行表达？"答案是，一个汉语演讲者可以让他的声音上下起伏，同时让个别音节起伏，无论他们的平均音高落在波浪的哪个部分。

　　作为统计上的空白，上一章提到了植物和动物的反应时间、光和 X 射线的波长以及不同物种之间的差异。无论我们有什么伦理基础使用动物劳动和食用肉类，由于人类和动物之间的差距，这个问题显然要简单得多。如果所有的中间环节都能够生存至今，那么它们应该享有什么权利呢？这个问题，如果不是无法回答的，那么就必须得到回答。

　　由于选择刻度 x 是智力自由裁量的问题，而 A 和 B 关于 x 的功能是一种近似（参见第 III 章分级思想，第 190 页），因此可能会发现，刻度 x 上的点不足以充分确定函数。例如，对于 200 个词的长度，我们可以有一个轶事或一个短篇小说。但是，如果我们看到了具有两个极值的统计分布，那么它将暗示着一个差异，即使在极值之间没有差距。然后可以通过考虑其他变量来研究问题。因此,通过重新考虑我们的变量,我们可能会得出结论:轶事只有一个要点,而短篇小说有几个相互矛盾的要素需要处理。此外,在心理学中所谓的自然简单反应实验中,发现反应时间的分布有两个极大值,进一步研究表明它们对应于肌肉反应和感觉反应。

在他的《性别与性格》一书中,O. Weininger 说,男性和女性仅在存在于所谓男性和女性中的两种性格比例上不同。然而,如果忘记在比率的统计分布中,正常个体或者更倾向于其中一种,他的观点就会夸大了。

2. 陡峭的曲线

在前面的部分中,我们有一个不涉及到有限问题的疑惑区域。如果这个区域足够狭窄,可以在问题中被忽略不计,那么我们就有了一个实际上的不连续性。因此,如果我们将氢气和氧气混合在一个烧瓶中,通入电火花,我们将立即发现瓶中生成了水,如果我们活着去检查的话。当然,这个烧瓶是由弹性物质制成的,首先会逐渐受到应力,直到达到破裂点,然后碎片逐渐分离。但是,对于许多目的而言,这种逐渐性是如此陡峭,以至于我们称之为不连续的跃迁,标志着烧瓶和破碎的玻璃之间的区别。

如果我们向一个悬挂着的灯具扔一把椅子,存在一定速度范围,椅子会轻轻触碰到灯具,但不会打碎它。这可以通过将椅子拿到灯具的高度,轻轻敲打它来验证。但是,与控制不了的变化相比,这个安全范围非常小,扔椅子所具有的变化范围非常大,因此我们可以实际上说,一把椅子要么不碰到灯具,要么一碰就会打碎它。

在上一章(第 240 页)中,地球表面被视为一个奇异点,标志着内部的直接距离定律和外部的反比平方定律之间的差异。但是,如果我们实际上挖一个有限大小的洞,让一个物体从上面掉下来,力的变化,也就是二阶导数的变化,将是逐渐的,尽管如果我们将它画在从月球距离到地面的比例尺上，它看起来像一个跳跃。

　　从这个角度来看，我们也可以相对地证明在青春期时使用"不连续性"这个术语的合理性，这个时期通过非常陡峭的曲线标志着一个人生命中的不同阶段。生物突变现象被视为演化连续性的一部分（第 VI 章脚注，第 251 页）。但是在另一个数量级上讲，突变足够陡峭，可以称之为跳跃。

3. 稳定均衡

　　为什么事物之间会相隔一段距离或出现陡峭的变化？也许通过研究广义平衡概念可以获得一些启示，因为它涉及差异问题。简单来说，我们可以让 x 代表广义变量（不一定是空间的），y 代表趋向最小值的广义"势能"（物理上、社会上等方面）。y - x 曲线的变化率或斜率将表示广义"力"，它衡量着下坡的趋势。

　　在图 1 中，A 是"稳定平衡"状态，即如果稍微移动它，它将返回到山谷。B 也是稳定平衡，尽管它可以被置于一个小的可移动范围内并返回。C 处于"中性平衡"状态，因为它不会被任何力量推动或拉回，保持中立。D 处于"不稳定平衡"状态，即如果它被轻微地移动，移动会受到力的影响，使其沿着山坡滚下去。E 不处于平衡状态，因为有一个力推动它向下移动。那么，这是熟悉的地面。现在，如果在这些山上下雨，不是明显的吗，雨滴会被山谷自动分类，分隔出它们滚入的流域？稳定平衡的中心，因此提供了一个类的统一性或同一性，与其他类分离开来。

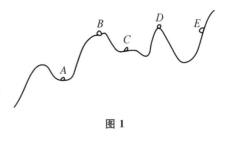

图 1

　　在化学反应中，有许多假设中的中间化合物，而在放射性中也形成了假设的元素。但只有那些处于稳定平衡的化合物和元素才被识别和命名。因此，我们发现了不相互融合的不同种类的物质。

晶体的鲜明特征和生物现象如叶序规律性[①]在更高层次的复杂性上也遵循同样的思想。

在铜管或木管乐器中产生音调,或者实际上在物理现象中的任何"定常波",只有某些明确定义的频率,它们之间的间隔是不连续的,可以被保持下去。喇叭手可以试图"哄骗"他的乐器产生音高的轻微变化,但他无法实现长音效果,这是长号演奏家所能做到的。但是,严肃的长号演奏家、小提琴家或歌手如何产生那些恰好是那些全音或半音的音符? 有时说,这类音乐家的任务比键盘乐器的音乐家难得多,因为他们必须从无数个错误的音符中选中唯一正确的音符。但从稳定平衡的角度来看,他们并不像他们看起来那么糟糕或那么令人钦佩。歌手通过训练获得了相对音高的某些平衡中心,在实际演唱中会稍微偏离,但如果他学会了准确的音高,偏差不会超出平衡的基准线,超出这个基准线歌手将感到需要重新调整或听众将感到需要更正。我们认为爪哇平均律五声音阶是不可想象的,因为爪哇人被训练出来区分和聚焦于那些对其他人来说不稳定的音符。

同样,语音器官的位置可以通过连续的变化来产生连续的语音音调。但在任何一种语言中,有少数习惯平衡中心,母语使用者不会超出限制。如果他想要用好的口音学习一门外语,他必须获得新的稳定平衡中心,就像欧洲人试图学习爪哇音阶一样。如果新中心靠近他的母语中心,那将非常难以获得。将"sir"发音为"soeur",或者将"parlez-vous français?"发音为"parley voo frongsay?"仅仅是使用最近的旧平衡中心替代新中心,因此形成了外语口音现象。一个多语者是一个已经获得许多中心平衡的人,他可以保持稳定和独特。

通过谨慎的方式,非习惯性的事情也可以建立稳定的中心。在

---

① 请参阅 W. M. 贝利斯(W. M. Bayliss)于 1914 年发表的《一般生理学原理》(Principles of General Physiology)第 383 页。

许多情况下，画一条线，区分合法和非法行为，或道德和不道德行为可能不一致。但如果一个人决心合法或道德，他将不会偏离判断的稳定平均水平。

　　作为一般性的例子，我们可以说，思想或概念通过其逻辑或方法论的稳定性得到确定。在这里，我们可以把它们的定义变化看作是位移，把不自然或笨拙看作是潜力。因此，"朋友"的概念相当稳定，让我们希望如此；但是如果我将我的朋友定义为通常理解的朋友类别加上我的宠物狗，那么这种偏离将导致使用"除了我的狗之外的朋友"这样的表达更加频繁，而"我的朋友"这个表达相对不常用。在这种逻辑压力的情况下，存在一种逻辑力量朝向稳定平衡点的方向。也许找到逻辑稳定平衡中心是所有定义问题的一个方面。（参见第四章，页 204 以下。）

4. 不稳定平衡

　　（1）如果物体聚集在稳定平衡点周围，那么处于不稳定或中性平衡的物体怎么办？如果一颗冰雹卡在分水岭或平坦板的脊上，它属于哪个山谷？这里让我们应用渐进和限制点的方法。在图 2 中，A 明显处于稳定平衡状态。B 也是如此。C 的稳定基础非常小。例如，冰雹可能卡在岩石的一个小浅裂缝里。在极限情况下，当基础趋近于零时，我们就有了处于不稳定平衡状态的 D。现在，只有通过抽象化才能将某个潜力 y 称为 x 的函数。在第四章的第 209 页中，我试图表明，函数只是一个理想的极限，在其中一个因素（或极少数因素）是卓越的，而所有导致轻微变化的其他因素都被认为是不相关的。同样的话也适用于中性平衡。现在，如果一颗冰雹停在一座山脉的光滑凸起的脊上，或者停在脊上的光滑板上，重力的主要因素实际上变为零，所谓的次要因素变为主要因素。例如，一阵风可能会将其吹向一侧或另一侧。因此，处于不稳定或中性平衡的物体实际上根本不处于平衡状态，而是在曲线的斜坡上，也就是受到一种力的作用，这种力在其处于主要稳定平衡时是太小，以至于无法推动其基础,或者在其处于主要斜坡时不会产生任何附加效果,但在主要因素平衡时会产生差异。

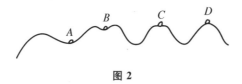

图 2

另一方面,如果空气静止,地球不旋转得太猛烈,那么光滑石头和光滑冰雹的分子粗糙度仍然足以使后者保持不动。但是这只是一个具有非常小稳定基础的稳定平衡状态。

因此,总的来说,我们可以说一件事要么处于稳定平衡状态,要么根本不处于平衡状态。根据唯一阈值的区分(pp. 223 - 226),我们可以说,在一个问题中,能够被视为偶然或无关紧要的因素能够破坏山顶上的稳定平衡,这将在该问题中被称为不稳定平衡。

将这一结果应用于产生差异的方法是,我们可以通过承认新的因素来重新制定我们的问题,这种精炼可以无限制地继续进行。但是,如果我们认为这已经足够解决我们的问题,但仍出现了看似不稳定的平衡情况,我们可以说扔硬币就足以决定这个问题。因此,无论是行动还是舍入小数的决定,都是可能的,除非我们要求无限数量的可能因素完全平衡,这在任何有限的问题中都不需要。

因此,站在两个基地之间的球员将会往左或往右跑,而不会停留在那里,因为被捉到的机会似乎是相等的。寻找电车的行人不会在两个站点之间缓慢逗留,因为在一个站点错过电车的机会与在另一个站点错过电车的机会相同。布里丹的驴在干草和水之间也许同样饥饿和口渴,如果这样的情况是可能的话,但是来自干草一侧的微风会稍微吸引它一边,然后不稳定的平衡就不再是平衡了。只有在学术的话语宇宙中,才可能有无限数量的因素完全平衡的情况。

(2) 在连续性的精神中,可以说每一点都重要,但更仔细地说,每一点都可能重要，但不必重要，除非它足以越过一个山脊或差异的门槛。在生理学中，有一个"全有或全无"的原则①，根据这个原则，如果刺激肌肉的神经，肌肉不会做出任何反应，直到强度达到最小阈值，超过这个阈值后，肌肉就会以全力做出反应。同样地，为在室内养着的植物点一支蜡烛对其新陈代谢毫无帮助。因为在植物接收到的正常光线的 1/100 以下时，任何光线都和没有光线一样。另外，缓慢渗出的水不会掉落，直到水的重量超过表面张力的保持力，此时整个水滴才会掉落。电荷相对连续地从静电机的梳齿上积聚，但将以单位跨越旋钮进行放电。根据辐射的量子理论，能量会连续地被吸收，但当集聚到其载体无法保持的程度时，它将被放射为一个单位。

（3）不稳定平衡点可以通过连接主要因素的二次因素的乘法，通过一种触发或杠杆作用被穿过。因此，缓慢地描述运动图片或汽油发动机的机制相当于将速度从外部降低到我们的意识范围之内。同样，我们做事的能力可以从低于所需阈值到高于它的地步进行倍增。我不能举起一块石头，但我可以使用杠杆来倍增我的力量。我无法准确地画出 30° 的角度，但是通过先画一个等边三角形然后将其平分，我得到的结果是比直接估计更准确的 30°。事实上，通过使用分析杠杆，通过自由手绘几何图形的技术值得研究。同样，意志力的结果可以通过建立触发连接而增加。一旦我开始弹钢琴，我就不能停下来，我很难克制自己开始弹钢琴。但是，将钢琴锁起来并把钥匙交给朋友可能在我的意志力范围之内。然后通过一种道德杠杆的方式达到了无法达到的结果。

总的来说，所有的方法都可以被视为杠杆，正如第二章所示。给定一个所需标准 S（图3）和一个有限

图3

①　请参阅皮尔庞特的《实变函数理论》，第一卷，第202页。

的触发器 A，无论是判断、技能、意志、力量、善意或其他什么，方法的问题将在于建立这样的联系，使得 A 可以被乘以到超过 S 的点 B，或者用分析语言来说，A 应该被转化成 B。这个问题在关于极限点的章节中也提到了（第 222 页），那里的重点是 A 与零的差异，也就是从无到有的差异，与这个差异相比，它似乎是无限的。而这里，重点是关于给定和精细化的标准 S，A 与 B 之间的差异。

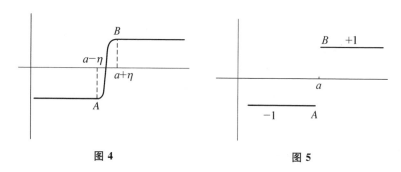

图 4　　　　　　　　　　　　　　　图 5

5. 关于奇异点的不同之处

　　一般来说，奇异点不一定是不稳定平衡点，除非在形式上是这样的。因此，取任何一组数列 x，取任何一点 a。我们仅凭形式上的规定，可以将其称为奇异点，具有不稳定平衡点的属性，尽管所涉及的变量可能没有任何动态特征。让我们考虑函数

$$f(x)=2/\pi \tan^{-}(-1) \quad [[n(x-a)]],$$

其中 $\tan-1$ 取在第一象限，n 相对于问题是一个较大的数。那么，离 a 稍微向左偏移一点的点 $a-\eta$，将导致 A 几乎等于 -1，而稍微向右偏移一点的点 $a+\eta$，则导致 B 几乎等于 $+1$。在极限情况下，

$$f(x)=2/\pi \lim_{-}(n=\infty) \tan^{-}(-1) \quad [[n(x-a)]],$$

这是符号函数 $\mathrm{sgn}(x-a)$ [1]，如图 5 所示，图中任何一点向左滑动进入－1，任何一点向右滑动进入＋1，无论我们从多小的触发器—η 或＋η 开始。这是一种用分析语言来表达，在更简单的语言中，我们可以任意地将任何一点作为分割点，这样，在它的一侧的任何东西，无论多么接近，我们都放在一个类中，而在另一侧的任何东西我们都放在另一个类中。这是差异意义的下限（见上一章第 233 页的埃及金字塔）。在不稳定平衡点的情况下，重要的动态因素作为变量进入。在本节中，将考虑其他重要差异的情况。

　　我们看到一些被称为波的东西，还有一些被称为涟漪，它们在长度上有着明显的不同，正如本章第一节中已经讨论的那样。进一步的研究表明，我们会发现所有中间长度的东西。接下来我们注意到，波的传播速度不同，小的涟漪超过大的波。此外，我们发现波既可以由表面张力传播，也可以由重量和惯性传播，在达到最小速度的某个长度（水约为 1.6 厘米）之上，波长越长，速度越快，在这个点之下，相反的情况则是真的。因此，我们提出将这一点作为中性点，并将所有长度大于此长度的扰动称为"波"，将所有长度小于此长度的扰动称为"涟漪"。在这个逻辑不稳定平衡中，速度变化的代数符号在每个侧面作为触发器，这种分类的差异可能会导致动作或事件的有限差异。

　　同样，在从红色经过黄色到绿色的连续光谱中，我们通过黄色时会经历一个改变"阴影"方向的点，如颜色金字塔中的一个角。因此，这个奇异点标志着系列的两个部分之间的显着差异。

　　在上一章中，我们说红色和绿锈是相同的，尽管不同。那么，关键在于红色和绿锈尽管相同，但在饱和度为零的分界点上存在差异。如果我们将纱线分类为两个篮子，微微的色调差异就会导致纱线命运的有限差异。

　　正式差异的辩护是它们可以在许多方面涵盖重要的差异。但

---

① 　请参阅皮尔庞特的《实变函数理论》，第一卷，第 202 页。

是通过心理或法律行动，一旦进行了任意区分，这种区别就成为事实上的区别。在连续的归纳情况下，强调了 a 和 b 的相同之处，第二个假设说："没有理由我不应该在明天做这件事，而应该在后天做。"但我可以说，"我将第十七个明天称为一个奇异的日子，并将其变成奇异的日子，通过在那一天实际开始那项工作。"当然，如果我的意志足够坚强，它将成为一个奇异的日子。通常情况下，由于每个点在某些方面都是独特的，所以有可能通过利用每一个停止可怕的归纳的机会，或者担心可能使期望的归纳无效的故障，来打败第二个假设。对于"没有理由不这样做"的回答是"没有理由"。

　　惯例和法律也可以从形式上做出实质性的区别。几十年前，在 $180°$ 经线附近划定了一条线，使得在其东侧的任何点，时间都比其西侧邻居少 24 小时。在国际日期变更线上，没有地理标志，但是涉及时间表、日期、电报通讯等问题时，就会有实际的有限差异。当我们从夏令时改为日光节约时间时，也有一个名称上的事实区别。在某一天将时钟从凌晨 2 点调到凌晨 3 点当然只是时钟指针运动的一个陡峭曲线的情况，但这种连续性与单点的法律意义无关。

6. 差异的限制

　　一个显著的差异不仅仅是它所称呼的那样，但也不至于是它所不是的那样。因此，重要的是再次看一下问题的另一面。（1）情况的连续性。在测试所提出的差异的有效性时，应牢记一个开放的可能性，即通过检查中间情况，问题是否存在不连续性，而不需要进行转换。除非有明显的标记，否则最好应用情况的连续性。因此，在上一章中讨论的冲击的笛卡尔理论的示例中，提出了一个零点的奇异点，这样，在一个或另一个方向上质量的轻微差异会使整个物体以 $2v$ 的速度有限的差异移动。如果速度或动量是质量差异的连续函数，它应该对小的情况差异有小的变化。这实际上是莱布尼兹反对笛卡尔理论的论点①。哲学上，莱布尼兹认为自然是连续的，因此笛卡尔是错误的。但在方法上，人们可以满足地说，在规定的问题中，函数可能是连续的，如果是这样的话，笛卡尔可能是错的，而在力学上，他确实是错的。

在反对亚里士多德的沉重物体下落更快的理论时，伽利略②假设了两个不同重量的物体被连接在一起，然后推断出，由于物体 a 以速度 A 移动，而较重的物体 b 以较大的速度 B 移动，两个物体将以 A 和 B 之间的速度移动，而不是比 B 更快，这正是亚里士多德理论所要求的。如果我假装成一个亚里士多德主义者，我可能会回答说，两个物体被连接在一起时实际上是一个整体，而在两个部分之间妥协效应的推理不成立。而现代的亚里士多德主义者可能会引用这样一个事实，即当两个分开的导体在最少的接触处连接在一起时，我们无法像它们分开时那样推理它们的电作用。只有当我们询问连接和不连接之间的区别，并展示在不同情况下，两个球通过一个蜘蛛网、一条绳子、一条链子、一根横杆、通过焊接连接的方式，实际的机械差异是逐渐而不是像电连接那样的，伽利略的论点才具有说服力。这种带有逻辑上的荒谬推导，因为在事实上经过确认的一系列情况中所表现的连续性，证明了亚里士多德理论所蕴含的奇点并不存在。

在空气动力学中，有一个结论是飞机在时速低于 100 英里时，空气阻力与速度的平方成正比，而在 100 英里以上，则与速度的立方成正比。在一定范围内，这是有效的公式差异，但通过连续的情况，我们发现 100 英里的速度仅仅是技术惯例下的一个奇异点，而不是根据精细的物理测量来判定的奇异点。因为在 100 英里左右的速度下，阻力随速度变化的程度并不是突然或者陡峭的，而是指

---

① 给皮埃尔·贝尔的信，1687 年，收录在莱布尼茨的哲学作品中，翻译由 G. M. 邓肯 1890 年版，第 33—34 页。

② 《伽利略：关于两门新科学的对话》，英文翻译版，第 63 页。

数方程式中 y 的值,当 v 接近 100 时就已经大于 2,当 v 刚刚超过 100 时也不完全等于 3。

（2）新的变量。——差异可能受到这样一个事实的限制,即在考虑其他变量时,与一组变量相关的明显区别可能会连续融合或变得恒定。因此,在解析上,在 $y=\mathrm{sgn}\ x$ 中,A 和 B 由分界点 0（图 6）清晰标记。但在 $y=(\mathrm{sgn}\ x)\cdot|x|$ 这相当于 $y=xA'$ 和 B' 在 0 附近越来越少不同。这只是将有限差异引回到它们的触发器。另一个简单的转换,我们又回到了恒等式。

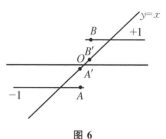

图 6

一个奇异性的丧失也可以来自于独立变量 x 的转换。因此,水的结冰点标志着水和冰之间的差异。在它下面,我们没有水而是 100％ 的冰,它上面我们没有冰而是 100％ 的水（图 7）。但如果我们考虑热量而不是温度作为 x,那么当热量添加到冰中时,将会出现中间比例,如图 8 所示,因此通过引入另一个变量,奇异点被拉伸成为一个连续的曲线。同样,在从一种物质变成另一种物质的化学反应中,如果我们从一堆物质的空间上穿过边界,我们发现没有中间物质,而是在穿过边界时出现了明显的变化。但如果我们考虑一个量转化为另一个量所需的时间,我们将发现这个变化是一个连续函数。

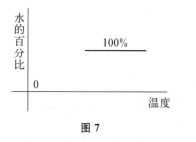

图 7

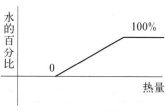

图 8

7. 特异点的差异

　　现在我们回到一个问题：特异点本身属于哪个类别，这部分已经在不稳定平衡的讨论中部分回答了。(1)"在疑虑的情况下"。我们经常听到这样的决策：在同一航道行驶的船只应该互相从左侧超越，但是如果船只相距很远则可以从右侧超越。在疑虑的情况下，从左侧超越。除非真的很饿，否则不要在饭间吃东西。在疑虑的情况下，不要吃。如果汽车靠近就不要穿过，如果远离就可以。在疑虑的情况下，不要穿过。我要买一个秒表或一只金表，看哪个更便宜。"其他条件相等"的情况下，我更喜欢秒表。名义上，我们已经确定了特异点。但是，如果有疑虑它是否是疑虑的情况呢？这个疑虑又是什么程度的疑虑呢？这个疑虑显然是无穷无尽的。更具体地说，假设我们仅根据演讲的材料来评判演讲者。在相等的情况下，语言更好的获胜。在进一步的相等情况下，更好的表达能力获胜。在进一步的相等情况下，更好的着装获胜，以此类推。换句话说，我们面临的是次要因素通过平衡主要因素而成为主要因素的情况，如在不稳定平衡下所述，实际结论是我们可以通过引入更多因素来解决这个问题，或者如果怀疑仍然存在，则通过自由裁量或随机决定，相信结果的统计平均值的安全性。因此，没有吃糖果和冰淇淋的舌头在不确定饥饿感的情况下不吃饭间食物，会有一个安全的平均解释。

　　(2)函数的零点。——在上一节中，考虑的点处于某种不稳定的平衡状态，其中该点必须向一侧或另一侧倾斜，无论触发器多么微不足道。两艘相向而行的船，如果不左舷也不右舷，将会发生碰撞，这又是一个不稳定平衡状态，但是涉及到另一组变量。但是，如果我们有一个形式上类似于稳定平衡状态的情况，其中点的微小偏差使差异足够小以被称为零，那么我们就可以将这个奇异点单独作为一类。(参见上面关于稳定平衡作为分类中心的内容)。这对连续函数的性质特别适用，因为它可以穿过所有中间值。如果函数

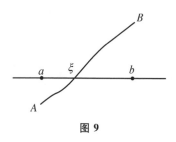

图 9

$f(x)$ 是连续的，并且 $f(a)<0$，并且 $f(b)>0$，那么在 a 和 b 之间某个地方，存在一个点 ξ，使得 $f(\xi)=0$，其中 ξ 本身可能是一个有趣的奇异点（图 9）。

因此，一副歌剧望远镜可以放大远处的物体并缩小近处的物体。因此必须有一个距离，在这个距离上，物体将看起来正好与透过歌剧望远镜时一样大。

因此，我看到潮水在桥下奔流，一天的某个时候向下流动，另一部分时候向上流动。因此必须有某个时刻水是平静的。

打棒球时，如果球靠近手，球棒会向手的方向震动；如果球靠近球棒的末端，球棒将会远离手震动。因此，在球棒上必须有一个点 ξ，在那里打球不会使手感到震动。这被证明是摆动球棒的冲击中心（图 10）。

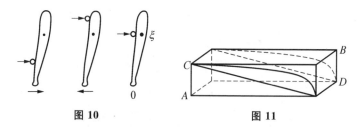

图 10　　　　　　　　　　图 11

如果我们有一根矩形梁 AB，端点 A 固定不动（图 11），它的强度会朝着支撑端变弱。如果通过对角锯切，只留下部分 CD，强度会朝着支撑点增强。伽利略说："既然如此，似乎不仅是合理的，而且是不可避免的[1]，存在一条剖面线，当多余材料被去除后，将留下一个形状如此的固体，它在所有点都提供相同的阻力"，也就是说，一种强度变化为零的形状。他证明了这是一个抛物线截面。

_____

① 《伽利略：关于两门新科学的对话》，英文翻译版，第 141 页。

（3）零的应用于测量。由于在许多情况下，判断零比判断数量更容易，因此我们经常将零作为一种测量方法。例如，在海上航行的滚动船上，很难直接测量水平线和太阳之间的夹角。但是这里有一个六分仪，通过反射和直接照明将太阳和地平线靠近。通过一个调整，它们之间的距离是一个符号，通过另一个调整，是另一个符号。因此，有一个调整，它们会恰好接触，这可以通过观察来相当准确地判断。

如果某些数量没有定义，它们可以通过已知数量的消去来进行定义。因此，pb 和 $p'b'$ 长度相等，但 pb 看起来更长。更长多少呢？但首先，询问"更长多少"是什么意思？定义这种幻觉的一种方法是：取一个点 a，使得 pa 显然比 $p'b'$ 短。因此，必须存在一个点 ξ，使得 $p\xi$ 看起来等于 $p'b'$。那么，$b\xi$ 就是幻觉的度量。这实际上是心理学中的熟悉领域。（在实际实验中，点 a、ξ、b 不应出现在同一条线上，如图 12，这只是为了说明的目的。）

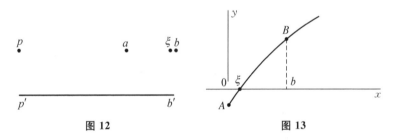

图 12　　　　　　　　　　　　图 13

同样，将黄色视为负蓝色，颜色对比度可以这样测量。在固定的蓝色背景下取一个薄条。让 x 表示正常情况下条的蓝度，y 表示条在背景下的蓝度。如果我们取一个灰色条（—它的蓝度 $x=0$），那么通过对比，它看起来是黄色的（$y=a-$蓝色）。

因此，我们有点 A（图 13）[①]。如果我们取一个明显的蓝条，它也会看起来是蓝色的，所以我们有点 B，其 y 大于零。如果 y 是 x 的

———————————

① 　参见第一章，有关跳水青蛙的内容。

连续函数,那么应该有一条某种中间色调的条,当它放在强烈的蓝色背景下时,它将呈现为灰色,即存在一个 ξ,使得 $y = f(\xi) = 0$。

这实际上是 H. Pretori 和 M. Sachs 在颜色对比度[1] 和 C. Hess 和 H. Pretori 在亮度对比度[2] 中使用的方法。

关于这样的奇异点,有一个普遍的警告是,我们永远不能在所有情况下简单地以 $y = f(x)$ 的形式看待它。正如之前所说,当一级因素的影响变得可以忽略不计时,二级因素的影响就不可忽略了。因此,如果一条带子不够窄,在临界点附近,我们可能会看到带有黄色边框的蓝色带子。用一副廉价的歌剧望远镜,可能存在一些关键距离,其中一些部分的视野会变大,而其他部分则会缩小。因此,除非我们确保在具体情况下,其他因素可以被称为偶然、无关或可以忽略的因素,否则甚至在相对意义上也没有干净的零点。

(4)极限点。上一章提醒要谨慎地推断极限点的奇异性。因此,本章应该突显极限点与其他点的差异。再次提醒,由于这在第五章已经被讨论,除了利用一些之后学习的材料外,不需要进一步阐述。

关于这样的奇异点的一般警告,在这个研究中都隐含着,就是我们永远不应该在所有情况下严格地取 $y = f(x)$。正如之前所说的,当一次因素的影响变得可以忽略不计时,二次因素的影响就不可忽略了。因此,如果条纹不够窄,在临界点附近,我们可能会有一个带有黄边的蓝色条纹。用一副廉价的歌剧望远镜,会有一些临界距离,在这些距离上,某些区域会放大,而其他区域则会缩小。因此,除非我们确信在具体考虑时,其他因素可以被称为偶然的、无关的或可以忽略不计的,否则甚至相对而言也没有一个清晰的零点。

(四)极限点。——上一章中提醒了要谨慎地推断极限点的奇异性。因此,这一章应该强调极限点与其他点的差异性。同样,由

---

[1] Pfluger 的档案(生理学),卷 60,1895 年,第 71 页及以下。

[2] 眼科档案,第 50 卷,第 4 期,1894 年,第 50 页及以下。

于这在第五章中已经处理过，除了利用一些后续研究的材料外，没有必要进一步阐述。

某些生物或社会力量总是向极限点推进，将其作为唯一的稳定平衡点。高水位标志不仅是水位的上限，而且可以通过植物生长来测量。如果植物在高于此水位的位置生长，它们将向下生长，如果在低于此水位的位置生长，它们在有机会向上生长之前就会死亡。因此，它们会尽可能地生长到极限。

在制定规则或法律时，始终要注意物事将会向其推进的极限点。如果公共销售短缺商品，开放销售的时间点并不都相同，但人群会向那个奇异的时间极限冲去，即开放的那一刻。

在铁路货物运输中，维护成本非常高，因此操作额外费用是可以忽略不计的。因此，如果两条平行线无限竞争，将会出现恶性竞争，直至不收取货运费用作为稳定极限。从另一个角度来看，关于线路的进一步存在，当然可能不是稳定平衡点，正如铁路历史所证明的那样。

8.　自然的连续性

在经历了这些具体同一性和差异性的实际案例，并通过将连续性和不连续性互相转化来使用后，人们可能仍会问，归根结底，自然是连续的还是不连续的。一个答案是方法论不会用到"归根结底"。连续性只有在我们选择变量和函数时才是准确或近似有意义的。水和岩板的温度关系是不连续的。水和冰的比例以及与热量的关系是连续的。简单水和冰在大范围上的关系是连续还是不连续是没有意义的，需要进一步定义。因此，总的来说，自然既不连续也不连续。只有一个函数可以是连续的[①]，而自然作为自然不是一个函数。我们可以通过适当的转换自由地使自然的某个方面连续或不

---

① 　在应用中，一个连续体的简单连续性可以被看作是函数 $x' = x$。请参见第一章，第 155 页。相对论理论将影响这些讨论的进一步阐述，但不会影响一般的具体观点。

连续,并承担相应的风险;如果我们成功地抓住了方法论杠杆的长端,结果是启示性和有用的;如果我们抓住了杠杆的错误端,那么结果是人为和浪费的。

自然连续性的问题,然而如果我们善意地审视其动机并尝试通过适当的陈述使其具有重要意义,那么它仍然没有被否定。其中最重要的动机实际上涉及独立变量时间的连续性。问"自然是否连续"通常意味着:"通过足够的细化,是否总是可能将任何现象的测量(无论它多么突然地改变)表达为时间的连续函数?"但是我们所说的时间是什么意思呢? 在实际科学中,无论是在物理学还是心理学中,时间都是通过所谓的"在时间内发生"的现象来衡量的,例如地球的旋转、沙子的流动、钟摆的振动、思想的流逝、紧张和放松的感觉。同时性、之前和之后、时间长度的工作意义都基于科学的日常事实。因此,我们可以说,从方法论上讲,把时间看作由所有在这些方面相关联的现象构成是足够的。

因此,现象 y 在时间上的相对不连续意味着,如果我们在 y 上放置一个普通的时间测量 t,那么 y 将出现明显的差异,而测量现象 t 却没有什么明显的变化。因此,当伽利略打开灯笼的快门时,光线"瞬间"照射到了数英里之外的山上。但是,通过用一个齿轮代替手动快门,菲泽使光线受到了一个变化速率与光线相比不可忽略的现象的影响,因此通过问题的重新表述,相对不连续性变成了相对连续性。

另一方面,在上述时间观念中,哲学问题是:是否存在任何变化的现象,其变化的量级如此之大,以至于无论已知或未知的任何变化现象,以任何有限单位衡量,都不能放置在其旁边,使得在测量上的足够小的差异会使问题中对应的差异变为有限? 但是以这种形式陈述这个问题,唯一可能的含义变得毫无意义。因为,如果肯定回答这个问题,我们的科学实践就简单地将该现象从时间序列中排除,并将其称为不同事物的同时存在,而不是同一事物的不连续变化。因此,假设万有引力是瞬间发生的,那么我们应该简单地说存在某个强度的力场，存在于某些点上，而不是说通过波或辐射进行瞬时通讯。因此，我们可以说，自然是时间的连续函数，因为时间的定义已被证明是最有用的。因此，自然的连续性不是一个哲学上的结论，而是在科学优势的大圆圈中进行辩论。

第八章　结论与进一步问题

1. 结果总结

　　如果问题、方法和结论是"平行连接"的,那么陈述这个研究的结论的最好方式是指向各个单独的章节并说:"Voila!"因为问题的陈述和研究方法本身就是结论的一部分,可以被批判和争议其有效性和意义。但是,为了方便参考,以下是各章的结果总结①:

　　第一章　问题。–将连续性的概念,以不同程度的数学精度使用,作为一条指导线,认为值得进行方法论研究。第二章　方法。–方法,一般来说,被视为杠杆,通过从某些实际出发获得更多的现实。这个研究中的典型方法是深入到具体事物中,找到它们中的渐变和序列,检查不同情况下的内外函数,以及在我们认为合适时改变我们的观点。第三章　分等级的概念。——当绝对地看待概念时,尝试看看它们也具有何种程度的意义。一些特定的结论如下:举例、比喻、隐喻、语言游戏等,是构成概念定义的不同层次的元素。在数学中,变量和常量之间有不同阶段的参数。被限制在一条线上的数学函数是将值限制在管或带中的一种限制程度。当其他因素的变化对现象没有"明显"的影响时,某个因素是现象的"主要"原因。第四章　串行顺序。——任何两个事物都可以按照自己定义的串行顺序进行比较。串行可比性是一个程度问题。对于一个串行顺序,我们能够陈述的真理越多,就越有证据表明它已经被定义得很好。只要科学中的使用波动和偶然误差低于相关性的阈值,我们就能对串行顺序进行非诡辩性陈述,这样我们就可以用其他名称来称呼某个事物,而不仅仅是它的定义。第五章　极限点——极限

---

①　这个总结与官方的"摘要"不同,可以在阅读或未阅读论文的情况下阅读。

情况至少在作为一种情况时是相同的，而在成为极限情况时至少是不同的。数学的精神是在下限，哲学的精神是在上限。科学和生活占据中间的位置。但通过变换的方法，极端的地方有一些方面是相同的。在有限的事物中，实际的、范畴的、事实上的等等与形式上的虚无相比具有无限的性质。在特定的问题中，上下阈值可以代替极限。因此，建议将极限重新定义为由这些阈值构成。这似乎符合数学的用法。在这个意义上，我们说，真理是真理的极限，意义或定义是标准的极限，道德是实际道德的极限等等。

这种奥卡姆剃刀的应用与通常的应用有一个重要的不同之处，例如，当物体被"还原"为感觉数据的极限类别时，我只是把它看作是"将现实的一部分对抗另一部分"，在其中某些人或某些问题可能会找到"机械上的优势"；但从一个环形的视角出发，在事物的中心引出问题，可能会在某些其他问题中，把定义反过来，例如，一位日常工作的物理学家或生理学家会发现感官数据远非终极的，而更愿意将它们"还原"成其他人刚试图将其还原为感觉数据的术语。

Ⅵ. 通过连续性达成同一性。——重要的同一性始终有着差异的背景。连续性的概念有助于发现同一性，前提是选择一个明智的变量 x，其中事物以某种非平凡的方式融合在一起。

这种应用奥卡姆剃刀的重要方面与通常的应用不同，例如，当物体被"简化"为有限感官数据时，我只是将其视为"现实的一部分相对于另一部分的对抗"，在这个对抗中，某些人或某些问题可能会找到"机械优势"；但是从一个以事物中心开启问题的循环视角来看，可能会发现在某个其他问题中，定义应该被颠倒；例如，一位工作日的物理学家或生理学家会发现感官数据远非最终形态，并且更喜欢将其"简化"为其他人刚刚试图简化为感官数据的术语。

Ⅵ 通过连续性实现的同一性。——重要的同一性始终背景有所不同。连续性的概念有助于发现同一性，前提是在选择一个变量 x 时要明智，以便以某种非平凡的方式看到事物的融合。

背景差异可能是一些特别感兴趣的点，如零点、大的程度差异或小的程度差异。还要重视看到当前立场的案例与其他案例之间的同一性。

连续数学归纳的一个偶然结果是一个定理，"连续数学归纳定理"，它是楔子论证的要点。像所有论证一样，这种论证的强度取决于其前提的强度。

Ⅶ　通过连续性实现的差异。——重要的差异始终存在于同一性的背景之中。差异不仅仅是差异，而是意味着分类、事件的替代问题、观念或感觉的差异以及行动决策。

差异可能源于 x 的大幅变化或陡峭的曲线，标志着奇点，特别是稳定和不稳定平衡点。

奇点可能不同于其他点，因为它们本身具有趣味性。当数量变换符号时，它所发生的地方可能会引起怀疑，或者作为测量的方法。

一种值得更突出强调的推理方法是通过案例的连续性进行推理，这可以用来检查可疑差异的点。

2. 总结：它们的循环性

什么是程度差异和种类差异之间的界限？从"观点"角度来看，我的回答是：这取决于情况。

自然界是否连续？这也要看情况。

但是凭借调和的气质和一个有些混乱的头脑，我倾向于看到事物相互融合，而不是分隔它们的障碍、线条和点。因此，我认为自然界原则上是连续的，并称这个论点为"连续性"。在同样的精神下，我还承认，如果一个人感到在思想世界中需要更多的不连续性，这个人可以重复这些章节的内容，称之为"不连续性"的研究。

在"某些程度上"的精神下，我进一步得出结论：除了是重言式的命题，没有普遍的命题是真实的，没有足够的理由，除了是循环的理由，特别地，数学和精确科学在它们是精确的意义上是循环的。

这些一般性结论的一个明显反驳是这样一种扫帚式的论断本身就是归谬法。对于这种攻击，可以通过求助于罗素和怀特黑德的类型层次结构来逃避，并说我是以更高级的哲学立场在讲话。但出于自己的立场，即使用内部方法进行战斗或撤退，也就是说，使用一个内部的方法，我只是简单地回答说，这些结论是安全的，恰恰因为它们本身就是循环的。然而，有些循环并不是恶性的。希望这些一般性结论，在引言中，如果阐述，将提供无益的形式主义的例子，在经过这些章节的具体案例的长时间应用之后，现在已经获得足够的含义，使它们的正式公告具有非平凡的意义。从中可以看出，这些结论不是这个研究的"终点"，除了在时间上，也不提供"连续性问题的解决方案"，而只是各种连续性问题研究的简明提醒，而"连续性问题"在最后必须包括在内。

3. 进一步的问题

在引言中，我说这项研究只是方法论中函数理论的一部分。要进行这样系统的研究，就需要对变量和功能的类型进行调查。变量的调查将是对物理单位维度研究的一般化。逻辑上，变量可以是连续的、密集的系列、函数等；在数学上，它可以是实数、几何点、角度、下标等；在更具体的应用中，它可以是时间、风险、强度、善意、电荷、困难等。

数学中的一个函数只是抽象地"定义"了。但在应用中，这种功能可能有不同的"模式"，可以说是。$y = f(x)$可以通过定义、分类、陈述、问题、假设、试验性假设、估计、猜测、习惯的概念或误解、声明、普遍法则、历史记录、观察、发现、感觉、义务、立法、命令或行动来提出。所有这些都需要仔细分类和研究。

3. 值得特别关注的一种功能关系是，其中涉及一些动态因素。例如，价格是供求关系的函数，但进一步的问题

在引言中，我指出这项研究只是关于方法论中函数的一般理论的一部分。要进行这样系统的研究，就需要对变量和功能的种类进行调查。变量的调查将是对物理单位的维度研究的一种概括。从逻辑上讲，变量可以是连续的、密集的系列、函数等；从数学上讲，它

可以是实数、几何点、角度、下标等;在更具体的应用中,它可以是时间、风险、强度、善意、电荷、难度等等。

在数学中,一个函数只是抽象地"定义"了。但在应用中,这种功能可能有不同的"模式",可以通过定义、分类、陈述、问题、假设、试探性假说、估计、猜测、习惯的观念或误解、声明、普遍法则、历史记录、观察、发现、感受、义务、立法、命令或行动来表述。所有这些都需要仔细分类和研究。

一个值得特别关注的函数关系是涉及某些动态因素的函数关系。例如,价格是供求关系的函数,但是有一个时间滞后因素使功能变得复杂。这是一个相当普遍重要的点。

奇异点只在"同一性"和"差异性"下被研究。但它们足够重要,应该单独加以研究。极大值和极小值问题在经济问题中尤为重要。在道德问题中,"中庸之道"可以概括为最优点或最佳路径的概念,这是一个极值问题。不同种类的平衡,只在"差异性"下被研究,也值得进行系统的调查。

在方法论中,函数理论也可以被看作是一种具体的数学,其中数学概念,例如极限的解释是具体的,超越了在数学物理中的范围。一些抽象的可能性,例如周期性的循环系列,如年、复数、n元函数的n个变量、广义坐标、抽象几何中的投影关系和"群"的属性等,都没有被涉及。再次强调,具体的数学只是一种方法,而不是一种教条,实际上发现的解释不应被视为理所当然。

存在时间滞后会使功能变得更加复杂。这是一个非常普遍重要的点。

4. 应用

当问题的主题是核心利益时,我们说我们将这些研究应用于问题,而不管使用什么方法或以什么顺序。但是"两者之间没有明确的界限",特别是整个论文既是方法又是主题,可以自由运用反思方法。在逻辑学中,常规理解是存在分类问题,可以从身份和差异,通过连续性，以及交叉分配的多维原则的角度来处理。概念，定义，法律，理论的连续性和弹性，从逻辑平衡的稳定阈值和中心的角度来看，本身可以形成一项研究。（参见第 3 节的术语，第 4 章第 204 页以及第 7 章第 267 页）

"相关性的意义和限度"，尤其是与阈值的观念相关的，值得进行比本论文中给出的隐含处理更为详尽的探讨。与概念、定义等的研究密切相关的是术语原则的问题。在这些因素（如用法、简洁、对称性、系统性、词源、色彩、中性等）中，哪一个因素的功能应被视为适用性的衡量标准？在更深层次的哲学问题方面，机械主义和生命力学，或者决定论和自由意志的定义可以从平衡的角度进行研究，这并非新颖的尝试。解释绝对和无限的问题是一个中心问题。对于相对和有限的参照是否能解释或解释掉，伦理学中的目的论和进化论伦理学是伦理学的具体化还是对真正伦理学的否定？某些形式的宗教是否真正提供了宗教的解释，或只是宗教的替代品？

在伦理学的特殊问题中，有一个涉及保守主义和自由主义之间调和的问题，这涉及到典型的连续性问题。

在行为是否合法的界限问题上，可采用连续的数学归纳方法进行肯定或否定的处理。

公正问题也可能涉及多变量函数。[①] 据说一个人（或一个国家）的好坏仅限于其承受得起的程度。这是一种重言或令人不安的真理？你和我能承受多少？这是一个问题而不是一个事实。

涉及宪法性、普通法、公平、先例、自由裁量的法律问题，是"疑虑情况下"的问题。在这个领域，我只能便宜地说，只有内部训练有素的人才知道如何处理方法论的杠杆。

在实验心理学中，对幻觉的测量已经进行了详细的解释（第七章，282—283 页）。

根据精确科学中所发现的优雅、相关性和象征的标准，通常用

---

① 　参见 F. Y. Edgeworth 的《数学心理学》第 95 页。

色彩金字塔来表示颜色似乎还有很大的改进空间。值得一试的是，探索到底能发展出多少"颜色解析几何"。[①]

应用显然还扩展到工业和个人效率（极大值和极小值）的问题。在教育心理学中，训练运动技能的方法将涉及到中介物、明确的位置、捏压等考虑因素。一个有用的学科，正如第七章（第271页）所提出的那样，是一种通过分析性知识的智力杠杆进行"自由手绘几何图形"的系统。

在声学、音乐、声音心理学和实验音韵学等边缘领域中，代表们之间存在很多交叉谈话，似乎值得澄清。变量的分类和定义将是这样一项研究的第一个重要步骤。

在音乐本身中，音高（循环和线性序列）、音程、节奏、速度、力度、力度变化等元素是方法学理论中最重要的主题。

最后，让我揭示一个事实，我的插图主要是从我在写作时所从事的主题中绘制的。每次我遇到一些新的事物，无论是自行车骑行、演讲、统计学还是双色运动图片，我都会找到一些更多的"例证"，这些例证反过来又影响到我的一般问题，并可能导致它们的解决、解决方案或消解。

因此，"最终"，目前的观点在形式上仅仅是一篇正式论文的结束，而在抽象概括和"通过合格证明无理由"方面，"没有理由"所有我未来的活动，包括由于时间范围的变化而可能拒绝（到目前为止所达到的大部分结果），都可以被看作是一个不断连续地书写连续论文的延续。

---

① 这个问题是由亨德森教授提出的。

Ⅰ 使用的文献

页码

154 Hobson，E. W. 实变函数论，第 222—223 页。

159 Scientific American，1917 年 10 月 20 日。

161 Russell，B. Leibniz 哲学，1900 年，第 64—65 页。

165 Aristotle,《尼各马可伦理学》第 Ⅸ 章，第 Ⅱ 卷，(J. E. C. Welldon 的翻译第 56 页)。

166 Crothers，S. M.《赎罪人的钱袋》，1905 年(第一篇)。

170 Galilei，Galileo《论两个新科学的对话》。H. Crew 和 A. De Salvic 的英文译本，1914 年，第 122 页。

175 Ruskin，J.《芝麻和百合》，1864 年，第 32 节(哈佛经典文库，第 28 卷，第 121 页)。

181 Hollingworht，H. L.，"心理物理连续体"。哲学、心理学和科学方法杂志，1916 年，第 12 卷，第 7 期，第 182 页以下。

183 Bosanquet，B.《逻辑》，第 2 版，1911 年，第 Ⅱ 卷，第 141 页。

192 Pearson，K.《科学语法》，第 3 版，1911 年，第一部分，关于因果的章节。

197 Huntington，E. V.《连续体论》，1917 年。

200 Lewis Carroll(道奇森，C. L.)《爱丽丝漫游奇境记》，"疯狂茶会"。

202 富兰克林，B.《自传》，第三条美德(《哈佛经典文库》第 1 卷，第 83 页)。

211 亨廷顿，E. V.《美国数学月刊》，1918 年 1 月。

223 刘易斯·卡罗《乌龟对阿基里斯所说的话》。《心灵》杂志，1895 年，第 278 页。

228 罗素，B.《我们对外部世界的认识作为哲学科学方法的领域》，1914 年，第 42 页。

234 伍德，R. W.《动物类比》，1908 年，第 1 页。

242 波因丁,J. H.和汤姆森,J. J.《物理教科书：热》,第 3 版,1908 年,第 116 页,脚注。

256 伽利略・伽利雷《关于两种新科学的对话》,英文版由 H. Crew 和 A. De Salris 翻译,1914 年,第 72 页。

263 魏宁格,O.《性别与性格》。385 贝利斯,W. M.《普通生理学原理》,1914 年,第 383 页。

269 贝利斯.W.M.《普通生理学原理》,1914 年,第 383 页。

272 皮尔庞特,J.《实变函数理论》,1905 年,I,第 202 页及以下。

276 莱布尼兹写给皮埃尔・巴伊尔的信,1687 年,《莱布尼兹哲学著作》,由 G. M. Duncan 翻译,1890 年,第 33—34 页。

276 伽利略《关于两种新科学的对话》,英文版由 H. Crew 和 A. De Salris 翻译,1914 年,第 63 页。

280 伽利略 同上,第 141 页。

295 埃奇沃斯,F. Y.《数学心理学》,1881 年,第 95 页。

Ⅱ 一些相关的著作

Biometrica，1901 至今，尤其是 Karl Pearson 的文章。
Boussineso，J. M.《真正的机械决定论与生命和道德自由的调和》，1878 年。

Mach，E.《热力学原理》，1899 年。

Mach，E.《力学科学》，1883 年。由 T. J. Mc Cormick 翻译成英文，1902 年。

Meyerson，E.《同一性与现实性》，1907 年。

Moore，E. H.《一般分析》。

Petzoldt，J.《数学和经济学》，发表于《科学哲学季刊》。

Poincaré，F.《科学的基础》，由 C. B. Halsted 翻译成英文，1913 年。

Poincaré，F.《最后的思考》，1913 年。

关于"连续数学归纳"的注记[①]

一、特殊情况。——假设函数 $f(x)$ 在某实变量 x 的某个区间内有定义。

假设一：该区间内存在一个点 a，使得 $f(a)=0$。

假设二：该区间存在一个常数 Δ，使得对于任何 $0<\delta\leqslant\Delta$，如果 $f(x)=0$，则 $f(x+\delta)=0$。那么对于该区间内任何 b，当 $b>a$ 时，有 $f(b)=0$。

证明。——

I. 如果 $b-a\leqslant\Delta$，则根据假设二，结论成立。

II. 如果 $b-a>\Delta$，则首先应用阿基米德公理，即存在一个整数 n 和一个分数 $\theta(0\leqslant\theta\leqslant1)$，使得 $b-a=(n+\theta)\Delta$，或者 $b=(a+\theta\Delta)+n\Delta$。然后，应用普通数学归纳法，因此：由假设一和二，因为 $\theta\Delta<\Delta$。

∴ $f(a+\theta\Delta)=0$

因此，再次由假设二得：(1) $f[(a+\theta\Delta)+1\cdot\Delta]=0$。

如果 $f[(a+\theta\Delta)+m\cdot\Delta]=0$，则由假设二得：(2) $f[(a+\theta\Delta)+(m+1)\Delta]=0$。

因此，通过结合 (1) 和 (2)，可得到：$f(a+\theta\Delta+n\Delta)=0$，即 $f(b)=0$。

二、一般情况。——设 $\varphi(x)$ 是定义在某实变量 x 的某个区间内的任意命题函数。

---

① 该论文载于《美国数学学会公报》，第 26 卷，第 17—18 页，1919 年 10 月。(于 1919 年 4 月 5 日在美国数学学会旧金山分会会议上宣读。)

假设一：该区间内存在一个点 a，使得 $\varphi(a)$ 成立。

假设二：该区间存在一个常数 Δ，使得对于任何 $0<\delta\leqslant\Delta$，如果 $\varphi(x)$ 成立，则 $\varphi(x\pm\delta)$ 成立。

那么对于该区间内任何 b，当 $b\gtreqqless a$ 时，$\varphi(b)$ 成立，证明与特殊情况相同，只是需要进行明显的措辞或符号更改。

注：该定理基本上依赖于阿基米德公设和普通数学归纳法，但不是后者的推广，也就是说它并不包含后者作为一种特殊情况。它不是数理逻辑中的定理，因为它与实变量 x 有关。但它比处理等式的普通定理更为普遍，因为 $\varphi(x)$ 可以是关于连续性、收敛性、可积性等的陈述，无法用简单的 $f(x)=0$ 形式表示。

该定理是"楔子的尖端"或"骆驼的鼻子"的熟知论证的数学表述：

假设 1：假设可以饮用半杯啤酒。

假设 2.如果任何量 x 的啤酒都是被允许的，那么只要 δ 不超过一个无法感知的量 Δ，就没有理由不允许 $x+\delta$。因此，任何数量都是被允许的。

和所有数学定理一样，结论的正确性取决于假设的正确性。在这种情况下，如果论证失败，通常是因为第二个假设所需的常数 Δ 不存在。以楔子为例。如果一个楔子在两个由弹性力推在一起的侧面之间被以一个恒定的力推进，当达到一个平衡点被抵消的增加阻力的分量时它将停止。在这种情况下，$\varphi(x+\delta)$ 仍然成立所需的 Δ 在区间内将变得越来越小，随着 x 接近危险点，超过该点，结论不再成立。

图书在版编目（CIP）数据

连续性：方法论的研究 / 赵元任著；石锋，潘韦
功译. — 上海：上海教育出版社，2023.8
ISBN 978-7-5720-2124-4

Ⅰ.①连… Ⅱ.①赵… ②石… ③潘… Ⅲ.①连续性
–方法论–研究 Ⅳ.①B026

中国国家版本馆CIP数据核字(2023)第144884号

本书英语原文刊登在商务印书馆出版的《赵元任全集》第十四卷中。本书的
翻译、出版获得商务印书馆授权。

责任编辑　徐川山
封面设计　陆　弦

连续性：方法论的研究
赵元任　著　石　锋　潘韦功　译

出版发行　上海教育出版社有限公司
官　　网　www.seph.com.cn
地　　址　上海市闵行区号景路159弄C座
邮　　编　201101
印　　刷　上海展强印刷有限公司
开　　本　890×1240　1/32　印张 14.375　插页 4
字　　数　400 千字
版　　次　2023年9月第1版
印　　次　2023年9月第1次印刷
印　　数　1–1,500 本
书　　号　ISBN 978-7-5720-2124-4/H·0069
定　　价　106.00 元

如发现质量问题，读者可向本社调换　电话：021-64373213